AF605864

AMERICAN ARTISTS, AUTHORS, AND COLLECTORS

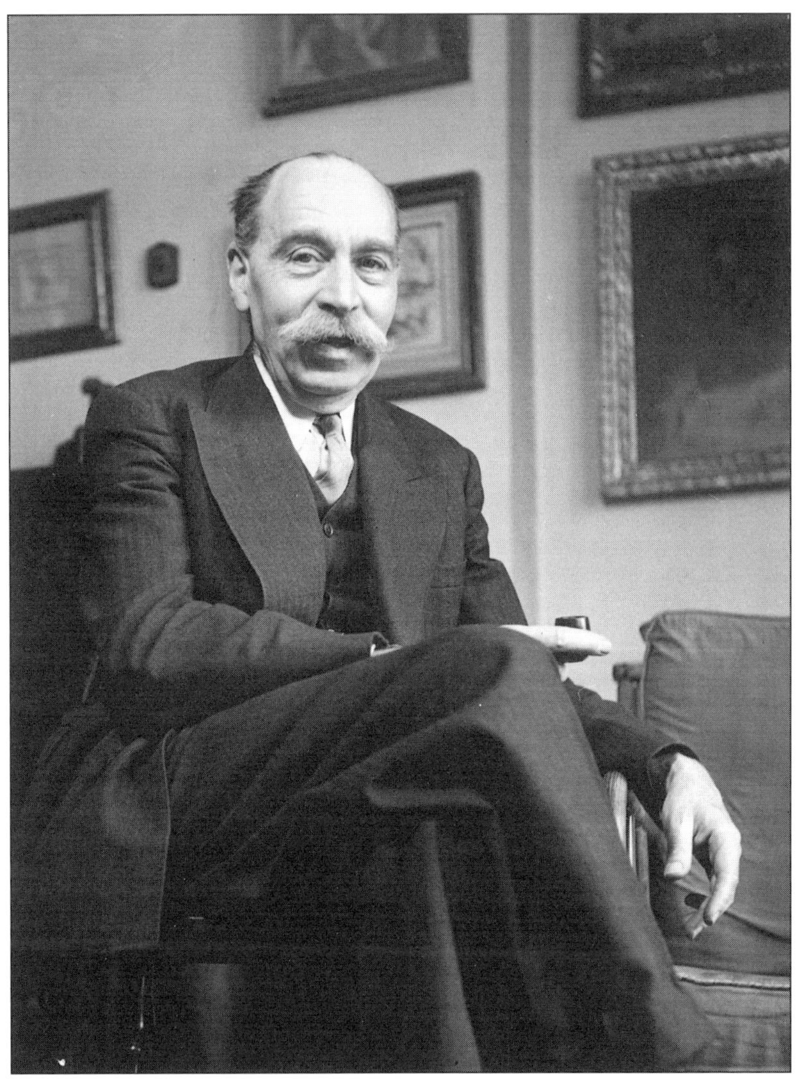

Walter Pach in his studio at 3 Washington Square North, New York City, ca. 1950. Photograph by Helen G. Salomon. Collection of Raymond P. Pach.

BENNARD B. PERLMAN

AMERICAN ARTISTS, AUTHORS, AND COLLECTORS

The Walter Pach Letters 1906–1958

STATE UNIVERSITY OF NEW YORK PRESS

Published by
STATE UNIVERSITY OF NEW YORK PRESS
ALBANY

Printed in the United States of America

For information, address
State University of New York Press,
90 State Street, Suite 700, Albany, NY 12207

Production and book design, Laurie Searl
Marketing, Fran Keneston

Library of Congress Cataloging-in-Publication Data

Perlman, Bennard B.
American artists, authors, and collectors : the Walter Pach letters, 1906–1958 / Bennard B. Perlman.
p. cm.
Includes bibliographical references and index.
ISBN 0-7914-5293-X (alk. paper) — ISBN 0-7914-5294-8 (pbk. : alk. paper)
1. Pach, Walter, 1883–1958—Correspondence. 2. Painters—United States—Correspondence. 3. Art—United States—20th century—Correspondence. I. Pach, Walter, 1883–1958. Correspondence. Selections. 2002. II. Title.

ND237.P15 A3 2002
759.13—dc21

2002017629

10 9 8 7 6 5 4 3 2 1

CONTENTS

ILLUSTRATIONS

PREFACE

When Raymond Pach approached me seven years ago regarding the publication of his father's letters, he confessed that the only correspondence in his possession was among family members.

There had to be more.

A two-year quest of my contacting the archivists in countless museums and universities, plus numerous individuals, resulted in a collection of some 1,600 letters.

Selectivity for this publication became essential, though the decisions as to which correspondence to include, which to delete, was bound to be subjective in nature.

The letters selected were chosen on the basis of two or three criteria: The stature and contributions of the correspondents; hitherto unpublished revelations embodied in the missives; and whether I had been able to amass both segments of the correspondence—to and from Pach.

Many letters contained herein are included in their entirety, although deletions were made (always indicated by a group of dots) when the contents seemed either redundant or of little significance to either the scholar or casual reader. Minor misspellings and typographical errors in the original letters have been retained. Changes were made only where there was a potential to misread, and these have been noted in the text. Some headings have been eliminated where redundant, and when included they have been shortened and in some cases abbreviated for consistency. Inside addresses have been eliminated except where their inclusion was important or relevant. Salutations, closings, and signatures have been kept as in the original letters. The source or sources of each group of letters is indicated, so that the specialist or merely curious may peruse all of the missives found by this researcher in toto.

ACKNOWLEDGMENTS

When I met with Walter Pach on September 5, 1952, for a three-hour interview, he displayed a complete disinterest in self-aggrandizement, downplaying his own role in the history of twentieth-century American art. Only through persistent prodding was it possible to coax this softspoken, educated gentleman to speak even briefly about himself.

As his contributions became more apparent to me over the years, it was a distinct pleasure to meet his son, Raymond, in 1987 when we assembled an exhibition of works by his father, Arthur B. Davies, and Walt Kuhn. The following year Raymond Pach requested that I write the catalogue for an exhibition of paintings by his parents.

When Raymond approached me in April 1995 to undertake the task of collecting his father's previously unpublished correspondence, I was intrigued by the project's prospects, and readily agreed. Just like Walter Pach, the man, his letters reveal how he consistently preferred to work without fanfare, behind the scenes. So it is to Raymond Pach, above all others, to whom I express my sincere appreciation.

Among the other individuals whose cooperation has proven invaluable are: Marie Adams, The Denver Art Museum; Susan Ahern, Towson University; Lorraine Anderson, Baltimore County Library; Susan K. Anderson, Philadelphia Museum of Art; Daniela Andrasko, The Metropolitan Museum of Art; D. Scott Atkinson, San Diego Museum of Art; Don Bacigalupi, San Diego Museum of Art; Annie Bayly, Archives of American Art, Washington Center; Avis Berman; Margaret Biller, Baltimore City Community College; Michala Biondi, The New York Public Library; Stacy Bomento, Philadelphia Museum of Art; Julika Bond; Elizabeth Botten, Archives of American Art; Mimi Bowling, The New York Public Library; Susan Brady, Yale University; Sally Brazil, Frick Art Reference Library; Arthur Breton, Archives of American Art, Washington Center; Robert Burke, Enoch Pratt Free Library, Baltimore; Molly Carrott, The Metropolitan Museum of Art; Susan Carey, Archives of American Art, Washington Center; Ralph Clayton, Pratt Library; Linda Clous, The Phillips Collection; Judy Collier, Goucher College; Erika Cooper, Peabody Library, Johns Hopkins University; Rolando Corpus, Philadelphia

Museum of Art; Eva Crider, Archives of American Art, Washington Center; Virginia Dajani, American Academy of Arts and Letters; Bernice Davidson, The Frick Collection; Claudine Davison; Robin T. Dettre, National Museum of American Art; Michael Donnelly, Pratt Library; Barbara B. Dreier; Katherine (Mrs. Thomas, Jr.) Dreier; Anita Duquette, Whitney Museum of American Art; Irene Dunne, Pratt Library; Marcia Dysart, Pratt Library; Marcia Eisenstern, Pratt Library; Nancy Emerson, San Diego Museum of Art; Andrea Feldman, The Museum of Modern Art; Jean Fitzgerald, Archives of American Art, Washington Center; Martha Fleischman, Kennedy Galleries; Diane Geiger, Archives of American Art, Detroit Center; Hanna Geldrich-Leffman, Loyola College; Christopher Gray; Chris Graybill, Pratt Library; James Grebl, San Diego Museum of Art; Rosa Halbert, Baltimore County Library; Leslie Heitzman, The Museum of Modern Art; Irene Himelfarb, Baltimore County Library; Joseph Hobach, The Phillips Collection; Jean Holliday, Princeton University; Lucy Holman, Pratt Library; Jeanie M. James, The Metropolitan Museum of Art; Jayme Jamison, Philadelphia Museum of Art; Harriet Jenkins, Pratt Library; Beth Joffrion, Archives of American Art, Washington Center; Sona Johnston, The Baltimore Museum of Art; William R. Johnston, The Walters Art Museum; William Jones, Pratt Library; Robert Kaufmann, The Metropolitan Museum of Art; Mattie Kelley, Bowdoin College Museum of Art; Sarah Kielt, The Frick Art Reference Library; Anne Kilroy, The Cleveland Museum of Art; Jackie Kinsey, Pratt Library; Eleanor Krell, Pratt Library; Virginia Krumholz, The Cleveland Museum of Art; Rachel Kubie, Pratt Library; Cheryl Leibold, The Pennsylvania Academy of the Fine Arts; David Levy, Pratt Library; Agapita Judy Lopez, The Georgia O'Keeffe Foundation; Ellen Luchinsky, Pratt Library; Pat Lynagh, National Museum of American Art; Ilene Magaras, Solomon E. Guggenheim Museum; Nancy Malloy, Archives of American Art, New York Center; Laurette E. McCarthy; Wilbur McGill, Pratt Library; Ursula E. McLean, Peabody Institute, Johns Hopkins University; Julie Mellby, Whitney Museum of American Art; Harriet Memeger, Delaware Art Museum; Lisa Mittman, Baltimore County Library; Jacqueline Matisse Monnier; Linda Muehlig, Smith College Museum of Art; Carol Murray, The Baltimore Museum of Art; Francis M. Naumann; Alene D. Oestreicher, The Baltimore Museum of Art; Emilo Ortega,Towson University; Kristin Parker, Isabella Stewart Gardner Museum; Douglass Paschall, Philadelphia Museum of Art; Carole M. Pesner, Kraushaar Galleries; Martin E. Petersen, San Diego Museum of Art; Daria Phair, Pratt Library; Susan Pichler, New York Public Library; Susan Raudin, Bowdoin College; Rona Roob, The Museum of Modern Art; Kenneth W. Rose, Rockefeller Archive Center; Lori Rosman, Pratt Library; Kathleen Ryan, Philadelphia Museum of Art; Katie Sasser, Bowdoin College; Karen Schneider, The Phillips Collection; Linda Seckelson, The Metropolitan Museum of Art; Nancy M. Shawcross, University of Pennsylvania; Tania Shichtmas; Eileen Meyer Sklar, Delaware Art Museum; Helen (Mrs. John) Sloan; Abigail G. Smith, Fogg Art Museum; Amanda Smith, Harvard University; Shawn Steidinger, The Metropolitan Museum of Art; Cathie Stover, Archives of American Art, Washington Center; Ruth Sudermeyer, Pratt Library; Fiorella Gioffredi Superbi, The Harvard Center for Italian Renaissance Studies, Florence; Judy Throm, Archives of American Art, Washington Center; Gilbert Vicaro, Philadelphia Museum of Art; Robert Wark, Henry E. Huntington Library and Art Gallery; Merri-Todd Webster, Pratt Library; Richard Whitaker, Pratt Library; Oscar White; Ryan Weber, The Detroit Institute of Arts; Patricia Willis, Yale University; and Judith Zilczer, Hirshhorn Museum and Sculpture Garden.

This publication has been funded in part
by a grant from Mrs. John Sloan.

INTRODUCTION

> When the Metropolitan Museum was founded, my father and uncle were its photographers, remaining so for many years. I have no memories farther back than those of being at the Museum.
>
> —Walter Pach

No American artist has had a more auspicious beginning in his chosen field. Within a year after his birth on July 11, 1883, Walter Pach was taken by his father, Gotthelf, from their home on upper Park Avenue to assignments at the Metropolitan on Fourteenth Street, where the infant is said to have crawled around on the museum floor even before he learned to walk.[1] By the time he was seven he was being encouraged by the museum's curator of paintings, George H. Story, who invited him to start copying the drawings of old masters in the Metropolitan's collection.

By all rights, however, Walter should have elected a career in photography. He was being groomed to become the second generation to head the family firm of Pach Brothers, official photographers to more than a dozen U.S. presidents beginning with Ulysses S. Grant. But a single photo assignment seems to have put a damper on that as Walter's chosen profession. While a student at the City College of New York, he worked for his father as a photographer's assistant during summer vacations. One job involved ascending the as-yet unfinished Flatiron Building, Manhattan's first skyscraper, to take panoramic pictures of the city. From a vantage point twenty stories above the street, Pach recalled, he used one arm to steady the tripod with the other tightly wrapped around an outside steel beam.[2]

During his last year at City College, he was enrolled in a drawing and aesthetics class taught by Leigh Harrison Hunt, a New York artist and writer. An indication of Walter's future interest and direction can be gleaned from his senior oration at the college, in which he stated that "as moderns—it is the tendencies of plastic art, music, and literature in our own era that we prefer to consider."[3]

Walter Pach's one goal in life was to become a successful professional artist and he craved to work at the easel on a daily basis. (Indeed, when I arranged an interview with him in 1952, he requested that I visit after the sunlight had begun to fade, for, as he put it, "I still paint every day.")[4]

Although he did gain a reputation as a painter and etcher, Pach became the consummate art educator as well. Through his writing of books, articles in some forty magazines and newspapers, and lectures in museums and colleges throughout the United States and beyond, he sought to teach the general public, as well as the art collector, the meaning and appreciation of modern art.

Pach wore the multiple hats of professor, art critic, historian, exhibition organizer, art consultant, and translator in order to accomplish this end. He helped in the formation of major American art collections and aided numerous museums in obtaining notable examples of both contemporary art and distinguished works from the past.

Upon graduation from college in 1903, Pach enrolled at the New York School of Art, where he took classes for the next three years with both of the school's leading instructors, William Merritt Chase and Robert Henri. The two men appeared to be opposites in their teaching styles and demeanor, yet one similarity was their praise for the Spanish master Diego Velásquez. Chase was labeled "one of the most ardent admirers of Velásquez"[5] at about the time that both he and Henri were making copies of the Spaniard's canvases in the Prado. And Henri informed his classes that "Velásquez . . . made a dozen strokes reveal more than most other painters could accomplish in a thousand."[6]

Pach attended Chase's summer class in Madrid in 1905 where he, too, copied Velásquez, as did his fellow students. Pach occasionally lectured to the group, for he could read and speak Spanish, as well as French, Dutch, Italian, and German. One of his classmates expressed an admiration for Pach's intellect by writing him:

> There is a large and always increasing demand for information by the public for *real* information about art from an artistic standpoint. . . . With your scholarly abilities I cannot see why you wouldn't make a fine writer on art subjects.[7]

Pach heeded the advice, for when he returned to Madrid the following summer with a class led by Henri, he devoted more time to researching an article about Velásquez than to painting in his style. The result was a treatise of nearly ten thousand words, which was published in *Scribner's* Magazine.[8] When Pach received a check for the article in the amount of $250,[9] he must have realized that his future livelihood would rest with the pen rather than the brush.

During the summer of 1907 Pach was once again with William Merritt Chase's class, this time assuming the dual roles of art history lecturer and instructor of painting in Florence. Pach stayed on in Europe after the Italian class ended, eventually taking up residence in Paris for nine months during the winter, spring, and summer of 1907–1908.

Thanks to his fluency in French, he gained entrée into the studios of well-known artists, resulting in several ground-breaking articles for *Scribner's*.

First there was the story about Claude Monet and "the scheme to bring [him] to America." According to Pach, "A French statesman who had recently visited our country conceived the idea . . ." (The statesman was Georges Clemenceau, who had married an American and was, in 1908, the premier of France.) Monet's response to Pach:

> "But I am old, now, to learn another country—one must know a place thoroughly before one can paint it. That's why I stay here in the country where I was born. I know it." So Monet will not go at once to make a record of America, though he expressed a desire to visit it.[10]

Now Pach also began to sharpen his writing skills by initiating what was to become an extensive, lifelong correspondence with individuals residing on both sides of the Atlantic. Among the first to whom letters flowed back and forth was Alice Klauber, a native of San Diego who had enrolled in Chase's 1907 summer art class in Italy [See p. 194].

Soon after interviewing Monet, Pach wrote to her from Paris:

> I did see Monet, and had a splendid two hours with him. . . . He showed me numberless pictures of all his career nearly. . . . Finally I came to the great question. . . . I said what was the opinion of some people on Matisse, and then asked: "Do you see these qualities?" There was not an instant's hesitation in his reply "Nullement." *French has no stronger* (polite) negation. He went on to say, quite fully, that . . . he has studied the [Matisse] pictures attentively . . . with all desire not to see another's mistakes added to the list of which his own misjudgment forms so prominent a part . . .[11]

The December 1908 issue of *Scribner's* contained another landmark piece by Pach titled "Cézanne—An Introduction." It has been heralded as the first appreciation of the artist to appear in an American magazine. Pach boldly characterized the Frenchman as "by all odds the strongest of recent influences in continental painting, and practically an unknown name in America!" Having viewed the Cézanne retrospective in the previous year's Salon d'Automne, Pach argued that "his greatness lies more in an intensely individual way of seeing nature than as an expresser of abstract artistic concepts."[12]

The explanations and arguments in favor of Cézanne were enlightening and even convincing to a portion of the uninformed public.

During his residency in Paris, Pach came to know numerous artists: Constantin Brancusi, whom he described as "that worker in the wooden shoes, living by himself in what seems a stone quarry . . ." and Raoul Dufy, "whose grandfather, having been a Scotchman, spelled the family name with a double 'f'";[13] Renoir, whose interview with Pach was the first one he had agreed to in thirty years;[14] and the brothers Marcel Duchamp, Raymond Duchamp-Villon, and Jacques Villon.

The amiable American would one day call upon Auguste Rodin and watch as the master sculpted a head in his presence,[15] while on two occasions Georges Rouault, who described himself to Pach as living "in the time of the cathedrals," came to visit *him*.[16]

By 1907 Pach was friendly with Gertrude and Leo Stein, and became a regular guest at their Saturday night soirees. Two years later Gertrude, who made a practice of writing portraits about the artists in her circle, including Picasso and Matisse, composed such a portrait of Pach:

> Some things are to him beautiful things, some things are to him desirable things . . . learning anything is to him a natural thing, succeeding in living is to him a natural thing, teaching any one is to him a necessary thing, teaching everything is to him a necessary thing. . . .[17]

It was at the Steins that Pach met Picasso and renewed his acquaintance with Matisse, to whom he was initially introduced during the summer of 1907 at the Steins' rented villa outside of Florence.[18] At first Pach found Matisse's work "just too incomprehensible for one of my background,"[19] but that changed quickly, in part because he was allowed to sit in on an art class taught by Matisse. At the urging of the art critic for the *New York American*, Pach, still in Paris, wrote an appreciation of Matisse for that newspaper. But when the editor viewed accompanying photographs of Matisse's work, he deemed them too unintelligible, and the article never saw the light of day.

Soon after Pach returned to New York toward the end of 1908 he met Arthur B. Davies and the two of them, together with Walt Kuhn, would select the foreign works for the 1913 Armory Show, an event destined to alter the course of American art. Davies had read Pach's article about Cézanne in *Scribner's* and then began sending French magazines to him for translation, as well as requests for photographs of art by French artists."I am more delighted than ever with Gauguin and his work . . . ," Davies wrote Pach in 1909. "I would wish to know more of this true artist . . ."[20]

Pach was also partly responsible for another major exhibition, the 1910 Independent Show. For years the National Academy of Design, the conservative molder of public taste, had made a practice of accepting more paintings for their annual exhibits than the galleries could accommodate, then eliminate those with strong evidence of being different in subject matter or technique. When the Academy's exhibition was held in December 1909, Pach was singled out for the ultimate affront when six of his entries were accepted, but none were hung in the show.[21]

The following month he attended a meeting with Robert Henri, John Sloan, George Luks, Everett Shinn, and Jerome Myers to plan an alternate exhibit, resulting in the 1910 Independent. Purposely planned to overlap the National Academy's spring annual and held in rented buildings, the exhibition featured more than six hundred works by over one hundred artists.

Between the fall of 1910 and January 1913 Pach was back in Paris. He studied for a time at the Académie Ranson with Paul Sérusier and Maurice Denis, two of the most avid followers of Gauguin who had belonged to the art group known as the Nabis ("Prophets" in Hebrew). In 1890 Denis had written an article titled "Définition du Neo-Traditionnisme," which began: "It is well to remember that a picture before being a battle horse, a nude woman, or some anecdote—is essentially a flat surface covered with colors assembled in a certain order."[22]

Whether Pach had actually read these words or heard them uttered by his mentor, he was already sympathetic to the Nabis philosophy of art inspired by the imagination and as an expression of ideas, as opposed to purely naturalistic representations. In Pach's article on Cézanne written two years before, he referred to the increase in artists and laymen who were "giving less attention to the externals and caring more for what is within. . . ."[23] This preference was to become the cornerstone of his critical writing for the rest of his career.

Pach continued to expand his friendships with European artists of the avant-garde. During November 1911 he met with several of the Italian Futurists—Umberto Boccioni, Gino Severini and Carlo Carrà—who had gathered in Paris prior to the first Futurist exhibit there. In 1911–1912 he was welcomed to artists' get-togethers in the Paris suburb of Puteaux, held in the adjoining studios of the brothers Duchamp: the painter Jacques Villon (who was born Gaston Duchamp) and Raymond Duchamp-Villon, sculptor. As Pach recalled years later:

> Two important events derived from these meetings. One was the splendid effort at collective expression staged by the Autumn Salon of 1912; the other was the exhibition entitled *La Section d'Or*, held simultaneously in the Rue la Boëtie.[24]

The 1912 Salon, seen from October 1 to November 8, marked the exhibit's tenth anniversary, so the milestone included a historical survey of more than two hundred nineteenth-century paintings, with canvases by Delacroix, Courbet, Corot, Manet, Monet, van Gogh, and Gauguin; Picasso and Matisse were among those represented in the contemporary section.

Arthur B. Davies had already approached Pach to suggest European artists for inclusion in the Armory Show scheduled for the following February, and Pach quickly envisioned the New York exhibition duplicating the Salon. Davies's letter of October 2, 1912, stated:

> Kuhn sailed for Hamburg to see the Sonderbund [Exhibit] at Cologne and to enlist for our show such artists with promise of the newest tendencies. . . . To those of us and men like yourself the possibilities loom tremendous . . .[25]

When Davies joined Walt Kuhn in Paris on November 6, they were guided by Pach to the studios of first-line artists, to the Steins, and to various galleries, with the hope that works would be loaned to the show. Pach's role was crucial. He once recalled a typical pitfall:

> One dealer . . . raised the issue of America's unpreparedness as to modern art; he was loath to let his pictures be used as a means to attract a merely gaping crowd. I was able to convince him that he must do his share in educating a new public . . .[26]

By the time Davies and Kuhn bid farewell to Paris and Pach, he had agreed to write biographies of each of the foreign artists, arrange for shipping the art to New York, serve as spokesman before the public and salesman at the armory, and produce pamphlets about Duchamp-Villon and Odilon Redon, plus a translation of Elie Faure's seventy-six-page essay on Cézanne, to be sold during the exhibition. For these services Pach was paid $1,200, becoming one of only two salaried employees (the other was Frederick James Gregg, art critic for the *New York Evening Sun*, who was named chairman of the Press Committee).

As Walt Kuhn acknowledges in *The Story of the Armory Show*:

> Walter Pach . . . furnished inestimable service to our undertaking. To his wide acquaintanceship among French artists and dealers, the advantages of his linguistic abilities and general knowledge of art, should be credited a large measure of our success.[27]

The reasons behind Pach agreeing to participate in the project were succinctly stated by him:

> It was, essentially, to get a better definition of living that the Armory Show was undertaken. America was living off the canned foods of art; there was fresh fruit, fresh meat on the tables of Paris, and it wanted its share. . . . It also set itself to end the reign of ignorance as to modern art that had prevailed in America since the bringing over of the Impressionists, almost thirty years before.[28]

The success of the Armory Show in ending America's "reign of ignorance as to modern art," though not immediate, was surely a strong beginning, and Pach was its major spokesman. It was he who consummated the sale of Cézanne's *The Poorhouse on the Hill* [retitled *View of the Domaine St. Joseph*] (late 1880s), to the Metropolitan Museum of Art, the first oil by that artist to enter a U.S. museum collection [See page 120]. Marcel Duchamp's infamous *Nude Descending a Staircase, No. 2* (1912) was also sold by him [See page 53], as was Matisse's *The Blue Nude* (1907), among dozens of other modern works.

Pach was represented in the Armory Show by five oils and a like number of etchings; his painting, *Flowers* (undated), was purchased by Henry Clay Frick.

When the exhibit moved on to Chicago, Pach accompanied it, causing him to bear the brunt of much of that city's hostility toward modern art. The day after his arrival, a newspaper reproduced a Pach painting alongside one by Matisse, beneath which were images of a pair of curious-looking people. The caption read: "Two of these Cubists are in Dunning [the local insane asylum], the other two are still at large. Can you tell which is which?"[29]

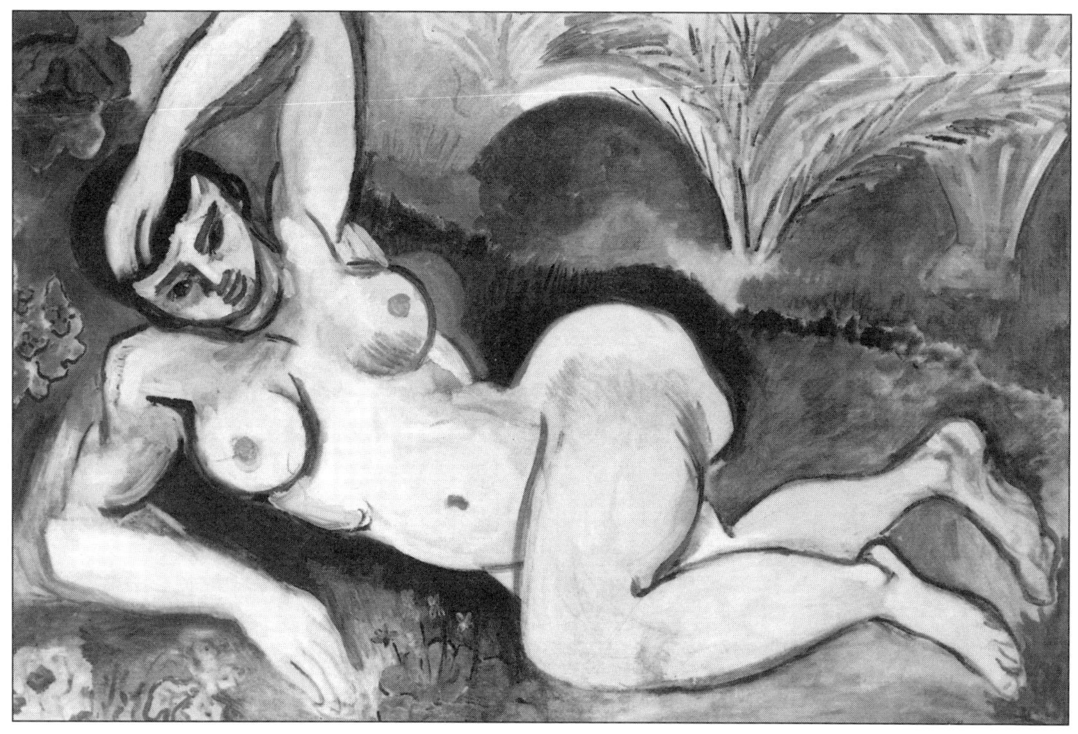

Henri Matisse, *Blue Nude ("Souvenir de Biskra")*, 1907. Oil on canvas, 36 1/4 x 55 1/4 in. The Baltimore Museum of Art: The Cone Collection, formed by Dr. Claribel Cone and Miss Etta Cone of Baltimore, Maryland. BMA 1950.228.

In the aftermath of the Armory Show, Pach's expertise was sought as new art galleries sprung up in New York. He organized exhibits of Matisse, Brancusi, and the Duchamp brothers for the Joseph Brummer Gallery, and in the fall of 1914 he traveled abroad to obtain work by the French moderns for the Carroll, Bourgeois, and Montross galleries. Although World War I had already erupted in Europe, the French capital appeared sufficiently safe for Pach to visit; besides, he was armed with a "To Whom It May Concern" letter from Theodore Roosevelt seeking official cooperation. As a result, Pach was successful in acquiring and transporting back to the United States art by Picasso, Derain, Redon, Rouault, Dufy, and Matisse.

The resultant one-man show of Matisse's art, comprised of nearly seventy-five drawings, paintings, sculptures, and prints, represented his first fully comprehensive solo exhibit in the United States when it opened at the Montross Gallery in January 1915.[30] (During Pach's visit with Matisse, the Frenchman showed his appreciation by etching a portrait of his American friend.)

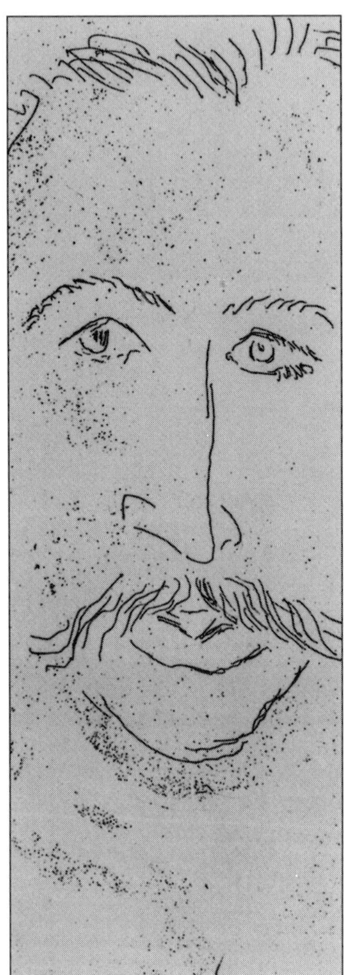

Henri Matisse, *Portrait of Walter Pach,* 1914. Etching, printed in black, plate: 6 5/16 x 2 3/8 in. The Museum of Modern Art, New York. Steven C. Clark Fund. Photograph © 2001, The Museum of Modern Art, New York.

Walter Pach was not only a promoter of European modern art, but its defender as well. Writing in *The New York Times* in March 1916, he admonished

> a young painter, back from abroad, who declared that the war had swept away Post-Impressionism, Cubism, and the other developments of art . . . and that those who were formerly ultra-modern in their tendencies, have become conservatives. . . .

On the same day that these statements appeared, another New York paper published interviews with Marcel Duchamp, Albert Gleizes, Jean Crotti, and Francis

> Picabia [who,] far from indicating any turning away from the principles of the Cubistic group . . . guaranteed their continuing the advance of new truths without a hint of going back to the old ideas . . .

Then, from a personal point of view, Pach added:

> Of the most important remaining members of the new schools—Matisse, Derain, Duchamp-Villon, Brancusi, Metzinger, Dufy, Rouault, and others, the writer can affirm, from having visited their studios since the war began, that nothing is further from their minds than any renunciation of the principles for which they have been contending for so many years.[31]

Pach's friend Marcel Duchamp was kept abreast of happenings in the New York art world by Pach, who sent him a copy of the catalog for the January 1915 Matisse exhibition at the Montross Gallery [See page 154]. The following April, Duchamp, expressed an interest in leaving France for America "*on the condition* that I could earn my living there."[32] Encouraged by Pach, he set sail for New York and was greeted at dockside by his friend.

As time would tell, even Pach had his limits when it came to the appreciation and acceptance of avant-garde art. In 1916 he and Duchamp were among the founding directors of the Society of Independent Artists. Anyone, amateur or professional, would be allowed to exhibit two works in its annual shows upon payment of a small initiation fee and dues. Democratic to the end, installation of the art would be done alphabetically, with no jury involved.

Perhaps Pach, for all his knowledge of Duchamp's creative outpouring, was unaware of the changes that had transpired since the *Nude Descending a Staircase*, for when Duchamp submitted a porcelain urinal titled *Fountain* (1917) and signed it with his pseudonym "R. Mutt," Pach joined other directors in voting it out of the show. As a Society press release sought to explain: "The *Fountain* may be a very useful object in its place, but its place is not an art exhibition and it is, by no definition, a work of art."[33] Duchamp resigned from the association, though he continued to correspond with Pach in subsequent years [See page 150].

The decade of the 1920s was a period when Pach was most prolific as a writer: he produced the translation of Elie Faure's five-volume *History of Art*, five books of his own, and more than sixty pieces for periodicals. Pach began contributing to *The Freeman*, an intellectual weekly, in 1920, writing thirty-one articles between June of that year and September 1923. Excerpts reveal the passion for his points-of-view:

> . . . why is there not more appreciation of art in this country? . . . we should have far more art-buyers . . . and we should be educating the public to the idea that possessing beautiful things is not the sole privilege of the very rich . . .[34]

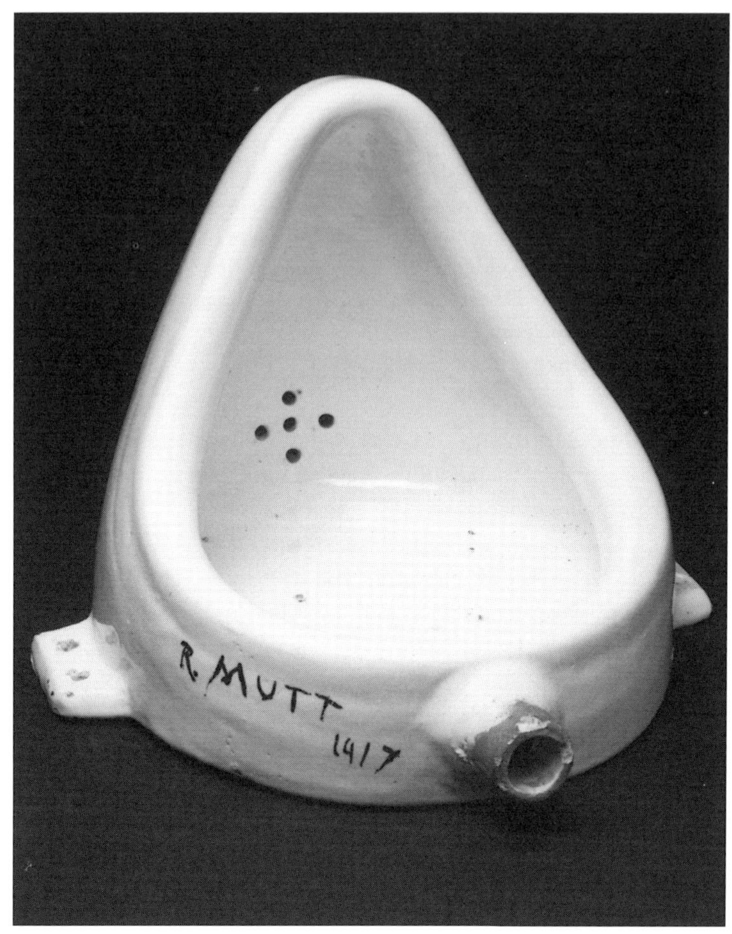

Marcel Duchamp, *Fountain (Second Version)*, 1950. Readymade: glazed sanitary china with black paint, 12 x 15 x 18 in. Philadelphia Museum of Art: Gift (by exchange) of Mrs. Herbert Cameron Morris. Photograph by Graydon Wood, 1998.

It is American life itself that must move on to the mature individuality out of which will naturally grow self-realization, style—art. We are outgrowing the formlessness of a pioneering people pushing out into the gigantic adventure of a new continent . . . [t]he unspeakable trash that the crowd likes—moderately—in our magazines and exhibitions [should not] be thought of as American art simply because there is so much of it.[35]

. . . pictures [by amateurs in the 1921 Society of Independent Artists exhibition] are not as bad as many of the "serious" works of the professionals; for, weak in craftsmanship as most of the amateur things are, they have at least the attractiveness of things done *con amore* [with love], whereas most if not all of the work done nowadays by men who paint solely to earn money is as unlovable as the other products of commercialism.[36]

> It was Cézanne—and to this he owes his immense importance—who saw that the reality we sought was not to be obtained by making an eye-deceiving counterfeit of nature, but that by erecting a structure of form and colour whose intervals and harmonies repeat the rhythm that the world establishes in our brain, we produce a "truer" thing than any imitative process can pretend to.[37]

It was through this publication that Pach became friendly with Van Wyck Brooks, a member of its editorial staff [See page 93], and Lewis Mumford [See page 204]. Pach referred to Brooks as "one of the most brilliant and likable men I know."[38] On the other hand, Mumford praised Pach in his book, *The Brown Decades*, stating that he

> placed the American artist on a footing with his contemporaries in Europe, and overcame, through his keen criticism and excellent expositions, the touch of provincialism that would in the long run have proved a serious handicap to American art.[39]

Another contact on *The Freeman* proved invaluable, for the magazine's publisher and business manager, B. W. Huebsch, aided in the publication of one or more of Pach's books. Pach's *The Master of Modern Art* (1925) probably did more than any other volume at the time to explain modernism methodically and sympathetically to a public still largely suspicious and unaccepting of the new art forms. In clarifying Cubism, for example, Pach wrote:

> Our knowledge of objects depends on seeing them from different sides. Braque and Picasso paint them so; the recombination of the planes . . . [provides] the means for relating, one with another, the phases of sight retained by memory . . .[40]

Three years later Pach's volume, *Ananias, or the False Artist*, appeared. In it he attacked an academician such as William-Adolphe Bouguereau as one with "the bad ideas of a generation or two ago, whom we blush to remember on our grandfather's walls" and Léon Bakst as "a slight and ill-schooled draftsman, without vision or conviction . . .[41]

Pach also castigated the American portraitist J. Carroll Beckwith for his "ingenious explanation of Germany's bloodlust" during the early days of World War I. Beckwith was quoted in *The New York Times* as feeling that

> France was responsible for it, for she had been systematically exporting large quantities of modern art to her neighbor . . . and it was German consumption of such stimulants that had driven the good, industrious nation to madness and war."[42]

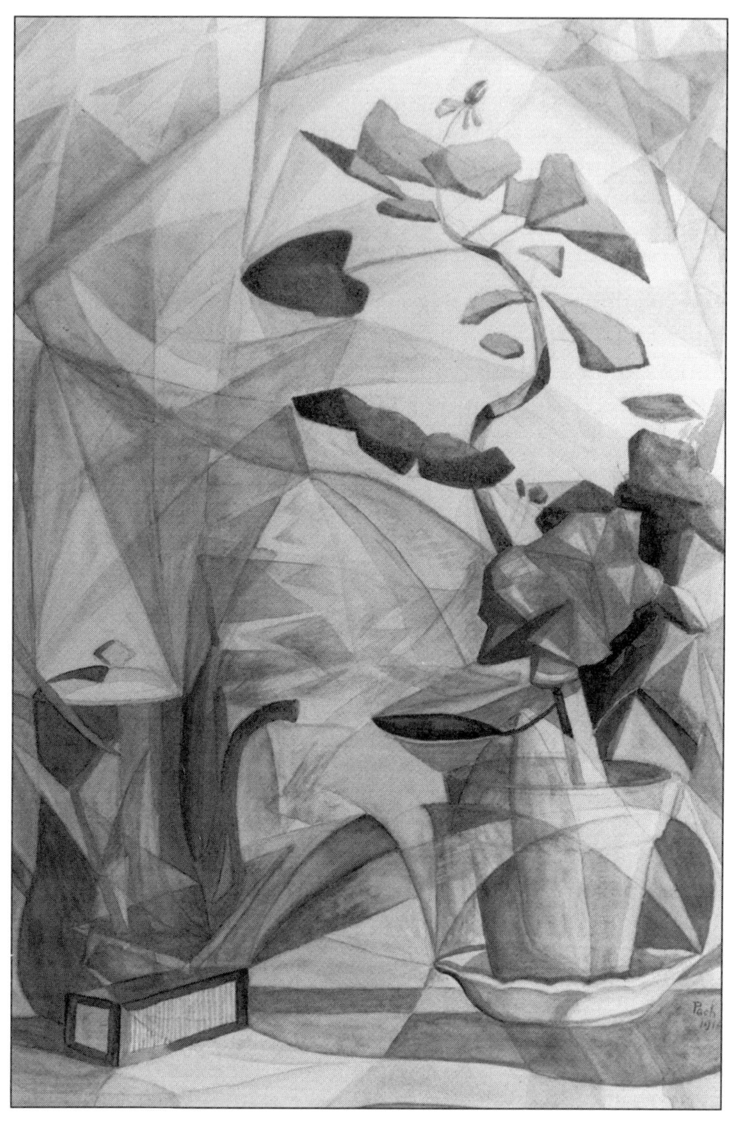

Walter Pach, *Untitled (Cubist Still Life)*, 1914. Watercolor on illustration board, 13 3/4 x 9 7/8 in. Whitney Museum of American Art, New York, Gift of Francis Steegmuller, in memory of Gerda and Beatrice Stein. 85.22.

Pach concluded that part of the blame for the false artist rested with the American museum, since it was

> the most important factor in the progress toward better taste on the part of the public. But not until the institution has reached the maturity of knowing how to deal with modern work will it fulfill its whole function.[43]

Pach's heavy writing schedule did not preclude his devoting considerable time to producing and exhibiting his art. Despite the brouhaha over Marcel Duchamp's *Fountain* and its rejection from the 1917 Society of Independent Artists show, Pach continued to expend his energies on the organization, accepting the position of treasurer in its inaugural year and retaining the post for the next fifteen seasons. (For five of those years his wife Magda, whom he had married in 1914, served as its secretary.)

In the Society's first exhibit, Pach's entries included *Sunday Night* (later retitled *St. Patrick's at Night*) (1916), a cubist cityscape. It is this style in which he had been painting since the Armory Show. Pach continued to exhibit with the Independents each year during the 1920s and 1930s, showing oils and watercolors of varied subject matter, as indicated by such titles as *Seated Nude*, *Flowers*, and *Street in Mexico City*.

The latter painting, exhibited in the 1923 Independent, was created as a result of Pach's having been in the Mexican capital the previous year to teach at the National University of Mexico. This was his first year-long experience of lecturing in a foreign land. "The work will be light and along the lines I know," he wrote a fellow artist, (except that it will be in Spanish, which I never before spoke publicly).[44] Pach observed that the most assiduous visitor to his sessions was José Clemente Orozco, a political cartoonist at the time who would shortly turn to creating murals.[45]

Pach was instrumental in having seven Mexican artists invited to exhibit with the Independents the following year, which number included Diego Rivera, Jean Charlot, and Orozco. He subsequently wrote an article about them:

> The special feature of this year's [1923] exhibition was the remarkable group of Mexican artists who were the guests of the Society. The admirable cultural life of these people across the border is very little known in the United States; . . . I can remember no previous showing of Mexican painting in our exhibitions.[46]

Walter Pach's own art received mixed reviews. Commenting on his abstract canvas of *Sunday Night*, Frank Jewett Mather Jr., art critic for *The Nation*, found it "very soothing and fascinating, without having the least idea of what it's all about. It looks rather hypnotizing."[47]

Pach had his first one-man show in 1925 at the age of forty-one. Of a solo exhibit the following year featuring his prints, a *New York Herald Tribune* critic wrote that

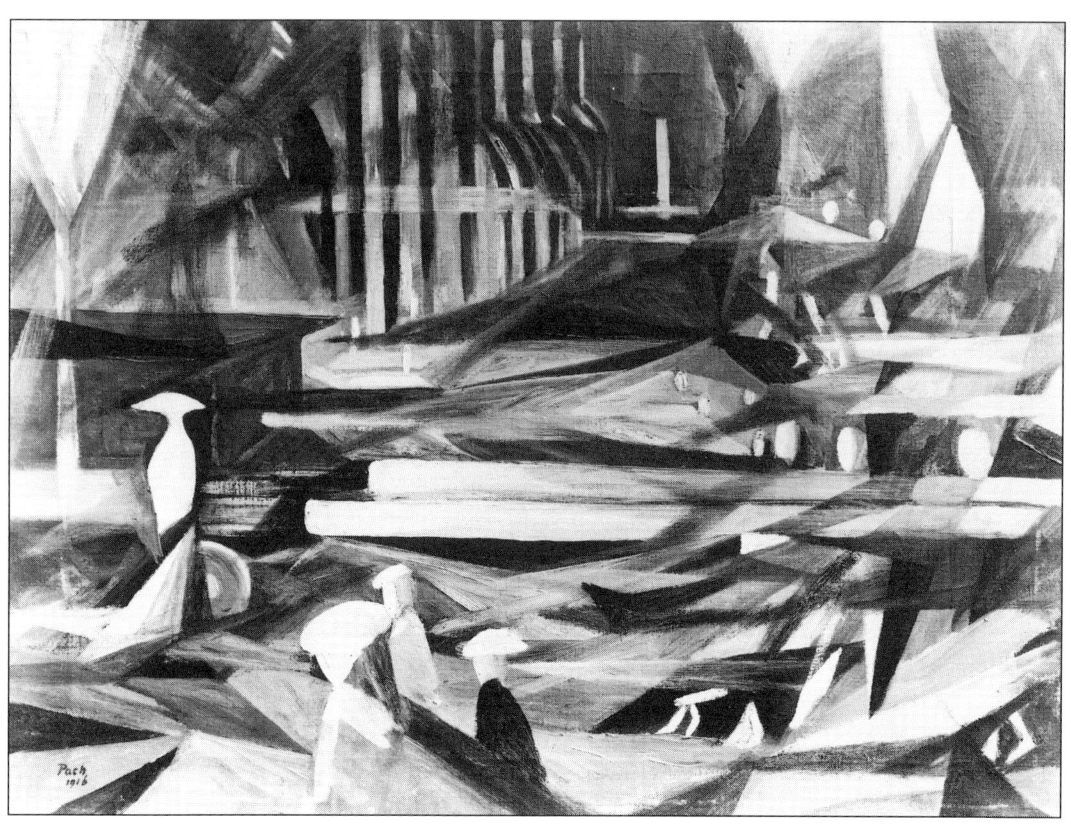

Walter Pach, *Sunday Night* (retitled *St. Patrick's at Night*), 1916. Oil on canvas, 18 x 24 in. Photograph courtesy Peter A. Juley and Son Collection, Smithsonian American Art Museum.

> Pach, hitherto known to us only as a painter, comes forward at the Weyhe Gallery with a quantity of etchings. To put it candidly, he is about three times as skillful with the [etching] needle as he is with the brush, and, in fact, leaves a capital impression with these plates.[48]

The Art News reviewed Pach's one-man show at the Kraushaar Galleries in 1927, its critic commenting that

> Pach paints in big masses; his edges are hard and his whole statement is precise, [his canvases] carefully balanced and deliberately planned . . . sometimes by a quite complicated system of forces . . .[49]

Another one-man exhibit in 1928 at the same gallery evoked this response:

> . . . although he has a tendency to report his findings in the field of modern painting with encyclopaedic dryness . . . in the present exhibition the painter has made himself more clearly heard and, in consequence, the show is by far the best Pach has had.[50]

Amid all of the painting and writing, the exhibitions, magazine articles, and books, Pach left for Paris to spend the summer of 1926 directing the first courses for Americans held at the École du Louvre. His teaching often involved lecturing both mornings and afternoons before rows of paintings in the Louvre Museum.

Four years later Pach returned to Paris to take up residence there, a move occasioned by the hostile reception voiced by some critics of his latest book, *Ananias, and the False Artist*. Shortly after its publication in the fall of 1928, Pach received a letter from Lee Simonson, editor of *Creative Art* Magazine. After thanking him for "being so pleasant about extending your article on Rivera at the last minute,"[51] Simonson described his own forthcoming review of *Ananias* as

> extremely hard hitting. I have maintained, as I told you personally that everything you say is true and all of it unimportant, and . . . that if you succeeded in what you desired to do you had merely found an institution that within ten years would be an academy, although under another name.
>
> In fact, I have attacked your point of view so hard, that I feel you should have the opportunity to reply—at our usual rates—in the next number. . . .[52]

Pach refused the offer.

Rockwell Kent, a former classmate of Pach's at the New York School of Art and "admittedly unmodern,"[53] produced a similarly negative review in *The Bookman*:

> Walter Pach has written . . . three hundred and forty-five pages of professional drivel. . . . What moral priggery to call Meissonier and his kind "false artists"! They are exactly what they tried to be, good photographic painters. . . . There's room in the world for every kind of art but no room in a decently ordered society for the artist who plays politics.[54]

And William Howe Downes, retired art critic for *The Boston Transcript*, took Pach to task in an *American Magazine of Art* article, writing that, in *Ananias*,

> he sets aside the goats on the one hand and the sheep on the other, quite in the Ruskinian manner. . . . It must be a grand and glorious feeling to be as sure as he seems to be of his own infallibility.

Downes elucidated:

> As an instance of intolerance, the treatment of John Sargent is especially to be noticed. Was it not disingenuous to pick out one of the poorest examples of Sargent's

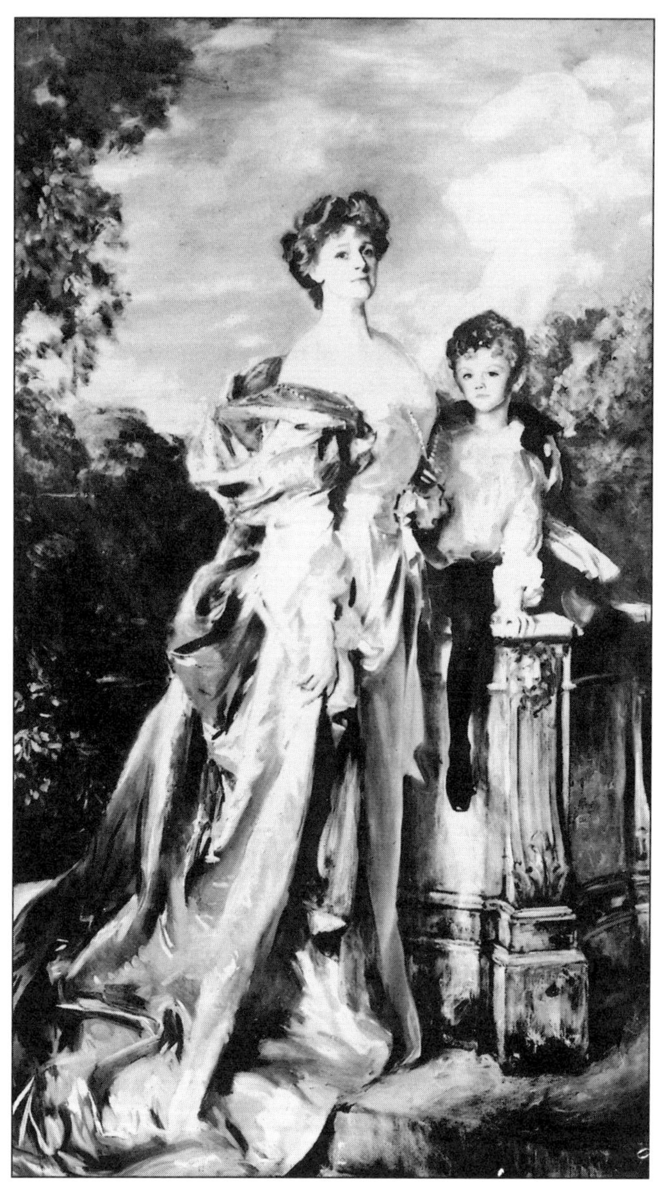

John Singer Sargent, *Lady Warwick and Her Son*, 1905. Oil on canvas, 105 1/2 x 60 3/8 in. Worcester Art Museum, Worcester, Massachusetts, Museum Purchase 1913.69. Photograph courtesy Peter A. Juley and Son Collection, Smithsonian American Art Museum.

> work in America—the picture in the Worcester Art Museum—as a target, when there are so many Sargents far better than that in our museums?[55]

What Pach had said in his book was that

> [Sargent] really hated the "society portraits" that crowded in on him in ever-increasing numbers. "I've simply got to finish that damn thing," he said of his big canvas of the Countess of Warwick and her son, "the boy keeps getting older and the woman keeps getting younger";—which did not prevent him from recommending the picture as one of his best works to the museum of Worcester, Mass., which purchased it accordingly.[56]

A footnote in *Ananias* indicates that the former of these two facts came from Sargent's friend and admirer, William Merritt Chase; the latter from the one-time director of the Worcester Museum.

Lost on the average reader of Downes's criticism of Pach was the fact that Downes had authored a biography of Sargent just three years before, in which he quoted from the *Bulletin* of the Worcester Museum that Sargent's *Lady Warwick and her Son* (1905) "was said to be a favorite with the artist himself; it was painted with a professed liking for the subject."[57] Adding insult to injury, Pach highlighted his disdain for the Sargent portrait by giving it the dubious honor of being reproduced on the dust jacket of his book.

Pach's three-year, self-imposed exile in Paris did not diminish his role as champion for worthy causes. Early in 1931 he initiated efforts to have a painting by Thomas Eakins accepted by the Louvre [See pages 158, 161ff]. Pach had interviewed Eakins many years before, and in a 1923 article titled "A grand Provinciale" he pointed out that "We have been long in realizing the importance of his work."[58]

Simultaneously, Pach was instrumental in arranging the sale of Jacques Louis David's masterpiece, *The Death of Socrates* (1787), to The Metropolitan Museum of Art, having learned that its French owner was willing to part with it [See page 124]. And when John Sloan was on the verge of resigning as president of The Art Students League the following April over his attempt to have George Grosz, the satiric German artist, hired to teach there, Pach cabled the school in support of Sloan [See page 373].

The sum of Pach's paintings, drawings, and prints produced during the preceding thirty months were displayed in a one-man show at Paris' Galerie Dru during March 1932. Some were portraits, others florals, landscapes, and Parisian street scenes; still others were created at the time, during a visit to Tangier, Morocco, which had long fascinated him because of that country's effect upon Eugène Delacroix, one of Pach's favorite artists. Yet the most surprising subjects in his exhibit were a series of watercolors of animals: A pig, fox, leopard, tiger, and wild boar. While Delacroix, well-known for such subject matter, chose to sketch his beasts in the Paris zoo, Pach enrolled at L'École d'Art Animalier, an art school that housed such animals on the premises.

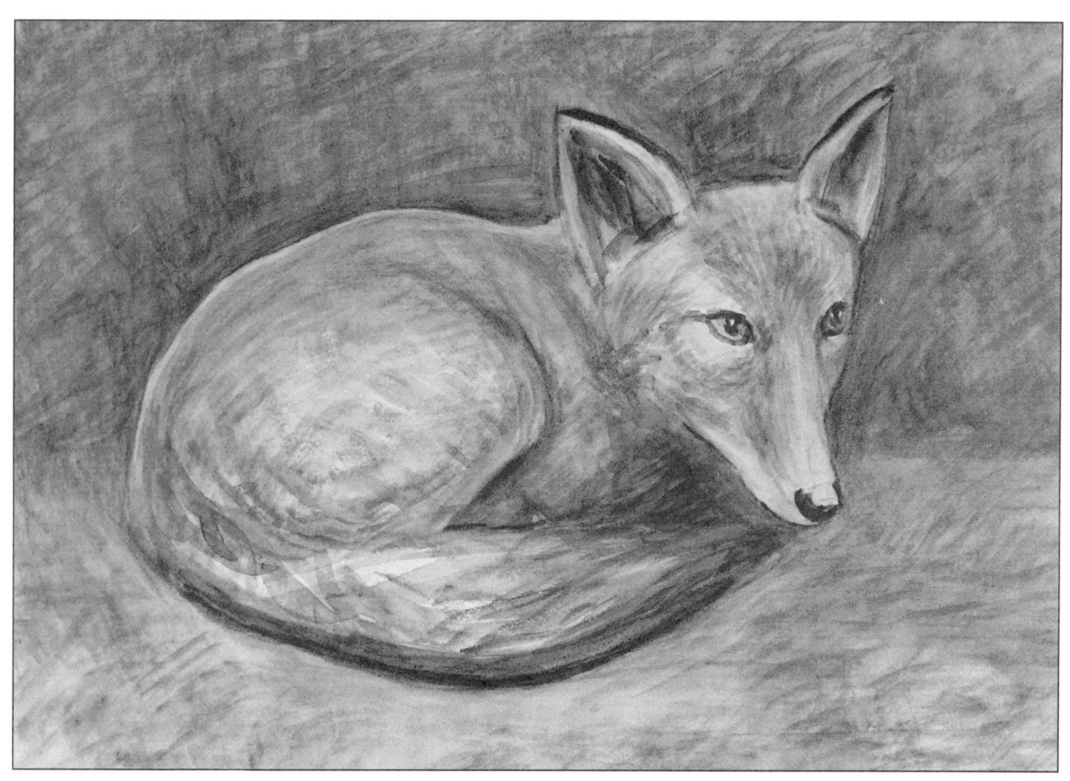

Walter Pach, *The Fox,* 1931. Charcoal and watercolor, 10 1/2 x 13 1/2 in. The Baltimore Museum of Art: The Cone Collection, formed by Dr. Claribel Cone and Miss Etta Cone of Baltimore, Maryland. BMA 1950.355.

Pach's fascination with Delacroix would culminate in his translation of *The Journal of Eugène Delacroix* from the French; the 731-page volume appeared in 1937.

Walter Pach's return to the United States in the fall of 1932 was heralded by *Time* Magazine in an article headlined "Pach Back." *Time* reminded its readers that

> [F]or years he has blazed a defense of modern painting up and down the columns of a dozen newspapers and magazines in language that would have pleased a frontier editor in gold rush days.[59]

Less than nine months later Pach was engaged in another crusade, this one involving the dismissal of Diego Rivera from his Rockefeller Center mural project and the boarding up of the art. As a member of a committee of artists and writers, Pach sought to personally negotiate a settlement with Abby and John D. Rockefeller Jr. [See page 326].

The reality of having to earn a living in New York City "at American prices," compared with the lower costs in Paris, occurred to Pach prior to his return to the United States. Early in 1932 he wrote to John Sloan:

> I've sent off some letters, lately, with regard to lectures . . . the idea has been turning around in my head that instead of working with a lay public, I ought to pass on what I've been learning of works of art to those who are most directly interested—to art students.[60]

Consequently, rather than continuing to present lectures primarily in museums, as he had been doing on weekends for thirteen years at the Metropolitan Museum and during the week at similar institutions throughout the country, Pach arranged to provide a series of illustrated talks beginning in 1932 at The Art Students League of New York.

In 1936 he continued to target students of art by becoming a member of the advisory board of the American Artists School in Manhattan, serving with Max Weber, Margaret Bourke-White, William Gropper, and others.

By June of that year Pach was involved in producing another book for, as he explained, "my friend Van Wyck Brooks . . . [is] eager for me to go through with my scheme of writing on the artists I have known."[61] The result was Pach's autobiographical *Queer Thing, Painting*, published in 1938. The unlikely title is typical of Pach's penchant for research and scholarship; he once revealed that those words had been uttered by J. M. W. Turner at a Royal Academy banquet a hundred years earlier.[62]

Because of the hostile reception of *Ananais* a decade before, Pach craved reactions to his latest volume. The first one he received came from Brooks, who wrote him that *Queer Thing, Painting*

> has moved me more than anything I have read this year. . . . Most of this book is wise, with the wisdom of the heart. It is steeped in your attitude in all these matters, that "humility is a primary need," etc., etc. You have the humility,—you couldn't know as much if you didn't! . . .[63]

At some point during the Depression of the 1930s, Pach sought to obtain a steady job in order to ease his own financial shortfall. By then the Pachs' son Raymond, born in 1914, was a student at Bowdoin College.

Between 1934 and 1938 Pach averaged publication of only two magazine articles a year, and royalties from two books—*Queer Thing, Painting* and *Vincent Van Gogh, 1853–1890*—could not be counted on to cover his day-to-day expenses. He had already concluded that "my painting, not being anything to depend on for a living, I thought of a museum position."[64]

An opportunity arose when plans for establishing a National Gallery of Art in Washington were announced. Pach wrote to his friend Paul J. Sachs, associate director of Harvard's Fogg Art Museum, in October 1939, seeking his aid in obtaining a position there [See page 345]. Although a curatorial post was not forthcoming, the lengthy resumé sent to Sachs was shared by him with David E. Finley, chosen to become the first director of the National Gallery, and John Walker III, its chief curator. All three men were members of a special advisory committee for the 1940 New York World's Fair, and within weeks Pach was hired to organize a sizable "Masterpieces of Art" exhibition for the coming summer's event.

With the title of "Director General" bestowed upon him, Pach was charged with the daunting task of seeking the loan of sixteenth, seventeenth, eighteenth, and nineteenth-century masterpieces to fill three pavilions erected on the fair grounds for their display. The "Masterpieces of Art" exhibit at the 1939 New York World's Fair had been limited to works from foreign collections; however, the outbreak of World War II scuttled any plans to borrow from Europe again.

Pach pressed his wife into service as a typist and sent out dozens of letters. Replies ranged from Edsel Ford's refusal to part with his Renoir to Duncan Phillips's proposal to lend works other than the ones Pach had sought. Pach was also required to crisscross the country in order to view private collections from which he could earmark substitutes for art that was unavailable.

The exhibit for the 1939 Fair had not included nineteenth-century art, so Pach had a field day choosing selections from that period. Among the European examples were works by David, Ingres, Delacroix, Corot, Daumier, Courbet, Millet, Degas, Manet, Morisot, Monet, Pissarro, Sisley, Renoir, Cézanne, Redon, Gauguin, van Gogh, Seurat, and Toulouse-Lautrec; among the Americans, Inness, Whistler, Homer, Ryder, Sargent, Eakins, Duveneck, Davies, Glackens, Prendergast, Henri, Luks, and Cassatt.

The artists represented were many of those who had been in the Armory Show. And, upon request, the Rockefellers contributed $500 to provide documents for the exhibit, a role Pach himself had played at the 1913 exhibition. Pach's expertise and untiring efforts resulted in the gathering together of better than two thousand works of art; then, after the exhibit opened, he found it necessary to be on hand on a regular basis.

The fall of 1942 found Pach once again in Mexico City, lecturing at the University. He revealed the reason for his move in a letter to John Sloan:

> The last two years—since the World's Fair job—have been a time of almost absolute financial drought for me. We have been living almost wholly on past earnings, and the prospects for the coming season looked worse than ever. The jobs I tried for were refused me; no sale of pictures, few lectures; and every attempt to earn by writing knocked on the head. So, as expenses here [in Mexico] are from a fourth to a third of what they were in New York . . . I am happy over our outlook.[65]

During the years of World War II, Pach had begun writing another book, *The Art Museum in America*, which was published in 1948. Reviews were favorable. *Art News*

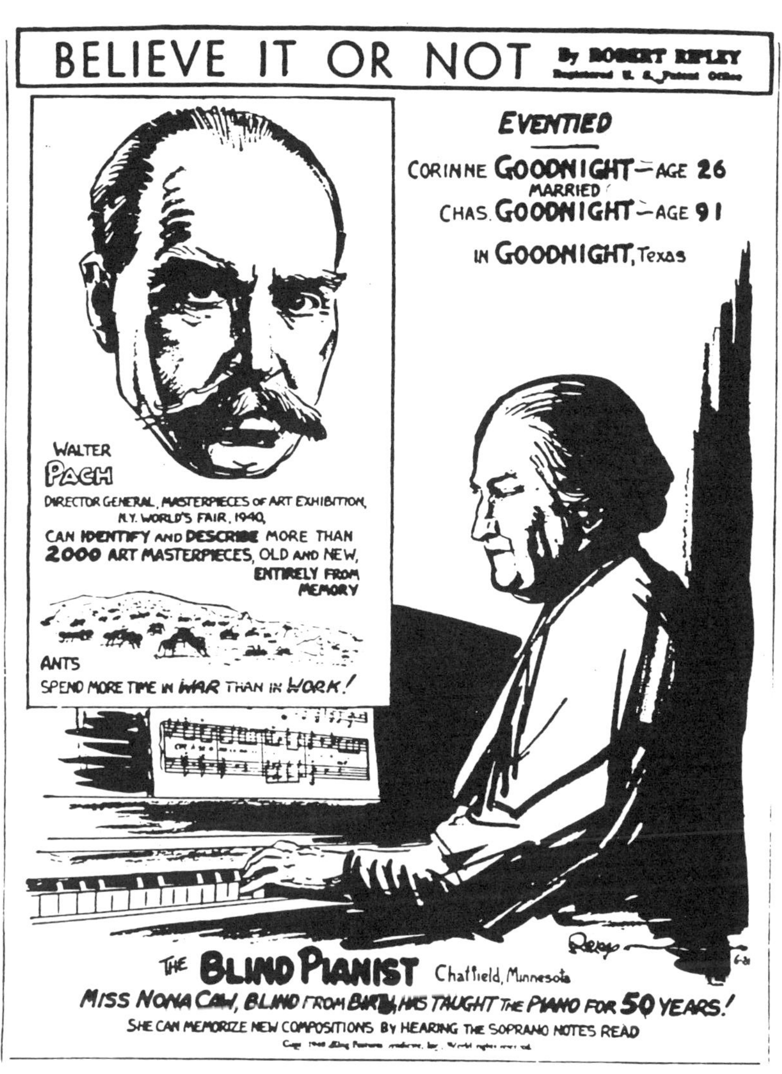

"Ripley's Believe It or Not!" from *The New York Journal-American,* June 24, 1940. Copyright 2001 Ripley Entertainment Inc.

described the author as "well qualified by his years of experience in the art world . . . [and] in his learned, rambling and high-minded survey of American museums, [he explains] how it grew and how it must continue to grow."[66]

The writer for *Art Quarterly* stated:

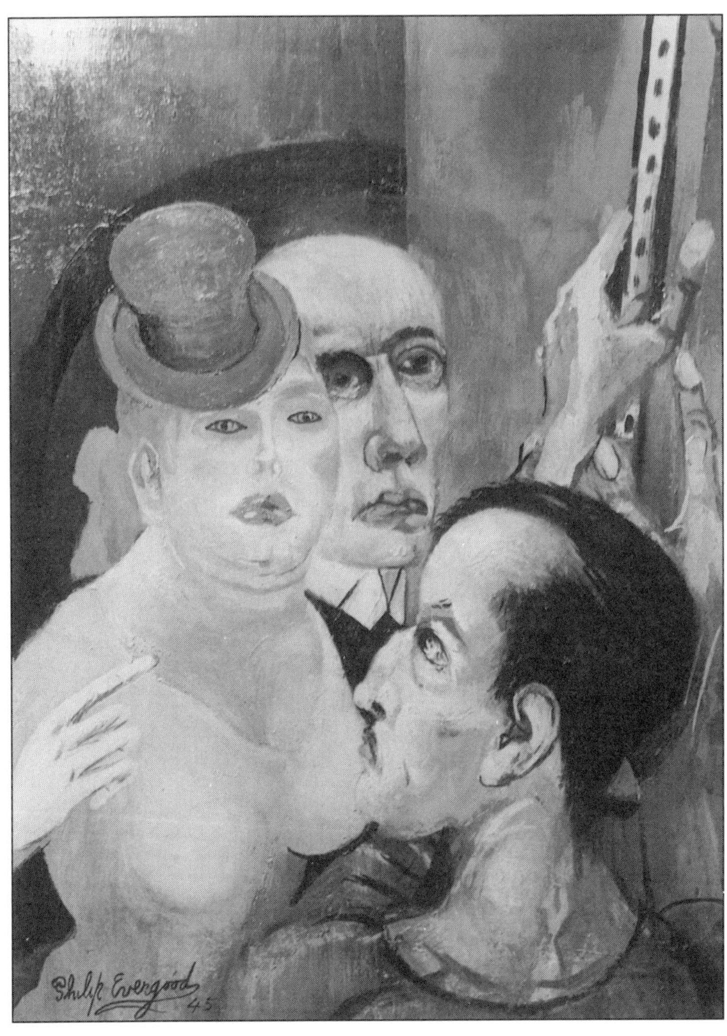

Philip Evergood, *No Sale,* 1945. Oil on canvas, 26 1/8 x 20 1/8 in. The Baltimore Museum of Art: Gift of the Shilling Foundation. BMA 1946.133.

The first thing which impressed this reviewer when reading Mr. Pach's book was the author's enthusiasm . . . that Mr. Pach is content with digressions is not one of the lesser *tours de force* of *The Art Museum in America.* The long chapter on "Recent Accessions," for instance, which might have been trite or dry, contains a wealth of anecdotes which could find no place in a dignified catalogue of paintings but which will be helpful to future scholars.[67]

Tucked away on page 220 of the volume is reference to

> certain acquisitions which have come to our museums, not through their own initiative, but as gifts from a small foundation established to promote the welfare of American artists. It derives from the bequest of an old painter, Alexander Shilling, and is administered by men of his calling.[68]

Shilling, an American painter and etcher who had died in 1937, bequeathed his modest estate to two friends with the suggestion that they use his funds to benefit artists. What Pach did not reveal, in his typically modest manner, was that since 1939 he had been overseeing a plan to use the funds to purchase works by painters and sculptors, then donate them to U.S. museums. Pach was designated chairman of the fund committee, which members included John Sloan; George Grosz; Edwin M. M. Warburg, of the Museum of Modern Art; and Talbot Faulkner Hamlin, professor of architecture at Columbia University.

During the ensuing years, works by Philip Evergood, Hugo Robus, Jacob Lawrence, A. S. Baylinson, John B. Flannagan, and others were donated; and The Metropolitan Museum of Art; Museum of Fine Arts, Boston; the Philadelphia Museum of Art; Detroit Institute of Arts; and the Art Institute of Chicago were among the institutions benefiting from this effort.

When Pach's responsibilities with the fund began winding down in the early 1950s, he initiated a new venture: an art gallery in the B. Altman's department store on Thirty-fourth Street. It opened in 1952 as "The Gallery of Fine Prints" and was thought to be the first fine arts gallery in the country housed within such an establishment.

The art was exhibited in three rooms on the store's fifth floor, where more than one hundred framed pictures could be accommodated. Displays were changed every six weeks or as pictures were sold. Through his numerous contacts, Pach was able to obtain etchings, engravings, lithographs, woodcuts, and the like on consignment; the artists represented included Rembrandt, Picasso, Matisse, Millet, and others.

The president of B. Altman's, John Burke Jr., felt that the gallery's major attraction was the fact that Pach personally chose all of the art offered for sale. To emphasize the point, Pach's name appeared in all of the news releases and newspaper advertising.

Shortly before Pach's sixty-seventh birthday he received a letter from the French Embassy in New York which read:

> On behalf of the French Government, I have the honor to inform you that the President of the Republic of France has conferred upon you the cross of Chevalier of the Legion of Honor, on the proposition of the Minister of Foreign Affairs, by decree of February 20th.[70]

While the reasons for the award were not spelled out in the communication, they undoubtedly involved a lifetime of promoting French art, art history, and literature, including the translation of Elie Faure's five-volume *History of Art*.

Although Pach was not similarly honored in this country, he continued to promote American artists of varied styles and reputations. Writing an article in the *Atlantic*

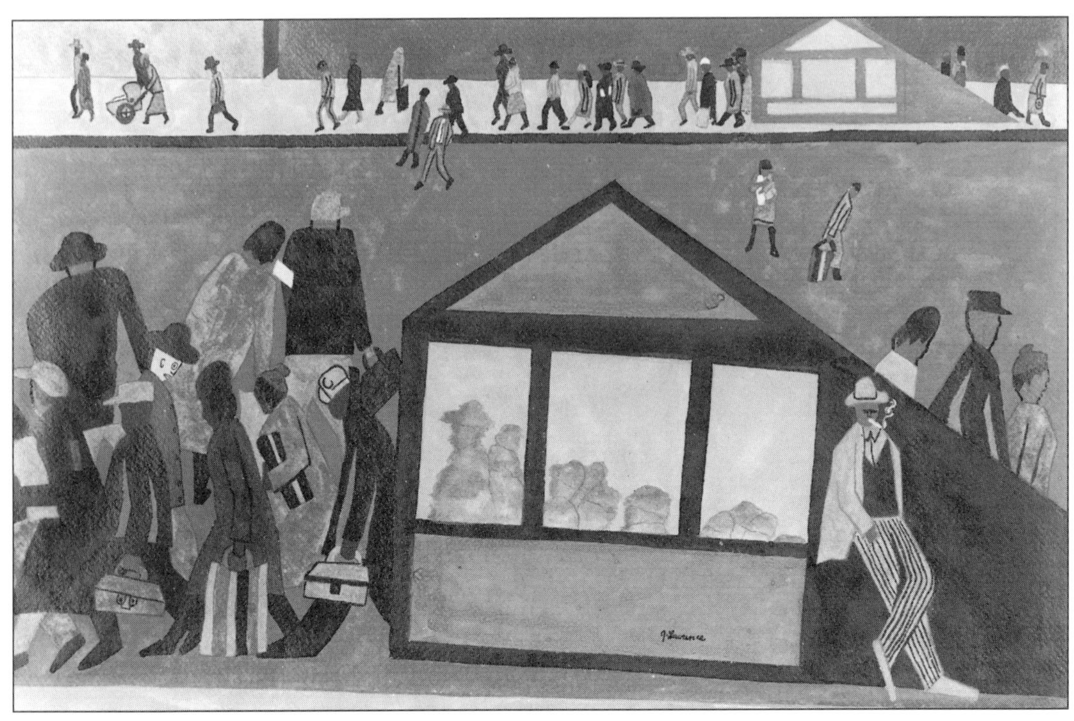

Jacob Lawrence, *Subway—Home from Work*, 1943. Watercolor on paper, 14 x 21 1/4 in. Virginia Museum of Fine Arts, Gift of The Alexander Shilling Fund. Acc. # 44.18.1. Photograph by Ron Jennings.

Monthly a year before he died, Pach argued convincingly that "there are submerged artists in every generation, painters whose excellence is not recognized until long after their deaths."[71] Among those to whom he affixed the label were John Vanderlyn, John Quidor, William Rimmer, Ryder, Eakins, and Prendergast.

Pach had continued to paint all the while. When the Laurel Gallery presented what would prove to be the final one-man show held during his lifetime, an *ARTnews* review read:

> WALTER PACH . . . Armory Show organizer, art historian, translator and ARTnews contributor, currently exhibits another of his many talents. His portraits and still-lifes are sensitive, conservatively realist works, executed in a competent if somewhat laborious technique. There are occasional lapses of taste, as in the garish blue and orange contrasts in a picture of ancient Mexican sculptures and fresh fruits. But for the most part, especially in the portraits and in a studio interior, Pach has his medium well under control, and creates a quiet poetry.[72]

By then Pach's paintings and prints were represented in many of the museums that today include his work: The Metropolitan Museum of Art, The Museum of Modern Art, the Whitney Museum of American Art, The Phillips Collection, and museums in Brooklyn, Philadelphia, Baltimore, Cleveland, Detroit, and Los Angeles, among others.

When Walter Pach died on November 27, 1958, the heading over his obituary in *The New York Times* read: "WALTER PACH, 75, PAINTER IS DEAD." For once his role as an artist received star billing. He would have liked that.

Editor's Note: For further biographical details provided by Pach himself, see his letter to Paul J. Sachs of October 26, 1939, on page 346.

Notes

Letter from Walter Pach to Paul J. Sachs, Oct. 26, 1939. Fogg Art Museum Archives, Harvard University.

1. Raymond Pach conversation with the author, Dec. 4, 1987.

2. Ibid.

3. Walter Pach Papers, Archives of American Art (AAA), reel 4220, frame 362.

4. Walter Pach conversation with the author, Sept. 5, 1952.

5. "The Collector," *The Art Amateur* 40 (May 1899), 115.

6. *The Art Spirit by Robert Henri*, compiled by Margery Ryerson. (Philadelphia: J. B. Lippencott & Co., 1923), 71.

7. Letter from Frank R. Wadsworth to Walter Pach, [postmarked] March 2, 1905. Walter Pach Papers, AAA, reel 4216, frames 745, 746.

8. Walter Pach, "The 'Memoria' of Velasquez," *Scribner's* Magazine 42 (July 1907), 38–52.

9. Walter Pach Papers, AAA, reel 4216, frames 760, 761.

10. Walter Pach, "At the Studio of Claude Monet," *Scribner's* Magazine 43 (June 1908), 765.

11. Letter from Walter Pach to Alice Klauber, Nov. 16, 1907. Alice Klauber Papers, Archives of the San Diego Museum of Art.

12. Walter Pach, "Cézanne—An Introduction," *Scribner's* Magazine 44 (Dec. 1908), 765, 768.

13. Walter Pach, *Queer Thing, Painting* (New York: Harper & Brothers, 1938), 173.

14. "Pierre Auguste Renoir," *Scribner's* Magazine 51 (May 1912), 606–612.

15. Pach, *Queer Thing, Painting*, 81.

16. Letter from Walter Pach to Ida Guggenheimer, July 7, 1930. Ida Guggenheimer Papers, AAA, reel 4039, frame 17.

17. Gertrude Stein, *Two: Gertrude Stein and Her Brother / and Other Early Portraits* [1908–1912] (New Haven: Yale University Press, 1951), 339.

18. Pach, *Queer Thing, Painting*, 116, and John Elderfield, *Henri Matisse: A Retrospective*. Exhibition catalogue (New York: The Museum of Modern Art, 1992), 136.

19. Pach, ibid., 117.

20. Letter from Arthur B. Davies to Walter Pach, July 9, 1909. Walter Pach Papers, AAA, reel 4216, frame 817.

21. Walter Pach conversation with the author, Sept. 5, 1952.

22. Ronald Pickavance, *Gauguin and the School of Pont-Aven*. Exhibition catalogue (San Diego: San Diego Museum of Art, 1994), 92.

23. Walter Pach, "Cézanne—An Introduction," 768.

24. Walter Pach, "Thus is Cubism Cultivated," *Art News* 48 (May 1949), 25.

25. Letter from Arthur B. Davies to Walter Pach, Oct. 2, 1912. Walter Pach Papers, AAA, reel 4217, frame 96.

26. Pach, *Queer Thing, Painting*, 180.

27. Walt Kuhn, *The Story of the Armory Show* (New York: Walt Kuhn, 1938), 10.

28. Pach, *Queer Thing, Painting*, 177.

29. Ibid., 197.

30. John Elderfield, *Henri Matisse: A Retrospective Exhibition*, op. cit., 240.

31. Walter Pach, "French Art and War," *The New York Times*, March 5, 1916, Sec. 2, 1.

32. Letter from Marcel Duchamp to Walter Pach, April 2 [1915], as published in Francis M. Naumann, "Amicalement, Marcel: Fourteen Letters from Marcel Duchamp to Walter Pach," *Archives of American Art Journal* 29 (1989), 39.

33. Francis M. Naumann with Beth Venn, *Making Mischief: Dada Invades New York*. Exhibition catalogue (New York: Whitney Museum of American Art, 1996), 88.

34. Walter Pach, "Art. Art in America. I," *The Freeman* 2 (Nov. 10, 1920), 206, 207.

35. Walter Pach, "Art. Art in America. II," *The Freeman* 2 (Nov. 17, 1920), 232, 233.

36. Walter Pach, "Art. The Independents," *The Freeman* 2 (March 9, 1921), 616.

37. Walter Pach, "Art. Modern Art. Cubism: The Earlier Years," *The Freeman* 7 (Aug. 15, 1923), 542–543.

38. Letter from Walter Pach to Manierre Dawson, Jan. 11, 1927. Manierre Dawson Papers, AAA, reel 64, frame 912.

39. Lewis Mumford, *The Brown Decades* (New York: Dover Publications, 1955), 208.

40. Walter Pach, *The Masters of Modern Art* (New York: The Viking Press and B. W. Huebsch, 1925), 77.

41. Walter Pach, *Ananias or the False Artist* (New York: Harper & Brothers, 1928), 75.

42. Ibid., 104.

43. Ibid., 113.

44. Letter from Walter Pach to Manierre Dawson, June 14, 1922. Manierre Dawson Papers, AAA, reel 64, frame 900.

45. Pach, *Queer Thing, Painting*, 285.

46. Walter Pach, "Art. The Independents," *The Freeman* 7 (April 18, 1923), 136.

47. Frank Jewett Mather Jr., "The Society of Independent Artists," *The Nation* 104 (May 10, 1917), 574.

48. "Brumback and Numerous Others [including Pach]," *New York Herald Tribune*, March 7, 1926.

49. "Exhibits in New York: Pach, Sisley, Beckman, Fitzgerald Collection," *Art News* 25 (April 23, 1927), 11.

50. "Walter Pach: Kraushaar Galleries," *Art News* 27 (Nov. 24, 1928), 10.

51. Walter Pach, "The Evolution of Diego Rivera," *Creative Art* 4 (Jan. 1929), 31–39.

52. Letter from Lee Simonson to Walter Pach, Dec. 18, 1928. Lee Simonson Papers, AAA, reel 4218, frame 222.

53. Letter from Rockwell Kent to Carl Zigrosser, as quoted in David Traxel, *An American Saga: The Life and Times of Rockwell Kent* (New York: Harper and Row, 1980), 154.

54. Rockwell Kent, "Ananias and the Bad (sic) Artist." Book review, The Bookman 69 (March 1929), 108, 109.

55. William Howe Downes, "John Ruskin and Walter Pach: Defenders of the Faith," *American Magazine of Art* 20 (Aug. 1929), 458, 459.

56. Walter Pach, *Ananias, or the False Artist*, 16.

57. William Howe Downes, *John S. Sargent: His Life and Work* (Boston: Little, Brown and Company, 1925), 215.

58. Walter Pach, "Painting. A Grand Provincial," *The Freeman* 7 (April 11, 1923), 113.

59. "Pach Back," *Time* 20 (Oct. 3, 1932), 34.

60. Letter from Walter Pach to John Sloan, Feb. 13, 1932. John Sloan Letters, Helen Farr Sloan Library, Delaware Art Museum, Wilmington.

61. Letter from Walter Pach to Ida Guggenheimer, June 28, 1936. Ida Guggenheimer Letters, AAA, roll 4039, frame 106.

62. Pach, *Queer Thing, Painting*, 3.

63. Letter from Van Wyck Brooks to Walter Pach, Nov. 9, 1938. Van Wyck Brooks Letters, AAA, roll 4218, frame 591.

64. Pach, *Queer Thing, Painting*, 89.

65. Letter from Walter Pach to John Sloan, Aug. 10, 1942. John Sloan Letters, Helen Farr Sloan Library, Delaware Art Museum, Wilmington.

66. "Bookshelf: The Art Museum in America By Walter Pach," *Art News* 47 (Jan. 1949), 10.

67. "Recent Publications in the Field of Art: Walter Pach, The Art Museum in America," *Art Quarterly* 12, no. 2 (1949), 195.

68. Pach, *The Art Museum in America*, p. 221.

69. Letters from Oscar White to the author, Aug. 17 and Sept. 20, 1995.

70. Letter from François Puaux, Acting Consul General, Consulat Général de France à New York, to Walter Pach, March 7, 1950. Collection of Raymond Pach.

71. Walter Pach, "Submerged Artists," *Atlantic Monthly* 199 (Feb. 1957), 68.

72. "Walter Pach," *ARTnews* 46 (April 1947), 49.

The Walter Pach Letters
1906–1958

The pen is the tongue of the mind.

—Cervantes (1547–1616)

WALTER C. ARENSBERG (1878–1954)

A collector, patron, and poet. The heir to a Pittsburgh steel executive, he amassed a major collection of twentieth-century avant-garde art. Walter Arensberg graduated from Harvard University with a major in English literature, and after considering a career in journalism turned to writing poetry instead. In 1907 he married Louise Stevens and they lived in Boston for the next seven years. His interest in collecting art was aroused when he attended the 1913 Armory Show, from which he purchased lithographs by Cézanne, Gauguin, and Vuillard, and an oil by Jacques Villon. Soon Arensberg became fascinated by the work of Villon's brother, Marcel Duchamp, and within a few years acquired more than thirty-five of his works. The purchases were facilitated by Duchamp's decision to leave France for New York following the outbreak of World War I, a move encouraged by Walter Pach who greeted him at dockside. Pach had arranged for Duchamp to stay at the Arensbergs' apartment while they summered in Connecticut. When Duchamp's *Nude Descending a Staircase No. 2* (1912), the Armory Show's most infamous painting, was put up for sale by the individual who had purchased it from the 1913 show, it was Pach who arranged the transaction for Arensberg (see February 3, 1919 letter from Frederic C. Torrey to Pach under "The Armory Show: Frederic C. Torrey"). From 1914 to 1921 the Arensbergs' New York apartment became the unofficial salon for the American Dada movement; it was there that Duchamp and Francis Picabia mingled with American artists and writers of a similar mind. It was also during those years that Walter Arensberg amassed a major collection of twentieth-century avant-garde art, which was donated to the Philadelphia Museum of Art in 1950.

The Pach-Arensberg correspondence dates from 1913 to 1954.

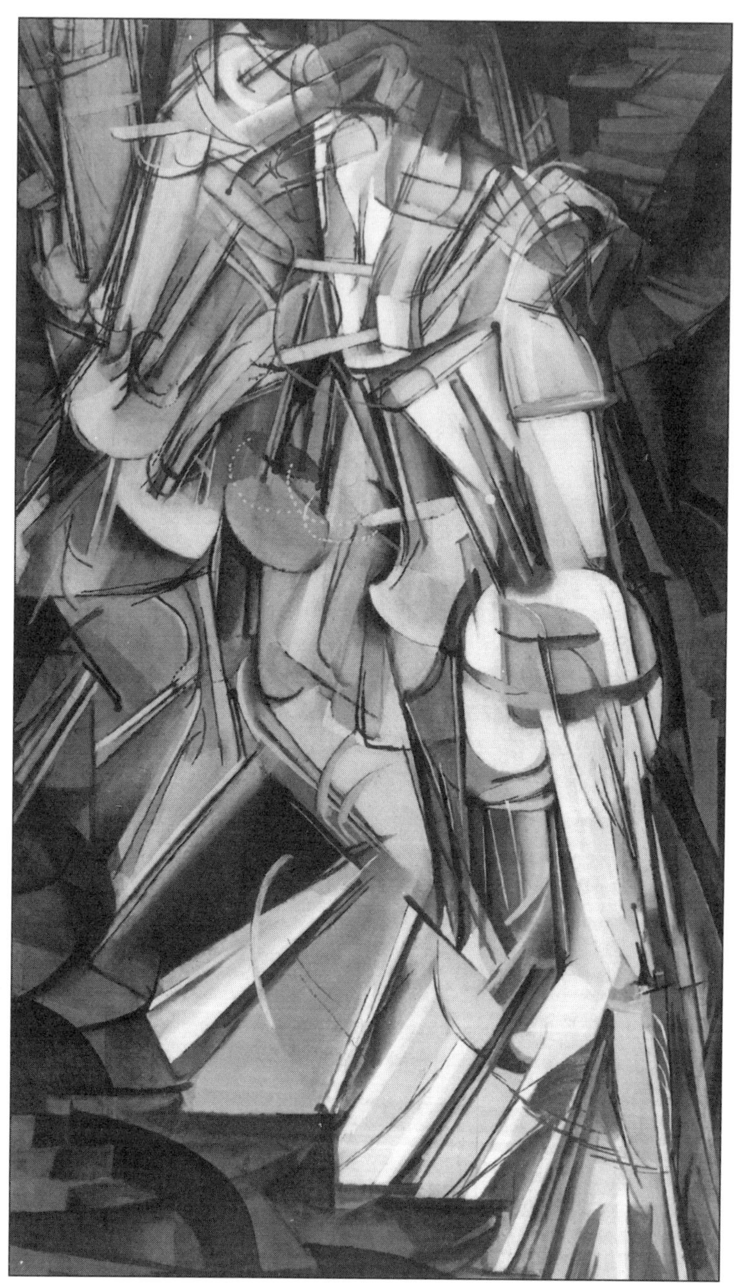

Marcel Duchamp, *Nude Descending a Staircase, No. 2*, 1912. Oil on canvas, 57 7/8 x 35 1/8 in. Philadelphia Museum of Art: The Louise and Walter Arensberg Collection. Acc. 1950-134-59. Photograph by Graydon Wood, 1994.

[Postcard]
1135 Park Ave.
New York, Nov. 30, 1913

Walter C. Arensberg, Esq.
Hotel Victoria
Boston

My dear Arensberg:

Our exhibition opens tomorrow in Pittsburgh.[1] I should have told you before but I guess all your friends will go to the [Carnegie] Institute anyhow to see it. We are likely to have it in New York in February.[2] The fellows have done magnificently for it.

Best regards, Walter Pach

1. Following the Armory Show's closing in Boston in May, 1913, Arthur B. Davies was approached to help organize an exhibit of French cubist works to be shown between June and August at department stores in Cleveland, Pittsburgh, and Philadelphia. When the display reached Pittsburgh, the local art society sought an exhibition by contemporary American artists who had been affiliated with the Armory Show. As a result, that exhibit, which opened at the Carnegie Institute on December 1, 1913, contained works by Kuhn, Glackens, Prendergast, Sheeler, Stella, Schamberg, Pach, MacRae, Allen Tucker, George Of, and Davies; it represented the first museum show of modern American art in the country.

2. The same American paintings displayed in Pittsburgh were exhibited at the Montross Gallery in New York the following February, the first anniversary of the Armory Show.

[Postcard]
New York, Feb. 24, 1914

My dear Arensberg,

The book I think you surely want is "La Littérature et les Idées Nouvelles" by Alexandre Mercereau, published by Figuière et Cie, 7 rue Corneille, Paris; price fr. 3.50. I should think that was the anthology but am not sure; anyhow it sounds good for you. I enjoyed yesterday afternoon immensely and thank you again for the appreciation. Please send me your present address. Good wishes to Mrs. Arensberg.

Yours, Walter Pach

Boston, Undated (March 2, 1914)

My dear Pach:

If you have been married since I saw you or if you are still waiting to be married,[1] you will scarcely have time for even a word from me. But I must thank you again for so much of the pleasure of my brief visit to New York. The exhibition[2] was tremendously fresh and fine. It takes life at what a breathless tempo! Many of the pictures—and your own among the most vivid of all[3]—are intact in my memory. And there I feel that they will remain, the reservoirs of profound experience. I have been wondering if you are not the illusionist of the movement. At any rate you bring to the study of appearance something incalculably more penetrating and faithful than mere observation. You certainly give the impression of telling the truth—the whole truth and nothing but the truth—like a witness in court who adds a good God damn for emphasis.

Thank you for the titles. I have already ordered all that you gave me. By the way, some day I will return the number of Pan which you lent to me.

It's not poetic justice—it's artistic justice that has made you a happy married man at this time.

Cordially yours, Walter C. Arensberg

1. Pach had married Magdalen (Magda) Frohberg on February 26.

2. An "Exhibition of Paintings and Drawings" held at the Montross Gallery from February 2 to 23, 1914. Among the thirteen exhibitors were William J. Glackens, Arthur B. Davies, Walt Kuhn, Maurice B. Prendergast, Charles Sheeler, Joseph Stella, and Pach.

3. He exhibited three cubist still-lifes titled *Progression, No. 1*; *Progression, No. 2*; and *Progression, No. 3*.

UNDATED (SUMMER 1915)

Dear Walter Pach:

I intended to write you at once of my disappointment in missing the Matisse monotypes.[1] Some forgotten errand developed at the very last, just as I was starting for your place from the Grand Central, where I had left the baggage early in order to have time. It was so good of you to give me the chance of seeing them that I don't want you to think I did'nt [*sic*] appreciate it.

Your letter came last night with the beautiful poem by Le Roy.[2] I shall urge Kreymborg[3] to use it, and if he will I will pay for it myself. You are a trump—you really do things. My heart goes out to the wonderful lad in the trenches over there who writes among the petals and the bombs. I wish I could do something for him. Do you think there is any thing I could send him that would give him pleasure?

I am glad you are at work on your book, but I most devoutly hope that you are not neglecting your painting. Don't be discouraged if the magazines you mention reject the story. It surely ought to find a publisher. I have been a fool and worse, I suppose, about my new book. I neglected till last week to start the MSS [manuscript] on its way, and find that I am too late for publication this fall. All the fall lists are already made out. I don't know whether to bring it out privately or to wait till spring.

I'm not awfully enthusiastic about the country, I find. Curiously, we have had from a friend here a very attractive description of Milford, Penna., so that we are tempted to try it some time. Lou[4] leaves Saturday to visit friends for a month, and I am going to see my mother. I shall pass through New York and see Duchamp[5] en route.

I'm already looking forward to the fall, when we can all foregather again. At present I am diluting the scenery with a visit to Boston about twice a week, where there is something to eat and drink and someone to talk to.

Dreams are more amusing than ever. Remember yours.

With very best regards to Mrs[.] Pach and the young man,[6]

Faithfully yours, Walter C. Arensberg

1. Pach had organized the first fully representative one-man show of works by Matisse in New York, held at the Montross Gallery from January 20 to February 27, 1915. It included nearly fifty prints and drawings.

2. Jean Le Roy (?–1918), a young French poet Pach had met in Paris in 1910.

3. Alfred Kreymbourg (1883–1966), founder and editor of *The Glebe* and *Others* magazines.

4. Louise Arensberg, Walter's wife.

5. Marcel Duchamp (1887–1968), who arrived in New York in June 1915. It was Pach who had extended him an invitation to come to the United States and had met him at dockside.

6. A reference to either Marcel Duchamp, age twenty-eight, or the Pachs' six-month old son Raymond, who was named for sculptor Raymond Duchamp-Villon.

Travelling toward San Antonio, Feb. 8, 1940 (at home, 148 W. 72nd St., New York, on February 21)

Dear Walter [Arensberg],

Thank you very much for your note and its enclosure.[1] You will believe that it was totally unexpected, but I can accept it just because of the spontaneity of the idea and, on the other hand too, because the acquisition of those pictures in the old days has proved a good investment. The proof is evident from the growth of your interest in painting—and that bunch of things at your house gave me pleasure not only because of their immensely high quality but because they made me realize that the interest I saw begin at the Armory Show in New York, that went on in Boston—and at Shady Hill,[2] where I remember some good evenings—and then took a new spurt in 67th Street,[3] had really developed again—and strongly developed—in these years when you have had only occasional contact with the main art centers. It is, then, a possession worth having; and I can take satisfaction in any share I may have had in contributing to it. Aside from that, Torrey[4] sent me the wire about [selling] the Duchamp[5] picture that time because he needed money for a sudden emergency, as he said, and neither then nor when I saw him in California did he ever suggest paying me a commission; no more did Matisse, in the matter of *his* picture. I had gone to Paris as the representative of Montross and of the Carroll Galleries (officially—in reality it was out of interest in having the work of the Armory Show continue) and he may perfectly well have thought I was on a salary from those dealers. I wasn't, (I got my expenses—not a cent over my expenses) . . . my interest has moved in the last twenty years or so. Modern art is, of course, the only kind we can produce, and so I am keen on it, as I am on living people, as compared with those of the past. But the art of the past is living, even when the men (the relatively few men) who made it are dead, and to see Delacroix and Ingres and David—or Jan Steen or Le Nain—is to see modern art better. . . . I have never consorted much with Derain—the man—, but one reason why I rate him so high as an artist is that his work shows an appreciation of "primitive" elementals and, with that, of the advanced technique of our time. It shows an application, also, of those things—and I will not admit for a moment that he is an eclectic, though the word seems easy (almost inevitable) to use in defining him. He gave Matisse many ideas at the Fauve time, he gave Picasso and Braque almost the whole of the Cubist idea at its inception, he has shown the way a third time with what I call—clumsily—his neo-realism; and, aside from all considerations of theory, I think the man at his best is enormous. (He is frequently far below his best).

There was a thing I may have misunderstood, when we were talking of that Duchamp-Villon horse's head—which seemed to me not less than stupendous. You asked me if, in my book on that artist, I had repeated Faure's observation that he saw all later sculpture coming out of Duchamp-Villon. I think I did, many years later, in *Queer Thing, Painting*; but Elie Faure made his remark only on seeing the plates in the memorial volume that I published in 1924, so of course I could not put his words into that book. The doubt that has been turning around in my head, since seeing you, is whether you got a copy of that book (paper bound, about 10 x 12 inches, twenty-five plates and text—the latter of great value as it is mostly D-V's). If Villon and Marcel did not send it to you, *please* let me know, as I have several copies yet. It was privately printed and is almost never to be found at book-sellers' shops; you really ought to have it.

This letter is a sort of postscript to my visit. I should be glad to hear from you, but I fear I am going to be unable to write again—for a very long time. That World's Fair[6] is going to come down on me like an avalanche, from the minute I hit New York—which I ought not to have left (only that I previously engaged to give these lectures).

It was so good to have that get-together with you and the always charming lady, and I do thank you for it again.

As ever, Cordially—Walter Pach.

1. A check made out to Pach.

2. "Shady Hill" was the Arensbergs' estate in Cambridge, Massachusetts, from which they moved in the fall of 1914 to New York City. "Shady Hill" subsequently became the home of Paul Sachs, of the Fogg Museum (see Paul Sachs letter to Pach, Jan. 4, 1949).

3. The Arensbergs' residence in New York was at 33 West 67th Street.

4. Frederic C. Torrey was the San Francisco art dealer who purchased Marcel Duchamp's notorious painting from the Armory Show (see Torrey letter, March 6, 1913) and subsequently sold it, through Pach, to Arensberg (see Torry letter to Pach, Feb. 3, 1919).

5. *Nude Descending a Staircase.*

6. Pach was charged with selecting the "Masterpieces of Art" Exhibition consisting of paintings from the sixteenth through nineteenth centuries for the 1940 New York World's Fair.

June 10, 1942
7065 Hillside Avenue
Hollywood, California

Dear Walter [Pach]:

I am writing to tell you that I have just seen your birdstone[1] in the travelling exhibition of Indian Art and that I think it is stunning. Do you ever consider parting with it? If you do would you be so good as to let me know?

Have you heard that Marcel [Duchamp] is arriving towards the end of this month? Best regards to Magda and yourself,

Sincerely yours, [Walter Arensberg]

1. A piece of North American Indian art. Arensberg raised the subject again seven years later (see telegram to Pach, January 14, 1949) and Pach agreed to sell it to him for $500 (see Pach letter to Arensberg, January 19, 1949).

New York, June 15, 1942

Dear Walter [Arensberg],

. . . The news about Marcel is grand . . . he's still the big man he was in the past,— and that must be atrocious over there—the life under present conditions, I mean.

About the Indian bird-stone: under other circumstances I'd say (as I'd like to now)—you take it, as a souvenir of the good hours we've had together. *BUT*, it's the only bit of Indian sculpture I have (excluding Mexican), I have a particularly soft spot for Indian art (The show in New York was something unbelievably great—even if you have the souvenir book they published, as I assume you have), and I am still devoted to my few possessions—which I hope you'll see with me some day. All in all, I know you'll understand if I say I want to keep this piece . . .

Incidentally—and by chance—my bird-stone is the finest I've ever seen (or felt, because you can't realize the subtlety of the surfaces, their undulating irregularity, until you run your fingers along them). Altogether the wonder of the old North Americans keeps growing for me. Have you the book of the Payne Collection? If not, *by all means*, send for it (enclosing $2.00 if I remember correctly) to The Dickson Mounds, Lewistown, Illinois. Every time I look at it, I get a thrill . . .

Best wishes to Lou and yourself, and here's hoping we see you again—before too long.

Cordially, as always, Walter Pach.

I'll keep you in mind if I ever do want to let go of the bird-stone; I fear it isn't likely.

R.F.D. 3, Brewster, N.Y., Sept. 11, 1947

Dear Walter [Arensberg]:

. . . [I have been] reading Juan Larrea's book "Guernica, Picasso" these last days. Outside of the art in the picture, which must impress you as it does me, there is, as Larrea points out in most convincing fashion, a whole world of interest in the psycho-analytic revelation and in the cryptic meanings of the work. That carried me back to discussions during your time in New York when, for example, you lent me Pfister's big book, and then to your visit of 1925 when you showed me the concealed message of certain pages in the Shakespeare-Bacon material. Principally, however, it is because of Larrea's philosophical penetration into the ideas in and behind the masterpiece that I want to recommend the book to you. It is published (or soon will be for I think mine is an advance copy) by Curt Valentin, of the Buchholz Gallery, 32 East 57th St., New York 22. . . .

The translation was terribly defective when Valentin appealed to me to take it in hand, last spring, and I had a very big job in straightening it out. The fact that I had a hand in it debars me from reviewing the book, as far as I've looked into that question. Now, to come brutally to the point I have in mind, I'm sure you could do something really admirable on the subject. I said 'brutally,' just now, because you've been away from such matters for a long while, at least as far as I know. But think the question over: the subject is a magnificent one (I think the *Guernica* is the greatest 20th Century picture, so far, and I'm convinced that Larrea's book will make a strong impression on your mind. He is a Spaniard, a very old friend of Picasso's, and has been living in Mexico for a number of years, having gone there after Franco's victory, if it is that. He edits that superb review *Cuadernos Americanos*, and wrote a book I may have told you of in Hollywood, an extraordinary thing called *Rendición de Espíritu*).

. . . I am painting; it is a difficult art, but very interesting. I see Marcel [Duchamp] at intervals—always the same, always so likable. The news from Villon is great: France appreciates him now; soon it will be America's turn, I think. . . . Do let me hear your idea of the Larrea book. . . . And, once more, my best to Lou and yourself.

Cordially—Walter Pach.

HOLLYWOOD, OCT. 2, 1947

Dear Walter [Pach]:

I am terribly sorry to have left your very flattering letter so long unanswered. I am answering now (in a hurry, I regret) so that you may be free to start looking for someone else. I just want to let you know that it will be impossible for me to do the review that you request. I just don't feel equal to the importance of the task, especially at this particular time when I am really working against a dead-line in connection with my own research.

I am going to write to you soon, a little more in detail, about this and that. It would be great if I could only have a few hours with you to exchange ideas.

Love to Magda.

Sincerely yours, [Walter Arensberg]

---

3 WASHINGTON SQUARE
NEW YORK 3, N.Y., JULY 20, 1948

Dear Walter [Arensberg],

I have just returned from a two months' visit to Paris; I had a week in London, also.

It was a thrilling time for me, after an absence of sixteen years, especially as I was living with Jacques Villon, who is *such* a dear fellow, and who has been going on to always more beautiful painting. . . .

I was . . . particularly impressed by the progress in appreciation that Paris has to show. Instead of the poisonous deadness of the Luxembourg, there is now the big Musée d'Art Moderne, where Matisse, Picasso, Braque and others each have an entire room devoted to their work. There are six Villons, with more of them in the offing.

Therefore, after my first visit there, I was the more shocked by the fact that—with magnificent ensembles of Maillol and Despiau—there was not a single work by Duchamp-Villon. I spoke of this to Villon, who was apologetic, who mentioned the museum's shortness of money—which it uses chiefly for the work of living men, but who finally had M. Dorival, one of the curators, come to lunch, and to see the sculptures by his brother. I was there, and I told M. Dorival how Brummer—by far the greatest connoisseur of our time—had had great exhibitions of Maillol and Despiau but, in discussing each of them with me, had said "Of course, he isn't Duchamp-Villon!"

In a nutshell, then, the Museum has made up for its omission by taking some six or eight works by the sculptor; it will have bronze casts made of the very large *Torso of a Woman* and the *Horse* (full size), though metal and labor are scarce and expensive.

With this fine result attained, I spoke, later, to M. Dorival about a representation of the third of the extraordinary brothers. Marcel is known almost solely by reproductions, in France today, but when M. Dorival spoke to M. Cassou, the director of the Museum, both were very keen for such an acquisition, if it were obtainable. M. Cassou authorized me, quite specifically, to write you of the matter; should you consider it favorably, he would be happy to take the final, official steps toward their adding a Duchamp to their collections.

I might add—though you doubtless know it—that you are the only one to remedy the grievous lack of recognition of Marcel's work in his own country, and in the most important museum of modern French art. Its collections entitle it to that description, outside of its place—Paris—still the incomparable center of modern art.

There is the example of John Quinn's placing of Seurat's *Circus* in France. He considered that a work of art belongs, morally, to the country that produced it, and he at once provided in his will that the Suerat was to return to France.

If that country had been obtuse about recognizing the genius of the great Neo-Impressionist, less blame is to be assigned in the case of Duchamp, whose best work came to America at so early a date—when he was only about twenty-five years old. And I think that the French are now showing such a will to repair their past errors that they deserve help in showing the real achievement of their country.

I should not hesitate to let my canvas of the *Chess Players* [retitled *The Chess Game*] go to Paris were it suitable to represent Marcel. But it is too early, and the few small works still in France are likewise insufficient to make clear his genius. Only such things as you have could do that, and I do think that you would have a lasting satisfaction if you decided to meet the wishes of the men at the head of that all-important French museum. They would be glad to make a payment for such a picture; but with the franc at three hundred to the dollar, the sum they could pay would—when translated into American money—doubtless seem a very small one. Still I mention it as an evidence of their good faith; I could not, obviously, discuss the matter of a payment without knowing your ideas about the matter as a whole.

I spoke to Marcel about it yesterday. While he considers the acquisition of his brothers' work as a big thing, he still says that he can not take any position about the disposal of his own work. He dislikes what he considers the officialism of the new French museum, and will not make any gesture to support the institution; but he told me just as positively that he was not opposing my idea. In short, his final word was that he is "neutral." (For myself, I can only say I am not neutral: there is still a great fight between good and bad artists, and I am on the side of the good ones, as I see the thing. The museum is the chief theatre of the struggle, and I think it should be supported when it is working for the general good). Villon strongly endorsed my idea.

As to yourself, please let me say that though I have hesitated to write this letter, and though I think you should not permit a dispersal of your great group of Duchamp pictures, the ceding of one work *for such a cause would*, it seems to me, still be within the best ideals for your collection.

With warmest greetings to Lou and yourself, I am, as always

Yours very cordially Walter Pach.

WESTERN UNION TELEGRAM

HOLLYWOOD, JAN. 14, 1949

WALTER PACH
3 WASHINGTON SQUARE
NEW YORK, N.Y.

WILL YOU SELL ME YOUR BIRD STONE

Walter C. Arensberg

NEW YORK, JAN. 19, 1949

Dear Walter [Arensberg],

. . . I am [not] completely declining your offer: but let me say just how the matter stands.

. . . I have never been able to get more than this one original sculpture, the bird stone. I bought it, years ago, from among about a million objects (mostly arrow heads, pots, etc.) in that Payne Collection in Illinois. A few years later, I went back there thinking there *must* be something else I'd want. But no, I got nothing but a couple of trifles (one nice clay thing from Honduras), and at that, I bought largely in order to take *something*. . . .

Several people have tried quite hard to get me to sell them the bird stone, but I've always refused to consider letting it go. Perhaps you've heard that we recently put up some things of ours in an auction, and the truth is that we want to build up our capital. There were certain pictures that the man from the Parke-Bernet Gallery wanted, but that I would not part with: we are holding on to the things we care for most. But Vollard used to say "Everything is for sale: give me enough money, and I'll buy you the Place de la Concorde." So, as to the bird stone: if any one offered me $5000, $2000, or $1000 for it, I'd feel I had no right to refuse—though if I had money, I should refuse any price.

The long and the short of the matter is that if you want to pay me $500 for the piece, I'll let it go. . . . I've never seen a bird stone comparable with this one. It's the biggest one I know, the subtlest in surfaces (you really need to follow its surfaces with your hand—the eye is not enough; and then it's a genuine piece[)]. . . . I wish Hollywood and New York were not so far apart. . . . I'd like to hear of your work (I know next to nothing about it); I'd like to show you some things I've been doing; . . . I'd like you to see our new Villons (he's coming on *gloriously*, and you'd be repaid if you came here for the show—in April, I think; he is doing *such* beautiful work). But—I'll just add best regards for Lou and yourself, and remain

Yours cordially—Walter Pach.

NIGHT LETTER—WESTERN UNION
WALTER PACH, FEB. 9, 1949

SUBJECT TO THE APPROVAL OF LOU WHO HAS NEVER SEEN THE STONE BUT WHO I AM CONFIDENT WILL LIKE IT AS MUCH AS I DO, WILL PURCHASE FOR FIVE HUNDRED. PLEASE SEND AT ONCE.

Walter C. Arensberg

NEW YORK, FEB. 10, 1949

Dear Walter [Arensberg],

Your telegram arrived this morning. The bird stone is now packed, and ready to go to the post office tomorrow.

It can travel much more safely dismounted, but you will see at once how simple a matter it is to set it up again. The base, of wood, has the wire in the holes where it belongs. . . . I don't know if you observed, when the piece was on exhibition, that it had been broken and repaired at the neck. This occurred before I bought it. Fortunately, the break was a simple one, and the absolute tallying of the two big fragments precludes any idea of a substitution or omission. . . .

Hoping things are well with you, I am

Yours very sincerely Walter Pach.

HOLLYWOOD, APRIL 2, 1949

Dear Walter [Pach]:

We have decided to keep the bird stone, which is really beautiful. It makes a wonderful mate to one just a little smaller that we already have.

Enclosed please find the check. The amount is so in excess of the values with which we are acquainted, that I am asking you to allocate three hundred to the old affaire Matisse. To let the actual price be known would be to destroy the market to which I have access. . . .

With all good wishes to you both,

Faithfully yours, [Walter Arensberg]

NEW YORK, APRIL 6, 1949

Dear Walter [Arensberg],

Many thanks for your letter and the check. . . . I wish you could be here for the Villon show which will open shortly. He is absolutely inspiring as he goes on getting deeper, stronger, more joyous, every year. I shall have an article on him in *Art News*[1] for May. I wrote it with a very different ending, a sort of triumphant note for Villon, France, and modern art, despite renewed attacks on it by Leo Stein, Berenson, Francis Henry Taylor, Lincoln Kirstein and others. The editor would not have that, nor my "editorializing" on France, etc. So I had to replace those pages; I am, however, not dissatisfied with the material I substituted. . . . With kindest regards to Lou, I am

Yours cordially Walter Pach.

1. "Thus Is Cubism Cultivated," *Art News* 48 (May 1949), 23–25.

New York, May 28, 1949

Dear Walter [Arensberg],

. . . For a year or two, Al Bing has spoken to me, before and after his trips to California, of offering you on my behalf the Duchamp of the *Chess Players*. I never consented to his doing so, for one thing because I enjoy having the picture . . . and then I have always thought that if I did sell it, the price should be one that would be in keeping with those paid for other modern masterpieces . . .

I am told on good authority that the Modern Museum here paid $20,000 for the big La Fresnaye, *La Conquête de l'Air*; and there have been other prices of similar proportions. All prices for unique things have to be more or less arbitrary, and I have set $6000 as the figure for the *Chess Players*. I mention it chiefly because Al Bing said I ought to give you first shot at it—if you wanted it. . . . If, on turning over the idea in your mind, you think you might be interested, do send me a line. . . .

Best wishes to Lou and yourself. As always

Cordially—Walter Pach.

New York, June 21, 1950

Dear Walter [Arensberg],

Marcel dropped in this afternoon to tell me of your letter and its offer to buy the *Chess Players*[1] for $4000, with an initial payment of $1500 and the balance at intervals running through 1951. I am glad to accept on those terms (Just name your own dates for installments). For one thing I believe the *Chess Players* is incomparably the most important work of its period, and therefore will round out your collection in the most emphatic way. Another reason that I am glad to see the picture go to you is that I shall now be free of the importunities of the dealers, several of whom have been coming to me periodically about the canvas. When I finally let Peggy Guggenheim[2] have the *Young Man*[3] picture, it was after the the [*sic*] series of visits from a chap named Lyon (more appropriately it might have been Hyena) whom she employed. I finally had to ask him not to return, but he telephoned that he wanted to get my opinion on the authenticity of a Delacroix (which he borrowed for the occasion) and I was curious about that, and let him in again—whereupon he began anew about the Duchamp. I get pretty well fed up on such business; now it is ended.

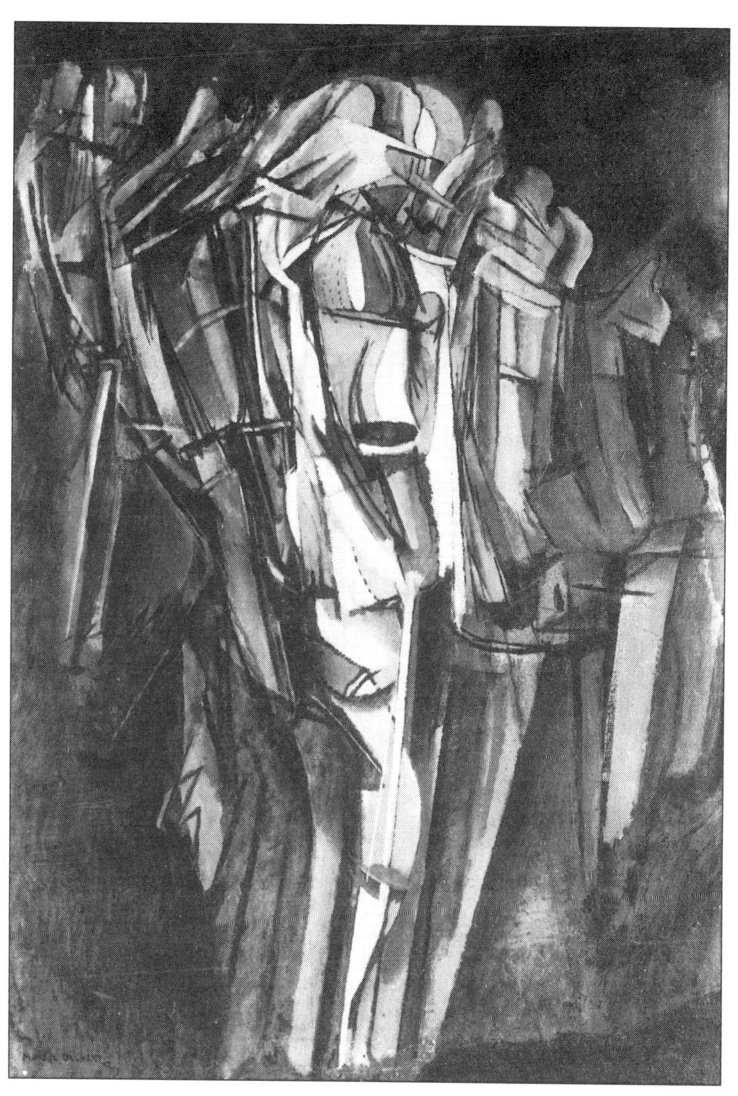

Marcel Duchamp, *Nude (Study) Sad Young Man on a Train*, 1911–12. Oil on cardboard, mounted on masonite, 39 3/8 x 28 3/4 in. Solomon R. Guggenheim Foundation, New York, Peggy Guggenheim Collection, Venice, 1976. 76.2553.9. Photograph by Robert E. Mates © The Solomon R. Guggenheim Foundation, New York.

As air mail takes so short a time, I will wait about shipping the picture till I hear whether you have any special instructions on that point—though I imagine it is to go to your Hillside address, like this letter. I always have my own pictures sent by Budworth, and as I still have the case in which the Duchamp came, that detail of expense will be avoided.

I don't know if you saw my article in the May *Atlantic Monthly*.[4] It was the remnants of my article on your collection at the Chicago Art Institute, which *Harper's* practically ordered and then refused.

All good wishes to Lou and yourself.

Most cordially—Walter Pach.

1. Marcel Duchamp's *The Chess Players* [retitled *The Chess Game*], 1910. Oil on canvas.
2. Peggy Guggenheim (1898–1979), expatriate millionaire and art collector.
3. Duchamp's *Sad Young Man on a Train*, 1912. Oil on canvas.
4. "Art Must be Modern," *The Atlantic Monthly* 185 (May 1950), 44–48.

Undated [June 29, 1950]

Dear Walter [Pach]:

I am enclosing a check for $1500.00 as a first payment on The Chess Players. You will notice that the check is drawn to The Francis Bacon Foundation, which was created by Lou and me both for the purpose of my research and for the purpose of creating and owning our art collection. Please, therefore, send your receipt to The Francis Bacon Foundation.

It looks very much as if we will be able to send you the balance of the amount for The Chess Players in July.

I congratulate you on your article about modern art, with your outspoken references to Francis Taylor.[1] Our own experiences quite confirm the opinion that he does not like modern art. Did I mention to you my idea that he was chosen as the director of the Museum on the principle that eunuchs are chosen as the heads of harems, namely, as persons who are uninterested in the contents?

We had no idea that you had planned an article on our collection. We would have been extremely interested.

I can't tell you how happy we are to be getting The Chess Players. We are glad that you are having it shipped by Budworth. Please have it sent direct to Earl Stendahl, 7055 Hillside Avenue, since he will uncrate it and hang it for us, and also, please be sure to have it insured and send us the bill for the insurance.

With best regards to you all,

Sincerely yours, [Walter C. Arensberg]

P.S. We were interested in the reference in your letter to The Chess Players as the most important picture of its period. Just what is your meaning? You are referring to it, I imagine, as the most important work by Marcel in that period. Is this correct? However in studying a photograph of it last night I was certainly impressed by its outstanding quality, so that, in a sense, it could hold its own with any work by anybody at that same time.

Enclosure
check number #3001 for $1500^{00}

1. Francis Henry Taylor (1903–1957), director of The Metropolitan Museum of Art.

New York, July 3, 1950

Dear Walter [Arensberg],

Thanks for your letter of the 29th of June, and the check. I enclose a receipt for the Francis Bacon Foundation, and shall have Budworth call as early as he can and get the picture off to you—addressing it to Mr. Stendahl and having it insured, presumably for its full value, and accompanied by the bill for his charges.

When I first read your comment on my remark that I consider the *Chess Players* the most important picture of its period I was vexed at having made too loose a statement, for I had intended to say the most important Duchamp of the period. However, as you suggest, reviewing other masterpieces of the time, even including the great things by Matisse and Picasso of the time (which sometimes appears to me as Picasso's best time—when he was perhaps at his most creative moment) I do think that Marcel's picture holds its own. Arthur B. Davies[1] (whom I do not often quote, but who did have some moments of intuition) said the *Chess Players* was the finest Cézannesque picture he had seen; but that is, of course, only its retrospective aspect—and not completely accurate, at that. What seems to me a more positive statement is that Marcel, having concentrated all his art of the time in this large canvas, with its extraordinary characterization of those two splendid artists, his brothers, and their wives, having done a thing so monumental in design and full in color, had to look further than naturalism for the scope of his painting, and so was led to that greatest evolution of his art—as it seems to me—the one culminating in the *King and Queen Surrounded by Swift Nudes*. So that my inadvertent phrase is not altogether devoid of justification, since a definitive work from nature had to precede the development of 1912—with which no one has caught up since, as far as I can see. The Duchamp at the Museum of Modern Art in New York[2] usually hangs between a Picasso and a Braque painted within a twelve-month [period] of Marcel's picture. I have often remarked to people that if one did not observe the dating of the three works, one might well think that the Duchamp was painted twenty years later than the Picasso and the Braque, both very good examples but not even anticipating the finer, more original conception of the other work.

Thank you very much indeed for what you say of my *Atlantic* article, and particularly for using the word *outspoken* as regards my words about Francis Taylor and his vicious rubbish. One or two people said I was gentlemanly in my reply to those critics, and I really wish they had used a different term. Yes,—years ago, you did use the word eunuchs for such people, and I replied that it was Théophile Gautier's word for them in the preface to *Mademoiselle de Maupin*; you said you had forgotten that. They are eunuchs not only in their impotence but in their hatred for those whom Gautier calls the Sultans, the men whom they have to serve. I have just had a mean experience with a group of these poor and malicious creatures; they got me to write the text for a book of Renoir reproductions, mauled it into an almost totally misrepresentative shape, and then substituted for my comments on the plates some detestable lucubrations of their own. The best a good lawyer could do for me was to get the title page to read *Introduction* instead of *Text* by Walter Pach and to get "Commentaries by The Editorial Board" into the Table of Contents. I hope people will notice this but I fear most will not. My only consoling thought is that Renoir will never see the thing. Taylor has cut loose again in the latest *Bulletin* of the Metropolitan.[3] He is a bad lot, but art will survive him.

Since you kindly say you would have been interested to see what I wrote of your collection, I send you—under separate cover and registered—the original manuscript, which is all I have left, the first typed copy having been lost in the mails (a rare occurrence) and the carbon having been used by the *Atlantic* as the basis for the article it published. What I send you is very much longer, everything about you[r] pictures having been cut out since the Chicago show was over. *Harper's* had practically ordered the article from me but—after keeping it for a long time—decided to use one by Emily Genauer,[4] and said they could not have two articles on art without letting months elapse between them. Such happenings have put me off of magazine work in recent years. The editors want [more of] a "liver" kind of stuff than I turn out. You will have difficulty in reading some parts of the article I send you; it got *too* long and I find that some of the passages which might have interested you are struck out with a red pencil. But I think they are still legible. I don't want the manuscript any more; so you can destroy it when you have seen it sufficiently.[5] But please do not let others see the drawings on the reversed side of the sheets. My sketches of the nude are very uneven in quality, and so I use the bad ones as paper for such writing as this Ms., and I have never before let any such sheets go out: it's just that I *do* think one or two things in the original article may interest you. The *Harper's* editor said that the Chicago show was not enough of a subject for them, so I put in the replies to those three critics and the other material. (You may note that there were, at first, four critics, but I think the *Atlantic* people were right in cutting out that little worm of a Kirstein,[6] though I regret some of the other omissions). Mr. Weeks, of the *Atlantic*, was so nice in his letters (I've never met him) that I'm intending to write a sequel to *Art Must Be Modern*[7]—which was *his* phrase after reading my text (to which I added a paragraph in order to justify the title). The new one will be *Art Must Be Classical*. Here's hoping!

Let me say again that I am really glad that you are to have the *Chess Players*. It is a grand work—as many have realized when seeing it on our wall. More will feel that, undoubtedly, when it hangs at your place. I got fine effects with it at night, with a lamp below it making it stand out and glow in the surrounding darkness. But it has been splendid in exhibitions with quite ordinary light.

Best wishes for your own work—of which I wish I knew something. Aren't you about ready to "fess up"? And best wishes to Lou; Magda joins me as to you both.

Most cordially Walter Pach.

1. Arthur B. Davies (1862–1928), the artist who, as president of the Association of American Painters and Sculptors, enlisted Pach's aid in assembling avant-garde French art for the Armory Show.

2. Duchamp's *The Passage from Virgin to Bride*, 1912, hung between Picasso's *"Ma Jolie" [Woman with a Zither or Guitar]*, 1911–1912, and Braque's *Man with a Guitar*, 1911.

3. Francis Henry Taylor had written in the June 1950 issue of the Museum *Bulletin* (volume 8, page 300): "If purchases of the modern art of Europe have been infrequent in the past decade, it is because . . . the Museum has limited purchase funds, and it would be absurd to compete with the Museum of Modern Art and with private collectors in an area where admittedly prices are too often inflated."

4. Emily Genauer (1911–), art critic on the *New York Herald Tribune*.

5. The manuscript was retained, and is in the Arensberg Archives at the Philadelphia Museum of Art.

6. Lincoln Kirstein (1907–1996), art critic and author of *Eli Nadelman Drawings*, 1949.

7. *The Atlantic Monthly* 185 (May 1950). 44–48.

Undated (Summer or fall 1950)

Dear Walter [Arensberg],

I've just remembered this letter from Marcel to a former owner of the picture (Chess Players). It is really a document so you ought to keep it.

W. P. [Walter Pach]

(Enclosure)

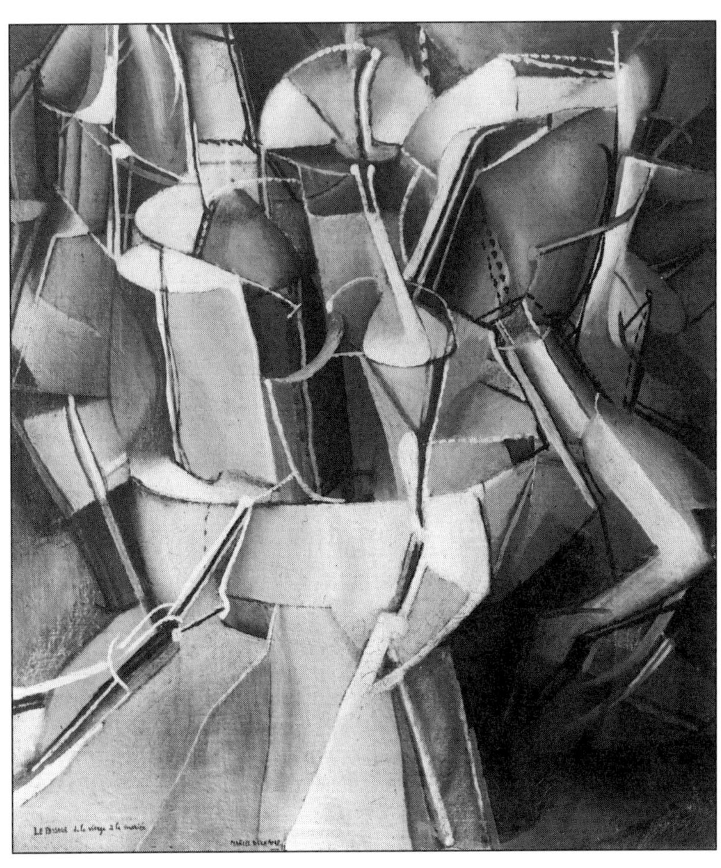

Marcel Duchamp, *The Passage from Virgin to Bride*, 1912. Oil on canvas, 23 3/8 x 21 1/4 in. The Museum of Modern Art, New York. Purchase. Photograph © 2001, The Museum of Modern Art, New York.

MONACO, HOTEL DE NICE, SEPT. 13, 1926

My dear Dr. Tovell[1]

The painting was done in the Spring of 1910—exhibited at the Salon d'Automne 1910.

I became, that year, "Societaire du Salon d'Automne" meaning that, from then on, I needed not to have the jury pass on my paintings any more.

It was reproduced in Apollinaire's book on Cubism (1913)—and I sent it to N.Y. to be exhibited at the Carroll Galleries in 1915, where Mr. Quinn bought it.

—From left to right: my brother, Raymond Duchamp-Villon Sculptor, who died from blood poisoning, as a physician during the war.

His wife lying on the ground.

My other brother, Jacques Villon, the painter whose paintings were also in the Quinn Collection.

His wife sitting at the tea table.

The painting is packed now and I will have it shipped as soon as I get back to Paris (Oct 1st) to your office address.

Veuillez agréer ainsi que Mme Tovell mes hommages. respectueux[2]

Marcel Duchamp 29 rue Campagne Premiere Paris

1. Dr. Harold M. Tovell, who resided in Brussels.

2. Would you please accept, as well as Madame Tovell, the expression of my respect and best regards. respectfully

---

NEW YORK, AUG. 14, 1950

Dear Walter [Arensberg],

. . . I'd really like to know whether the *Chess Players* didn't exceed your expectations when you saw it. . . .

We miss the big picture, a unique thing, and a grand one, in my opinion. Still, it was on the wall of our living room for a number of years, so that it is pretty well registered in my mind. And I'm glad that *you* have it. Marcel is too.

We have a number of Villons, and are very happy to see two of them on the wall where *The Chess Players* used to hang. Between them is a very powerful Géricault and—as I wrote to Villon after making that unusual juxtaposition—it is quite astonishing how the old, dark picture and the late, brilliant ones turn out to be very good neighbors indeed.

All good wishes to Lou and yourself; Magda joins me in them.

Yours cordially Walter Pach.

NEW YORK, DEC. 2, 1953

Dear Walter [Arensberg],

Some ten days ago . . . we made a stop at Philadelphia on our way.

Doubtless you have heard of the perfectly admirable presentation that has been made of your Mexican objects, so I will not do more than confirm that from my own feeling about the show. . . . [I] was astonished at the number and importance of the pieces you have added since my last visit to you in 1943. There were some things that just got me by

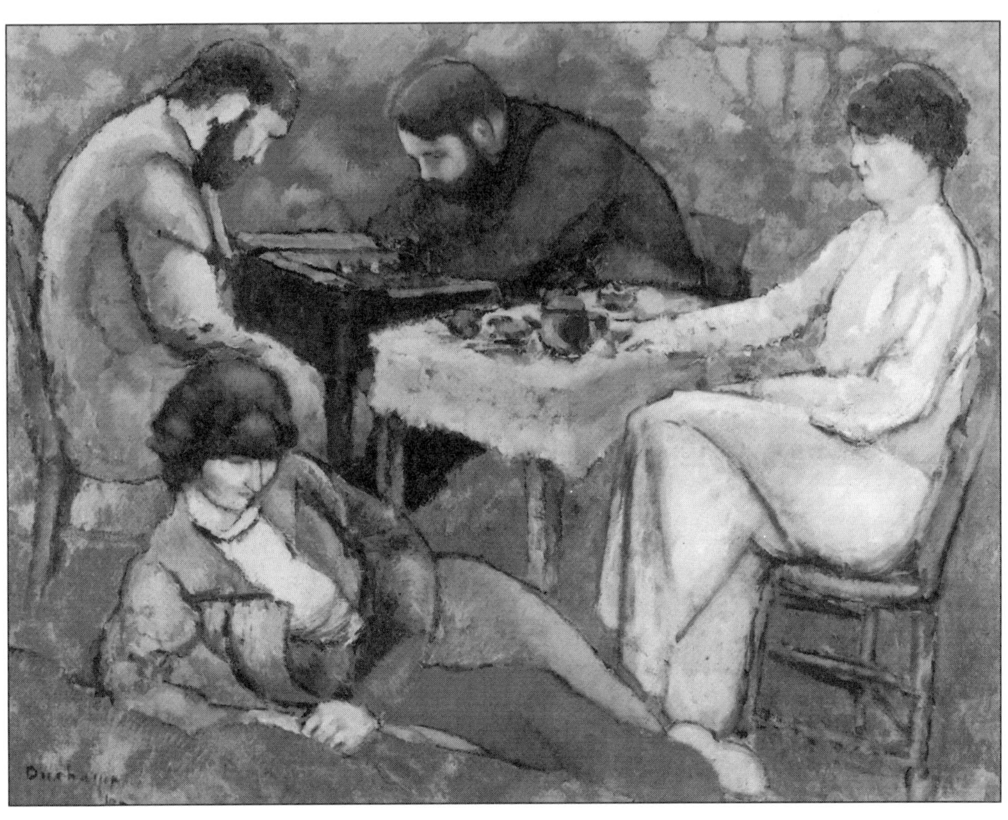

Marcel Duchamp, *The Chess Players* (retitled *The Chess Game*), 1910. Oil on canvas, 44 7/8 x 57 11/16 in. Philadelphia Museum of Art: The Louise and Walter Arensberg Collection. Acc. 1950-134-82. Photograph by Graydon Wood, 1994.

the throat . . . it's a grand bunch of stuff you've brought together, and I don't know whether it isn't more important for the public to see than the modern pictures that are cropping up on every hand now . . . every socialite and her boy-friend are talking modern art now (which doesn't spoil it for me), whereas the grandeur of those old Mexicans is still unappreciated by all but the fewest people. So this is to say thanks for opening up this tremendous vista for the numberless people who are going to profit by your things.

With warmest regards to Lou, I am

As always—yours—Walter Pach.

Source of Letters: Arensberg Archives © Philadelphia Museum of Art.

THE ARMORY SHOW: FREDERIC C. TORREY

The International Exhibition of Modern Art, held in New York City from February 17 to March 15, 1913, became known as the Armory Show because it was displayed in the rented headquarters of the 69th Infantry Regiment Armory at Lexington Avenue and Twenty-fifth Street. The exhibit contained nearly 1,300 paintings, sculptures, drawings, and prints; though only approximately one-third of these were by European artists, it was their contributions, and specifically Marcel Duchamp's *Nude Descending a Staircase, No. 2* and Henri Matisse's *The Blue Nude*, that attracted the greatest attention among a puzzled and often outraged public. (When the exhibit was sent on to Chicago, a replica of *The Blue Nude* was burned in effigy by students of the Art Institute there.)

Frederic C. Torrey (1864–1935) was the San Francisco art and antiques dealer who purchased the Duchamp *Nude* from the show on March 5 without having ever viewed the canvas. Pach not only consummated that sale, but when Torrey expressed a willingness to sell the painting six years later, it was Pach who effected its purchase by Walter Arensberg.

VICKERY ATKINS & TORREY

GALLERIES 550 SUTTER STREET, SAN FRANCISCO: CALIFORNIA

MARCH 6, 1913

The Association of American Painters & Sculptors,
122 E. 25th St.,
New York City.

Gentlemen:

I enclose herewith, check for $444.00 payable to the Treasurer of your Association. This amount is intended to cover the following items: $115. for four small panels by D. Putnam Brinley, catalogued under Nos. 843–4–5–6. It is understood that Mr. Brinley is to sign these panels and send them to me without frames at the close of the exhibition; $324. for a painting by Marcel Duchamp, catalogue number 241, entitled "Nu descendant un escalier." At the close of the exhibition, please have this painting delivered to the Newcomb Mfg. Co., 42 W. 13th St., New York City, who will undertake the packing and shipping to me.

I also provide $5. which I understand to be the price of the edition de luxe of the catalogue which had not appeared at the time I was in New York.

Yours very truly, Federic C. Torrey.

SAN FRANCISCO, JAN. 3, 1919

My dear Walter Pach:

A Happy New Year to you and yours!

Through an error in their mailing room no copies of that tremendously valuable publication the American Art News reached us since mid-summer but not until I became curious about the status of the proposed picture tax did I notice the omission. So I caused the missing numbers to be sent to us and have just been going through their accurate pages. Possibly you have not taken this trouble and so will have missed the amusement of the following in the issue of Oct 19. under the San Francisco correspondence.

"Walter Pach, Curator of Hindu Art at the Boston Museum, gave a course of lectures at the summer session of the Chase School at "Carmel" [California].

I hope the baked-clay records of Babylon upon which archaeologists build so confidently were not made on the same reportorial system! . . .

Considering the present high price of gasoline do you think any one would pay a thousand dollars for the Un Descendant *[Nude Descending a Staircase]*? Walter Arensberg wrote to me about purchasing it that year I met him in N.Y. but I was not in a selling mood. It has lately occurred to me to write now and offer it to him but it occurs to me at the moment that someone with your knowledge might be quite as much interested, and if so would be glad to know of my willingness at the moment to let it go. . . .

Sincerely, Frederic C. Torrey

San Francisco, Feb. 3, 1919

My dear Walter Pach:

Your telegram referring to the shipment of the "Nude"[1] to Arensberg[2]—whose address I am assuming to be as before—33 W. 67th—reached me Friday PM. I sent over the wagon for it Saturday but it did not get back early enough to be boxed and shipped on Sat. It thus goes forward by express today, and I delayed acknowledging your telegram until I could report that it was actually on its way.

Your speedy action takes my breath away as I had assumed the matter would for a time fall rather into the domain of fireside gossip. Inasmuch as Arensberg had actually approached me—three years ago—to buy the thing although I was not minded as at present to part with it at a price within reason—I naturally felt he was the most likely candidate, and I am greatly pleased that he has taken it. When I received your first telegram I did not tell Mrs. T. to whom I had not confided my intention to part with the painting if occasion offered: and I imagined more or less shamefacedly, if she would object if I parted with it. The explosive nature of her reply "I SHOULD NOT"!!! requires properly small caps italicized if there are such things! You had hardly turned eastward before she bundled the Matisses off into a closet, and she looks upon the departure of the "Un descendant" as a red letter day on the hill. And yet we live happily together! Matrimony certainly requires a sense of humor to comfort certain of its aspects.

However—in *some* things her aesthetic judgment and yours—and mine—run as the lawyers say on all fours. Notably on the Spanish Dancer who came on the scene shortly after you left. Alice wanted me to tell you that she had [said] you will know already his point of view. I am myself strongly moved in the direction of the article in current Dial by Lomonossoff.[3] I want that Russian experiment to be given a fair chance. The "refugees" that have come through here have been of the propertied class and their grievances are very real—but they naturally don't want their own possessions "experimented" with. One can make a tragic affair of being deprived of one's pate-de-foie-gras: And many a woman would give her Pekinese dog a funeral much as she would by no means give her cook, or her maid. I feel like suggesting to some of these landlord-refugees that they should rather be thanking God they have lasted so long. That they got to 1918 is the incredible thing.

We are all interested in your plan for Mrs. Pach's visit across the water in the summer, but rather skeptical as to its being so soon possible. We would much rather have her consent to turn westward again and let us see how Raymond has grown up—

I haven't heard any rumors as yet as to Summer School plans—indeed it is rather early no doubt for that. The "flu" has greatly disorganized college work,—for a time it was closed, and a subsequent period of masks is just now over.[4] (Masks off in S.F. on Saturday last. Berkeley a few days earlier.) By the way, you have doubtless heard from Mrs. Martinez of the recent death of her father Herman Whitaker, the writer.[5]

I have come this far in a long letter without having attempted to thank you for your agency in the Arensberg matter. I am also conscious of a shock at this moment as I realize that you sent me two telegrams *prepaid*, which isn't at all according to Hoyle! However I wont at the moment try.

We are all well, including all the living things at the ranch. We all send our best regards to you all—except Sandy who doesn't care about any of us but Raymond to whom I'm sure he sends his love.

Sincerely, Frederic C. Torrey

1. Marcel Duchamp's *Nude Descending a Staircase*.

2. Walter Arensberg, who Pach arranged to purchase the painting.

3. George V. Lomonossoff, "A Voice Out of Russia," *The Dial* 66 (January 25, 1919), 61–66.

4. At one point during the influenza epidemic of 1918–1919, it was advised that wearing a surgical mask would help thwart the disease.

5. Whitaker (1867–1919) had written a series of novels, many of which focused on the American West.

San Francisco, Feb. 7, 1919

Dear Walter Pach,

Just a hurried line to acknowledge receipt of your Regis[tered] letter (last night) with Arensberg's check. The illusion of circumstance made it look as big as a house!

The painting which I advised you earlier had been shipped on Monday, was in fact so shipped bearing the valuation 1000. But next day we were advised that it had not gone forward as their limit of valuation had been exceeded. (Under new regulations unknown to us)[.] So we reduced valuation to 500. and it was sent out on *Tuesday*. I am not quite sure how long it takes for a parcel direct N.Y.-S.F. but I have hope it might be in A's hands before Sunday. If it does not so reach him[,] this day's delay may account for it. . . .

Best regards to all,

Frederic C. Torrey

Source of Letters: Archives of American Art, Smithsonian Institution, Walt Kuhn Papers, Reel D72.

BERNARD BERENSON (1865–1959)

Historian, art critic, and preeminent expert on Italian Renaissance painting. Born in Lithuania, he emigrated to Boston at the age of eleven, graduated from Harvard College, and, with several hundred dollars subscribed by a few Harvard professors and friends, including Isabella Stewart Gardner, he set out for Europe. Bernard Berenson would remain there for the rest of his life. Eventually employed by Lord Joseph Duveen as a paid expert, Berenson began his long career of acquiring priceless Italian paintings for collectors such as Mrs. Gardner, as well as such institutions as the Metropolitan Museum of Art and the National Gallery in Washington. A prolific writer on Italian art and artists, he produced some twenty-eight books between 1894 and 1958 (with three more published posthumously). These include: *The Venetian Painters of the Renaissance* (1894), *The Florentine Painters of the Renaissance* (1896), *The North Italian Painters of the Renaissance* (1907), *The Study and Criticism of Italian Art* (1916), and *Drawings of the Florentine Painters* (1938).

Walter Pach was initially taken to Berenson's villa, "I Tatti," outside of Florence, by Leo Stein, Gertrude's brother. In 1920 Pach wrote an article in *The Freeman* regarding an exhibition at the Metropolitan Museum in which he accepted the attribution of a painting as being by Cimabue (ca. 1250–after 1300), an artist whose very existence was questioned by many art experts. Berenson's own article in support of the attribution had not yet appeared.

The friendship between Pach and Berenson followed, resulting in a correspondence that spans the years from 1921 to 1955.

I Tatti Settignano Florence, Nov. 9, 1921

Dear Mr. Pach,

I received yr. letter of Sept. 9. & the catalogue as well as the photo. of the fascinating St. Francis at Brooklyn.[1]

Thanks, and thanks.

The Francis is curiously like the naive art of all the eccentric regions of Europe.

Go far enough away fr. the centre, provided you don't hit a neo-ultra-plus quasi futurist, & you still find phenomena of candid naif simplification of the already attenuated & anaemic.

I recall the hours spent with you as am[on]g. the most delightful we had in our last visit home. I have spoken of you since returning to my exile, & I look forward with genuine zest to seeing you here some day.

If you write anything likely to interest me, I am sure you will please send it to me.

Sincerely yrs, B. Berenson

1. *Saint Francis of Assisi*, an Indian painting on buffalo or elk hide from the Church at Jemez, New Mexico, dating from the late seventeenth century. Collection of The Brooklyn Museum. Pach featured it in his article "The Art of the American Indian," Dial 68 (January 1920), 57–65, 434–445.

Florence, Feb. 6, 1924

Dear Mr. Pach,

I hasten to thank you for the number of Harper's wh. came the day after I wrote.[1] I have read it with interest, with zeal & with envy. I wish it were given to me too to see in their own land the great monuments that you speak of so feelingly. It was a mysterious, all awesome, a very terrible &, in rare moments, a subtly beautiful phase of art. At least that is the impression I get from what originals I have been able to see. When you come over you shall see a black stone that with almost nothing at all has been turned into a coiled serpent ready to spring, as well as two or three other small things not altogether unworthy of attention

With best remembrances

Sincerely yrs, B. Berenson

1. The January 1924 issue of *Harper's Monthly* contains Pach's article, "The Greatest American Artists" (volume 148, pages 252–262), concerning the Aztec, Toltec, and Mayan Art of Mexico.

FLORENCE, AUG. 11, 1924

Dear Mr Pach,

Your good letter of July 12 is still unanswered. I was waiting for the leisure to read yr. Masters of Modern Art. The opportunity came at last & this morning I finished it.

I wish I could give you the support you ask for. And I have found yr. book informing, stimulating, provoking & sincere. But I cannot even begin to see what you do, in Cubism. Your claim for it remains un-intelligible to my sexagenarian intellect. True, if I were writing about the art of the last 100 yrs. I also should have to speak of Cubism, but I should give it a merely therapeutical value or at utmost a notational interest. By fluke . . . or thro' sheer force of genius a person who imagined he was a cubist, & logicised himself into a systematic theology with regard to it, might produce a work of art. Nor can I follow yr. statement that Cubism is in the line of succession to the Classic Art of the last 100 yrs. Yes, chronologically just as its political equivalent Leninism is the chronological successor to Tsarism.

But why go on? To make my meaning clear would take a volume & I doubt whether anybody would bother to read it just now. I am willing to let even this most deplorable aberration of Gallic logicism have its free rein. And good luck to you. But much as I believe in you, I cannot second you in this effort.

I wish you had come here & looked instead of remaining in France to paint. Painting & writing will never go together. One or the other must be sacrificed & in yr. case it would be a pity if it was the writer who succumbed. True I don't know yr. painting.

With all good wishes

Sincerely yours, B. Berenson

P.S. I know no published word of sense about the relation of Signorelli to Piero della Francesca.

HÔTEL SUBE, ST. TROPEZ, SEPT. 5, 1924

permanent address:
13 East 14th St.
New York City (we leave here next week)

Dear Mr. Berenson,

For three weeks, since I got your kind letter about my book, I have been wanting to write and thank you for it. I believe the reason I have postponed writing until now is that I felt tempted each time to take up the points you mention—and I felt it would be unfair to tempt you to write again. So you must not do so even if I do mention one or two matters. I see that the chapter on Cubism is going to seem to many people the crux of the book, though I am rather more interested in other parts of the modern period.

Since receiving your letter I have looked at the book a number of times, or rather at the illustrations, to see whether the points you bring up make me look on the works of Picasso, Braque and the others in a different light. I fear I am much as I was in former years when people told me certain pictures were beautiful and I could not see them (pictures I now like). It shakes my faith in the efficacy of words, for now I see these Cubistic works as beautiful and cannot unsee them. At all events I am glad you speak of Cubism as Gallic (despite Picasso's being very much of a Spaniard) for that takes it pretty far away from the Leninism you mention—which is German-Russian and very foreign to the French genius with its love of freedom. I feel quite sure there is no parallelism between art and the political movement when people in America call the moderns Bolshevists it is just to give them a bad name, and I should be sorry to think there was a better reason for their doing so than their opposition to changes.

Without wanting to hoist myself to the plane of Delacroix (who is a very special admiration of mine), I should like to cite him as a painter who wrote. Have you the two volumes of his splendid essays which were recently republished by Georges Cris et Cie in Paris? In some ways they are more important than the "Journal" or the "Letters" which were accessible before—as these were not. The various book together make up quite a literary *oeuvre*,—though I know only too well how much right there is on your side in speaking of a painter's difficulty in writing.

Thank you for encouraging me to continue with the writing; thank you also for all the trouble you took with the book and the letter on it. I shall work at my Piero-Signorelli problem.

Yours most cordially, Walter Pach

Florence, Sept. 13, 1924

Dear Mr. Pach.

Altho I am distressingly busy . . . & over-worked, I must write to thank you for yr. note of the 5th. I am truly touched by the candour & transparent sincerity therein manifested—the genuine humility wh. is the beginning & end of all wisdom.

Of course you know I did not mean what the Ku-Kluxcan [*sic*] or Coolidgites mean when they speak of the latest phenomena in painting as Bolshevik. But in a prophetic, devastatingly deep way that's what they are. And they may serve a kindred purpose, namely to bury the dead forms. But they are undertakers, gravediggers, & at best manure-makers only. Artists they are not & Picasso not at all. He, she & it are *impasses*. I wish you were here for talks. We could at all events agree about the breadth & depth of the gulf betw. us. And that would be a great satisfaction.

Thanks for drawing my attention to the two vols by Delacroix. D. was too much of a writer & theorist, & to my palete [*sic*], his art is therefore less sound. I cannot help thinking that you very much over estimate him. He is too much the illustrator. His colour—to me—is not convincing, & his form too submissive to the canons of another art, namely literature—Let me hear from you not too seldom.

Sincerely yrs., B. Berenson

Florence, June 9, 1926

Thanks, dear Pach for yr. kind & interesting note. I do not want prayer, praise, approval or agreement, altho I should welcome them all as a byproduct. What I do want is discussion.

Now ultimately there are two & two only goals for the study of the art of the past. There is the aesthetic one wh. should attempt to love art & enjoy it for ever. And there is the humanistic one which regards art as an experience that humanity is always having & yet is always different. To feel these differences or so many different & yet consecutive moments in the life of the race seems to me the end & the reward of culture.

For which reason it is no mere bit of antiquarianism to decide whether the new Metropolitan acquisition is or is not by Antonello [da Messina]. If it is then there is no succession of moments but their telescoping & confusion in the history of the humanization of our race. I feel more & more that an entirely new generation after Antonello had to arise before a design like the Antonello Madonna could have been achieved.

Ma besta[1]

Thanks for your article in Harper's. It is a triumph that a "bloody monthly"—as Thackeray used to call the mags—should venture to publish such an Anti-Rotarian protest. Am I not still vilipended and lapidated because I dared so long as 35 years ago to protest ag.[ainst] the prostate worship of Sargent & later of Monet—as they pronounced him in America? But at the end of the article you too join the gang of "somehowgood-ites." Of course you can't be quite so insipid when you are geometrizing as all the new artists do, or when you are smirking & coying. But the young gents are just as much mere shadows, just as much mere echoes, just as much glossolagists as their Bouguer[e]au precurrsors [*sic*]. However if your soul demands opti[mi]sm, give it its heed.

Yes, I saw yr. article in L'Amour des Arts,[2] & I not only remember receiving & reading yr. paper on Mexican art but writing to you about it. I am glad to hear yr. painting is taking on, altho I deplore yr. giving to it the time you should dedicate to writing.

I wish you could get Harper's to accept fr you a series of articles on the Gardner Collection.[3] If they don't, nor any other of the Americ. [an] "higher monthlies" "l'Amour de l'Art" certainly would.

Address here is better still c/o Baring Bros. London until further notice. We are leaving in a few days & shall be gone for months to Germany etc. till Sept. & then to Paris & London.

Ever yrs., B. Berenson

1. "Ma besta[nte]," But enough.

2. "L'art au Mexique," *L'amour de l'art* 7 (1926), 285–294.

3. Bernard Berenson played a major role in advising and acquiring works from the Italian Renaissance for the Isabella Stewart Gardner Museum in Boston.

Florence, Aug. 19, 1926

Dear Pach.

Yr. note of Apr. 24 found me in Sicily, & I got back only a little while ago, after a good bout at what there was to see there, & in Campagia.

I was pleased to hear fr. you, & delighted to learn that you were coming abroad & to lecture on French painting in the Louvre. I hope you are enjoying it thoroughly, & living & growing in the process. All the same I wish you could have seen yr. way to running down here for good talk. I should like to see where you stand, but I fear you will never take the place yr. gifts as a critic would lead you to, if you can not detach yrself fr. painting yrself. It is a pity, for critics are ever so much rarer. It is reasonable that so it should be, for criticism is to art what art is to nature. Art is a rest in the flight fr. the pall mall of nature to the crystal sphere of pure intellect—but a rather restive rest peppering to get up & be doing—

I am going to spend the next 3 wks. exploring N. Italy with a view to my revised & I fear final lists.

Sincerely yrs., B. Berenson

Fabriano, May 10, 1927

Dear Pach,

It did not occur to me that my last book could be of any interest to you. But the first reviews to reach me from both England & America frighten me into believing that no "Angry-Saxon" critic will so much as notice the one & only contribution the book makes to a criticism that is based on a question of design.

The Madonna in the last article—now acquired by the Metropolitan Museum—is in essence an uncompensated diagonal or if you prefer musical lingo an undissolved discord. My claim was that such an idea could not have occurred to any one in Antonello's life-time. I now am more convinced than ever that in so far as it took on at all, it was nearer 1520 than 1478, & that even this later date appealed more to Italianates like Scovel than to real Italians.

If it would amuse you to discuss this problem in connection with a review of my Three Essays in Method, Miss Belle Greene will procure you a copy. You alone are likely to want to do it & to be able to do it. Let me hear yr. news & plans.

Sincerely yrs., B. Berenson

New York, July 7, 1927

Dear Mr. Berenson,

Herewith are advance pages of the review of your book—to appear next Sunday.[1]

After a month in which I was going over photographs etc., and trying to think my way through to an article, I found that the book was to appear this week; the editor wanted the review for the issue of the paper nearest in date, so the final writing of the paper went quickly—not too quickly, but if I could have laid it aside for a few days I think I should have changed one or two expressions—especially the one about admitting the possibility of the centrifugal composition. That could be conceded only as a "per impossibile," as you say.

I don't know whether I shall be more or less content (or discontented) with the article after a month, but it does, at least, bring the matter into full discussion (and the Herald-Tribune is a good medium for that). To do that I gave the major part of my space to straight reviewing; and I know from experience that one is heard more readily at the Museum (which is the important place for the discussion to be heard) if one does not raise one's voice too loud. I am sure there will be results from the article, and if I hear of any that seem worth while, I shall let you know of them.

I saw the Gardner Collection this spring for the first time, but I hope to make an excursion to Boston this summer to see it again, also the things on loan at the Fogg Museum. I am rather sure that Harper's would not want a series of articles on the collection of Mrs. Gardner or even one article, probably. Also the next thing I must do is write a book on the theme of that Harper article I sent you last.[2] And I have promised

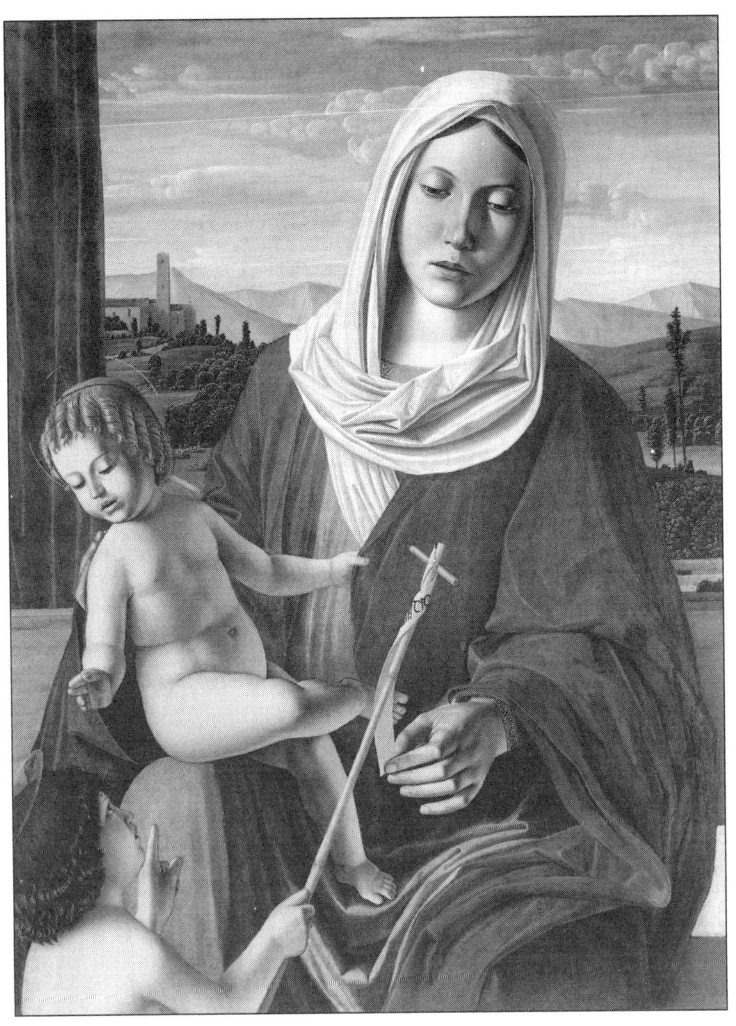

Michele da Verona (Michele di Zenone), *Madonna and Child with the Infant Saint John the Baptist*, n.d. Oil over tempera on wood, 29 x 22 3/4 in. The Metropolitan Museum of Art, Anonymous Gift, 1927. (27.41).

to do another piece of work after that. But I shall, this time, make some notes on the Gardner Collection and perhaps be able to use them later on.

With regards and good wishes for your journey,

Yours very sincerely, Walter Pach

1. Berenson's *Three Essays in Method*, published by The Clarendon Press, New York.

2. The article was "What Passes for Art," *Harper's* 155 (June 1927), 89–97, which deals with "bad artists of the past" and "bad modern men." The resulting book, *Ananias or The False Artist*, was published by Harper & Brothers the following year.

GRAND HOTEL
STOCKHOLM, JULY 25, 1927
ADDRESS BARING BROS. LONDON

Dear Pach,

I have read yr. review with the greatest pleasure & the keenest appreciation of your intelligent & friendly comprehension of what I am driving at. However, like Cortissoz[1] you seem to assume that I make absolute claims for a quantitative method of art study. Far from it. For me real criticism begins only where archae[o]logy ends. My Three Essays[2] is an ironical & veiled attempt to demonstrate that there is a big part of the job that any well trained mediocrity can achieve. The real shame is when critics in high places have not got even that far. But your review still leaves room for an inquiry regarding the vertical design of the impossible Antonello.[3] If you were disposed to pursue it & got it published at home, I should be much gratified.

Great artists like Antonello are not prophets but fulfillers of prophecy. To me it seems that there can be no purpose to the study of the history of art if it does not convince students that such a composition as that of the pseudo-Antonello was impossible in Antonello's life time, not to speak of being totally opposed to the almost Egyptian frontality, verticality & horizontality of that most *primitif* of Renaissance painters.

No more now as I am busy seeing all I can of Sweden in the few days I can spare. If by happy accident you should be in Paris in Nov. you would find me there at Hotel Beau Lita, Rue de Prosbourg, and I hope to hear from you soon & often.

Sincerely yrs, B. Berenson

1. Royal Cortissoz (1869–1948), art critic for the *New York Herald Tribune*.

2. *Three Essays in Method*.

3. Antonello da Messina (1430–1479), artist of the Early Renaissance in Northern Italy.

16, Lower Berkeley Street
London W.1.
Oct. 7, 1927

Dear Pach.

I have suggested thro a friend that Harpers approach you about a series of articles or a book on the Isabella Gardner Collection. If they do come to you, try to undertake the job. You would learn a good deal doing it, & I would give you all the assistance I could. And if you refused it, God knows whom they will get!

I have no leisure myself, & besides as the collection has on the whole—excluding antique & Oriental rubbish—been made by me, I prefer to let others judge its merits. Of course I prefer an unprejudiced judge. In Boston I naturally am no prophet. On the contrary, from the way they talk you would think I had done an irreparable injury by getting the collection together. But with Anatole France's Pontius Pilate I can say "*L'avenir me vendra justice*"[1]

With best regards

Sincerely yrs, B. Berenson

1. "The future will give me justice."

Permanent address: c/o Morgan & Co., 14 place Vendôme, Paris
Until September 1st or so,—Château des Palmiers,
Les Lecques—St. Cyr (France), Aug. 2, 1930

Dear Mr. Berenson,

. . . A year ago we gave up our apartment in New York, put our furniture and pictures into storage, and came away to live in Paris—I was almost going to say 'came away to live'—only that would be too ungrateful to the pleasant people and things in America: but there *was* a drive and restlessness that I got to feeling too much, and I did not progress in my thinking and working as I wanted to. Paris is so much better for that—I find the same stimulus there as before the war, and I believe my work shows the effect (not so much of the stimulus as of the quiet and the chance to go on consecutively with one day painting after another).

In the way of writing I did only one thing—an article on Delacroix as a classicist for *L'Amour de l'Art*—it was in the June issue, to synchronize with the great exhibition at the Louvre. I did not hear of your being in Paris for that, and possibly you have not heard that they propose to continue it till the first of October (instead of the first of August as originally announced—they had not yet the consent of the lenders when I left Paris for my present vacation in the Midi). If you have not seen the show and can possibly get to Paris before it closes, my respectful advice would be to do so. Of course, I know I am saying this after what might be called a Delacroix winter—I was looking at his things, hunting them for purchase (I managed to get just a couple of small ones—or three, exactly), and reading his writings, but despite what may be a somewhat personal preoccupation, I do believe I can say he belongs with the great—perhaps greatest men of the past. The show at the Louvre made me feel so more than ever.

Last fall I made the acquaintance of Lionello Venturi,[1] then returning from America. I asked him if he still believed in the "Antonello Madonna" in the Metropolitan Museum. He said "More than ever"; with me it was less than ever; so I was interested, in London—(I don't know if the matter still interests you)—to note the hands of Benedetto Diana's *Redeemer*. They have an angularity of drawing which made me think of the Madonna's hands in the New York picture. The tonality and quality of the color was also to be related with those of our painting. I do not recall Benedetto Diana clearly. If you are writing me some time, would you say whether you see any chance of him as the author of that curious work? I always have thought of it as early 16th Century (I say so because Belle Greene once spoke if it as nearly modern—I am not sure but that that was partly through vexation with the Metropolitan people: they do give one plenty of reason for such a feeling). . . .

With regards to Mrs. Berenson and yourself, I am

Yours cordially, Walter Pach.

1. Venturi (1885–1961) was an Italian art history professor and gallery director whose area of expertise was fifteenth- and sixteenth-century Italian painting.

Florence, Aug. 22, 1930

Dear Pach,

It is delightful to hear fr. you at such close range, & to hope that there is a chance of seeing you before very long. I am getting old & immobile, or rather no longer stand agglomerations of anything, whether houses, or people, or works of art. On the whole I would rather not see the entire output of a master.

So that, understanding & appreciating your kind intention, even you can not persuade me to go in for a surfeit of Delacroix.

Besides, I know him well, & have known [him] ever since 1887.

And so with what you may have seen at the Victoria & Albert Museum of Medieval Art, I want it all *par petits piquets*,[1] & not in an avalanche. I do not ask anybody to take after me. If they had my make-up & my experience they would of themselves. And others must feed as they will, or they can. I say all this to explain that Paris frightens me as London does or New York does. And no event can induce me to go there.

I'd rather go to Lepcis, Tinej[d]ad, or Kairouan,[2] as I hope to do in Oct. I like to go far afield & if possible when tourists don't, & there to soak, & muse, & loaf, & enjoy what over forty years of looking & turning over have taught me to enjoy.

And what a feast it is, when spread out discreetly & soberly, not like a meat-&-game marked on a wholesale pastry cooks!

I am putting the last touches to the lists of Italian Painters. Then I must revise my Drawings of Florentine Painters. Whereupon shall, if I survive, set to work on a book to be called The Decline & Revival of Form in the Figure Arts. The Lord only knows what will become of it.

No, B. Diana has nothing *specifically* in common with the Necropolitan "Antonello" that is much closer to Cristotero da Parma. Remember I should be delighted to see you. I do hope you will come our way before long.

Sincerely yrs., B. Berenson

1. In small steps.
2. Towns in Libya, Morocco, and Tunisia, respectively.

[ABOARD THE] NORTH GERMAN LLOYD [STEAMSHIP] BREMEN, AUG. 26, 1932

Dear Mr. Berenson,

Our three years' vacation from New York being at an end, we are on our way home—for New York is still home, in some curious way, even if Paris is so much nearer our interests. And just now we've been having a visit with my wife's family, who are Dresden people. I enjoyed the gallery all over again, very much as I did twenty-eight years ago when I first went there. At that time I fell in love with the *Neuvermählte*, Titian's Lavinia as a bride (and I believe it is really she). I wanted to give up the rest of my trip in order to stay there and make a copy of the picture. This summer I did so—and also one (small ones, but exact, in water-color) of a picture I would not have thought of, if I had noticed it in 1904: Poussin's *Flora*, which is one of the most celestial things of that master—who keeps going higher for me each year. Also I was so proud to find, in 1905 when I visited Vienna, that the painter I now care for most of all—Rubens—

had had the same idea of the Lavinia as I, for he copied it too (and what a copy!) We were in Madrid last summer, coming back from Morocco, where we had been for two months, and it was the Rubens pictures that meant most to me, though I went, after an absence of twenty-five years, with the expectation of finding the Titians the supreme things of the gallery. . . .

. . . to speak further of my very infrequent writing, I've an article on the classicism of Barye[1] going through in L'Amour de l'Art, probably to appear in October.[2] If you see it you'll rejoice with us over our possession of that wonderful nude that is reproduced with the article, the only nude that Barye ever *painted.* We got some fine things in Paris (Delacroix, Géricault, Jongkind, and some others) but nothing like that Barye. He has come to be almost the most sympathetic master of the century to me, though I ask no one to be even patient with such an idea.

Here at the end of my letter I say how much I enjoyed seeing your article on those glorious Signorelli drawings. It gave me an unusually sharp twinge of home-sickness for Florence,—but we were not fated to come this time. We shall yet!

As always most cordially yours, Walter Pach

1. Antoine-Louis Barye (1796–1875), a French sculptor who specialized in producing relatively small bronzes of animals, often in combat.

2. "Le Classicism de Barye," *L'Amour de l'Art* 9 (November 1932), 318–320.

---

39 West 67th Street
New York, March 15, 1933

Dear Mr. Berenson,

. . . This place [Pach's new Manhattan address] is to our liking—more than any we've ever had in America. I've not had the right use of it yet, having been hauled around the country to give lectures—always on modern art. Fortunately for me, there is much interest in that, even now, but sometimes I'd prefer to speak on other things. At the Metropolitan Museum I did: one lecture on Classicism and Romanticism, and one on [Jacques-] Louis David and his Successors—both subjects that I feel strongly about and to which I devoted much thought during the three years in Paris. . . . I am casting about for a combination which shall permit me, next season, to pay my way and yet do my own work. At present, university work seems most possible. Publishing is in too low an estate, and my friends at the Metropolitan say there is nothing I would want in that place—which is moreover crying poverty in the loudest tones. I fear they are justified . . .

The three years of our absence were used by New York to become much more up-to-date: The Havemeyer things helped the Metropolitan very much; and the collectors, with the *Modern Museum* or Modern Exhibition Rooms as their show place,[1] are ready for any daring—though I (who am supposed to see this as a triumph) am not convinced that any really important progress has been made. I hear little about collecting that seems genuinely intelligent, I have heard little—if anything—of valid criticism; the painters improve (there is one, A. S. Baylinson,[2] who interests me very much indeed), but I am impatient for better things. Just now, with the new brooms in Washington promising to sweep clean, there is a note of optimistic expectation, but I fear I should be a pessimist if a fortunate share of good health and of interest in my painting did not keep my mind off the ills of the world and its slender knowledge of art.

The best picture at the Metropolitan to come since I left is the Signorelli *Madonna*—though Bryson Burroughs, when I said that, added a word of generous enthusiasm for the David *Death of Socrates*, which I got for them.[3]

Your card expresses a kind wish that we could have a good talk. I reciprocate with all my heart . . . I thought of you in Boston not long ago where I went to speak at the Museum (modern art, even there: modern American art) and when I saw Mrs. Gardner's things again. I was in Detroit too, where Valentiner[4] has certainly gathered some fine things. I met Edsel Ford[5] and thought he might go far in understanding. I liked him and Mrs. Edsel Ford.

All good wishes to you.

As always—most cordially, Walter Pach

1. Before the Museum of Modern Art moved into its own home at 11 West Fifty-third Street in May 1931, it occupied space on the twelfth floor of the Heckscher Building at 730 Fifth Avenue.

2. Pach was familiar with Baylinson's art because the latter had exhibited in every one of The Society of Independent Artists annuals beginning with the organization's inception in 1917.

3. See Pach letter to Burroughs, January 30, 1931 ff.

4. Dr. W.[illiam] R. Valentiner (1880–1958), director of The Detroit Institute of Arts.

5. Edsel Ford, Henry Ford's son, owned some notable French paintings, including Renoir's *The Cup of Chocolate*.

---

148 West 72nd St.
New York, Aug. 21, 1935

Dear Mr. Berenson,

About seventeen or eighteen years ago, I was asked to write an article on you for an Encyclopedia. I had trouble in getting biographical material; at last your nephew,

Lawrence, referred me to a source where I could get the facts—out of which the year of your birth remains in my mind. Lately . . . I realized that you were seventy, this year, so it seemed an appropriate time—(though I don't know the month and day on which to send you congratulations)—to write at least a line in connection with the auspicious year, and to wish you many more of them, with lots of good pictures to look at—on your own walls, as much as possible.

Every time that I recall the fact that during our years abroad I did not get back to Italy, I have a twinge of regret . . . I wanted to paint—and I could not even get over to London for the Italian exhibition, even less for the French show, though I should have loved to see it. About the Persian show I had rather slight regrets. An hour or so at the Louvre (or, now, at the Metropolitan) among the Persian things will hold me for quite a long while. I am incurably European, I guess,—Mexican things being my next interest, even more than those of China (which—to be sure—I do not know as well as I should).

But I do hope to get back to Italy some day . . .

It is three years since we returned to America, and my finances have not picked up any. They have rather tended to become more difficult. . . . I have been somewhat disappointed in people: despite the severity of the depression, I don't think they had the right to drop art to the extent that they did. . . .

Kindly convey my best remembrances to Mrs. Berenson and believe me

Very sincerely yours, Walter Pach

CONSUMA, SEPT. 13, 1935

Dear Pach.

My 70th birthday, wh. happily brought me a discreet number of congratulations, brought none more welcome than yr. letter. I was glad to be in touch with you again, & before I am again overwhelmed by the various calls made on every septuagen[ar]ian who has done any thing & thus become an institution, I give myself the pleasure of scribbling a few words to you. In the first place let me say that I am truly glad that yr. painting is giving satisfaction to yrself. One can live on all air if one is happy in one's work.

Then I must tell you that I am delighted with what you say about exhibitions like the . . . one . . . at the Petit Palais. I oppose it with all my impotence for the present & affection has in the future. I notice that even the organizer of the circus became rather uncomfortable over it.

How I wish I could have seen the Morgan portr.[ait] cleaned, the one you speak of as [Andrea del] Castagno. By the way it is [Antonio del] Pollaiuolo & not as 40 yrs. ago

I persuaded the world. I know better now, & as a matter of fact it is not round enough for Castagno & its contours are altogether Pollaiuolo. Th. is of interest to me not as a question of attribution but of perceiving definite differences of purpose & quality altho for gesture & "pathos" either master might seem its author.

The book I have been at work on for years is the revision of the Drawings of Flor[entine] Painters. It has been rendered peculiarly difficult & disagreeable by the foulness piled over Michelangelo by a lot of German animals, the worst of whom is a biped named Panofsky[1] who passes I understand for a great sage, spell-binder & brightener in your part [of the world].

Happily this is nearly finished, & now I have serious difficulties in finding a publisher to undertake such a venture.

I dream,of writing on the decline & recovery of form in the visual arts. But plans at 70 with a diminished income, so diminished that I may have to leave I Tatti, with a world in the throws of returning to the empire of Diocletian, are not to be taken too seriously.

I am writing from a house in the forests of the Pratomagno, 5 or 6 m.[iles] fr. Vallombrosa, over 3000th high, & scarcely an hour fr. I Tatti. It is an ideal place for work, & for living the life that suits me. Th.[is] still is a land of shepherds, charcoal burners & cow herds. Th. is the country Virgil loved, the kind of world the gods of old created & still inhabit. And how they laugh at the fuss & feathers of the proudlings below.

Do write again & before long. And remember me to yr. wife.

Sincerely yrs, B. Berenson

1. Erwin Panofsky (1892–1968) was a German art historian active in the United States, who wrote on Late Medieval and Renaissance art in Northern Europe and Italy.

NEW YORK, AUG. 3, 1936

Dear Mr. Berenson,

Since your beautiful letter of last fall . . . I write again to say that I continue to paint and occasionally to write. (The Virginia Quarterly for January—perhaps our best review now—had an article of mine on the Alba Madonna of Raphael—in view of American needs; and in "Parnassus" for April I had a paper on the outlook for modern art). Also by way of news of myself, I make my début as a teacher of painting—save for a few pupils in my studio—with a newly founded school at Columbia University, an outgrowth of the School of Architecture there. It is a big step for Columbia, where Dr. Butler has always been doubtful of art work. For me it is a chance to try out some theories of art teaching. I expressed them—verbally—in what I called A Course in

Tradition at The Art Students' League, four years ago. Now I shall try to put them into practice. I am eager (and—just in this connection) for that book on form which your letter mentions. To me that is the pivotal thing in European art, and what chiefly makes it superior to the art of the Orient.

You speak of Panofsky. Lately when I was lecturing for a month at Bowdoin College (where I had most pleasant visits with Mrs. Sessions—we often talked of you) one of my hearers was a most admirable professor of German who had attended Panofsky's lectures in Hamburg. My friend—for I now count him one—was passionately interested in art when a student at the University in Hamburg, and he said one reason why he attended my lectures was because they were different from Panofsky's—he said I was talking about painting, whereas with Panofsky, one could not tell whether he was talking of religion or philosophy or what it was: certainly there was no evidence of his having penetrated an inch into the field of art, or almost that he knew there was such a thing. That is not a great deal of consolation for the added difficulties you have had about the Michelangelo drawings, but perhaps it helps a little. Far better, if I could make you feel the pleasure I had again lately, would be an idea of what I got recently from your *Drawings of the Florentine Painters*.

Do you know the Piero [della Francesca] that our friend Clapp[1] recently got for the Frick Collection? The work of that supreme man comes out well in reproduction of course, but this is again so glorious a thing that it needs to be seen.

And do you know Mr. Grenville Winthrop?[2] A year or two ago I already thought his collection the most exciting in any house in America, but lately he has been buying again, and *such* paintings by Ingres, *such* drawings by David and Géricault that they took my breath away. That is one period that I am very particularly keen about. His Italian pictures are not of the best, but the collection as a whole gives me immense pleasure. He talks of bequeathing it to Harvard, and it was his intention to keep it in his New York home even then. But the Fogg [Museum] people want it in Cambridge and I think that a mistake—even though my feeling toward Boston is of the friendliest. The art-life of America is so focussed in New York that I think Mr. Winthrop's treasures would have their maximum of effect here. It is a pity that he had a falling-out with poor Bryson Burroughs (whom I still miss so much) and thereon decided not to give the things to the Metropolitan—an error in logic, for the institution lives on when the man is gone. I wish some one could make him see that.

I had my first visit with Henry Goldman[3] this year, strange as that may seem. He told me that the picture I wrote of as a Daddi is now spoken of by some as a Giotto. If my feeling counts, Daddi is the better name; certainly the picture is a grand one. And I did like the whole collection.

There is enormous activity here in mural work, due to the federal appropriations for the artists—many of whom never had so much money (many others, however, being

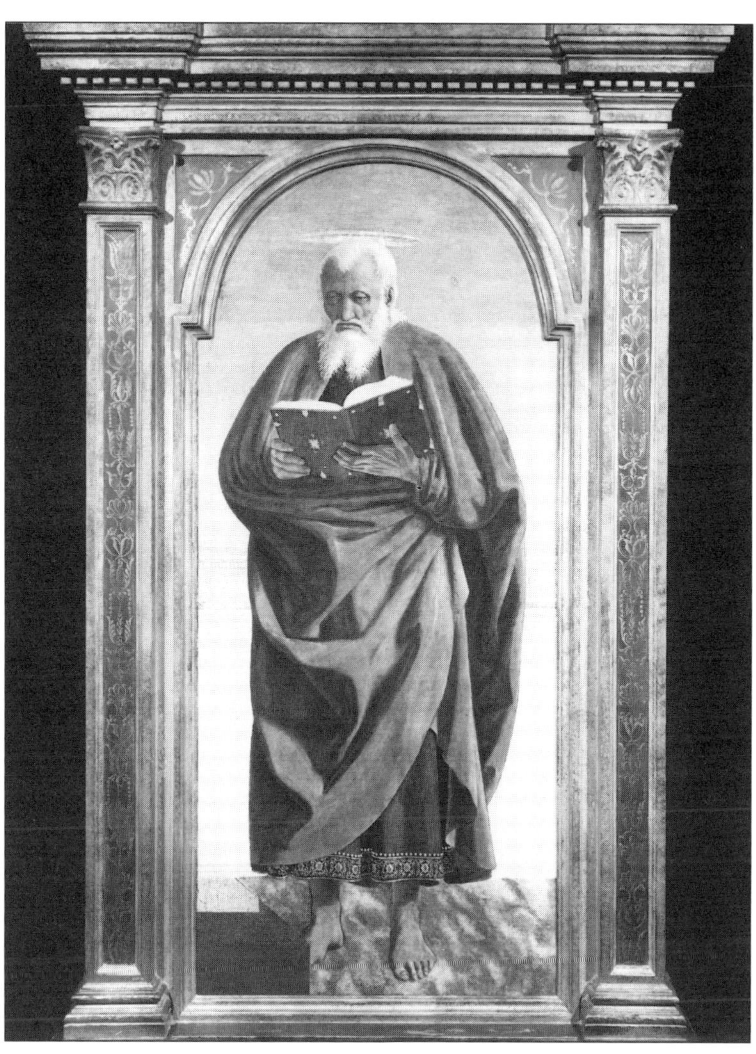

Piero della Francesca, *Saint Simon the Apostle,* 1454–69. Tempera on poplar panel, 52 3/4 x 24 1/2 in. © The Frick Collection, New York. Acc. 36.1.138.

poorer—and those not on relief having a very hard time). The example of Mexico made many people look for a "renaissance" here, but we have not the centuries of art behind us that the Mexicans have and we shall have to take our time. Still, good is being done, and it is likely that government support will continue even when the depression—in its worst forms—is over; that is very desirable, I think, though we must face the extremely difficult task of keeping *all* the money from going to mediocrities. . . . I like our new Titian *Venus* very much indeed.

With many good wishes.

Yours cordially, Walter Pach

1. Frederick Mortimor Clapp, director of the Frick Collection.

2. Winthrop (1865–1943), whose collection included Early American portraits as well as nineteenth-century European art.

3. An art collector.

GRUSBACH, MORAVIA, AUG. 26, 1936

My dear Pach.

Yours of Aug. 3 found me in bed with a little leisure, wherefore I answer it at once. Later I shall be caught in the vortex of Paris & London.

I am ever so glad to hear fr. you for you are one of the last surviving acquaintances who, in the study of art, have not gone over to irrelevant geometricity, even more irrelevant but skyscraping pedantry, still more irrelevant metaphysics & most irrelevant of all, waste-basket material of anecdotage.

What I hear fr. America about art writing—in so far as it is not frankly commercial—& about art teaching is enough to drive one to drink. Students seem ready only to be fitted for posts by Sachs or befuddled by Mackowsky, & so greatly prefer the lat[t]er.

So I am happy to learn that you have got a footing at Columbia, & I know I can count on you to do what you can to let aesthetic sense prevail.

I used to know Greny Winthrop, but years have passed, as you know, since I have been home, & I have lost touch with him. I have heard of his collection & that like the Blisses at Washington he meant to leave them to Harvard but to remain where they were. If you see him again give him my remembrances & tell him how glad I should be to hear from him.

Goldman's Madonna is one I used to give to Daddi. I now regard it as by an artist closer than Daddi to Giotto but not Giotto himself. The leading German Jew critics give it to Giotto as they tried to give away rug to the great master it vaguely recalls.

I have begun the book on the Decline & Recovery of Form, & I may publish the introduction as a separate book. The whole will take many years, & if it gets published may help to restore reason in the now so crazed Kingdom of art. But is that realm crazier than the other realms of cidevant human, now tooth-and-claw biped!

I have just spent six weeks studying Roman remains, & Byzantine frescoes in Yugoslavia. It is a wonderfully varied but always beautiful & unspoilt country where one felt so far away from Hitler, Mussolini, Stalin & Co.

Send me anything inexpensive that you publish and let me hear of things more serious.

Ever yrs., B. Berenson

Florence, Nov. 30, 1936

Dear Pach.

I have been back some 10 days, found a mountain of printed matter awaiting me, & today got at last to yr. "Raphael" in the Virginia Quarterly. Of course it interested me. I, however, expect nothing fr. the state on corporations, or inflated contributions like Rockefeller, Frick etc. etc. All such bodies can vie & alas! abuse art, but cannot promote it or even encourage it.

So on the whole the photo of yr. fresco gave me more pleasure than the article.

In yrs. of Sept. 24 you speak of Van Wyck Brooks. When you see him will you tell him that I should be pleased if he came to see me when he next stops off in Florence.

I found Paris more of a world-capital than ever, & had five weeks of museums, collections & humanized bipeds. It was a treat after even London, altho that too is relatively civilized, & may be heard of in the next few years as the political new Jerusalem.

I wish I could have a long talk with you.

Ever yrs., B. Berenson

[on a train out of] New Orleans, Feb. 16, 1940

Dear Mr. Berenson,

It crossed my mind this morning that you are going to be seventy-five years old this year and, to celebrate such an event as well as to wish you many years more of happy work, I take my pen in hand.

Sometimes I think it has almost gotten out of hand, I have used it to the tune of a book a year since 1936: a short work on van Gogh being of that date, my translation and editing of Delacroix's *Journal* being of 1937, *Queer Thing Painting* appearing in 1938, and in 1939, my *Ingres*. Van Wyck Brooks, who often speaks of you, says it is the best I have done. If he has not gotten around to you yet in his history of American literature, he will. Probably the latter case is the real one, for his *Indian Summer* of New England, which ought to be just about going to the publisher at this time, goes down only to 1895, 1 think. To me, his insight into American thought, and his writing about it are extremely fine—the best work of the kind we have today, and by far. I only wish I knew more of his subjects, for I read but little.

I continue to paint every moment I can get for that pursuit, and I continue in the uncongenial necessity of making a living. At this moment, I am on a lecture tour, having spoken at such places as Chicago, Bozeman (the Montana State College), Seattle, Portland (Oregon), San Francisco, Los Angeles, San Diego, San Antonio (Texas), Houston, and New Orleans. Now I am on my way to Flint and Detroit, Michigan, then home, thank goodness. I shall have been away just five weeks—and have worked hard. A chief item on that score is the acceptance of "entertainment;"—what is really demanded is that the visitor entertain—with the smallest practicable allowance of time for eating and sleeping. At that, as I wrote my wife about my defencelessness before the onslaughts of my "entertainers," the worst of it is that I sympathize with them in their loneliness and their desire to get ahead. They are doing so: when I was last in San Francisco—in 1918—it was a desert, parched and leafless, as far as art was concerned. Today there are three museums with works of value, and the human progress keeps pace with this movement. I am not a fanatic on progress,—reading Delacroix's *Journal*, if nothing else did the thing, would have made me sceptical about the word. But sometimes, as in the case of California, it is valid; and that deserves notice in a world as full of agonizing spectacles—and stupidities as ours is today. For some weeks before I left New York I was working on the 1940 *Masterpieces of Art* show at our World's Fair. Dr. Valentiner found that he could not take leave of absence from The Detroit Museum again so as to reorganize the show, organize a totally new one, that is—and the work fell to me. I should not have gone off on this tour, save that I could not properly withdraw at so late a date. So I have been running the office by air mail and telegraph,—my wife representing me in New York. Usually my work has been purposeful and—in intention, at least—creative. The *Ingres* is history (and assembling of the master's words, as they are to be found in no other single volume); but it is also an essay on the Classical and the Romantic, and an inquiry into their functions. I regard that as a useful thing. The World's Fair show is partly to yield diversion to holiday crowds (I always try to face the least elevated statement of a case), but it is partly to satisfy the eager interest of a public that has a pretty creditable attitude toward art. And, with all the flub-dub and drum-beating of such occasions, they have done service and had lasting effect on art-appreciation in America. There is a good deal of material here to choose from, and most people lend; some, like Grenville Winthrop, refused to do so. But I hope to compose a nice bouquet of works. That will be a satisfaction, if I succeed. Yet I'm free to say that I wouldn't give these months of work to the job if I didn't have to make a living. I am urgently reminded of the fact that I must, every so often, and of the uncertainty of my future.

I wrote to Paul Sachs[1] about it, not very long ago, and he suggested my getting myself appointed to the staff of the new National Gallery in Washington. It is a government job, and so within the control of the Civil Service. Their examination was, of course, child's play for me, until it came to one point. To avoid getting people on the pension roll, they have a regulation that appointees must not be over fifty-three years of age—and I am fifty-six. John Walker,[2] whom I do not know, but who writes me that you have often mentioned me to him (thank you!) is looking into the matter. I offered to waive all claim to a pension, but his first thought was that the Civil Service people would be adamant: that rules are sacred to them. With the enormous and concentrated work of the Fair to occupy me in the coming months, I shall not give much thought to later activities for a good while; but ducking the question is not grappling with it. So the thing will have to be faced again. I've always hoped to find a once-for-all answer to my problem, but have not succeeded so far. When poor Bryson Burroughs[3] died, I somewhat considered applying for the job, but decided not to do so. Harry Wehle, who is the curator now and to whom I mentioned the idea some years afterward, said "I don't think this would have been a position for you: you've too much of the crusader in you." John Quinn's[4] word was 'missionary'—which I never accepted; and I don't think that even 'crusader' is accurate. I think some things are true, that some are untrue, and that there is immeasurably more of general agreement about them than people admit, as a rule. If I get any thing like a free hand with my Fair, I think I can make nearly every one call it good. (And I expect to have a pretty free hand. If any idea for a next move by me should occur to you, in your observation tower, I'd be grateful if you'd let me know of it [)].

My son—aged twenty-five—just made his début as a singer. I was in California—to my immense regret, but the reports are that his recital went very well. It was quite wonderful for me to hear him give a trial performance, a short time before I left home. It made me think of how the world looked to me, simple and clear, when *I* was twenty-five. He is a fine boy, but I don't want to be a boy, I'm satisfied to be fifty-six (even if The Civil Service won't have me); I hope to be on the job at seventy-five. I'm sure you are, and I'm eager to read of it. Good luck, then, and my best wishes.

Cordially yours, Walter Pach

P.S. A book, recently published, which I venture to recommend to you is *Indian Arts in North America*, by George C. Vaillant; Harpers, $5. Dr. Vaillant began with Egyptology; he is now curator of Mexican art at The Museum of Natural History. His interest has moved on to the great peoples of the land that is now the United States, especially Ohio. I am mad about their work, the best of it. Tomorrow I visit a small town, hoping to buy from an Indian collection there.

In Santa Barbara, California, I saw Mr. Samuel Ilsley,[5] a charming man, who spoke of you.

1. Sachs (1878–1965), director of Harvard's Fogg Art Museum.

2. Walker (1906–1995), chief curator of the National Gallery of Art in Washington.

3. Burroughs (1869–1934), curator of the Department of Paintings at The Metropolitan Museum of Art.

4. Quinn (1870–1924), New York attorney and patron of Modern Art.

5. Ilsley (1863– ?) an author and playwright.

Florence, March 30, 1940

Dear Pach,

Yr. letter took a long time coming, but is no less welcome. I am glad to hear fr. you again & to learn of yr. doings in this long interval that I have had no direct communication from you. I never lose an occasion to say that I think of your gifts, and of the genuineness of your purpose. Walker knows all that, & to my knowledge agrees with me. I am confident that if it is in his competence to further your interests he will not fail to do so.

I am obliged to you for the name of the book on the art of our Indians, & I am ordering it at once. It may amuse you to learn that when I was fourteen I began an historical novel on the Ohio Mound Builders. I don't remember its getting very far, but the interest in the subject was there. It has never quite died.

My working days are over I fear. For one thing I feel afraid that I have nothing to say that would not sound commonplace; for another I am too much absorbed in what is going on in this part of the world where fighting is going [on] between the Allied Perseus & the German Dragon while U.S. Andromeda waits for the result. I should not have said "German" but *Nazi*. For the real German *elite* I have more admiration & affection than ever, & if Perseus wins this they too will be liberated.

Do write again before too long & always count on my interest in your doings.

Ever yrs, B. Berenson

New York, June 15, 1941

Dear Mr. Berenson,

Your last letter ends with a wish that I write again, and I hope you will not judge my appreciation of the compliment by the length of time before this writing. When your lines came, I was up to my eyes in the work of the *Masterpieces* Show at the [New York] World's Fair. Valentiner had done it the year before and had skimmed a good deal of the cream of the collections here, so—as director last year—I had to work very hard to keep from falling behind. Many people said, however, that they liked the 1940 Show better than the other. It was largely the 19th Century work—untouched the year before—which made our show stand so high, that and the French art, which had been too slightly treated. We had six Poussins, and I found them rising in power, month after month. At that, I had studied those in the Louvre more than almost anything else, during my last three years in Paris, and I copied the great "Flora" in Dresden. My friend Diego Rivera says French art can not die because it has the faculty of getting new strength from whatever other land that is producing, but I am scared this time. I have abundant hope though, and think this country is making strides in coming to a realization of its role in the world of today. It certainly needed to. At the risk of following Nero's example while the world burns, I will say that with the beautiful Fontainebleau School show we had, and the great treasures of the Louvre, the most impressive show of the year was of the American Indian art. I hope you did get Vaillant's book; its photographs of the magnificent mound builder work must have made you feel that your boyhood attempt at a novel about them was pointed in a fine direction. Lately, I was in Columbus, Ohio, again, and saw a new find, a head of grand quality that is so Mexican in character that one is sure there was communication between the two places.

I spoke to our new director at the Metropolitan[1] on a lecture about that show but was told "No one is interested in the Indians." That is a bit discouraging, but the way the new staff is doing over the arrangement of the pictures at the Museum makes me think that we are to see some real progress. For one thing, they have abolished the American room which one entered immediately after issuing from the first gallery, with its Raphael, Titian and Rubens. The juxtaposition never ceased to give me a shock, and was a bar to the patriotic pride in our art which the room was supposed to encourage. I suppose even this war will leave us still with a will o' the wisp regret about the failure of Henry Mencken's prophecy of 1918: he said "The one good thing to say is that now a man who boasts of his patriotism will be as ridiculous as a woman who boasts of her modesty." We're not there yet—in fact we're in for some bad times; but I keep on hoping.

One interesting thing here about the period is the number of art people it has brought us. In the last days I have seen G. M. Richter, Suida, Curt Glaser, and Paul Rosenberg. One man I have come to like very much is W. G. Constable, now at the Boston Museum. I am scared, for his sake, at the reports I get from everyone about the Piero della Francesca, as they call the portrait of a lady recently acquired there. I have not seen it myself, and am trying to keep an open mind till I do. The Boston people seem to be full of confidence.

Don't you think it's time for you to come and see it (since its cleaning, which was imperative, they say, because of the repaints). Every one would be happy to see you here, and none more so than

Yours always sincerely, Walter Pach

1. Henry Francis Taylor was appointed director of the Metropolitan Museum of Art in 1940, and served until 1955.

Till Oct. 1 only
Casa al Dono
Vallombrosa (Prov. di Firenze), Aug. 30, 1941

Dear Pach.

Yrs. of June 15 reached me less than three weeks ago, & proved most interesting. I am always happy to hear fr. you & [word illegible] yr. personal news as well as your news of the art world. ¶[1]Yes, I got the book on the art of our Indians which interested me. Some of the reproductions delighted me. You surmise a connection with Central America. There can be no question that it is so. I believe that the entire Mississippi basin to its utmost reaches was flooded with Aztec influences. In fact I possess proof of it. I wonder whether you are acquainted with an essay on "Prehistoric Art" by a certain Th.[omas] Wilson that appeared in the "Report of U.S. Nat. Mus[eum] 1896." You will find there repro.[ductions] of stone objects & bronzes found in Georgia & Tennessee that show unmistakably the connection with Central America The bronze on Pl. 59 is so Aztec that one might suspect it of being an importation. ¶If a photo. of the head you speak of at Columbus O. exists, or has been reproduced do ask them to send it to me. ¶I share Rivera's conviction that French art will rise again. With all & for all its crimes & absurdities, & despite the Catalan torment wh. stunned it, French art remained the only living, striving creative one, even tho' so low temporarily in vitality. ¶I am glad you appreciate Poussin more & more. I am proud in recalling that I placed him among my foremost admirations fr. the moment I saw him for the first time in June 1887 in the Louvre. Had I been a dealer I could have bought some of his finest for coppers[.] ¶We have been spending the summer in this paradise wanting for nothing & surrounded by friends. None so [illegible] the overwhelming majority of Italians in all classes. The longer I live here the more do I experience this. ¶I have a booklet ready to be called "An Approach to Art-History." I fear it would sadden you as such a proof of [illegible] decay. ¶Tell me more abt yrself & yr. family.

Sincerely yrs, B. Berenson

1. The paragraph marks (¶) were placed there by Mr. Berenson.

NEW YORK, NOV. 5, 1941

Dear Mr. Berenson,

Your letter of August 30th reached me about ten days ago. I at once wrote to Dr. Shetrone, the (very fine) director of the Ohio State Museum, and have received the enclosed photograph (which accounts for the large-size envelope). The sculpture was found in Ohio, and is undoubtedly of local origin; but, in type, it suggests the Mexicans as nothing else does that I have seen.

I wrote Dr. Vaillant about your letter, including the citation of the "Report of the U.S. National Museum." He is likely to know of that already, as he is a tremendous student. His "Aztecs of Mexico," which appeared recently, is a very fine book. He has just become the director of the Museum of the University of Pennsylvania.

I am trying for a similar position—at the Rhode Island School of Design, in Providence. They have a very fine museum there. I don't know at all what my chances are. Hitherto, I have not wanted jobs; but today, with the uncertainties we face and the extreme difficulty of making a living through painting, writing and lecturing, I really hope they take me. It will doubtless mean loss of freedom, particularly in the earlier time at the work, but I don't know whether failure to be appointed won't mean far worse things.

Your words about enjoying Poussin on your early visits to the Louvre struck an especially sympathetic chord in me, as I had recently been to Boston and seen, at the Fogg Museum, an entrancingly beautiful *Annunciation* by him. It comes from an English collection (Norris is, I believe, the name) and is over here "for the duration" [of the war in Europe]. Their big Rubens "Queen Thomyris and the Head of *some one*"[1] is a perfect marvel. Also it is having much success, which—I fear—is more than can be said for the little portrait given to Piero della Francesca. Of the latter, some people have said 'modern fake,' which I'm quite positive it is not. I did not have enough time with it (I'm not sure that for all my study at Arezzo, etc., I could have decided absolutely, in any case). My impression in Boston was that it was due to an early and very faithful follower. But I must say that it gains in recollection,—perhaps because I have a photograph here, and—in that—it does look "too beautiful" (if you'll excuse those sentimental words) for anyone but the master. Do you know the work? Mr. Constable tells me that it changed enormously when the overpainting was removed.

By the way, you've heard—have you not?—that the Metropolitan has removed the "Antonello" label from the Madonna that you studied in detail some years ago. As Burroughs wrote in the Bulletin of the Museum, at the time, you were the only one to stand out against it; I recall that there was quite a formidable list of men in favor of it. So that the decision ought to give you at least a minor satisfaction—beside the solid pleasure I think every one must feel when there is a new demonstration of the fact that art problems do not rest on mere personal reactions ("Truth on one side of the Pyrennes, falsehood on the other"), but that, given time, honest and competent men are bound to reach the same conclusions. I have written that at least one (in *Queer Thing, Painting*) and have said it many times. Yet people are forever saying there are no basically true things in art principles. To me, that's heresy. And I make no slightest claim to infallibility.

How good it would be if I could spend an evening with you over such matters! Perhaps I can—or several evenings—when the book you mention is accessible,—"An Approach to Art-history." I do hope that may be soon.

Yesterday I got from Van Wyck Brooks (who often speaks of you) an advance copy of his "Opinions of Oliver Allston"—the latter being himself, as the publisher tells on the jacket. I know two chapters in it that he gave me: "Primary Literature" and "Coterie Literature," and they are *extremely* important. They will be bitterly assailed however, and—just in a detail or two—I fear he gives a chance to attackers. I think they will hardly be able to obscure the value of the argument as a whole, however.

It is good to hear that Italy continues to be such a human place to reside in. I am glad—for your sake, and for the unfortunate human race.

My kindest regards to you and to Mrs. Berenson.

Yours very sincerely, Walter Pach

1. Cyrus.

---

3 Washington Square
New York, Sept. 30, 1945

Dear Mr. Berenson,

If my memory serves me right, my last letter to you was shortly before the War cut off the mail to Italy. I shall not attempt to give you any account of myself during that long time save to say that I continue painting and writing, and that I was again sent for by the National University of Mexico—where I spent the year 1942–'43 (July to July), giving one lecture a week with long vacations to visit Yucatan and other enchanting places that I had not known before. The ancient art of Mexico has continued to rise in my esteem, and with it the closely related art of the old peoples of our country. I have, for over a year, been at work on a book in which I bring in these arts pretty frequently though they are not my main theme. That is the art museum in the United States, the book being ordered (or subsidized) by The Rockefeller Foundation.[1] But calling it, as I do, *The Museum of the New World*, I am able to speak of the ancient Americans whose grandiose art is conspicuous by its absence at the Metropolitan, the Boston Museum and most of the other chief places. Valentiner, in Detroit, was the first in America to give it a place with the Old World arts. . . .

. . . I was grieved when I learned of the loss of Mrs. Berenson. I met her only on the few occasions when I could call on you in New York in 1919, but the memory of her gracious personality and her devotion to you has remained with me through the quarter-century since then. Please forgive my being so inept in begging you to accept my sympathy which is very real, none the less. . . .

And now—yourself! . . . What I wonder about most is not your experiences of the war, but how your ideas are working out and whether there is any chance of our seeing them in print. You used to write me such grand letters; but with the things you must have on your mind, and with present conditions (I hope not *too* bad for you) I would not want you to reply to this—unless you just felt like doing so, for some reason. If so, do please tell me of anything you are publishing.

With many good wishes,please believe me as always

Yours very cordially, Walter Pach

1. Pach's volume, titled *The Art Museum in America*, was published in 1948 by Pantheon Books, New York.

FLORENCE, NOV. 29, 1945

Dear Pach.

It is just a month since I had yours of Sept. 30. It has taken all this time to find the leisure to read yr. article on the rôle of modern art. The death of my wife on the one hand, & the absence of Anglo-Saxon youngish women working as secretaries overburdens me, & my working hours are diminished by *age*. Let me in the first place hasten to tell you that yr. son must come to me the moment he gets here. If he can profit by me, I shall be happy to see him often, & do what I can for him—I have enjoyed yr. article as I do everything you write. You are sincere, & sufficiently informed, & sufficiently thoughtful to have acquired the rare right to be considered *sincere*.—I share yr. view that art knows no past nor present, no nationalities, no races. I am as ready to find it in Oceania or in Thibet, Kamstchatka or in Benin. That is why I made such an effort to impose a distinction between Illustration & Decoration. Decoration is universal. Illustration, c.f. subject matter, alone is locally determined.

Some four or five years ago I wrote a book to be called Aesthetics (Ethics) & History. Wherein again I hammer this nail. I have let it lie, but mean to take it up again soon. In the interval I have started a "Decline & Recovery in the Figure Arts," & was well on the way when I had to go into hiding. There I kept a diary wh. may appear soon. Previously I had written an "Introduction to a Diary" wh. may appear at the same time.

Pity, there are such spaces between us. It would be great fun to converse.

All good wishes for a Happy New Year,

Sincerely yours, B. Berenson

NEW YORK, SEPT. 12, 1946

Dear Mr. Berenson,

Your letters are always so indulgent as to bespeak an interest in mine, so I take up my pen once more. . . .

This book [*The Art Museum in America*] seems to me to be especially for laymen—who are making progress here, but still need to be told of the wealth of art works available for them. One that I take exception to in the book (especially as to its condition) is the Masaccio *Madonna and Child* in the Mellon Collection at the National Gallery. It seems to me so doctored up that one can see nothing of Masaccio there—if indeed his hand ever *was* visible in it; the silhouette is impressive, to be sure—I have had great interest and pleasure in the recent book by Valentiner, *Origins of Modern Sculpture*. In a way, he carries on your idea of relating ancient and modern arts; I think that is one of the most useful things that can be done. In the forthcoming Magazine of Art (Washington) I shall have an article on Jacques Lipchitz;[1] I like his sculpture very much.

I believe my painting has moved ahead.

It is still too soon for us to think of a return to Europe, but I count on doing so; indeed I am hungry to go. Doubtless then we shall revisit Italy, and I shall then have the personal visits with you that you kindly speak of.

With warmest good wishes,

Yours very sincerely, Walter Pach

1. "Jacques Lipchitz and the Modern Movement," *Magazine of Art* 39 (December 1946), 354–358.

FLORENCE, JAN. 10. 1947

Dear Pach.

I waited for yr. son before answering yrs. of Sept. 12. He came a little while ago, but since then holiday correspondence has taken up all my time. I enjoyed your son's talk very much. He seemed more of an out-&-out intellectual than I expected of one who was to be a singer. His wife is a *bel pazzo di donna*,[1] & distinguished looking. Both promised to return when they could—So you too are finding difficulties in getting a book published, & one at that which should be as appealing as yours on our museums. I have tried four, each of whom . . . [illegible] felt bound to refuse my diary. It seems our publishers cannot afford to print a book unless they are sure it will sell at least fifty thousand copies—I have just finished a book on "Aesthetics & History." I suppose I shall have to let Princeton or Harvard print it. One cannot say any of the university presses attempts [to] publish a book, i.e. push its sales.

I do hope you will come over. It would give me real pleasure to see you again.

With all good wishes for 1947

Sincerely yours, B. Berenson

1. Beautiful crazy woman.

NEW YORK, SEPT. 3, 1947

Dear Mr. Berenson,

. . . You speak of the difficulty of publishing, and even I can remember a time when cultural books were welcomed—as they are not today. Mine on our museums was refused by a dozen or more publishers; it has lately been taken on by Pantheon Books, a very sympathetic firm, composed of Europeans, principally. They do beautiful work. Yet even they did not feel like tackling a new edition of my first book *The Masters of Modern Art*. I proposed it to them because Francis Henry Taylor has been urging me for a couple of years to get it into print again, with a new chapter on occurrences during the twenty-three years since it was published.

I am now working on notes for such a chapter. I could do a purely factual piece of writing, covering the rather small number of significant men who have appeared, not one of them being of really important stature, if my judgment is right. But just this fact seems to me to demand something more than objective treatment. Thirty or forty years ago, there was a rapid succession of big movements and big men. I do not think the change from that has come about because of external events, the wars, etc. . . .

But I think the cause of our latter-day conditions is to be sought elsewhere. From Ingres and Delacroix to Matisse and the Cubists there was an increasingly marked struggle to use form and color in their purity, and free from the tyranny of the objective. With that effort's reaching its extreme of realization, a new direction was demanded by art. I think that the mystery of Marcel Duchamp, the supremely gifted young man who renounced painting after a series of masterpieces, is to be explained by the fact that the transition from non-objective painting to a new form could not be made without a considerable period of research. There had to be new foundations laid, and by more than one man. He did some work along those lines, and is now a sort of spiritual guide to the group roughly called surrealist. He collected many of the works for the present (or recent) show of the school in Paris. But, as he has told me, he regards not a single one of these men as a really great artist—as yet, anyhow. "C'est la cathédrale—anonyme," as he puts it, "chacun apporte la pierre."[1]

Well, I am trying to contribute a stone of my own, though I shall never be ranked with the surrealists. (As a *rule*, I don't *admire* them much). I do see the need for a radically new point of view. . . . That is why the world has had to depend on the veterans—Matisse, Picasso and the rest—while waiting for a new group of important young men; or so I shall say in this new chapter to my book. . . .

Meanwhile, *tante belle cose*,[2] and please be sure that I shall always be happy of news of you—either in print or in a letter. As ever

Yours most cordially, Walter Pach

1. "That's the cathedral—anonymous, each one brings a stone."

2. Such beautiful things.

PARIS, SEPT. 17, 1951

Dear Mr. Berenson,

. . . I had expected to be home and at work in July, or August at the latest. But fate, in the form of a Greek girl I had met in Athens, decided otherwise. I had come away to Italy without speaking to her of the idea she inspired in me, but after reflecting on it for twelve days, I wrote asking her to marry me. Her reply—not a decisive one,—naturally—led me to take a plane back to Greece and, some three weeks later, we *were* married. Considering the difference in our backgrounds (She had never before left her country) there was a good bit of risk for us both in the step; but I am convinced that that is a thing of the past, and that we are going to make a go of it. America will be very new to her, even after Paris, but I'm counting on a continuation of our present happiness, even so. . . .

I wrote Paul Sachs of your kind words about the drawing of the Mexican girl that he bought for the Fogg Museum from me (it was Matisse's choice among my things also) and our friend wrote that he was glad of the news.

With all good wishes for your health and your studies, I am, as always,

Most sincerely yours, Walter Pach

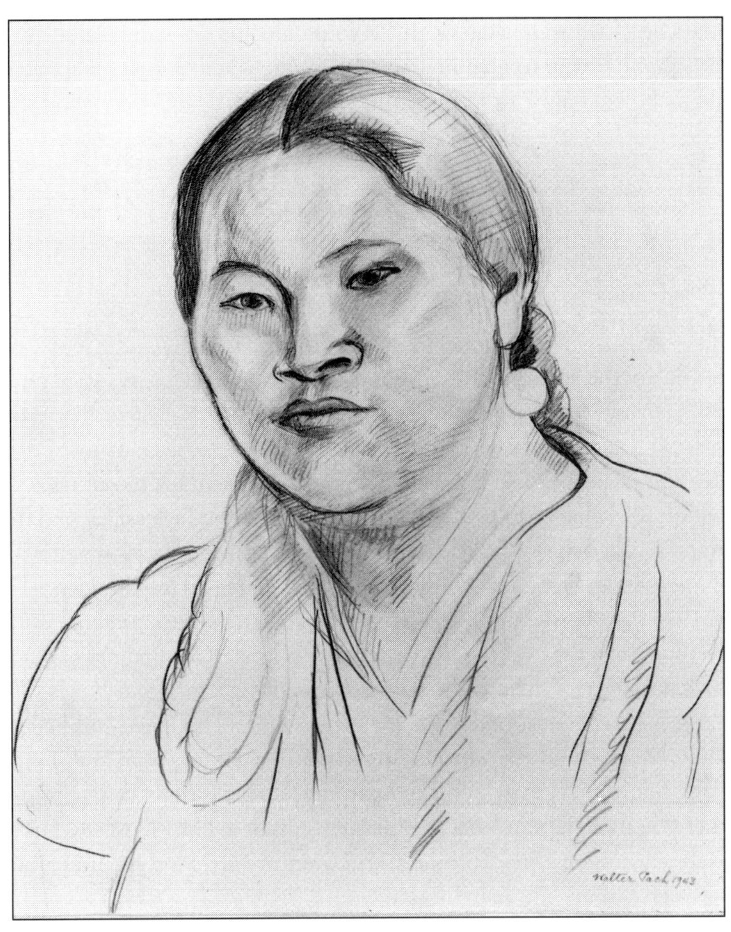

Walter Pach, *Portrait of Maria Modesta Martinez, an Otomi Girl (Mexican)*, 1943. Graphite on cream wove paper, 16 5/8 x 12 3/4 in. Courtesy of the Fogg Art Museum, Harvard University Art Museums, Bequest of Meta and Paul J. Sachs. Photograph by Katya Kallsen.

SETTIGNANO, SEPT. 23, 1951

Dear Pach.

My heartiest & most affectionate congratulations on your marriage, & may you and your Greek wife be as happy as you deserve to be. What luck! Do send me her photo!

A few days ago I wrote to thank you for your valuable book on American Museums. I forgot to remind you to give my regards to Van Wyck Brooks, & to assure him that it would make me happy to receive him at I Tatti[.] Again, every good wish!

Sincerely yours, B. Berenson

NEW YORK, JAN. 23, 1952

Dear Mr. Berenson,

. . . You speak of the art world sinking out of sight and sound for you. One result of my brief visit with you last May is to convince me that it is only partially that that is true. There is always a lot of "meaningless noise" that one does better not to hear anyhow. . . . Now, even when you are most skeptical about contemporary painting, as in that recent book,[1] you do not cast doubt on the value of art as a whole—and that is what Taylor does, and that, again, is why Mr. Kent[2] recalled the Oxford definition for Babel in its application to Taylor's book. . . . The activity in French art continues in a way that gives me confidence. The events beginning in 1914 have been enough to account for a pause in the appearance of new masters, but even more than the events, it is the need to assimilate the findings of the time since Cézanne which accounts for the present period of search and struggle. . . .

The Matisse show we just had was a joy; it was also a challenge—to keep up one's courage and invention amid the surrounding turmoil, as he has done. . . . I'm reading Wölflin for the first time (I read so little; I can save so little time for reading). I don't know whether you include him with the German-minded, but I must say I'm getting a lot from his contrasting of 15th, 16th and 17th Century art. And he's in earnest and struggling—which too few are doing today.

Now I'll stop, till some time when I have more entertaining things to write about. But I'm a bit isolated my self—which is why I don't complain for you: I-rather like it this way.

Yours most cordially, Walter Pach

1. *Babel's Tower* by Francis Henry Taylor.

2. Henry W. Kent.

NEW YORK, DEC. 29, 1953

Dear Mr. Berenson,

. . . in these last days I received offprints of the enclosed article,[1] and I hope it may be of at least passing interest for you.

It was begun in Florence, about the time I saw you in 1951, and was continued in Greece, on my return there, then in Paris and finally in New York—where it was refused by the larger magazines, and had to be given as a present to *Archaeology*—which had to cut it down by about a third for lack of space. Even so, I like it, especially for its proving, through the Delacroix and Barye works (from my own small collection), how basic is the art of Greece—to the point where those two great men did works that are almost Greek without ever seeing the originals (and I think there is no similar Greek sculpture from which Barye could have drawn his inspiration). Don't you think that is pretty good evidence? . . .

The years pass—but not my appreciation of your kindness. And so, many more and happy New Years to you—and lots more of writing, for the delight of all of us. As always

Most cordially yours, Walter Pach

1. "A Modernist Visits Greece." *Archaeology* 6 (Autumn 1953), 137–141.

NEW YORK, FEB. 3, 1955

Dear Mr. Berenson,

. . . One of the things that interested me lately was an article in the Paris review, *Diogene*, in which Raoul Ergmann publishes *Les Chances d'un Dialogue: Berenson et Malraux*; (July 1954, No. 7). While the writer seems to me completely fair to Malraux . . . I think he inclines quite perceptibly to your side of the "dialogue," which is not a hostile one. On the rare occasions when I see a Paris review, I am struck by the vivacity and penetration of the French writers. Without being excessively humble, I believe, about American expressions of intellect and art, I cannot avoid a comparison very much in our disfavor, on such occasions. Lately, the Whitney Museum, on moving to its new building adjoining the Museum of Modern Art, gave a review exhibition of its collection of recent American art. While competently selected, on the whole, and giving about as good an account of painting and sculpture in this country as could be given, the work shown fell so immensely short of the intelligence, finesse and creativeness of the French that I had to wonder, all over again, at the ignorance or the effrontery of those writers here who claim that we have overhauled Paris in the "contest of art" (the words are bad enough in themselves), or even that we have left the French behind. I suppose it's another manifestation of the isolationism-chauvinism one sees among political personages—who may lead us into another war. . . .

And then, one principal reason for these lines is that I want to offer you congratulations on your ninetieth birthday (I know it's this year, but don't know the date). They are real congratulations, since they are not a matter of those ninety years, but of what you've done in them and, above all, what you're doing in them—your *Seeing and Knowing* (as I said in my review of it) going so far ahead of what you'd done with the material previously. So, avanti sempre,[1] and accept, please, many good wishes from

Yours cordially, Walter Pach

1. Always going forward.

Settignano, April 21, 1955

Dear Pach.

Thanks for yours of so long ago—Febr. 3. Good of you to recall that I am in my 90th year. That by the way is the reason why my answer to yr. good letter has been so long delayed. I waste so much time dozing, resting.

Needless to say I agree with all you write about the present state of art appreciation in our beloved country. It has become a heavy industry, a "racket," endorsed by the self-indulgent heiresses (& heirs) of giant money makers. They are pre-potent now, & all we can do while they reign is to carry on to the best of our ability. I have just read Van Wyck Brooks' book on [John] Sloan. I cannot recall seeing paintings of his. . . . As you are so often mentioned in Brooks's pages I wonder how much of his thinking & saying is due to you. I should love to see you again.

Sincerely yrs, Bernard Berenson

Source of Letters: Bernard Berenson Archives, The Harvard Center for Italian Renaissance Studies, Villa I Tatti, Florence, Italy, which contains additional Berenson/Pach correspondence.

Also available through the Archives of American Art, Smithsonian Institution, Bernard Berenson Papers, Reel 4217.

VAN WYCK BROOKS (1886–1963)

Biographer, literary critic, and historian. A graduate of Harvard University, he was appointed an instructor of English at Stanford in 1911. With the publication of *America's Coming-of-Age* (1915), Brooks was labeled both articulate and a literary radical; he berated those who chose to separate art and the imagination from everyday life. Brooks was awarded the 1937 Pulitzer Prize for History for *The Flowering of New England*, the first of his five-volume set titled *Makers and Finders: A History of the Writer in America, 1800–1915*. He authored more than a score of books including *The Ordeal of Mark Twain* (1920), *The Pilgrimage of Henry James* (1925), *The World of Washington Irving* (1940), *John Sloan: A Painter's Life* (1955), and *The Dream of Arcadia: American Writers and Artists in Italy, 1760–1915* (1958).

Correspondence between Van Wyck Brooks and Walter Pach began in 1920, when Brooks was appointed literary and art editor of *The Freeman*, a new weekly journal, and Pach wrote his first articles for it. Their letters continued until 1958, the year of Pach's death.

ON SHIPBOARD, JUNE 2, 1926

Dear Van Wyck,

We were so sorry to miss your visit the time you called in 56th St. I hope the—for us—unaccustomed grandeur of our exterior will not deter you from trying again when we get back in September. On the interior we're just the same as in the old ranch on 14th St.

This trip is made at the invitation of New York University which, in connection with the Louvre authorities, is conducting a series of summer lectures in that museum. I am giving two courses. With the work and with the shortness of time, I shall not try to paint,—I can't satisfy myself (or attempt to satisfy myself) unless I have all the time. So I shall call this a vacation and, returning right after the courses, shall get to work hard in September. . . .

. . . this past winter was a good one for seeing modern French painting in New York (the sale of the Quinn Collection makes certain its continued and increased success). . . .

I have a grand idea for a book and shall try to write it this summer. Its general subject (I don't know the title) is *Bad Pictures*.[1] There is no such book. . . .

We hope you will have a Summer quite to your liking and that we shall see you early in the fall.

Yours cordially, Walter Pach

1. The book, ultimately titled *Ananias, or the False Artist*, was published by Harper and Bros. in 1928.

---

87 KING STREET
WESTPORT, CONN., JAN. 8, 1929

Dear Walter,

Your letter has come, and thank you. I am answering it for Eleanor,[1] as I am already working on the book.[2] We can easily have it finished so that it can be in Harper's hands by April 15th, and we send you chapters from time to time, beginning very soon, so that you may revise them and turn them in, if that is satisfactory to you. Please arrange the matter of remuneration in any way you think right, for I am sure that any arrangement you make will seem right to us. We hope everything goes well with you and that we may have a chance to see you before long.

I am yours sincerely, Van Wyck Brooks

1. Van Wyck Brooks's wife.

2. Elie Faure's *History of Art, Modern*, which Pach translated from the French in collaboration with Brooks and his wife. The volume was not published by Harper & Bros. until 1937.

WESTPORT, JAN. 15 [1929]

Dear Walter,

. . . The translation gets on apace, only I find that the prospect of *having* to finish it by April 15th is making Van Wyck nervous, the one thing, you know, that mustn't happen. I have every belief that it will be done by then, or even sooner, judging by the rate at which it is going, but I find I must ask you to ask Harpers to let us have until May 15th, if we need it. Of course for us nothing in the world is worth making Van Wyck worse. . . .

Faithfully your friend, Eleanor S. Brooks

WESTPORT, MARCH 18 [1929]

Dear Walter,

Thank you for your letter, which I truly expected to answer before but it is the translation itself that has prevented me. You know I never shared your and Van Wyck's confidence as to the ease and speed with which it could be done. Frankly I find it the very devil as to both style and meaning and I saw Van Wyck send you in the first installment with misgivings.

You see, in the old days I made an accurate translation first, as good a one as I could, then Van Wyck went over it and touched up the style. But with so exacting an illness in the house I am lucky if I can work on it for three hours a day. This was too slow for him, so he made the first trans.[lations] himself, and with such difficult France [*sic*] of course it was full of mistakes. Then I had to correct it and he did not again go over the style. I hope you will find this next installment better, and please do not apologize for retouching those sentences. . . . I wish we had the time to revise it half a dozen times ourselves. Faure is really ver[y] difficult, not his ideas, which I can almost always get, but his expression which is almost always involved and often inexact. For instance, as you know, he frequently mixes metaphors.

In this case there seems nothing to do but rewrite him. But we hate to take too great liberties with his work.

Hastily, but with much love from both of us to both of you.

Ever cordially, Eleanor S. Brooks.

48 West 56th St.
New York, April 6, 1929

Dear Eleanor,

Your letter of March 18th expresses very much what I have been feeling of late as I went over Faure's pages: vexation at his callousness about the trouble he gives his readers. As big a man as he is, he ought to be made to rewrite those heartlessly difficult sentences of his. I stick to my admiration of very nearly twenty years' standing for his ideas, but it is sheer egoism to put them forth in such form. . . .

We are eager to see you both soon, as we always are, and send you our warmest greetings.

Very cordially, Walter Pach

Westport, May 12 [1929]

Dear Walter,

It is a shame that you have not heard from us or had the translation before this, but you will remember that when we accepted it I made sure that there should be no rush before fall, if we found it difficult to do and you assured me that fall would do. It was Van Wyck, not I who thought it could be done in a few months. You see, his illness had made it very hard for me to work on it and the first rough translation made by him was so full of errors that I have had to re-write every sentence. Then he has had to go over my English and it has all been very slow. On top of this has come what has been for me a terrible tragedy. He has gone to Bloomingdale hospital at White Plains.[1] You can imagine that terrible weeks preceeded [*sic*] this decision and even more terrible one[s] have followed it. You will understand how vitally important it is for his future that *no one* should know of this. . . .

A great deal of affection to all three of you.

Eleanor

1. A psychiatric institution.

Westport, May 26 [1929]

Dear Walter,

Your note and its in closure [*sic*] are here. It was good to hear from you. These months have indeed been beyond words, and the understanding and sympathy of friends means more than I can well put into a letter. This particular and wretched crisis started when the *Independent* was bought by the *Outlook* and Van Wyck's weekly page disappeared. It wasn't much, but it had given him a feeling of really contributing to the family budget and having that precious thing, regular work. But I suppose it might have come on any how. . . .

. . . Tell Magda to write me sometimes. Meanwhile my love to you both,

As ever, Eleanor Brooks

---

c/o Morgan & Co., 14 place Vendôme,
Paris, Oct. 25, 1929

Dear Eleanor,

I have your note of October 8th announcing the sending of the last chapter, which came, has been revised, and has gone back to Harpers today—which ends the job as far as I am concerned—*Laus Deo*[1]. . . .

Magda sends her warmest regards, as I do.

Always most cordially yours—Walter Pach

1 Latin for "Praised be to God."

Westport, Feb. 8, 1932

My dear good friends Magda and Walter,

You cannot imagine how heart-warming your letter was, when it came the other day. How many times we have talked and thought of you, since I came home, now nearly a year—and it is good to have this full account of you both and your doings, inward & outward. I have so many things to write to you about, that I don't know where to begin, so let me begin with the personal things and end with Art and Literature (which are always with us)! We are so interested to hear that you, Walter, are having an exhibit in Paris and wish you all good luck. . . . My *Life of Emerson* is coming out in April and I shall send you a copy, and I am bringing out a new collection of essays in September, partly revised from old *Freeman* papers. Then I am planning a new and very long historical work, with enthusiasm—but experience teaches that one should sing small about one's plans. . . .

. . . apropos of our Westport neighbors (among whom I should love to feel that we may include you—soon—for a long visit, at least!) that we see much of the blessed Prendergasts. Eleanor loves their quiet sincerity, and Charles P— is surely a true primitive old master to whom only Vasari[1] could do justice in the way of anecdotes. We stroll with them almost every day for a few minutes, after the morning's work is over, on the beach, which is sheltered from the wind, on these sunny & mild winter days. . . . It will add to the pleasure of every day to feel that we can look forward to seeing you all in September.

Ever your friend, Van Wyck Brooks

1. Giorgio Vasari (1511–1574), whose *Lives of the Artists* (1550), dealing with the eminent architects, painters, and sculptors of Renaissance Italy, is injected with numerous anecdotes.

---

39 West 67th St.,
New York, Oct. 9, 1932

Dear Van Wyck,

I spoke to Bryson Burroughs the other day about Mr. Stimson's work.[1] I do not think he knows it very well—though he does know it. Also he mentioned the fact that Henry McBride had praised Mr. Stimson to him—he was not quite sure whether it was as an artist or as a teacher, for McBride studied under Mr. Stimson.

Burroughs seemed to see no likelihood of his being in Westport, so he thought the best plan was for you to bring the two water-colors or some drawings into his office. He thought the chances for acceptance of these smaller works were better than they would be for one of the larger oils. . . .

Hoping that you and Eleanor will look in on us soon, I am

Yours cordially, Walter Pach

1. John Ward Stimson, an early American admirer of William Blake, taught at the Artists and Artisans Institute in New York; it was there that McBride, the future *New York Sun* art critic, studied with him.

New York, Dec. 2, 1932

Dear Van Wyck,

. . . I got a note from an official of the radio company saying that the people there had liked my talk also and that there was a chance for the "trio" that I mentioned the day you were here (literature, music, and art). My musician is all set, in fact he first proposed it. Now, how about you?

I can't say what money there would be in it, but if it were only a modest sum I should, myself, be glad to earn it, these days. But of course I'm only twenty minutes away from the broadcasting station; for you it would mean a trip to town each time. . . .

Will you let me know by return of mail . . . whether you would consider the thing. . . .

With best remembrances to Eleanor

Your cordially, Walter Pach

Westport, Aug. 17, 1936

Dear Van Wyck,

. . . I recall—with greatest pleasure—our visit to Brummer's, years ago, which more or less caused me to write on Eakins for the *Freeman*. (I re-read that in your bound copies—and do think it's a good article). I think that last thing even more after reading Lloyd Goodrich's book on Eakins. . . . It bristles with information, conscientiously heaped up, and will always have value for that. The illustrations, however, are the inspiring part for *me*: with only the most agreeable feelings toward Goodrich, I am knocked edgeways by a sentence like this: "Relatively few Americans had studied in Paris, in comparison to the horde of young men who in the next decade were to flock to the city and make her the capital of the art world." If he'd said art-student world he would be nearly as wild still, for A Capital gets its rank as the residence of royalty or of government, not from its visitors. And just when I am doing my derndest to be an Americophile! (This set-back won't be serious in that respect: Eakins is the real feature of the book). What I'm really dissatisfied with is Goodrich's presentation of Eakins' ideas. Here is a tough sentence from an article by William C. Brownell, quoted in the book. Telling him of his opposition to a protracted period of drawing from the antique, Eakins said: "At best, they [casts of "even sculptors of the best Greek period"] are only imitations, and an imitation of imitations cannot have so much life as an imitation of nature itself." Now I am all for Eakins' theory that the student should work from life as soon as possible (Eakins sometimes allowed only a week for cast-drawing,—sending the student to the living model thereafter) but that word *imitation* is a facer. I don't believe that he saw no more in Phidias than imitation. I am writing to a pupil of Eakins' to see if we can't work out a more intelligible statement of that big man's ideas. . . .

The best of all good wishes to you and Eleanor from the pair of us who are so happy in your house.

Cordially, Walter Pach

Nov. 18, 1937

Dear Walter,

Two or three weeks ago your publisher sent me the Delacroix journal.[1] I don't know whether or not you had a hand in this kind gift, but in any case I have meant to thank you for it. I have been reading the book,—with various interruptions, and have not yet finished it, but I've read enough to see what an achievement it is. In the first place, the translation is masterly. I've sweated over enough books to have some right to say it! And then, in all your writing, I don't remember *anything* more wholly satisfying than your introduction. It is simply masterly also, such fine prose and so beautifully covering the subject. Of course, its a glorious book—to me a revelation, for I did not know before how unusual was Delacroix's mind and what marvellous insight he had in a hundred directions . . . the book is truly a great book and you've done it in a noble fashion, and every writer & artist must thank you everlastingly for it. . . .

With love to Magda from us both,

As always your friend, Van Wyck Brooks

1. *Delacroix's Journals*, translated by Pach, were published by Covici-Friede of New York in 1937.

---

148 West 72nd Street
New York, Nov. 18, 1937

Dear Van Wyck,

Thank you ever so much—and yet again—for the letter I got from you this morning. I know that many a young writer has thrilled at a word of encouragement from you (not to speak of the thousands on thousands of people who have been heartened by the way you define and illumine the profession of the writer—and so of all artists—in your books). But I doubt whether you have often given more pleasure than you did me, with the lines you were good enough to send me. . . .

Next to my personal share in your letter—almost on the same level with it—I must put my immense satisfaction over your deepened acquaintance with Delacroix. It was in 1902 that he entered my consciousness and, between his pictures "and his writings (there are still the *Essays* and the *Letters*) he has been growing deeper for me ever since. . . .

Magda—who also loved the letter—joins me in hearty greetings to Eleanor and yourself.

Cordially always, Walter Pach

WESTPORT, NOV. 9, 1938

Dear Walter,

I have only not written before about "Queer Thing, Painting"[1] because,—well, *because*,—there were plenty of reasons. But I've let it sink deep down inside, and it's just come up for breath again. It has moved me more than anything I have read this year,—barring some of the old folks whom I have been reading. I was ashamed already when I sent you the postcard about the "American Vasari" [Bernard Berenson].[2] I have known the grand old gossip since I was fourteen but he did not have your kind of brooding mind. You haven't written one sentence of gossip, in even the great good sense of the word. Most of this book is wise, with the wisdom of the heart. It is steeped in the devotion that you have brought to the world of arts,—every page bears the stamp of conviction. And its knowledge and its feeling!—I bend before you. . . . I had better begin now by making my few objections, in order to hand you later my full bouquet!

I make these objections with diffidence in the spirit of your own remark about Sarah Bernhardt and Réjane, for I feel about art and artists as you feel about actresses;—"I saw them only across the spotlights, and it is for others to tell about them" and how well I agree with, and hope I share, that "humility is a primary need," etc. You *have* this humility,—you couldn't know as much if you didn't!—though I well know that some folks think you lack it. It is because of this that you move and convince; and I, who really know that I know nothing about this realm of art,—that is, I know enough to know just this,—can offer objections only in a kindred spirit. . . . Let me offer my other objections at once in as few words as possible. . . . I think you praise some collectors too highly. I must say flatly about [J. P.] Morgan that I do not believe you; and I think you are rather too kind to our friend John Quinn. I think he may move more [previous word scratched out] *outside* than you paint him as being. I knew him and I know the type,—more or less. . . . I think it says something about his real grain that he *paid for* old [John Butler] Yeats'[3] funeral but did not attend it. (John and Dolly Sloan and I had all the fun there. We rode in the coach behind the hearse. Sloan broke the ice by saying his father was an undertaker,—funerals were an old story to him,—and he thought that Yeats would like us to enjoy it. And *we did*, as if the grand old soul had been sitting with us.). . . . Meanwhile, warmest regards to Magda—and a world of thanks to yourself.

Always yours sincerely, Van Wyck Brooks

1. Subtitled "Forty Years in the World of Art" and published by Harper and Bros. in 1938, it is part autobiography but primarily about the multitude of French and American artists Pach had known.

2. That particular Brooks postcard is not presently in the collection.

3. Yeats, the Irish portrait painter, had died in New York in 1922.

Westport, Dec. 29, 1939

Dear Walter,

. . . I am horrified to see how many weeks have passed and I have not written about your *Ingres*[1]. . . . Well, it's a glorious achievement, and, dear Walter, I think by far your best book. Did not the serenity of of the subject get into your nerves?—as much of the classical feeling got into your style; for you never wrote before with such a *masterful* clarity and directness. Your treatment is deeply impressive, and you won me over completely in the face of many earlier prejudices—against the "oil cloth or cast iron" business. The book is magnificent in all aspects, and I am lost in the wonder of it, that you can write books like this,—and in six months too,—without feeling the joy of creation that you get from painting. The book brought back all my gratitude to you for all that you have taught me about art, the happy hours that I have spent, in reading you and talking with you, in which I have always felt my horizon expanding. You don't know what a privilege it has been to me to share a little of your love of art, to drink from your inexhaustible reservoir yet and match my little knowledge with your great knowledge. I feel lucky to know you and Magda, and Eleanor feels quite as I do, and we both send you every affectionate greeting and every hope for a great and productive new year—

Ever your friend, Van Wyck Brooks

1. Pach's book about Jean-Auguste-Dominique Ingres (1780–1867), the great French neoclassic artist.

New York, Jan. 10, 1940

Dear Van Wyck,

. . . I start on a big tour next week, flying to Montana where I lecture for two days, and then going to Seattle, down the coast by degrees as far as San Diego, thence to San Antonio, Texas, to New Orleans, to Detroit (with places in between). I get back toward the end of February, and plunge headlong back into a job I have started, that of organizing on wholly new lines The Masterpieces of Art show at the World's Fair.[1] Had I not engaged to give these Western lectures, I should cut out the trip. I really ought to be using the time for the show at the Fair. Perhaps it will come out all right anyhow. Lord knows how I hope it does: I'm getting paid—but it is to make a success. . . .

You do not content yourself with just a friendly handshake, but give me chapter and verse about the insight into Ingres that you have obtained—you and dear Eleanor. . . . Lately I entered the Picasso Show in a refractory mood, having been engaged on Ingres, and other masters of a different period. Little by little, Picasso spread his net around me and I saw things in his way. (That does not mean that I see him as a very great man. He *is* a phenomenon, but also an artist—very surely). . . .

Thank you again for what you've done for me. With affectionate greetings to Eleanor, I am

Yours, Walter

1. The "Masterpieces of Art" Exhibition at the 1939 New York World's Fair had been organized by William R. Valentiner, Director of the Detroit Institute of Arts. Pach replaced him for the 1940 Fair. Pach's major difficulty stemmed from the fact that, with World War II raging in Europe, he was unable to borrow works from the many individuals and museums with which he had contacts overseas. As a result, Pach's four century survey of 373 European and American paintings was comprised solely of works in United States collections.

New York, Aug. 29, 1940

Dear Van Wyck,

. . . I won't try to speak about your book (with which I am about four-fifths through—for the present) . . . if my memory of the "Flowering"[1] is sufficiently precise—this is a better book,[2] perhaps because of the intensity with which (as I recall) you had to work at this one.

No, what I want to write *for* you-is a sketch of the ideas that occurred to me after reading certain passages on the painters of the Indian Summer period. . . .

The places I mean especially are on Pages 191 and 195 where you speak of Whistler and Sargent with reference to the place of technique in painting. The first thing is to be sure we're using the word *technique* in the same sense. *I* think that if it's taken in its more limited meaning, as Chase used it (almost as a synonym for brush-work, or virtuosity) it *can* perfectly be claimed for Sargent indeed, pre-eminence in technique—though it can't for Whistler, whom Chase, again, called a great fumbler; and Whistler did have unending trouble with his painting.

I'm pretty sure it's the broader sense of technique—as the element to be distinguished from idea or meaning—that you had in mind when writing. It is, for me, by far the more significant conception of the quality, and, in reference to it, I have tried out our two painters again, here at the Fair, where we have excellent examples of them (Sargent's *General Wood* has seemed to me, for a matter of decades, his nearest approach to a great portrait—which was why I selected it). Even these works, however, are far from excelling "in technique all but the greatest of the Frenchmen,"—in my idea of the matter. Eakins would be nearer that, I think, and I imagine you had him in the back of your mind when speaking of those who "remained in the frying pan" and turned out to be our big men. His work has structure, which is a fundamental of technique; Sargent and Whistler lack it. At his best Eakins' work has Scale (rightness of aesthetic proportion—the other two men are merely naturalistic in that respect); Eakins' drawing frequently has abstract harmony, Sargent's practically never, Whistler at times—and then in a pretty pallid way. All these are elements of technique. But unless one makes that "greatest of the Frenchmen" a very inclusive term indeed, I am sure I can find a large number of Frenchmen who go beyond even Eakins. As for the really great Frenchmen, the few geniuses of the century, they are on a level that no American painter has even approached. Obviously, these are just affirmations, not capable of being proved, though I am sure I could get plentiful confirmation of them from the best judges of the matter (with myself as the one to select those judges, as some one might add; but I think he is the man who would deprive us of all standards, and who brings us to complete isolation).

The reason why I spent my years in Paris was that I wanted to have the most complete and prolonged contact with the great tradition there. *It exists nowhere else*, which is why men like Jongkind, Guys, van Gogh, Picasso and Brancusi have remained there. I think none of them could have attained the stature he did had he remained in his own land. You are absolutely right about Copley's American period being his best—but then he went to England, where the influence was bad. Vanderlyn, another great American, did superb work in Paris and (as much as I know his painting) did not equal it in America. Of course he got up against the hardest conditions here, in that early time. But it is certain that if some work done after his return was very fine, his later career as a whole marks a decline.

I did not mean to get into this difficult (and—most likely—unprofitable) question of the artist's going away from his own country. As we once decided under your apple-tree, the problem of the painter differs from that of the writer in this respect. My

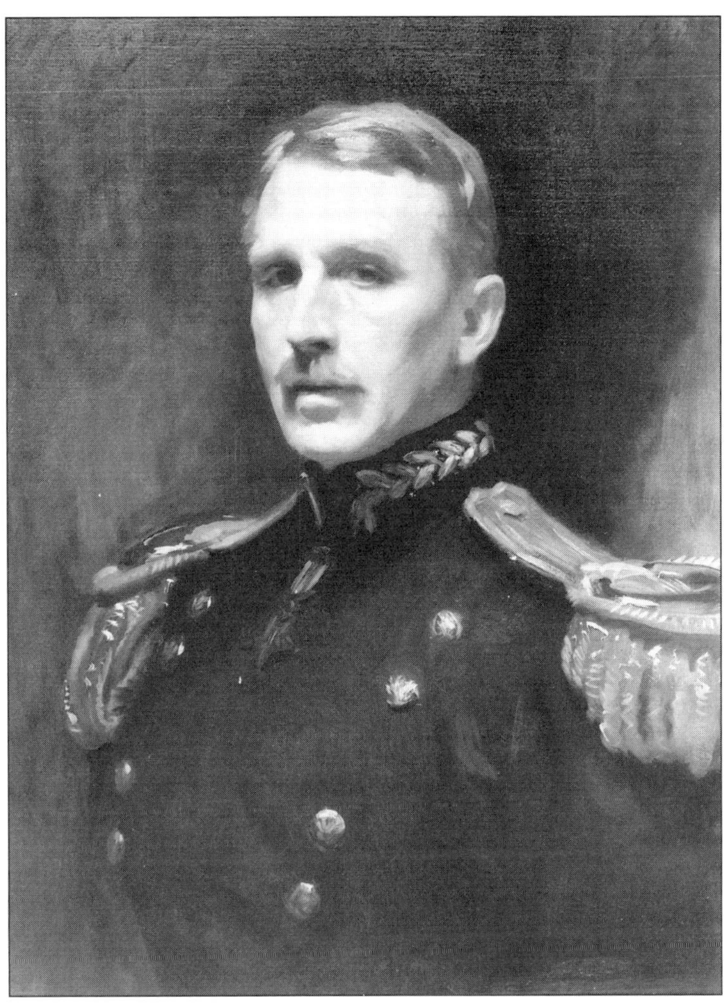

John Singer Sargent, *General Leonard Wood*, 1903. Oil on canvas 30 x 25 in. Collection unknown. Photograph courtesy Peter A. Juley & Son Collection, Smithsonian American Art Museum.

old stand-by (I think I've never before offered it to you) is to ask what American literature would have been if the old colonists had not brought along the Bible and Shakespeare, not to mention the Greek and Latin writers who were soon to follow—with Milton, Cervantes, and the rest. Not only were there no such influences in America for painting and sculpture, till centuries had passed, but the men who essayed those arts here had to combat the prejudices, ignorance and indifference of a public to whom the classics meant nothing. I know how much of the same evils there is in Europe: The point is that the minority of competent appreciators is a vastly larger one there—though our own is growing, thank goodness. . . .

I'm afraid this sounds pretty lecturious—and the whole point I had to make was that I am so stirred by your book that I wanted to make a small thanks-offering, even if I risk seeming to differ with you—as I'm sure I do not. I just harp on my own little string. Yours is the good music.

Cordially, Walter Pach

1. *The Flowering of New England*, for which Brooks won the 1937 Pulitzer Prize for History.

2. *New England Indian Summer 1865–1915* (New York: E.P. Dutton, 1940).

[POSTCARD]
BOOTHBAY HARBOR, MAINE, SEPT. 2, 1940

Dear Walter,

That is a grand letter. I can't answer it today, for we are packing up & leaving for home tomorrow. But I will tell you later how *uncanny* it is that you should have taken up that particular paragraph,—the only paragraph in the whole book which (after a dozen rewritings) left me unsatisfied. More of this anon, and our love to Magda.

Van Wyck Brooks

BREWSTER, NEW YORK, AUG. 22, 1941

Dear Van Wyck,

Since you were good enough to say you would be interested to know what I could find in your paper—acting in the role of a devil's advocate, I have looked it through again; but I fear I shall make a poor job of anticipating the opposition, for I am too much on the side of primary literature to see eye to eye with the coteries. But here goes for a few observations:

I think that when you invoke the authority of mankind in favor of writers who have long been called great, your opponents will be apt to translate your word "mankind" as a sort of "continuing rabble of the intellect" that has sanctioned rubbish, and rejected the great men,—until they have been canonized. In defiance of this rabble James Joyce utters blasphemies—not really against the Newman of hymn or against the great poets (who are beyond all offence) but against the mob that has mouthed and snivelled the great works, dragging them down to the level of the mob, as I remember "Lead kindly light" being cheapened by the way it was sung when I was at School. I think the claim that Joyce is a "defender of the classics" rest on his breaking with the vulgarians who, by mere force of numbers, are the ones who really travesty the classics by mixing them up with people like Rex Beach.[1] You may say that Beach does not have more than one generation in his support; in fact he has a good bit less than that,—but then the same is true of Gertrude Stein.

When you speak on P. 20 of certain men as "detached from the life of mankind which they scorn and condemn," I think I hear them replying—"not so; we detach ourselves from Mr. Brooks's segment of mankind: what remains will quite suffice us, for it will include the most intelligent—and the best."

P. 20—You speak of "younger writers" as saying that these men "possess the sense of their age." Don't you concede too much? I should think you were giving them credit enough if you said "many of the younger writers." (P.S. I thought you had said "*the* younger *writers*" so this almost cancels out).

When you come to Baudelaire, Rimbaud, and Mallarmé, I must say—this time for myself—that you are touching on men who have given me enormous pleasure (though I hasten to add that I set no store by my appreciation of poetry; I read so little of it). Certainly these men were authentic, and if they had not the sweep of Milton, for example, can it not be maintained that their period offered no incentive or inspiration for the epic mood? Most of those (all of those?) who essayed it fell into bathos at the time of those three men.

On P. 18, you say "their influence [that of the coterie] has to be cleared out of the way in order that primary literature may be reinstated." Taking the same ground as in my preceding query, can it not be said that when the age itself once more gives the signal for primary literature, men will bring it forth? Meanwhile is not "coterie literature" the thing we really have to offer? (Here I am saying what I do not think—as you doubtless understand).

And please do believe that I am sincere in saying you must not waste time in answering this letters. Acknowledge it if you like—and, best of all, by word of mouth when we can have a visit again. I hope it may be before too long. And do, please, give our affectionate regards to Eleanor.

Yours—Walter Pach

1. Rex E. Beach (1877–1949), a novelist and playwright.

Westport, Sept. 4, 1941

Dear Walter,

It was lovely of you to send me that fine letter, and I do thank you for it. I see your objections, and I shall get it hot and heavy, but if I have over-stated a little perhaps I'm in reaction too. Anyway, all these statements of mine will have a somewhat different colour when they are seen in the context of the book,[1] though one of the things I am reacting against is this whole conception of "mankind" as "rabble." I admire Tolstoy because he did not share this, and I think it is a largely modern notion that "mankind" has no feeling for the fine. And after all Tolstoy was a very great genius, and surely his feeling is entitled to as much respect as the feeling of the writers I attack. (I don't catch the allusion to Rex Beach. Mechanical twaddle like his has nothing to do with "mankind.") Also the fact that one "breaks with vulgarians" does not make one a defender of the classics. And I only object to writers like Mallarmé, beautiful writers whom I enjoy too, because writers of their type at present are the sole gods of the critical world, while writers like Victor Hugo are regarded as less than contemptible. However, I don't ask you to agree with me, but only wait till I send you my book, in which I make my whole case. And *then* you mustn't dream of writing me again, though I hope we may often talk of these letters. This is just a sincere thank-you letter.

It will be fine to see you next week. Your address again strikes me as superb. I have not yet made up my own few "remarks," and hope I can do justice to the occasion. Do let's arrange for another day here before you go back to town. Our love to Magda.

Always yours, Van Wyck Brooks

P.S. I don't think "popularity" means anything one way or another. But it might be noted that "mankind" recognized Victor Hugo at once—also Dickens, Ruskin, Dostoevsky, etc. and as for "giving the signal," is not this for "great writers" to do, not "the age"?

1. Brooks's *Opinions of Oliver Allston* (New York, 1941).

New York, Nov. 1, 1941

Dear Van Wyck,

At various times there has been question of my going into a museum. Years ago, a number of important positions were proposed to me, but I always declined, as I wanted to keep to painting, and could get through—financially—by various means. But today those means have a very poor look: I didn't sell one picture at my show, last spring, and writing is harder to place than I've ever found it. . . .

So I'd better get a job—*if* I can. There is one: the directorship of the museum of the Rhode Island School of Design, in Providence. I'd like to have it—much as I'd hate to leave my studio—and New York.

I know just how you feel about moving into the field of art questions. And yet—I do think you could say in a (short) letter to Mrs. M. S. Danforth, 101 Prospect St., Providence, R.I., (she is the president) that you have known my relation to the art of Eakins, Prendergast and others, my constant striving to keep the attitude toward American art on the same level as that of the French whom I know better than most people in this country, and that such interests, together with my work in writing, lecturing, etc. *should* make me valuable in her institution. . . . I do think that anyone with your record of study and defence of American culture would be listened to with respect. . . . Best remembrances to Eleanor.

As always, cordially—Walter Pach

[POSTCARD]
NEW YORK, NOV. 26, 1941

Dear Van Wyck,

Thanks for sending on the letter from Mrs. Danforth. I got one by the same mail from her, saying she wanted to see me when she is in New York, soon, but adding that they want a younger man. I don't regard that as final. We shall see. . . .

My best to dear Eleanor and to you.—

Walter

[POSTCARD]
NEW YORK, JAN. 23, 1942

Dear Van Wyck,

If you can find time when in New York, do have a look at the works by Quidor now exhibited at the Brooklyn Museum (which is a station of the I.R.T. subway).

Quidor, 1801–1881, one of the very remarkable artists of this country—and almost unknown—illustrated Washington Irving, and such a contemporary comment

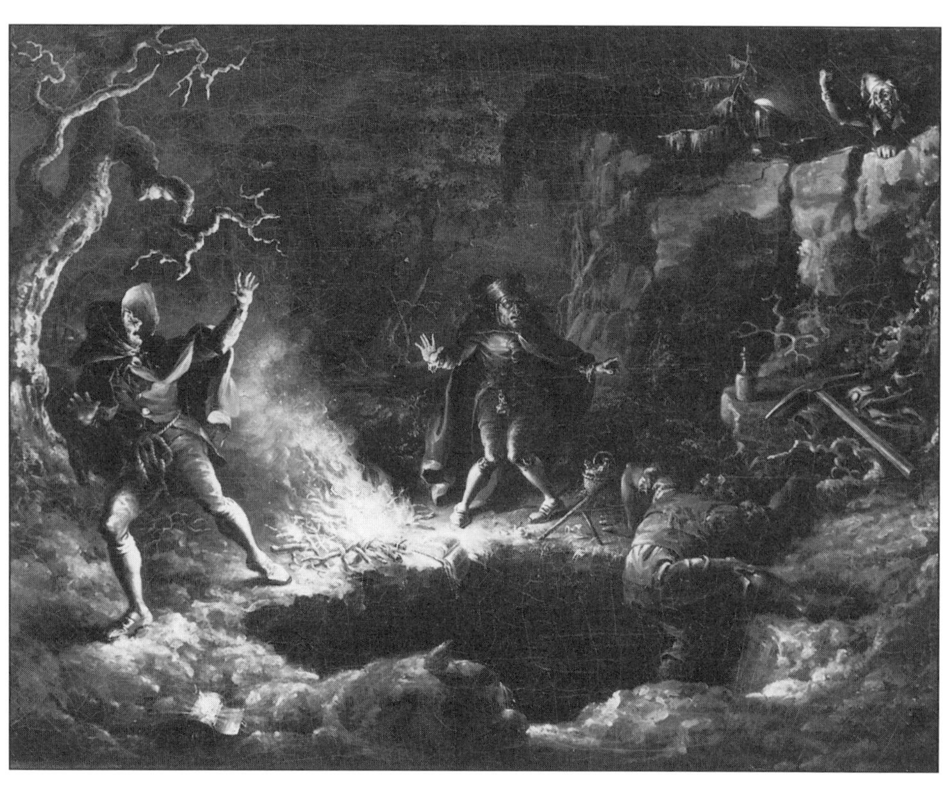

John Quidor, *The Money Diggers*, 1832. Oil on canvas, 16 5/8 x 21 1/2 in. The Brooklyn Museum, Gift of Mr. and Mrs. Alastair Bradley Martin. Acc. 48.171. Photograph by Dean Brown.

could—I think—be useful to you. I am sending you a brochure with his work. Mr. Baur, the curator of paintings at Brooklyn, did the research work on Quidor. He would much like to see you if you come, and you would take to him, as he is an earnest and delightful fellow.

Yours always—Walter

WESTPORT, JULY 16, 1942

Dear Walter,

I fear this must be a farewell note for the moment, for we gather from Magda's postcard that you will be off in a day or two. Good luck to you both, and may you have the best of times. I wish we might join you in Mexico. . . .[1]

Every sincere good wish to you both, and we'll look for a golden harvest when you return.

Van Wyck Brooks

1. Pach accepted an offer from the University of Mexico to give a series of lectures there, as he had done twenty years earlier.

Av. Michoacan 81
Mexico City, Sept. 20, 1942

Dear Van Wyck,

The two months—almost exactly—since we crossed the border have had wings to them, but I must not let any more time fly past without a line to you. . . .

Well, we have a peach of an apartment, with a fine studio, and are painting quite blithely. Later I hope to do better, but I'm started. I want to paint about half the people I see, especially the Indian girls. They are a marvelous type. And we have fine people to talk to—about the great intellectual activity here, and it *is* remarkable, and sympathetic. Sometimes it is hard to follow for me, as when Diego Rivera—who has the whole war doped out—insists that it is all a war of Fascism versus mankind, which, he says, is why the Allies refuse to open a second front—their purpose being to have Russia eliminated as a menace. That's too deep for me; in fact—I doubt it. But then, as you know, I am a slacker in the matter of thinking on politics (my defense being that my head is no good for such things. I also question the value of some other people's heads, in this respect. As to art-matters, Diego is simply great—and his painting is immense. I think you'd like to talk literature with him, also). . . .

Magda is well and happy, and would wish to be remembered most warmly. As ever,

Cordially—Walter Pach

[Postcard]
Mexico, Nov. 28, 1942

Dear Van Wyck,

So glad—both of us—to hear from you, except that what you say of Venturi-Rivera-Weber (Max) just burns me up. I must write you of that; . . .

Good wishes—Walter

Mexico, Jan. 13, 1943

Dear Van Wyck,

. . . I have here your letter of November, and surely hope you got the line I wrote you on receipt of it—first to reassure you about your having been a while in answering me, and to let you know how strongly I felt over Venturi's[1] jackass stupidity about Diego Rivera—who *is* an artist of the first rank today. There are few, indeed, of his rank, and in some ways he is uniquely important. I constantly admire his work more, while realizing drawbacks connected with the personality of the man—fascinating as he can be. You say I know Venturi. I answer that I do so only in a superficial way. From the first, in Paris, I found him so egregiously wrong—not only on modern art which he quite misunderstands (his admired Max Weber, e.g., is just a zero, or less) but on the Old Masters as well—that I have kept at a distance from him. I think he is a pleasant man, and on the right side of some things. But I loathe controversy and—with him—I must either keep silent or contradict. I get disturbed, almost upset, over such differences with men who ought to know better. I dare say you could duplicate such remarks from your own experience of men in the literary world. . . .

Magda joins me in affectionate good wishes to you, to Eleanor, and the boys.

As ever

Cordially—Walter Pach

1. Lionel Venturi (1885–1961) a professor of the History of Art in Turin, Italy, who moved to Paris and then the United States because of his opposition to fascism; he would return to Italy in 1945, after World War II.

3 Washington Square
New York, 3, N. Y., Oct. 11, 1944

Dear Van Wyck,

. . . There is a bad show of American painting again; I've not seen it, and may be able to keep out of the galleries of the Metropolitan where it hangs. One good reason for not seeing it is that it might make me too vitriolic in the book I'm writing—and where I want to say the best things I can about American art.

You've twice asked why I don't do a history of it, and the present book gets along toward the subject. It is on museums in America;[1] and they contain American art. They contain much more, of course, and there are all the general, theoretical considerations that you will readily imagine. It's a big chapter in American culture, and a force for the development of our people. . . .

I hope your recent spell of illness is altogether of the past—and that we may be seeing you and Eleanor.

As always,

Cordially, Walter Pach

1. *The Art Museum in America: Its History and Achievement*, would be published by Pantheon Books in 1948.

Aug. 26, 1946

Dear Magda and Walter,

I'm afraid we shall have to call the party off. Eleanor's condition has taken a curious turn for the worse, & I fear it is only a question now of a very few weeks. She may go back to the hospital,—I shall find out this afternoon,—and meanwhile I can only send you my love. . . .

Affectionately yours, Van Wyck

Don't write, dear Magda & Walter. There is really nothing to say at present. I will keep you posted about her condition.

New York, July 23, 1947

Dear Van Wyck,

I am reading Leo Stein's "Appreciations,"[1] and think it is a book that you will want to have a look at, some day. It seems to me much better than what he wrote before; I never liked his Aesthetics book;[2] it was just like chewing straw, for me. This one has some juice . . .

With warm greetings to you both, I am as always,

most cordially yours—Walter

1. *Appreciation: Painting, Poetry, and Prose* (New York: Random House, 1947).

2. *ABC of Aesthetics* (New York: Boni and Liveright, 1927).

New York, Nov. 4, 1950

Dear Gladys and Van Wyck,

Thank you for your friendly lines of last Sunday.

So much has taken place since I last wrote that I have been just too driven to pick up my pen again. Now my mind is a bit easier, so I give you the news.

After three days at that admirable Neustadter Home, the doctor there said her case must have more intensive study, for which our doctor had me take her to St. Vincent's Hospital where she was quite happy until—they came to the decision that an operation was necessary to get at the root of her trouble. It was—as they strongly suspected—a tumor of the brain. On Tuesday last this was removed, and with complete success. Her recovery from this extremely severe operation seems now to be well assured . . .[1]

Trusting that all goes well with you both, I am

Yours most cordially, Walter

1. Despite the optimistic outlook, Magda Pach died six days later, on November 10, 1950.

New York, Feb. 28, 1952

Dear Van Wyck,

This evening I finished your book . . .[1]

I can't help saying you take Gertrude Stein too seriously. Of course, you can show me pages and books of guff about her and her drool. But you speak of her lording it at the rue de Fleurus,[2] and she was brazen enough to get away with it, as far as concerns her victims in America, and some in England. There may be *some* in France, but the opinion of people there is almost surely what Picasso expressed when he said to me of Leo Stein, whom he hated (naturally) "Look at the way he treats his sister,—and she *tried*, anyhow, to do something." He was strong for Gertrude in some ways, but as far as her work went, all he could say was that she had tried.

Leo was better, more honest, for one thing. But you'd have trouble, in France, finding anyone to condone his pontificating, and his intimations of having recognized Matisse and Picasso at a *very* early time. They were not selling much, it's true, but French artists had already given them such general admiration that it was sure that they would sell. It is the artists whose opinion decides such matters—and not the Americans returning home with hardly a glint of understanding of art—and "selling" Leo Stein to

The New Republic as a great critic. Paris is hard to know; modern art is hard to know; and supposing, (as I do at a few rare moments) I thought of myself as having reached some understanding of modern art, I haven't the time to wrangle with the people who are befogging the public mind with their talk of modern art. I had one go at it, in The Atlantic Monthly nearly two years ago, when I said some things about Francis Taylor,[3] Berenson and Leo Stein, but what I've got to do is stick to my painting.

You don't need any encouragement to stick to your writing—and I shall be keen to see what you're doing now.

With remembrances to Gladys

Yours cordially, Walter

1. *The Confident Years: 1885–1915* (New York: E.P. Dutton, 1952).

2. Gertrude and Leo Stein had lived in Paris at 27 Rue de Fleurus, where they held open house on Saturdays frequented by artists, writers, collectors, dealers, friends, relatives, and acquaintances.

3. Francis Henry Taylor, director of the Metropolitan Museum of Art.

New York, Feb. 1, 1954

Dear Van Wyck,

You can't know, really, how good of you it was to write me that postcard about my books. But what in creation could have made you re-read five of them? I'm sure I can't imagine, but I *can* say thanks, and above all for finding the Ingres book "thrilling". . . .

I shall read your John Sloan manuscript in big gulps, the first time, and carefully, the second time, if you're still minded to let me see it in the spring.[1] I don't know just when my article on him will be out in the *Atlantic*, but I think very soon,[2] as Mr. Weeks[3] wrote me, some time ago, that he was sending it to the printer after one last editing. I don't think that will be a very drastic business; anyhow, I've forgotten what I did write, some two and a half years ago, so I shall probably not be impressed by any changes, at this time. . . .

Hoping that you and Gladys have a grand time in the South, and with warm thanks again, I am

Yours—Walter

1. Brooks's *John Sloan: A Painter's Life*, which was published in 1955 by E.P. Dutton & Co.

2. "John Sloan" by Pach appeared in *The Atlantic Monthly* 194 (August 1954), 68–72.

3. Edward Weeks, who wrote for the *Atlantic Monthly*.

New York, March 4, 1954

Dear Van Wyck,

. . . if you are minded to read something new of mine, and if you see the *Saturday Review* regularly, I'm having an article on the 13th or 20th of March (I believe).[1]

It's in the shape of a review of Berenson's two new books, but really it's my breaking of silence as to abstract art; I'm sure that the "modern decadents," as I call them will dislike it, but I've waited quite long enough about saying these things, and I just needed to. . . .

Warm good wishes to you and Gladys; Nikifora[2] joins me in them.

Yours always, Walter

1. Walter Pach, "A Pair of B.B.'s" [Review of Bernard Berenson's *Caravaggio: His Incongruity and His Fame* and *Seeing and Knowing*], *Saturday Review* 23 (August 3, 1954), 20–21.

2. Pach's second wife.

New York, May 5, 1954

Dear Van Wyck,

. . . Since you say of the Sloan book that there are questions which I alone can answer, and since I am as interested as you can imagine to read the book as a whole (the only way to see a given passage in its context and in perspective) I am wondering if there might not be a carbon copy that you could let me have for a brief time. . . .

With our warm good wishes to Gladys,

Yours always—Walter

New York, June 10, 1954

Dear Van Wyck,

Thanks for your letter.

It gives me a chance (lacking on that crowded visit from you) to say how very much I enjoyed the [John Sloan] book, and how much I think it will do for an understanding of Sloan's work. The more I read of "professional" art criticism, the less I think of it and its utility. Your evocation of the period and milieu, your sympathy with the man, his rugged sincerity, and his insight into the predominantly illustrative quality of his earlier work (an insight that carried him through in his determination to do something better)—all that will tell the contemporary,—and also the future public to what it *should* know. I am happy if any of my suggestions have made you feel safer about your statements.

As I want to drop in at Kraushaar's very soon anyhow, I shall speak to Antoinette[1] about that very late portrait of Yolande[2] that seems so particularly fine to me. Perhaps I shall ask her to set aside also a few other of my special favorites, for your consideration in September. I do want to stress the point again that Sloan thought his late works were his best. I certainly do, in the big majority of cases.

With remembrances to Gladys, and the hope to see you soon.

Yours always cordially, Walter

1. Antoinette Kraushaar, who was then running the gallery at 1055 Madison Avenue originally established by her father, John F. Kraushaar.

2. *Yolande Van R.*, painted in 1946–1947. Sloan had depicted the same model on several occasions during 1909–1910.

New York, Jan. 1, 1958

Dear Van Wyck,

I imagine that, when you got my card with merely provisional thanks for *From a Writer's Notebook*, you understood that you were in for one of my effusions—part of the price you pay for writing a book. . . . I *have* enjoyed it—so particularly indeed that I think it contains many of your best pages. . . .

As I have been a pretty consistent yea-sayer about your work, I feel entitled to express a certain doubt . . . about the passage beginning on Page 72. You say "everyone, in fact, needs incomprehension, and even oceans of it, and this is especially true of writers and artists." You cite "The stolid egoism of the English household" as the milieu for poets—and for artists too, presumably. But England has not produced artists of genius, though there has always been a full share of incomprehension there. I can't see it as a cause (even a contributing cause) of the talent or genius of English writers. I recognize your not having said it explained, all by itself, the excellence of English literature. But I think that writers and artists do their best when they express the thought of their public and know that their contemporary public is with them. I think that Shakespeare was, in the main, greatly enjoyed by the public of his time, even if understanding that would approach completeness could come about only when his plays were in print and could be savored at leisure. . . .

. . . with my admiration for men like Ingres and Delacroix, Barye and Corot, I often remind myself that they were born in the Eighteenth Century, and have to console myself quickly by recalling that I am keen for Picasso and Villon as well. (The latter has just done a thing that goes well ahead of all his past production, but at that, he's eighty-two years old, and I can't see much of value in the men who've come since. It's an uncomfortable thought that the blame for that is or may be my own; still, there's no one I respect who tells me of any new genius. I really think there's a drought—perhaps caused by the two wars).

Well, here's my effusion. I confidently hope it won't stop you from writing more books.

All good wishes—in which Nikifora joins emphatically—for what the new year will bring to you and Gladys.

As always,

Cordially yours, Walter Pach

Source of Letters: Van Wyck Brooks Papers, Rare Book & Manuscript Library, University of Pennsylvania, which contains additional Brooks/Pach correspondence.

Also available through the Archives of American Art, Smithsonian Institution, Van Wyck Brooks Papers, Reels 4218, 4219.

BRYSON BURROUGHS (1869–1934)

Curator of paintings at the Metropolitan Museum of Art from 1909 to 1934. Initially an artist, he studied at the Art Students League under Siddons Mowbray and Kenyon Cox, and later in Paris at Julian's and the École des Beaux-Arts, where his work was critiqued by Puvis de Chavannes. In 1901 Burroughs won a medal at the Pan-American Exposition in Buffalo, but his career as a painter was stifled five years later when he joined the staff of the Metropolitan as its assistant curator of paintings. The association between Walter Pach and Burroughs commenced at the time of the Armory Show, when Burroughs purchased, through Pach, Cézanne's *Colline des Pauvres* [*The Poorhouse on the Hill*] (late 1880s) for the Metropolitan. It was the first painting by that artist to be acquired by an American museum. Nearly two decades later Pach and Burroughs joined forces again to enable the Met to acquire Jacques-Louis David's *The Death of Socrates* (1787).

METROPOLITAN MUSEUM OF ART
DEPARTMENT OF PAINTINGS
NEW YORK, MARCH 24, 1913

Walter Pach, Esq.,
c/o The Blackstone,
Michigan Avenue.
Chicago, Ills.

Dear Mr. Pach:

Will you please give me all the information you have about our Cézanne.[1] Probable date of painting, the place, if you know it; its history as far as you know. It comes from Vollard, doesn't it? If so I might write him for the history.

I like the picture better and better and have not yet finished congratulating myself.

Very truly yours, Bryson Burroughs, Curator

1. *Colline des Pauvres* [*The Poorhouse on the Hill*], late 1880s. Oil on canvas. The painting was loaned by the Paris art dealer Ambroise Vollard to the Armory Show, from which it was purchased by Mr. Burroughs through Walter Pach, sales agent for the exhibition. It was the first Cézanne acquired by any museum in the United States.

Dear Walter Pach,

I have believed for a long time that the so-called sketch for the Raft of the Medusa in our Museum was a copy, basing my belief on the identity of the details of our picture and those of the picture in the Louvre, as well as a certain fixity and perfunctoriness in the work.

I am ashamed to say that I never have read Clément's book. If his statement about the figure in the left-hand corner is borne out by furthur investigation we are fully justified in removing the picture.

With best regards,

Sincerely, B. Burroughs

METROPOLITAN MUSEUM OF ART
NEW YORK, OCT. 23, 1930

Dear Walter Pach,

I am so sorry but there was a mix-up in the matter of your water-colors. Mr. Bing telephoned me about them a couple of weeks ago and I told him that the meeting was

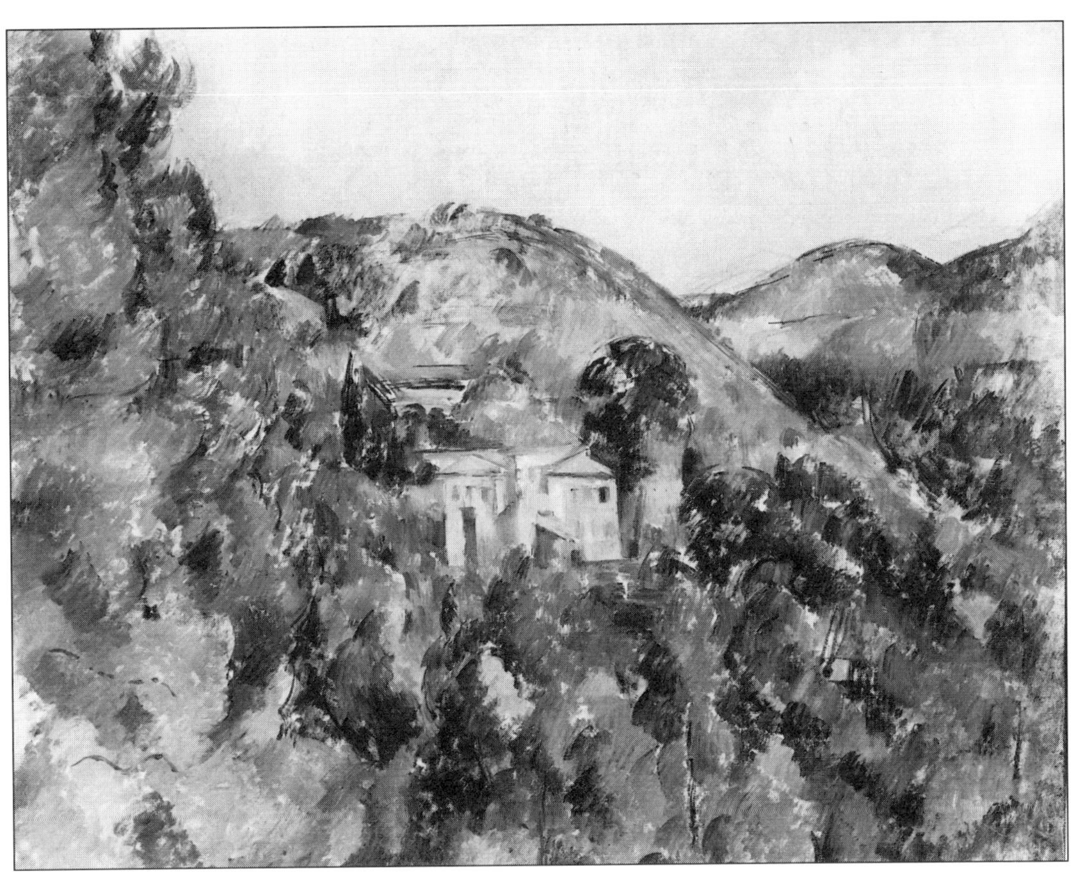

Paul Cézanne, *Colline des Pauvres [The Poorhouse on the Hill]*, retitled *View of the Domaine Saint-Joseph*, ca. 1877, Oil on canvas, 25 5/8 x 32 in. The Metropolitan Museum of Art, Catharine Lorillard Wolfe Collection, Wolfe Fund, 1913. (13.66).

to take place on the 20th. Mr. Bing said that in that case he would have them properly mounted and send them to me in time for the meeting. I kept asking the registrar's office about them as the time of the meeting drew near but they had received nothing.

It appears that they were left in my office and somehow no one told me about them so the package was lying unopened on the big table in the outer room. This afternoon the matter was cleared up.

They are excellent water-colors I think and represent you very well indeed—One can see that you did them with great pleasure and spontaneity. Your foreign stay is certainly doing a lot for you and I congratulate you on these works.[1]

They cant come up now until the 17th of November owing to the sloppy and un-businesslike and detestable lack of system in my office which is engendered by my

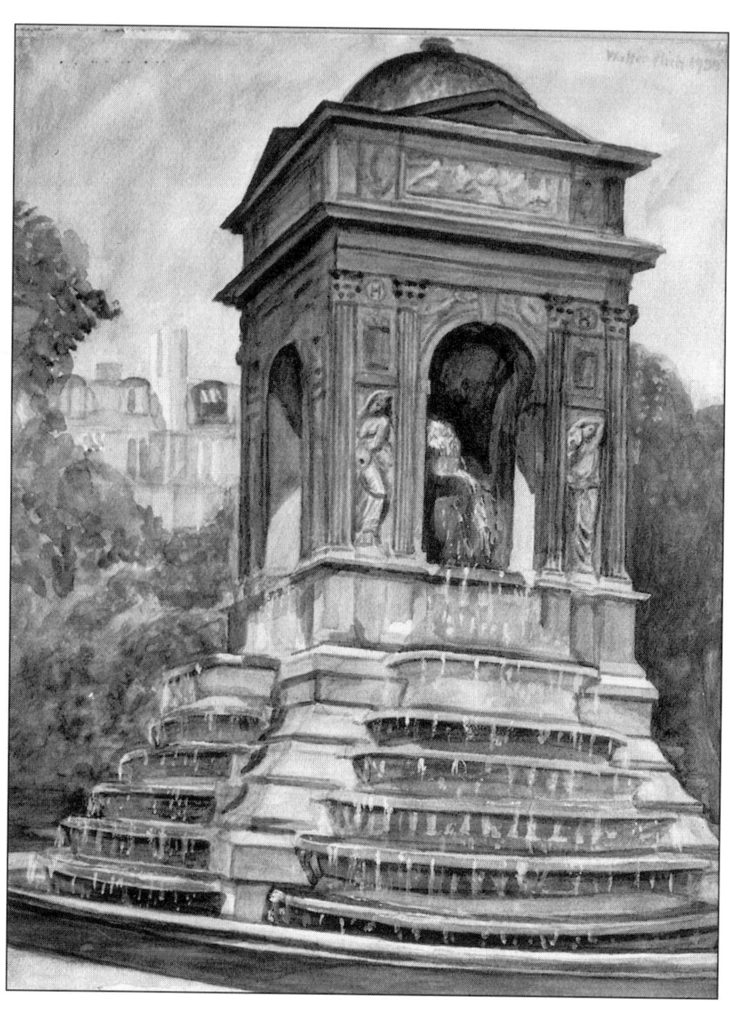

Walter Pach, *The Fountain of the Innocents, Paris*, 1930. Watercolor, 13 5/8 x 10 1/2 in. The Metropolitan Museum of Art, Anonymous Gift, 1930. (30.125.1).

own sloppiness and detestability. I foresee no trouble in their reception. The modern style has not the bitter enemies it used to have.

Yours, Bryson Burroughs

1. The four Pach watercolors acquired by the Metropolitan Museum are *The Fountain of the Innocents, Paris* (1930), *Les Invalides* (1930), *Cyclamen* (1929) and *Portrait of a Girl* (1930).

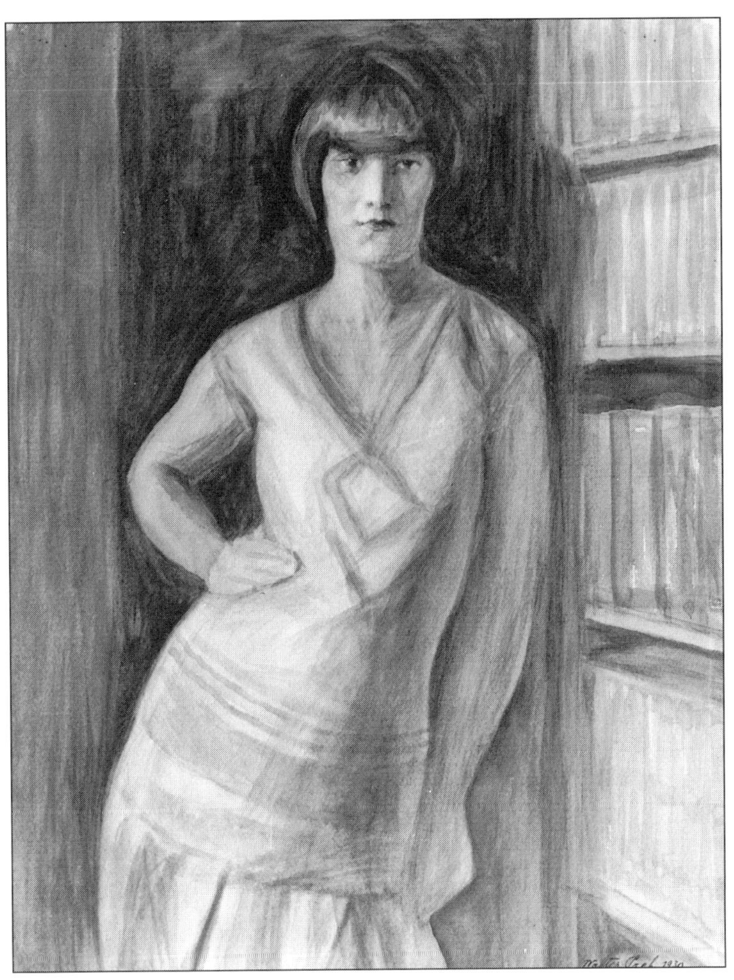

Walter Pach, *Portrait of a Girl*, 1930. Watercolor, 13 5/8 x 10 1/2 in. The Metropolitan Museum of Art, Anonymous Gift, 1930. (30.126.2).

PARIS, JAN. 20, 1931

Dear Mr. Burroughs,

Having you agree so cordially about the quality of the Pontormo[1] took away some of the regret of having it turn out to be no museum picture. I have now stumbled on one that is surely that and, though I am not going in for picture hunting as a practice, I thought I should send you the photograph of this David.[2] It is his *Socrates Receiving the Hemlock*[3] of the Salon of 1787, about which Sir Joshua Reynolds wrote that it was "the greatest effort of the art since the Sistine Chapel and the Stanze of Raphael. This work would have done honor to Athens at the time of Pericles. Ten days of observation have only confirmed the general idea which I had formed—which is that it is perfect in every way."

The picture was a command from Trudaine, from whose collection it went to the family whose descendents own it today. They want to sell it only so as to divide up an estate and not to make money, as they are very rich. The price is $18,000. The size is about 44 x 72 inches or somewhat less. The condition of the picture is flawless. It is described in various books on David.

If our Museum does not want it, could you, fittingly, pass it on to J. B. Potter or Fiske Kimball or Harold W. Parsons[4]—or some one else? Or if you don't like to, will you kindly return the photograph to me? I send it under separate cover.

My show at Kraushaar's opens the first week in March. I hope you can spare a moment to look at it.

With kind regards to Mrs. Burroughs, I am

Yours very sincerely, Walter Pach

1. Pontormo (1494–1556/7), an Italian Mannerist painter.

2. Jacques-Louis David (1748–1825), leading exponent of Neo-Classicism.

3. Titled *The Death of Socrates*.

4. John Briggs Potter (1864–1949), Keeper of Paintings and advisor to the Department of Paintings at the Museum of Fine Arts, Boston; Fiske Kimball (1888–1955), director of the Philadelphia Museum of Art; Harold Woodbury Parsons (1884–1967), a New York art advisor and buyer of paintings for various museums.

Feb. 6, 1931

Dear Mr. Pach,

Your letter came about a week ago and the photograph yesterday. I am exceedingly interested in the David and will bring it to the attention of the trustees at the meeting on the 16th. They are in a most economical mood just now and are turning down everything but I shall make a strong effort. It is really a remarkable opportunity and the Museum is most grateful to you.

Can you find out for us from the owners if they would be willing to send the painting here for consideration at our expense if the trustees should desire to examine it? And do you think that any concession in the price could be hoped for? Also has it a frame of the time?

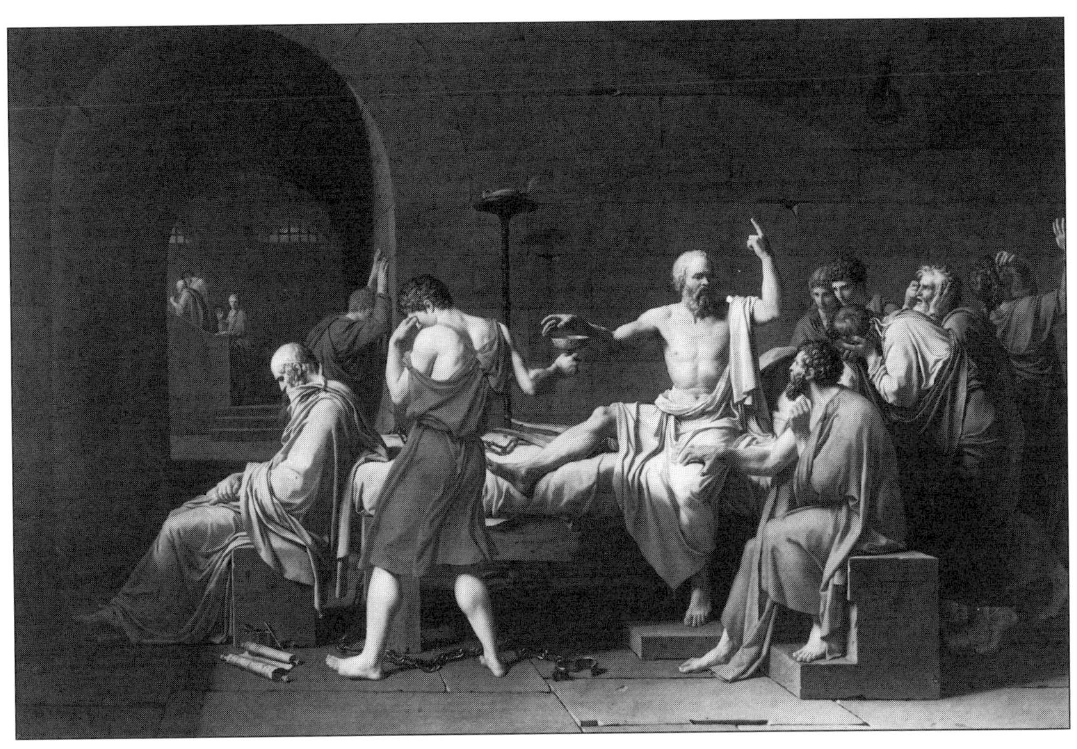

Jacques-Louis David, *The Death of Socrates*, 1787. Oil on canvas, 51 x 77 1/4 in. The Metropolitan Museum of Art, Catharine Lorillard Wolfe Collection, Wolfe Fund, 1931. (31.45).

Many, many thanks for the trouble you have taken and will take in these charitable enterprises.

Bryson Burroughs

THE METROPOLITAN MUSEUM OF ART
NEW YORK, MARCH 17, 1931

Dear Walter Pach,

You are certainly a brick to take all this trouble and the Museum is much beholden to you however the David matter turns out. For myself I have good hopes—several of the trustees have displayed a real interest in the matter.

The monthly meeting took place on the 16th and we can hardly expect the painting to be unpacked before several days but I have arranged for an immediate decision when it is unpacked. You will probably have heard from the Museum by cable before you receive this.

Now for a personal matter. Last Saturday I went to Kraushaar's to see your show.[1] He has arranged it very nicely. The fourteen oil paintings are in the gallery all symetrically arranged and the effect of the room is excellent. My favorites here were The Beach and Simonne. Simonne particularly stands out in my memory. Another painting, Youth, was on an easel in the back room. This could not be placed without destroying the balance of the various panels which now give such a decorative effect to the gallery.

The water-colors are in the alcove on the street side of the gallery. The watercolor portrait of Raymond (your son, isnt it?) is your best watercolor so far to my mind. Others that appealed to me here were the model reposing and the one you call Paris Autumn, and the sketch of the Institute with the statue of Voltaire made me a bit homesick. There is a little café (or was) from which one gets just that view and many's the Zinzano à l'eau de Seltz that has irrigated my dusty throat as I've looked at Voltaire and the trees and the Louvre across the river. You've already got one no doubt but I am enclosing the catalogue I carried away with me.

As to the Eakins matter[2] I should be honored to cooperate as you are already aware, when Mrs. Eakins invites me even without Jean Guiffrey's most gratifying compliment. Bless him for a dear!

I will write you as soon as anything happens.

Yours, B. Burroughs

1. "Paintings and Water Colors by Walter Pach" at the C. W. Kraushaar Art Galleries, 680 Fifth Avenue, from March 11 to 28, 1931.

2. Pach was seeking to have the Louvre Museum accept a painting by Thomas Eakins for its permanent collection.

The Metropolitan Museum of Art
New York, March 28, 1931

Dear Walter Pach—

The picture was delivered to us at last, and has been duly passed by the Customs. It is grander even than I had imagined—what a noble work—We are all very much excited and most enthusiastic—Such condition! Not even rubbed! It will be one of the masterpieces here, one of the outstanding works of permanent interest—

always provided the sub-committee decides that in their consciences they can approve of it—Only Blumenthal[1] has seen it yet and he is chilly. He finds it badly drawn, (dont laugh—he can safely be classed among the most intelligent of the trustees in matters of art) but has come around to a mild approval—The others ought to see it by Tuesday—. . . .

You see, I am sort of confident that the excellence in conjunction with the fame of the picture will make itself felt on those gentlemen who have its fate in charge—

But all this is for your ear alone—Let not our clean linen be shown in public—

I am in touch with Mrs Eakins at last and hope to see Lloyd Goodrich[2] tomorrow who know just which pictures are still free—What a splendid idea—Eakins-in-the-Louvre

My best compliments to you for all your beneficial labors!

Yours, B Burroughs

1. George Blumenthal, a trustee and seventh president of the Metropolitan Museum.

2. Goodrich (1897–1987) was at the time curator at the Whitney Museum of American Art.

[Telegram]
March 31, 1931

WALTER PACH
MORGANBANK PARIS (FRANCE)

DAVID BOUGHT HOORAY

BURROUGHS

The Metropolitan Museum of Art
New York, April 14, 1931

Dear Walter Pach,

Well—you've had my cable! En effet the David is bought. And I think, if you ask me, that its about the swellest picture we have acquired for a long time. Such marvellous science and such condition! And none of us here forget the fact that it's due to you that we have been able to get it.

You must send the Museum the bill of what expenses you had in the affair. There were a couple of cables I know and there must have been lots of cab fares. Jot them down and send to me. That's the least we can do.

I haven't written you before as I've been waiting for the Eakins matter to crystallize. Mrs. Eakins has been most sympathetic. Amongst the pictures which still belong to her the head of the cowboy (1) and the portrait of her father front face (2) would be my choices. But neither could be regarded as his *very best* to my mind, and I have broached to Mrs. Eakins a little plan I've concocted to which she agrees. It's this—to try to wangle Clara (1) or The Bohemian (2) out of the Pennsylvania Museum, i.e. try to induce them to offer one of the *very best* to the Louvre. What do you think of the idea? Clara was always one which seemed to me a top-notcher. I didn't propose it here as I knew the Trustees would not see it.

I am going to write Kimball[1] when I can find a half hour of recueillement[2] (it will be needed to produce the proper letter). I will only broach the general idea in the first letter. So if you have strong feelings in regard to any other which could be preferable just cable Burroughs Metmusart Newyork and the title.

Of course if [*sic*] may fall down flad [*sic*] but one can cite many reasons why it would be a grand gesture on the part of the Pennsylvania Museum and they own seventy-five paintings by Eakins; more by now!

Yours, Bryson Burroughs

1. Fiske Kimball, director of the Pennsylvania Museum (now the Philadelphia Museum of Art).

2. Contemplation.

THE METROPOLITAN MUSEUM OF ART
NEW YORK, MAY 3, 1931

Dear Walter Pach—

I got your cable of Apr. 27 and am delighted that you think the Penn. Mus. Eakins idea *splendid*. The Linfort portrait belongs to Mrs. Eakins, but it is larger than what I imagined as suitable—about as large as the Barker in fact.[1]

The Penn. Mus. Eakins project takes shape gradually—Mrs. Eakins is enthusiastic—Fiske Kimball wrote me in response to my suggestion that he was sympathetic to the idea and w1d. take it up with his Trustees. He wrote me later, or rather [illegible word] of that mus. wrote me, proposing "Clara" as suitable for the purpose [illegible word] a possible condition wh. I must report to you at length—I epitomize as follows. The Eakins' deed of gift specifies that the Eakins ptgs. can be exchanged but not given or sold [illegible word] of course as Mrs. E. is willing. It occured to the Penn. Mus. staff that the transaction could be more satisfactorily arranged if an exchange could be effect[ed] for "let us say" a Derain.

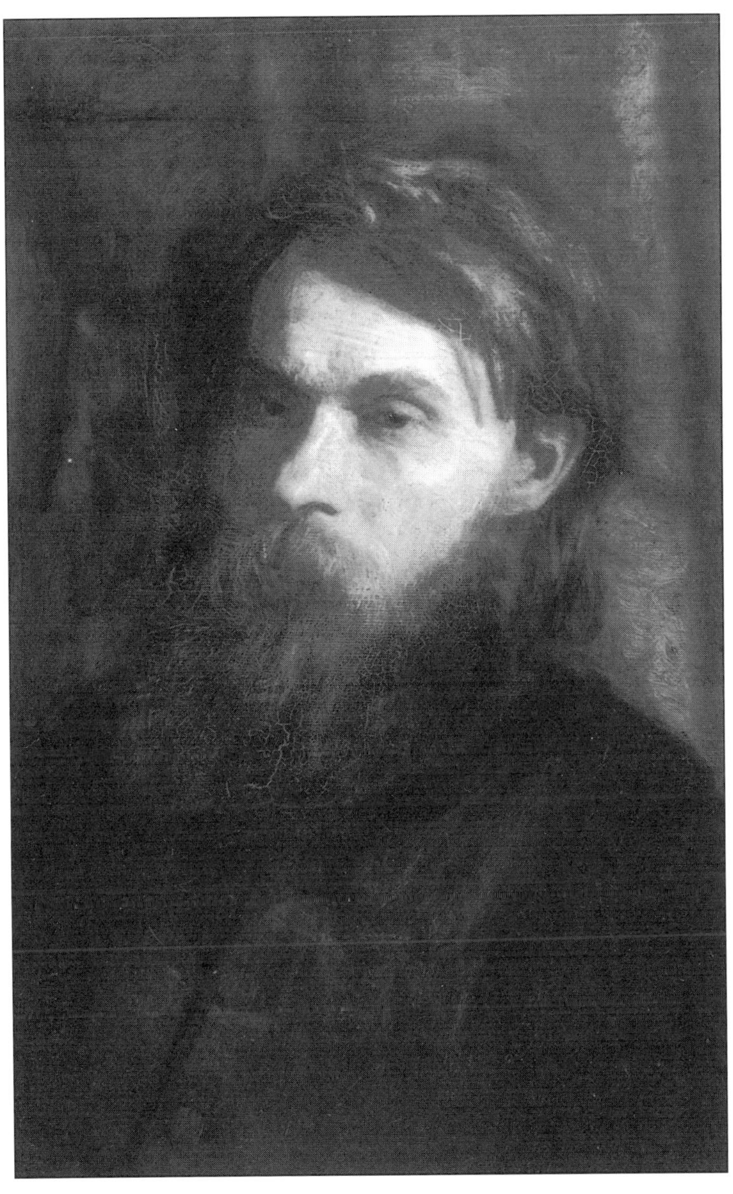

Thomas Eakins, *The Bohemian (Portrait of Franklin Louis Schenck)*, ca. 1890. Oil on canvas, 23 7/8 x 16 3/4 in. Philadelphia Museum of Art: Gift of Mrs. Thomas Eakins and Miss Mary Adeline Williams. Acc. 1929-184-15.

I then wrote that this wld. complicate things hopelessly—that a large Eakins objected *to by* Guiffrey[2] because it would necessitate committee action—that the purchase by the Louvre of a Derain, which not even the Luxembourg has as yet, for the purpose of exchanging it for an Eakins wld. necessitate a series of committee actions that the existance [*sic*] of the French Gov't itself might be endangered—

To wk. Kimball—Pach was going to raise money to buy the Eakins, let him raise money to buy the Derain instead.

So I wrote today—saying the suggestion that the Penn. Mus. give an Eakins to the Louvre was broached as something they might wish to do, being so will provide it themselves in honor of a great artist who was a Philadelphian—a picture by whom in the Louvre wld. be his apotheosis—an honor to Phila, to the United States and to France;—that Derains cost a hell of a lot, about 5000 $ or so and that many of Eakins admirers wld. object to subscribing for a Derain as the woods were full of them and more coming in each week and that in a few years they wld. find their way to the museums:—that if an Eakins were given that many wld. be glad to chip in to buy a handsome 17th century frame (in wh. his pictures look so swell) so that a fitting setting be given to what wld. be, with Whistler's Mother, a movement to Am. Art in the greatest museum of European Art—etc etc.

Kimball is a go-getter and he wants to squeeze what he can out of every occasion losing sight of sentimental aspects. I think he'll come round and from what I hear of Mr. Price(?) who is back of the Penn. Mus. in all its splendors, I believe he can be counted on to do the superb thing.

Please comment on what I've done—I should have wished to consult you, as the principal in this matter, but that is not practical. Have I taken too much on my own shoulders? I have had to do according to my own methods—

I've had great pleasure in writing about the David which grows on me more and more—Kent[3] sends you his regards—Louise[4] and I are to be in Paris about July 7th-15th. Will you be there then?

Yours, Burroughs

1. For further details about various suggestions of an Eakins portrait for the Louvre, read the Susan Eakins/Walter Pach letters in this volume.

2. Jean Guiffrey, head of the Department of Paintings at the Louvre Museum.

3. Henry Watson Kent, secretary of the Metropolitan Museum of Art.

4. Burroughs's wife.

THE METROPOLITAN MUSEUM OF ART
NEW YORK, MAY 11, 1931

Dear Walter Pach,

I am sending you herewith a copy of the letter I've just received from Fiske Kimball which explains itself perfectly and most satisfactorily. I am also sending you a print of the Clara which is the picture selected by the officials of the Pennsylvania Museum on their own initiative and which happens also to be my own first choice as an appropriate representation of Eakin's [*sic*] work for this purpose. I saw the picture again last week going to Philadelphia for the purpose of looking at their Eakinses and felt my previous judgement was amply confirmed by my present judgement.

Please give my cordial greetings to Jean Guiffrey.

Sincerely, Bryson Burroughs

PENNSYLVANIA MUSEUM OF ART
MEMORIAL HALL, PHILADELPHIA
MAY 8, 1931

Bryson Burroughs, Esq.,
Metropolitan Museum of Art
New York City

Dear Burroughs:

Your very gentle and interesting letter of May 2nd regarding the Eakins matter is received.

With the circumstances explained, I should certainly not think of asking people like my good friend Pach to put up their own money in the matter along the lines I had suggested, which would require a substantial sum. In the light of your last letter I shall recommend to my Board that a gift be made to the Louvre. I think it would perhaps be wise to find first from Guiffrey whether the "Clara" would be acceptable. Before I put it up to my Board, will you do that, stating of course that it is a tentative approach, and subject to our action, if the picture would be acceptable? You had better send a photograph to him.

I don't quite feel as you do in the matter of the frame, because apparently Eakins himself did not feel that way. He frequently, to be sure, used any old frame which came to hand, but one thing he always did was to kill the gold scrumbling over with drab color. As you know, he seems to have preferred even to mould frames so treated with a plain broad flat band of a brownish tone, which is so characteristic of him. I should be perfectly content, however, with whatever you and Pach may care to do about the frame. Very probably it would be best in Paris to do as the Parisians do!

Sincerely yours,
[signed] Fiske Kimball
Director

Hotel de la Colline
Villefranche-sur-Mer, June 24, 1931

Dear Walter Pach—

Josephine has forwarded me yr. letter of May 22 and also reported later developments in our darling project wh. seems to be all to the good.

It will be a great pleasure to see you and yr. wife in Paris provided you have not disturbed your plans in any way to remain there until our coming—My ambiguous statement had for foundation that we intended to arrive about the 7th and stay until our boat sails on the 17th.—of July. I would love to see the David-Weill Coll. in your company and also to call on yr. friend. If you are not there I will be likely—judging from the way I act ordinarily—to satisfy myself by going to the great collections where I always find something wh. I have never noticed before—and where the greatest things are. The Louvre is to me the richest jungle in the world and always remains so—

It is a great comfort the way the Eakins matter has turned out and I am really glad to be out of its final arrangement—leaving that in your hands, as it should be, and in the hands of Jean Guiffrey and the committee. I think the fact that the Penn. Mus. has decided to offer one of Eakins pictures is a fine action, and the Clara, all things considered would be to my mind, a worthy choice—It was my choice, indeed, before it was the choice of Fiske Kimball—so I was much pleased when they selected that work. The Luford [painting] belongs to Mrs. Eakins still, and though perfectly complete from our point of view, it is a work wh. was never finished, whereas the Clara is finished in that miraculous way Eakins finished, with each tiny form wrought out in that almost Van Eyck fashion, but with the greater qualities of large form and solidity, and of most convincing characterisation, material and spiritual reality—also perfectly attained—But lo! I talk like a Bulletin article, which is very foolish in this place, writing in the garden after lunch with this beautiful harbor below, showing through roses and grape vines and laurel. . . .

Yours—with cordial greetings
Bryson Burroughs

Bord S.S. "De Grasse," le 19 Juillet 1931

Dear Walter Pach—

I should have liked enormously to have seen you in Paris and to have swapped enthusiasms with you. . . .

Guiffrey, whom I saw several times, is delighted about the Eakins and, most appreciative of your efforts in regard to it. He has asked me to report to the committee the American possibilities for the French Exhibition next winter in London, which I shall be very glad to do—It ought to be a splendid collection—four hundred masterpieces, of which about half will be 19th century,—Robinson[1] was the great impediment in the lending of the Museum pictures and the chances seem pretty good that the Museum will be able to cooperate in regard to Courbet, Manet and Degas. It will be a satisfaction, and most advantageous all round if we can do so. A new era of liberalism and cooperation is about due with the passing of so many ancient trustees, and Robinson, though so excellent a director in many ways was apt to look upon the Metropolitan as an entirely isolated activity. It's a stirring time.

Did I tell you that we were going to Milan in the hope, primarily, of seeing the part of the Très Belles Heures which belongs to Prince Trivulzio? We saw it. Those pages painted by Hubert Van Eyck (I am sure for my own part that he is the painter) are miracles, pure miracles! The reproductions give no idea of them—They are like nothing else and having been protected from light and air and never retouched, they show the effect that the artist saw as he finished them. There is some silver leaf in one of the pictures, simulating the outdoor light as seen through the window of a dim room, and this silver is *scarcely tarnished.* When you think how sensitive silver is to oxidization you can understand how pristine the robust pigments have remained—Trivulzio has also a great altarpiece by Mantegna and a head by Antonello—supreme things.

Is there any hope you will be coming back this winter?

Best regards to you and Mrs Pach—Louise sends her greetings—

Yours, Bryson Burroughs

1. Edward Robinson (1858–1931), director of the Metropolitan Museum of Art from 1910 to 1931.

The Metropolitan Museum of Art
New York, Jan. 9, 1932

Dear Walter Rach:

I was sorry not to have been able to send you a more sympathetic word about the Géricault—Your cable *did* spell excitement and of course I knew you had reason for it—

but the trustees dont understand that sort of thing at all and again and again they have refused to commit themselves to anybody's judgment. Even after all my years of caution and carefulness they will give me no leeway of personal decision—The only way to handle them is to show them a picture and quote some *printed* opinion,—something that has been printed in a book—that they might respect but your opinion—my own opinion—is something they pass by without any absorbtion [*sic*] of it. Tell me what the picture is and I'll look it up in Clément[1] and in literature and prepare a dossier and on going to them with that, there is a chance that something might come of it. Now, in particular, when the Museum is facing lean years, write the probability, (it's more really than that) of having to use all the unrestricted funds for maintenance,—and economy is in the words and minds of all in authority, they are rigorous to know just what each cent goes for, and eager to know everything about any possibility that comes before them.

Coffin[2] is fine and liberal and I look for great improvements under his tenure but the others are pretty much as they were, even although so many of the old-timers have passed away. The *tradition* remains. They are much more afraid of mistakes of commission than of omission—As you probably know there is the greatest opportunity now, in the selling of Hermitage pictures (It's all hush stuff—so dont quote me, but a fact nevertheless) than has taken place since the upheavals following the French Revolution—But to profit by it would take great boldness and a pile of money—so they say let's confine ourselves to carrying on and if pictures come to American collectors there's always a chance that they will gravitate here.

There are half a dozen of those Gerard David replicas—the one you remember was here, a panel belonging to Mr de Forest[3]—lent by him—but now removed.

I think you are eminently fitted for Museum work and had occasion some time ago to say so to the Cincinnati people who happened to approach me for advice—But the present is not a favorable time for finding good positions—Did you hear that *all* the Detroit staff had been laid off on account of Detroit penury? And that the Pennsylvania Mus. in Philadelphia is in financial straits—the salaries, I hear, have been cut in half—though only half the hours of work are required. It's the same all over the country—the hard times I mean.

Do write me the particulars of the Géricault—the David has an enormous success and.looks *grand*! We bless you for it—Best regards to Mrs. Pach—

Yours—B. Burroughs

1. Charles Clément's *Géricault étude biographique et critique*, Paris, 1879.

2. William Sloane Coffin, sixth president of the Metropolitan Museum of Art and a trustee since 1924.

3. Robert de Forest had been president of the Metropolitan Museum until 1931.

The Metropolitan Museum of Art
New York, March 26, 1932

Dear Walter Pach—

Your letter of Feb 15th with the reproduction of Géricault came to me and I have been waiting for the free half hour to acknowledge and comment—the moment has now come and I have more to acknowledge and comment upon—your [one-man exhibition] catalogue, namely, with its delightful and whimsical foreword—How I envy you the power to write like that and in French too! The Marocaine [Moroccan] reproduced is one of those I suppose, you were doing when I was looking for you in Paris last spring—very handsome she looks too—and I can't blame you for running off to Africa while the running-off was good—Your exhibition, as I look from your catalogue to my calender [*sic*], closes today it seems—My best wishes for its complete success!

The Géricault reproduction is of a grand picture—that is evident, notwithstanding the engraving's crude blacks and the tear in the lower corner—I am in a low state of mind just now on account of trustees, and I feel that it would have done no good to have had the reproduction to show them—they would have surely turned it down. Don't pin any faith on the taste of trustees, my dear, and dont feel bad about the Museum missing the picture—Let it drop—in any event for the moment—and dont waste precious dreaming-time in imagining that anyone at the Museum will ever be allowed a margin of freedom in buying—You *would* have great difficulty in putting-up with the impertinences and decisions of higher authorities—You would always have the refuge and sanctuary of painting—at off moments, as I have—Without that life would be quite unbearable at times—. . .

Best regards & good luck—

Yours, Bryson Burroughs

Source of Letters: The Metropolitan Museum of Art Archives, New York, New York, which contains one additional Burroughs/Pach letter.

Also available through the Archives of American Art, Smithsonian Institution, Bryson Burroughs Papers, reel 4218; and the Walt Kuhn Papers, reel D72.

ARTHUR B. DAVIES
(1862–1928)

Painter, printmaker, and mastermind behind the 1913 Armory Show. Born in Utica, New York, his early penchant for art ranged from magazine illustrations to painting Bull Durham Tobacco advertisements on the sides of barns. His early oils were landscapes that combined elements of Inness and Ryder; these dream visions drew immediate praise from art critics who soon labeled him one of the foremost artists of the day.

When he rented a New York studio atop the Macbeth Gallery, Davies became an advisor to art dealer William Macbeth, recommending to him such artists as Robert Henri, Maurice Prendergast, and Rockwell Kent, who were subsequently shown there. Davies acquired the Macbeth Gallery for the show of The Eight in 1908, and financed the 1911 Independent Show organized by Kent.

Davies was a member of the Association of American Painters and Sculptors who hoped to organize an exhibit of their own work, but after being elected the group's president, he transformed the plan into the country's landmark exhibition of modern French art, the 1913 Armory Show. His awareness of such artists as Cézanne, Gauguin, and others was made possible by having Walter Pach translate French art publications for him. When Davies journeyed to Paris in the fall of 1912, he met Pach and Walt Kuhn there, and it was Pach, a resident in the French capital for several years, who introduced him to gallery owners, avant-garde artists, and major collectors, all of whom willingly loaned works to the forthcoming New York exhibit.

Although Davies was moved to paint in a Cubist manner at the time of the Armory Show, he reverted to romantic subject matter a few years later.

53 W. 39TH ST.
NEW YORK, MAY 27, 1909

Dear Mr. Pach

I can not find an error in the essay,[1] it is a beautiful lyrical piece of writing and in line with the best we know today. what you have put into it of yourself I am sure must interest a newer significant minority and I wish I might realize your hope for me.

Faithfully yours, Arthur B. Davies

1. Apparently Pach's article about Davies was never published (see Pach to Alice Klauber, August 31, 1909).

NEW YORK, JUNE 1, 1909

Dear Mr. Pach

I am sorry I have made engagements for Wednesday and if we can plan for some afternoon of next week that will suit Mr. Of[1] I think it would be better wed. afternoon next week is also out for me. Mr. Keeble can come by alone Thurs. or Friday and I would rather not take the chance of so many at once as I cannot be quite easy with strangers at any time. I could possibly show some things to Mr. Keeble I would rather develope more before showing you & Mr. Of. The Harper's editor I have met the like before and wish the history forgotten. I shall return the Druet catalogue as I have sent for same photograph and will be pleased to show them to you when they arrive, I am

Faithfully, Arthur B. Davies

1. George F. Of (1876–1954) was an artist who also ran a framing shop in Manhattan. While in Paris he had acquired several works by Matisse which he showed to Pach when they first met in 1908, and to other artists including, presumably, Davies.

NEW YORK, UNDATED

Dear Mr. Pach

I am more delighted than ever with Gauguin and his work. while there are many things I dont care to know, I would wish to know more of this true artist, who has the spiritually enlarging vision, eloquence of power and restraint. The opportunity for comparison with the work of Degas in the "Kunst [?]"[1] is most interesting and good for one, muscular nervous, desolately stimulating contra the prerequisite eternal calm—Thank you very much indeed . . .

Faithfully, A. B. Davies

1. "Art–" [rest of word illegible].

New York, Undated [April 8, 1910]

Dear Pach

I received from Prendergast[1] this morning the enclosed clipping on Matisse, which you, like myself have probably only seen extracts. please return after reading. The Rodin apostrophe to the Venus of Milo and himself—I read last night. If you have not read Furtwängler[2] on the Venus you will find him mighty interesting. He calls it an eclectic work of the 2d B.C. the motive a creation by Scopas: considerably contaminated by Melos local traditions . . .

Yours, Arthur B. D.

1. Maurice B. Prendergast (1861–1924), known to Davies since 1900 when they painted together near Davies's home in Rockland County, New York.

2. Adolf Furtwängler, *Meisterwerke der griechischen Plastik* (Berlin: 1893). English translation by Eugenie Sellers, *Masterpieces of Greek Sculpture* (London: 1895).

New York, May 14, 1910

Dear Pach

Couldn't you come in at about One o'clock Monday and go out for luncheon with me? I found your article on Matisse the most enlightening of any I have read so far. High changes of matter but not its modesty of spirit would make it ever fresh for a good many people

Your hastily, Arthur B. Davies

New York, June 19, 1912

My dear Pach

Your letter and the promise its contents offer have been quite exciting in this far away Teddy-ridden land so fully barbarous have we become. and I must get at the question. Just how shall we arrange the money and the shipping of the Cezanne? I thought it best to send the small deposit to show the sincerity of the desired option, and the wish to identify the painting as a strickly [*sic*] fair one. I have found a customer for the picture who will give the $2000.00 or if need [be] $2200, but the duty is always a drawback and if we can get price down to $2000.00 all will be quite promptly met by immediate payment. I can assure you of my great confidence in your judgement of the Cezanne as to quality etc, and I shall be only too happy to welcome it for the common good. On the arrival of the photo[,] I will cable results, yet I feel perfectly sure all will be entirely satisfactory.

The picture can be sent to Wm. Macbeth 450 Fifth Ave. who will see it through the customs, get the valuation right on the invoice properly legal—be perfectly straight[,] do not leave it to the uncertain appraiser here. I really hope if this picture should make the effect other more important canvases may be purchased later!! I have a message from Mr. Macbeth for you regarding photos of Rockwell Kent's pictures[.][1] if you state the ones you want he will send them to you direct as he says he does not know who has names of the paintings.

I have found such difficulty in writing any letters but such as this one of so imperative a nature and yet I have several beginnings addressed to you scattered over the years since your photo, and the cards the books have been received, and my heartiest thanks and truly cordial feeling is the same as ever. I have so much to say on the situation in art matters, as affecting individuals . . . under a true patriarchal art—not institutions—I must not take your time and will really write you a good letter soon. With kindest regards and a hope I may see you in Paris in October[1]—I am Faithfully yours

Arthur B. Davies

1. Davies found it necessary to postpone his trip, and did not arrive in Paris until November 16, 1912.

---

337 East 57th St.
New York, Oct. 1, 1912

Dear Walter Pach

The Cezanne is now reposing in Mr MacBeth's safe, awaiting the call of the owner.[1] I have been deeply impressed by its classic beauty—reminded more of the

Old Han bronzes than anything of Latin or Greek origin. Everyone has been most reverential. Geuthner of Worcester offered at once an advance on whatever the purchase price was. And by-the-way he wants a Cezanne if it can be put through his group of trustees—his greatest obstructionist has recently died—If I can predict there seems to me to be a very much brighter outlook here this fall for work of [a] positive kind of art. Certainly the negative improvements by museums and schools is near the limit. We had the devil's own time with the custom house over the detail of invoice neglected or improperly filled out. The point of when Count Costa bought the picture & of whom. only because he & Cezanne being dead the appraiser waived the matter. The duty on the old frame is hard to understand but is passed without demurr [*sic*]. I consider the picture a great acquisition for American wealth and would weigh it against many an old master. And yet the child is with us eternally and eternally lost each day, and our so called artists are simply fattened brains prospering by economic plundering.—I shall try to write you again about the Cezanne after the new owner sees the work—The reason for writing now is with reference to Walt Kuhn[2] and the coming exhibition at the 69th Inf. Armory in Lexington Ave. Kuhn sailed for Hamburg to see the Sonderbund at Cologne to enlist for our show such artists giving promise of the newest tendencies. —good work of an International character anywhere—The hanging space will be very large and lots of new men we hope to bring to the front. I had expected to go over with him at any rate meet him in Paris just now domestic troubles[3] are delaying and the unfinished work of preparation for the exhibition—To those of us and men like yourself the possibilities loom tremendous yet so many can only see another opportunity of showing their work. —we look for the higher organic life in the intuitive future. I believe you can do much for Kuhn in every way and I also believe he has a really healthy outlook with considerable ability in doing through paint his life as he knows it. So I am asking a favor of you again for which I hope I may reciprocate happily some time. I am sending a letter to him in your care, which is of value and owing to the uncertainty of the handling of letters at the Am. Express Co. I wish you to hold until his arrival in Paris. You will get a lot of information from him. and I have great confidences in his honesty of purpose and gameness in putting through successfully anything he is fairly up against. There is so much I want to letter about but must get this off by to-day steamer. Thanking you most heartily for all your trouble with the Cezanne and for your patience with my procrastination

Faithfully, Arthur B. Davies

1. The Cézanne had been owned by Count Enrico Costa, a resident of Florence and a friend of Berenson's; following Costa's death in 1911 it was purchased, through Pach, at Arthur B.Davies's behest for Davies's patron, Lizzie Bliss. The oil was titled "Landscape" when exhibited in the Armory Show.

2. Walt Kuhn (1877–1949) was Davies's closest friend. He was a member of the board of the Association of American Painters and Sculptors, which group sponsored the Armory Show; was its executive secretary, publicist, and head of the Catalogue and General Printing Committee.

3. The previous April, Davies had fathered an illegitimate child by his live-in model, and she resisted his traveling to Europe while she was left with the care of an infant.

[TELEGRAM]

NEW YORK, MARCH 21, 1913

Sir William VanHorne is very sorry he lent Cezanne is it possible to withdraw.[1]

Davies.

1. The work, titled *Portrait of Madame Cézanne*, was included in the show when it opened in Chicago on March 24. In 1988 it was contained in a private collection in Switzerland.

[TELEGRAM]

NEW YORK, MARCH 28, 1913

Walter Pach
care of Art Institute, Chicago, Ills.
Doctor Loewenstein decides not to buy the Vangogh[1] when will Kuhn return.

Davies

1. Though Dr. Helen C. Loewenstein did not acquire the van Gogh, she did purchase works by Charles Camoin, Emilie Charmy, and Jacques Villon from the show.

[NIGHT LETTER]

CHICAGO, APRIL 4, 1913

Davies
122 East 25th St
NYC

Duchamp Villon (seven rue lemaitre puteaux paris) writes that is uneasy about delaying his pictures but with more information will probably be satisfied address me care [Chicago Art] institute No new developments

Pach

New York, Undated [April 5, 1913]

Dear Pach

Kuhn returned yesterday morning with a batch of delayed answers to our many questions. We are looking for James today. The money for Duchamp-Villon goes by todays steamer "Oceanic," Cherbourg. We are still in the House of Bondage every thing has been ready now these two weeks and a lot of Druet's[1] and the German stuff should be on the water returning. Whether it is because of a new [Association] secretary in office or an extra rush of imports. However Mr. Hecht is a crank and goes his own way for his evidence. Regarding the Belle Green[2] bronze of Brancusi's Mlle Pogany, Clarke told me we could get a bronze made here by the Roman Bronze Co for about $350. to $400. as good as those made abroad but not a[s] cheap, I have not written to B.G. as she is evidently in mourning over the loss of her "meat" J.P.M.[3] and she may wait now to curtail her expenses. The "Library"[4] will be under her control unless the "House" lady[5] gets the best of her and she gets the *grand bounce*. Of course Brancusi should have a premium. We are looking forward to a genuine recreation in Boston as to the art interest.[6] I certainly think you have reason to feel sore over the insults,—unspeakable: We have found the Copley Gallery people gentleman with a degree of confidence, almost artistic. Our present scheme of shipping direct from Boston to Paris avoiding our repacking anyway here will be a great saving of expenses. If this is not possible the boxing for Paris can be done in Boston sent direct to the stores for inspection by customs people. I have the intention of notifying Druet of the first shipment to satisfy him temporarily, in fact the customs have delayed this matter entirely. I wish you would have O'Brien pack the Van-Horne Cezanne and ship to Macbeth immediately[.] also I promised Mr. Andrews[7] the owner of the Ryder "Pegasus" it would not be away over a month. if this painting could also come with the Cezanne I would be happy on that score[.] I doubt the Chicago appreciation of such good wine yet . . .

with best wishes and regards
Faithfully, A. B. Davies

1. Galerie E. Druet, at 20 rue Royale in Paris, specialized in modern paintings.

2. Belle de Costa Greene was hired by J. P. Morgan to organize and manage his literary collections, which included rare books of hours and Gutenberg bibles.

3. J. P. (John Pierpont) Morgan (1837–1913), the financier.

4. Morgan's library was Belle Greene's domain.

5. Mrs. Morgan.

6. The Armory Show opened in Boston's Copley Hall on April 28 and closed on May 19. Because of the limited wall space in the hall, no works by American artists were shown. Both the crowds and sales there were disappointing.

7. J. R. Andrews.

Source of Letters: Archives of American Art, Smithsonian Institution, Arthur B. Davies Papers, reels 4216, 4217.

KATHERINE DREIER (1877–1952)

Artist, art patron, and founder of the Société Anonyme. Born in Brooklyn, she studied art for a decade at the Brooklyn Art Students League, Pratt Institute, and with private teachers, including Walter Shirlaw. Her work consisted mostly of academic portraits and still-lifes, but during a stay in Europe, from 1911 to 1913, her style revealed a more contemporary bent along the lines of van Gogh.

Ms. Dreier loaned a van Gogh oil to the Armory Show, and purchased lithographs by Gauguin and Odilon Redon from it. She also exhibited two of her own oils in the show, and it is probable that she initially met Walter Pach at that time.

In 1917 she helped organize the first Society of Independent Artists exhibition and exhibited there too. Three years later Katherine Dreier founded the Société Anonyme: Museum of Modern Art, together with Marcel Duchamp and Man Ray. Its goal was to educate the American public, and to this end she organized more than eighty shows, initially in two third-floor rooms in a 47th Street brownstone, but eventually in museums as well. Some of the exhibits she organized circulated to other cities, and Ms. Dreier lectured at many of the venues. She introduced American audiences to the works of Leger, Mondrian, Kandinsky, and Paul Klee, among others, and also promoted avant-garde musicians and dancers.

The activities of the Société Anonyme lessened after the founding of The Museum of Modern Art in 1929, and it was formally dissolved a dozen years later when the collection was donated to Yale University.

Dec. 16, 1920

Mr. Walter Pach,
New York, N.Y.

My dear Mr. Pach:

Thank you so much for lending us your picture of Derrain [*sic*]. It was mighty good of you to do so.

I wonder if you can come to my rescue? I am to hold three lectures on Modern Art in January and I am referring to pictures which were shown at the Armory Exhibition February 1913. 1 don't know what has happened to my catalogue—I can find it neither at my home nor at the Museum of Modern Art. Could you, therefore, tell me which of the Italian Futurists exhibited in the Armory? Did you bring over any of them this year? Also is there by chance any catalogue left of that Exhibition which I could have as well as another copy for our Reference Library? Are there any postcards left of that Exhibition belonging to the modern group? I would appreciate this co-operation enormously.

Very sincerely, [Katherine Dreier]

---

13 East 14th St.,
New York, December 21, 1920

My dear Miss Dreier,

Your letter of the 16th only reached me today.

There was no representation whatever of the Futurist group at the International Exhibition of 1913. The Futurists were invited to exhibit and were told they could have a room to themselves if they wanted it, so as to keep their artistic individuality intact. After some time they told me it would be impossible to send their pictures to America because of other engagements.[1]

The only Futurist work that has been exhibited here, to the best of my belief, is that of Mr. [Gino] Severini, which Mr. Stieglitz showed at "291" and of which I think some examples are still being taken care of by Mr. Stieglitz. Severini would be very glad if they could be sold,—and they are interesting works.

I don't know at all where you could get a catalogue or post-cards of the International. The only way would be to write to the various men connected with it. I have one copy, but want it myself—frankly.

Yours very sincerely, Walter Pach

1. In addition to concern among the Futurists that the Armory Show could only serve to increase confusion between the cubists and their group, they had been asked to participate in the "First International Roman Secession Exhibition" in Italy, and the dates of the two shows overlapped.

SUMMER ADDRESS:—WEST REDDING, CONN.,
TELEGRAMS:—DANBURY, CONN.
FROM OCTOBER 7TH ADDRESS:—
88 CENTRAL PARK WEST.
OCT. 4, 1926

Walter Pach
c/o Metropolitan Museum
New York City

My dear Mr. Pach:

I am in the midst of arranging a very important Exhibition of International Modern Art for the Brooklyn Museum and I am writing to ask whether I may not have the pleasure of having you send one or two of your paintings over to the Brooklyn Museum to be included in this Exhibition. Please send them as soon as possible and address them as follows:

	Brooklyn Museum,
For the	Eastern Parkway,
Société Anonyme.	Brooklyn, N.Y.

As we are in the midst of arranging a Special Catalog, a copy of which each artist represented in the Exhibition is to receive, besides a hundred of which are to be sent to museums throughout the world, I would like very much to have you send me a photograph of yourself with a short biographical sketch to be included, if you are participating.

Besides this, I am wondering whether it would not interest you to meet me some time at the Brooklyn Museum and go over a few of the very interesting pictures and pieces of sculpture which we have for articles which you might be interested in writing for some of the magazines. I should be only too happy to place this material at your disposal—but on one condition, that, of course, you mention that these pictures or sculptures are part of the big International Exhibition of Modern Art which the Société Anonyme has arranged for the Brooklyn Museum.

If you saw Duchamp in Paris you may have heard him mention this Exhibition, for he has been most kind in helping me to arrange it. In fact, I have had the most marvelous cooperation from all the leading men of Europe in our group. Besides Duchamp,

Leger helped in Paris, Mondrian of Holland, Bragaglia of Rome, Kandinsky from Russia and Schwitters and Campendonk from Germany, so that with all this assistance it naturally is quite an unusual assemblage we have gotten together.

With kind greetings and hoping that I may count on your cooperation, believe me,

Very sincerely yours, [Katherine Dreier]

---

48 West 56th St.,
New York, Oct. 7, 1926

My dear Miss Dreier,

Thank you for your letter of October 4th. Duchamp did tell me something about the exhibition at the Brooklyn Museum, and I am sure that it will be of the very greatest interest.

I shall be glad to send two paintings to it:—The Birth of Venus, and Flowers.

As to biographical material:—I was born in New York City in 1883; I studied under Leigh Hunt, William M. Chase and Robert Henri, continuing my study in Europe, for the most part independently, but with the influence or advice of many of the great French artists whose work I was seeing and some of whom I came to know in the years between 1903 and 1913, during most of which time I was in Paris. I am represented by etchings in the Metropolitan Museum, the New York Public Library, the Cleveland Museum and other public galleries. I have written, principally on modern art, for publications like Scribner's, Harper's, The Freeman, La Gazette des Beaux-Arts, L'Amour de l'Art, etc., and have lectured at many of the museums and universities here, beside the University of Mexico and the École du Louvre (in the courses arranged there by New York University). I have published "The Masters of Modern Art" and "Georges Seurat," and am the translator of Elie Faure's "History of Art."

. . . .

It will be a great pleasure to see the works in Brooklyn with you, and I hope when the exhibition is on you will let me know what time you will be there. I am in some doubt as to whether I shall be able to write any articles this winter, as I have just engaged on some work which looks as if it will demand every hour that I can take from painting. I shall know better about this later on, however; I should like to do some writing if I can arrange my time for it.

With regards, I am

Yours very sincerely, Walter Pach

SOCIETE ANONYME : MUSEUM OF MODERN ART : 1920

NEW YORK, JAN. 14, 1949

Mr. Walter Pach
c/o Marcel Duchamp
210 West 14th Street
New York, N.Y.

Dear Mr. Pach:

I wonder if you recollect what years Wanamaker's held the Modern Exhibition at the Belmaison.

I find that Gwodzeski[1] was represented, and since we have a few of his water colors in our Collection of the Société Anonyme, I was wondering if you could help me out by telling me anything you recollect regarding him. I believe he also was in the Quinn Collection.

I have always envied you, having that beautiful Duchamp painting, "The Chess Players," and I was so grateful when you lent it to Yale University Art Gallery last year for their exhibition. It means so much to me whenever I see it.

With kindest regards to you and your wife, believe me,

Sincerely yours, Katherine S. Dreier

1. Gustaw Gwozdecki, a painter and the founder/director of the Academy of Fine Arts in Paris beginning in 1913.

---

3 WASHINGTON SQUARE
NEW YORK, JAN. 19, 1949

Dear Miss Dreier,

I wish I had a clearer memory of the dates of that Belmaison Gallery—somewhere before/and or/after 1920. I did not go there very often. I suppose it's too obvious a suggestion to say—ask Wanamaker's.

At least I can say you are right about Quinn's having had Gwodzeski: in the catalogue it says "Three drawings, Nudes." I never knew the artist, or about him.

It was a satisfaction to me to have the Duchamp of *The Chess Players* in your show at Yale. It has always been one of the most impressive things we have—and, at the same time, one of the most appealing.

With kindest regards

Yours very sincerely, Walter Pach

New York, Sept. 6, 1949

Dear Mr. Pach:

I find that Guy Pène du Bois, in his book "Artists Say the Silliest Things," mentions that you were in the same class with Patrick Henry Bruce when you all studied with Henri.

I wonder if, by any chance, you could tell me approximately when he was born. I have entered it 1884 with a question mark. It is interesting that as far as we know Bruce's paintings are only to be found in the public collection of the Société Anonyme and in the private collection of Henri Pierre Roché in Paris.

If you can give us any data regarding him, both Roché and I would be tremendously appreciative of it, for Roché hopes, eventually, to write a brochure on Bruce.

It will interest you to know that Wanamaker never answered my letter, and so I have simply mentioned the exhibition at the Belmaison in connection with certain artists who exhibited there.

I also want to thank you very much for telling Marcel Duchamp about the coming exhibition in honor of the 100th anniversary of the birth of William Chase. I am having the Chase I have photographed and will send you a copy in case you hear of anybody who would be interested. I am asking a very modest price for it, for I must try and get some returns from somewhere to finish my research work for the Catalogue.

With all best wishes, believe me,

Cordially yours, Katherine S. Dreier

Source of Letters: Yale Collection of American Literature, Beinecke Rare Book and Manuscript Library, Yale University, which contains additional Dreier/Pach correspondence.

MARCEL DUCHAMP (1887–1968)

Painter, sculptor, and a principle pioneer of Dada. Born in Blainville, France, the younger brother of the painter Jacques Villon and the sculptor Raymond Duchamp-Villon, his art as a teenager was impressionistic and by 1910 resembled Fauvism. The following year Marcel Duchamp began creating canvases that combined Cubism with the multiple-image illusion of motion associated with Futurism; his *Nude Descending a Staircase, No 2* (1912) became at once the most infamous and famous painting exhibited at the Armory Show.

Walter Pach first viewed Duchamp's work in Paris' Section d'Or (Golden Section) Exhibition in October 1912, after which Pach was instrumental in having his paintings included at the Armory. As sales agent for the exhibition, Pach was responsible for selling the *Nude* and Duchamp's other three oils on display there. In 1915, a few months after the outbreak of World War I, Duchamp wrote to his American friend expressing an interest in coming to the United States if he could earn a living here. Pach encouraged the move and met Duchamp when he disembarked in New York City.[1] When the Society of Independent Artists was established in 1917 with the anti-academic precepts of "no jury, no prizes" for its exhibitions, Duchamp tested the accepted norms of art and esthetics by submitting to its initial exhibit one of his early "readymades," a urinal titled *Fountain*. Duchamp was one of the Society's founders, yet the board, including Pach, cast its democratic ideals aside and voted against inclusion of the piece. Duchamp resigned; he would not be represented in a Society annual until twenty-four years later.[2]

The correspondence between Walter Pach and Marcel Duchamp dates from 1913 to 1943.

1. Duchamp had previously worked as a librarian, and after Pach informed John Quinn of that fact (see Pach letter to Quinn, April 15, 1915), Quinn was able to assist Duchamp in obtaining a position at the Pierpont Morgan Library before year's-end.

2. The Duchamp oil in the 1941 exhibition was *Le Passage de la Vierge a la Mariée* (*The Passage from Virgin to Bride*) (1912), and it was loaned by Walter Pach. The painting was subsequently purchased by The Museum of Modern Art.

Neuilly sur Seine
9 rue Amiral de Joinville
Wednesday, July 2 [1913]

Dear Mr. Pach,

I have heard through my brothers all the good news regarding the exhibition in America.[1] I am very happy; and I thank you for the dedication with which you have defended our painting.[2] 1 wanted to write you for a long time, but I am so lazy that I am no longer trying to find an excuse for it.

There is also a matter of economics: Has the last 600 franc check been sent? —or is it just delayed? —I have not received it —Could it be lost in the mail? I am asking for your answer on a simple postcard —Are you working a lot?

I am very depressed at the moment and I do absolutely nothing. These are short unpleasant moments.

I will leave in August to spend some time in England.

The weather is very nice at Puteaux on Sunday, and you must miss taking part in our games in the garden.

Will you be back with us soon? Don't you miss Paris a little. We have had a visit from Mr. Torrey,[3] who is an excellent man. He seemed very happy to make our acquaintance—

Good bye, dear Mr. Pach, send us some news soon. Very cordially yours,

Marcel Duchamp

1. The Armory Show.

2. Duchamp's *Nude Descending a Staircase, No. 2*.

3. Frederic C. Torrey (1864–1935), who purchased the Duchamp *Nude*.

---

23 rue St. Hippolyte
Paris, January 19, 1915

My dear friend.

A thousand thanks for your nice letter. It really pleased me. I communicated it to the family,[1] who will write you too.

First, all my congratulations for your fatherhood. Please give Mrs. Pach all my wishes of long life for young Raymond —You must feel profoundly happy with the outcome.[2]

Jacques Villon must have written you; He still is near Amiens, but he has been at rest for two weeks.[3] that is about 20 kilometers at the rear of the trenches; The situation has not changed since you left. We still read the war communiques twice a day.

There is less impatience: a kind of hibernation of the blood: I feel better this way because I do not have to talk of and hear talk of this matter.

Raymond is still at St. Germain. From time to time, he speaks of a probable departure; but nothing is definite at the moment. Yvonne[4] is still at the hospital, delighted with her life as a nurse; she would not give her place for an empire (of Germany). I go there every ten days to spend the evening.

In Paris, life is dull as always. Since yesterday, we must avoid any light that could indicate Paris to the Zeppelins; from 6 o'clock on shops are half-closed, there are no longer light-signs; the streets are barely lit and at the first alert it is totally black. One goes to the movies, because plays are even less interesting. My sister-in-law Villon[5] will probably leave for the North as a nurse sometime soon. She is happy about it, she might be able to see her husband. This is less probable.

I have been considered by the discharge board: and I have been condemned to remain a civilian for the entire duration of the war. They found me too *sick* to be a soldier.[6] I am not too sad about this decision: you know it well.

So I keep on working with regularity, for a few hours each day, I am very tired at the moment. I have not yet finished my red thing on glass.[7] I think I will complete it at the end of February.

I have not seen any artist for a long time. I do not know if Brancusi has left Paris. I do not think so. I will pay him a visit one of these days.

The Montparnasse is still as ever. I am writing you from the library, where life is even longer than in peace time. This tells you how little there is to do.

News of the sale of the watercolor[8] and the prints gave us great pleasure and we are happy if your efforts have not been in vain, my dear Pach.

Is life in New York still following the consequences of the war or is this crisis over? Surely it is.

Thank you also for the catalogues. Here, there are naturally no exhibitions. Flags are the only things in color that one can see.

There are a few concerts on Sundays, rather meager, without German music.

Write a note from time to time. I am also very lazy about writing myself.

Will you come to Paris this Summer as you had told me?

Please give my regards to Mrs. Pach and give a kiss to young Raymond for me.

Very amicably yours,

Marcel Duchamp

1. His brothers Raymond Duchamp-Villon (1876–1918), the sculptor, and Jacques Villon (1875–1963), the painter, both of whom were serving at the time in the French army.

2. Raymond Pach, born the previous month, was named for Raymond Duchamp-Villon.

3. He was drafted into the infantry soon after the outbreak of World War I in August 1914.

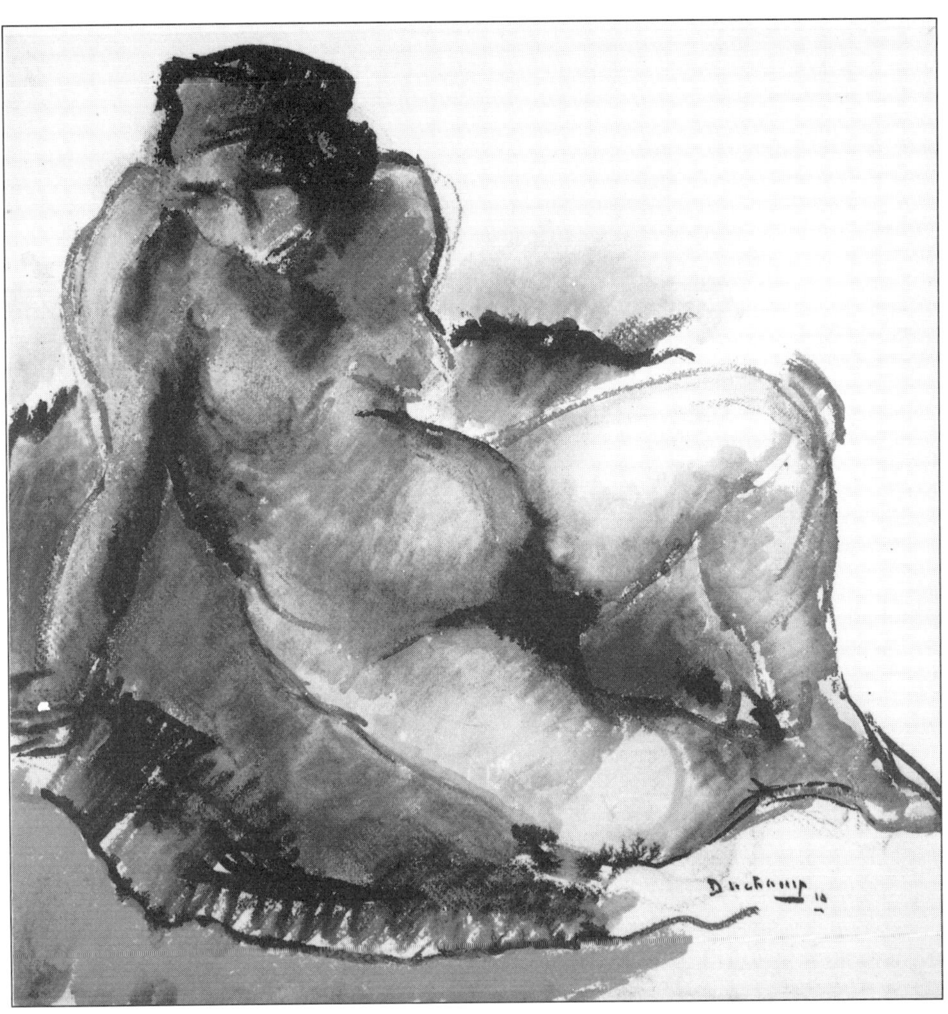

Marcel Duchamp, *Nude (Dark Skin)*, 1910. Watercolor 18 x 18 in. Philadelphia Museum of Art: The Louise and Walter Arensberg Collection: Acc. 1950-134-933.

4. Raymond Duchamp-Villon's wife.

5. Gabrielle Boeuf, wife of Jacques Villon.

6. Duchamp was prevented from serving due to a rheumatic heart.

7. A possible reference to his 9 *Malic Molds* (1914–1915).

8. The watercolor must have been Duchamp's *Dark Skin* (1910), purchased from the Carroll Galleries by John Quinn earlier in the month this letter was written.

Paris, March 12 [1915]

My dear friend,

I read your letter to Raymond and the good news about you. I also got the reproduction of my drawing in the newspaper.

I just received the Matisse catalogue; this exhibition must have been very interesting by its importance and its diversity.[1] I recall very well his painting of the "Gold Fish" and the reproduction is good.

Here the war lasts. . . . We always have excellent news from Villon; good health, good morale, almost gay: he amazes us all with his endurance; one talks of the "big spring blow" which ought to be decisive; . . . one expects to see the end of the war this summer (before vacation). . . .

Since my return I have been working a lot; I am finishing the bits of glass I had begun and am preparing the top of my painting.[2]

Raymond is still happy at St. Germain, his wife is a nurse there at the hospital as you know; I go there pretty often we play games of poker and we imagine ourselves being very far away from the events— . . .

I have heard that Delaunay[3] was or is leaving for America. Do you know anything about it?

The artistic life of Mont Parnasse is still as always although I know very little about it now. I have not met any painter of my acquaintance. . . . I must absolutely go see Brancusi.

From Picasso, from Braque, from Derain I have no news.

How are Mrs. Pach and young Raymond. . . .[4]

Good bye now, dear friend, I promise to write you more often . . . a thousand tokens of my friendship—

Marcel Duchamp

1. Pach organized the first fully representative one-man show by Matisse to be held in the United States; it was shown at the Montross Gallery in New York from January 20 to February 17, 1915, and consisted of fourteen paintings, eleven sculptures, and nearly fifty drawings and prints.

2. The "bits of glass" are those referred to in the previous letter. "Preparing the top of my painting" is probably a reference to his full-size sketch for *The Bride Stripped Bare by Her Bachelors, Even (The Large Glass)*.

3. Robert Delaunay (1885–1941), who had developed his colorful, circular abstract compositions labeled Orphism by the time this letter was written.

4. This Raymond refers to the Pachs' three-month-old son, who was named for Duchamp's brother, Raymond.

Paris, April 2 [1915]

My dear friend,

I received your letter of March 9 which brought us the good news of the sale at the exhibition. On behalf of Raymond and Villon I am reporting to you how happy they are. . . .

Now here is what interests me particularly: I have absolutely decided to leave France. As I had told you last November, I would willingly live in New York. But only *on the condition* that I could earn my living there. 1st. Do you think that I could easily find a job as a librarian or something analogous that *would leave me great freedom* to work (Some information about me: I do not speak English, I graduated with my Baccalaureate in literature (don't you laugh!!), I worked for two years at the Bibliothèque Ste. Geneviève as an intern. —2nd. I will leave here at the end of May at the earliest. Do you think that this is a good time or should I rather wait until September. I have told no one about this plan. Thus I ask you to answer me on this topic on a separate sheet in your letter so that my brothers do not know anything before my resolution is completely made. . . .

Very cordially yours, Marcel Duchamp

Cafe-Restaurant L. MOLLARD
Hotel Anglo Americain
April 27 [1915]
113–115–117 Rue Saint Lazare
Paris, April 27 [1915]

My dear friend

. . . I . . . sense great discouragement in your letter! You miss Paris, yes, I understand this very well because here you were living the free life of an artist with all the joys and all the hard times that one likes to remember —My stay in New York is a very different matter. I do not go there to seek what is missing in Paris. I do not hope to find anything there but individuals —If you remember our talks on the Boulevards St. Michel and Raspail, you will see my intention to depart as a necessary consequence of these conversations. —*I do not go to New York I leave Paris.* It is altogether different.

For a long time and even before the war, I have disliked this "artistic life" in which I was involved. —It is the exact opposite of what I want. So I had tried to somewhat escape from the artists through the library. Then during the war, I felt increasingly more incompatible with this milieu. I absolutely wanted to leave. Where to? New York was my only choice, because I knew you there. I hope to be able to avoid an artistic life there, possibly with a job which would keep me very busy. . . . Yet, since you warn me against New York, if I cannot live there any more than Paris, I could always come back, or go somewhere else. —I have repeated to you my preoccupation to earn enough money to live there securely. It is a necessary consequence . . . I am very happy when I learn that you have sold these canvases and I thank you very sincerely for your friendship. But *I am afraid to end up being* in need to sell canvases, in other words, *to be a society painter.* —I will probably leave on May 22nd or possibly 29th . . .

I hope (?) to find here the promise of a position. (This is problematic). In any case, I beg you not to believe that my brothers think you might be pressuring me. The three of us have too much confidence and friendship for you. I am sure that they will find at least some comfort in knowing that I will be there with you. . . . All my respects, and all my friendship and a military salute for young Raymond.

M. Duchamp

PARIS, MAY 21, 1915

My dear friend.

I received your letter of May 7. In fact, I understand your uncertainty. One has to take these moments as calmly as possible while keeping up hope. . . .

I went to the Transatlantic Company. There is no departure on May 29. The "Rochambeau" will leave on June 5. And it is almost certain that I will leave on that day. . . .

Regarding my stay there I am determined to take a job even if it prevents me from painting. Too bad! Above all, don't you worry in the least, my dear friend. I am bothered enough to cause you so much trouble. But I hope to make it up to you. . . .

Marcel Duchamp

[JULY 28, 1915]

My dear Pach—

I saw your father at "Nicholas."[1] He told me to come pick up the sample of my photo. It is very good. Now tell me: is it for Vanity Fair, or for me? Do I have to bring it to this publication? Give me your instructions.

One thing that will interest you more: Mr. [John] Quinn telephoned me on Saturday morning at 11. I had been to see him at his house for two minutes and he invited me for the same evening . . . I was able to understand better what you had told me. Besides our conversation remained general, and the more difficult for me since no one spoke a word of French.

But I managed—Did not say a word about you, or course—Discretion—Not a word about [Arthur B.] Davies either. —Mr. Quinn, in fact, could be for me a hearty supporter. I appreciated him even more than the first time. He is very anxious to know whether Cubism was killed by the war and he has general questions about art and Europe over the next three years: As soon as my English will allow me to do so I promise to make him give up this "political" vision of art . . .

Cordially yours, M. Duchamp

1. This probably refers to having seen Pach's father in the offices of *St. Nicholas: An Illustrated Magazine for Young Folk*, located in The Century Co. building.

Source of Letters: Archives of American Art, Smithsonian Institution, Marcel Duchamp Papers, reel 4217.

English Translation: Francis M. Naumann, "amicalement, Marcel: Fourteen Letters from Marcel Duchamp to Walter Pach," *Archives of American Art Journal* 29, nos. 3, 4 (1989): 36–50.

SUSAN MACDOWELL EAKINS (1851–1938)

Artist and wife of painter Thomas Eakins. Her father, a well-known Philadelphia engraver, encouraged her interest in art. After viewing Eakins's canvas, *The Gross Clinic*, in 1876, she was sufficiently impressed to enroll as a student of his at The Pennsylvania Academy of the Fine Arts, in which classes she remained for seven years. During that time, Susan Macdowell's work was included in six of the academy's annual exhibits and was awarded two prizes. Following her marriage to Eakins in 1884, however, she subordinated her own career to his. After Thomas Eakins's death in 1916, Susan Eakins undertook the task of placing his remaining works in various exhibitions and museum collections. In 1929 Mrs. Eakins accepted the offer of the Philadelphia Museum of Art's director, Fiske Kimball, to donate a large body of Eakins's art to his hometown institution. One of the canvases, a portrait titled *Clara* (ca. 1900), was selected by the Louvre Museum, through the efforts of Walter Pach, for inclusion in its permanent collection. In a 1933 magazine article,[1] Pach explained how this came about without revealing that he was the "American painter residing in Paris for a time" who

> chanced to possess a picture by his older compatriot. . . . He took the picture under his arm, trudged up the endless spiral staircase to the attic of the museum . . . and showed his treasure to M. Jean Guiffrey, the head of the department of paintings, and to the late M. Raymond Koechlin, the president of the *Amis du Louvre*, who had dropped in for a chat with the curator.
>
> Neither of the gentlemen was familiar with the work of Eakins. But M. Guiffrey was keen for a picture by the artist at once. . . . "Will you give part of the cost of an Eakins, if I raise the rest by subscription at home?" asked the American. . . . None was needed, however, for Mrs. Eakins . . . would not hear of setting a price on a work for the great gallery where her husband had profited so deeply in his student years [so] a

fine canvas was obtained for the Louvre from the collection of works by Mr. Eakins given by his widow to the Pennsylvania Museum.

The Walter Pach-Susan Eakins letters date from 1926 to 1937.

1. Walter Pach, "American Art in the Louvre," *Fine Arts* 20 (May 1933), 20, 48.

MRS. THOMAS EAKINS
1729 MOUNT VERNON STREET
PHILADELPHIA, OCT. 10, 1928

Dear Mr. Pach

. . . Just now I am in the midst of disorder, having some of the old rooms repaired, and it does seem such work takes all attention and considerable labor moving things around. I have, however, been able to keep the path way around the pictures clear, while the repairing is going on . . .

As a rule, I do not think people want to hurry in selecting pictures. And whether it is the desire to purchase or not, I am always pleased to show my husbands pictures

The portrait of Charles Linford, had a small hole in the background, and it is away at present being repaired by Thomas Stevenson.

About the Rush picture,[1] I have decided that it would be best to make a group of all canvases & studies pertaining to the subject, and if possible keep it in Philadelphia. I have them gathered together in my studio. . . .

Very sincerely, Susan M. Eakins

1. *William Rush Carving His Allegorical Figure of the Schuylkill* (1876–1877). Oil on canvas, 20-1/8 x 26-1/8″.

PHILADELPHIA, OCT. 21, 1930

Dear Mr. Pach.

. . . I think I wrote you that an exhibition was proposed of Eakins works—in New York City—but it is not at all determined or sure. I have been preparing for it, new frames and a careful examination of the canvases by the good painter Charles Bregler—a beloved & devoted pupil of my husband. Mr. Bregler has found painting done on some of the pictures, probably done while away on exhibition, also so often varnished as to obscure the original tone. His work has been so fine and surprising, that I

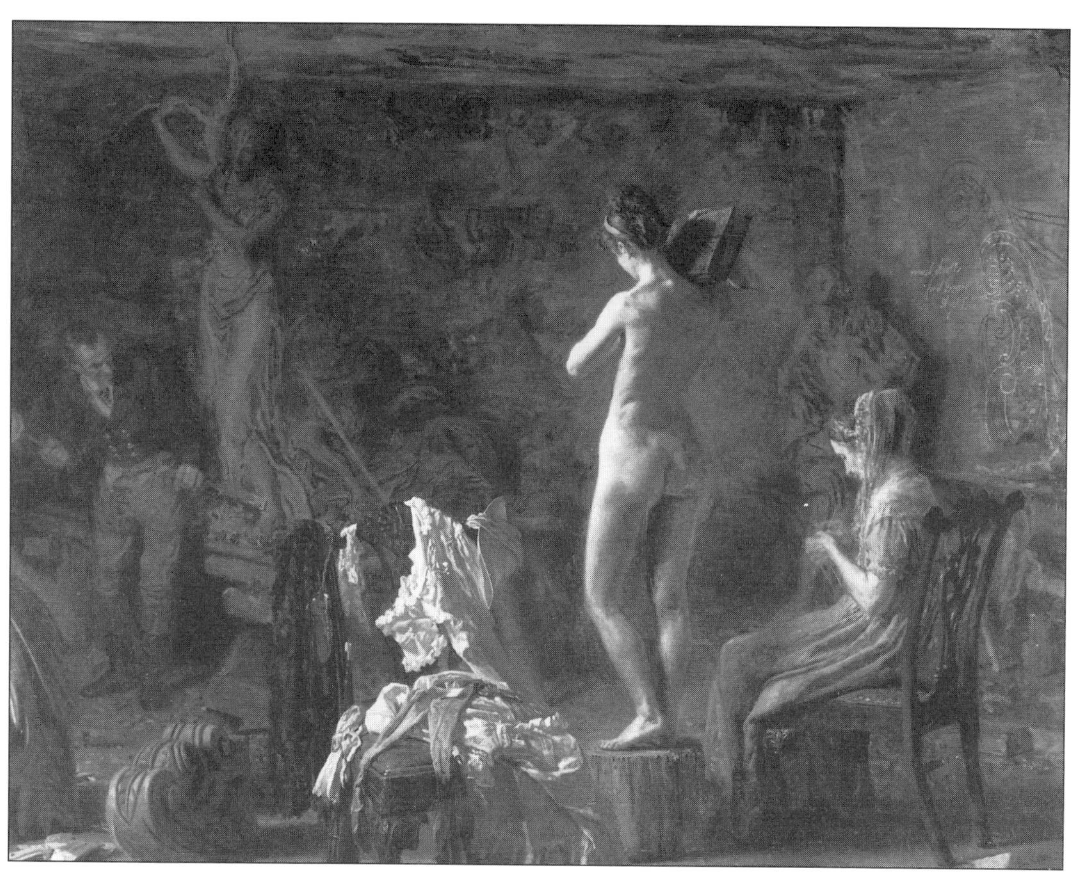

Thomas Eakins, *William Rush Carving His Allegorical Figure of the Schuylkill*, 1876-77. Oil on canvas on masonite, 20 1/8 x 26 1/8 in. Philadelphia Museum of Art: Gift of Mrs. Thomas Eakins and Miss Mary Adeline Williams. Acc. 1929-184-27. Photograph by Graydon Wood 1992.

am having fine glass placed over some, hoping that will insure their safety against ignorant, if not mischievous retouching. Whether I can exhibit or not I am glad to have Mr. Bregler take care of them for me. . . .

I have made a rough little drawing of this study which was made while working in the schools in Paris, it may help you to decide, and if you would prefer to have it sent on to you, and find it is not the one you saw at Brummers[1] do not hesitate to return it when you return to the States [Pach was in Paris]. I like the modeling particularly of the neck, and will be glad to have it back, but if it is the one you want, I am glad to give it to you. I have often wondered what became of the many studies

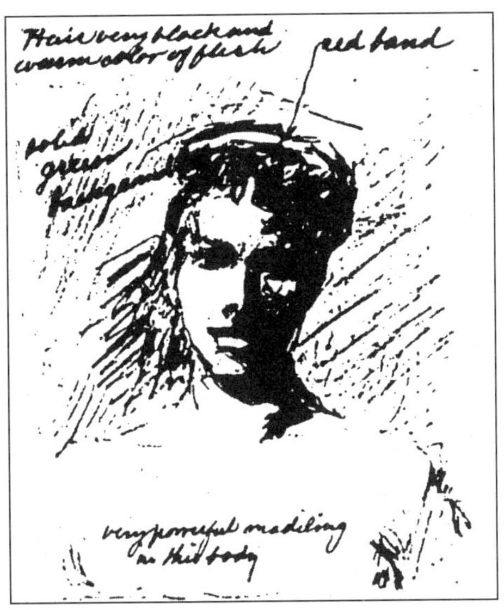

my husband made in the school,[2] also he thought it most excellent to make memory studies of what he was working at from the models. He brought only a few back with him. . . .

Very sincerely yours, Susan M. Eakins

1. Joseph C. Brummer Galleries in New York.

2. École des Beaux Arts, Paris.

PHILADELPHIA, JAN. 25, 1931

Dear Mr. Pach.

. . . It is very kind of you to interest the Louvre in the Eakins work—presently I hope to send you some photographs—I think possibly not before March, as nearly all the pictures (my walls are bare) are in New York—and I would like to get very good prints to send—I could have them photographed in this house. I too, like the Charles Linford portrait, as a possible one—I would prefer to present a picture, rather than sell—so we will not worry about prices—I feel tenderly about Paris, where my husband studied and loved his master Jerome [Gerome].

. . . A very curious, I think stupid mistake, is made in the articles on the Eakins work—they report that the little seated figure of Thomas Eakins, was his favorite attitude while painting. He only took that position when painting the lower part of large canvases. Imagine him painting the "Gross" or "Agnew"[1] or any life size subject squatting on the floor—I remember at the Metropolitan Museum 1917 exhibition they wanted the seated figure—I rebelled—I like it, but, the standing figure represents Mr. Eakins best . . .

I hope I have not tired you.

from Susan M. Eakins

1. *The Gross Clinic* and *The Agnew Clinic*, his two largest oils.

PHILADELPHIA, FEB. 19, 1931

Dear Mr. Pach

Thanking you for your kind interest with regard to presenting an Eakins painting for the acceptance of the Louvre. In compliance with my promise to you, I am sending photographs of the paintings, which I believe would most surely represent the character of my husband's work

The "Hamilton"[1] is so completely American in subject and character, is my choice. The canvas is 80 inches high–50 inches wide The "Barker"[2] and the "Wallace"[3] equally fine in understanding

The Barker canvas 60 inches high—40 inches wide

The Wallace canvas 50 [inches high—]/[inches wide]

Charles Bregler who was a pupil of my husband, and an artist himself is most interested and appreciative of the work, thinks with you that the Linford[4] is beautiful, but agrees with me in the choice of Hamilton as does Samuel.Murray, Clarence M. Cranmer and David Wilson Jordan.[5]

My sister in law, Mrs. Wm. G. Macdowell who owns the portrait of my father with the big hat,[6] suggested that for the Louvre. She is heart and soul with me whatever is done. I cannot find a photo of that portrait. I hope however they will be interested to have one of those I have suggested.

I am including a photo. of my husband, taken while he was a student in Paris—I believe it should add to the interest.

The photographs of the pictures I suggest—I believe were made from plates—The Metropolitan Museum owns, made during the Exhibition of Eakins 1917.[7]

There have [been] two exhibitions of Eakins—the last one, at 5 East 56th St.[8] is still going and in their show have the three I send the photos of, I think they will close soon.

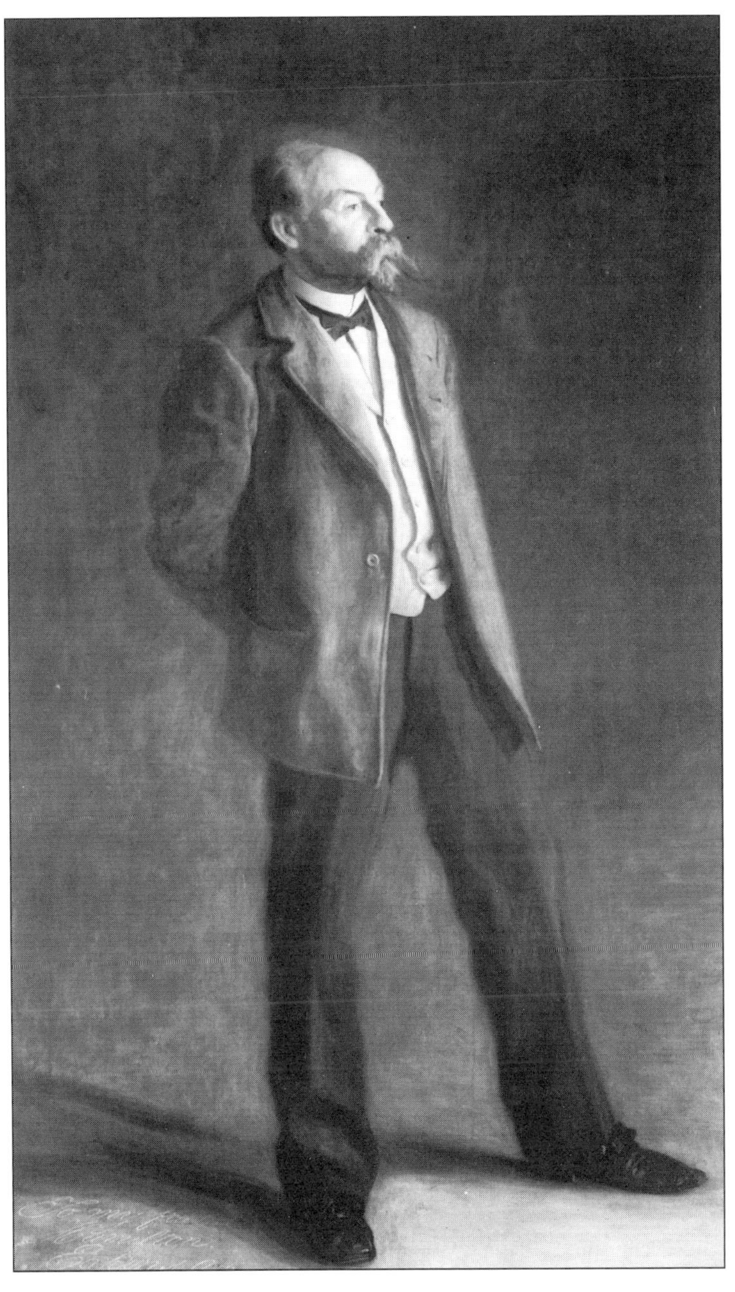

Thomas Eakins, *Portrait of John McLure Hamilton*, 1895. Oil on canvas, 79 1/16 x 49 in. Wadsworth Athenum, Hartford, The Ella Gallup Sumner and Mary Catlin Sumner Collection Fund. Acc. 1947.399.

I did not go to New York—at all, so cannot describe any thing of the many interesting affairs of New York, you told one of your water-colors to be at the Metropolitan Museum—Besides not being there, I have not met any folks interested in Art, who have been in New York. Mrs. Macdowell is still very much troubled with sciatica—I feel so sorry for her, she is so uncomplaining and cheerful, and does love to be interested—and yet is unable to get about comfortably.

Mr. Cramer [*sic*] goes often to New York and has met up with Mr. Brummer,[9] whom he is very fond of

Cranmer is a good fellow—been a sport all his life, and I think it delights him to think that Joseph Brummer likes a fight

We have had a long spell of clear weather, so near like Spring that the trees and birds are deceived—poor things. I look for a blizzard or something unusual to pay for our gentle winter.

I hope Mrs. Pach and you have kept well, and able to enjoy fully your life and painting in France, also best wishes for your boy.

I hope I have not tired you.

Very sincerely, Susan M. Eakins

1. *Portrait of John McLure Hamilton*, 1895. Oil on canvas. Hamilton (1853–1936) was a Portrait painter.

2. *Portrait of Professor George F. Barker*, 1886. Oil on canvas. The painting had been awarded the Thomas B. Clark prize for "the best American figure composition painted in the United States" at the 1888 National Academy of Design Annual. Barker was a Professor of Chemistry at the University of Pennsylvania and had collaborated with Eakins on his Eadweard Muybridge Commission.

3. *Portrait of J. Laurie Wallace*, c. 1885. Oil on canvas. An Eakins pupil who posed for several of his instructor's paintings, Wallace became an instructor at The Art Institute of Chicago.

4. *Portrait of Charles Linford*, c. 1895. Oil on canvas. Linford (1846–1897) was a landscape artist.

5. Murray (1870–1941) and Jordan had been Eakins students; Cranmer wrote for the Philadelphia *Ledger* and was Susan Eakins's agent for the sale of her husband's paintings after his death.

6. *William H. Macdowell with a Hat*, c. 1898. Oil on canvas.

7. The Metropolitan's Memorial Exhibition, held during November 1917.

8. She meant to write 5 East 57th Street, site of the Babcock Gallery.

9. Joseph C. Brummer, who owned a gallery in New York.

Philadelphia, Feb. 21, 1931

Dear Mr. Pach

I am following my letter of Feb 19th with this letter to tell you Mr. Cranmer[1] has just informed me that the Bertelli Gallery on 56th Street had arranged for the sale of the John McClure Hamilton. They did not understand that this picture was one I wanted presented for the choice of one for the Louvre.

This of course prevents my offering the "Hamilton"[2] but they distincly [*sic*] understand now that the "Barker"[3] and the "Wallace,"[4] are out of their hands until I free them for further exhibition.

I hope I am not giving you trouble.

I would like very much to present a picture, at the same time, I realize the considerations that ensue as to choice of subject, & size & so forth.

With kind regards

Very truly, Susan M. Eakins

1. Clarence Cranmer, a Philadelphia newspaperman who became Mrs. Eakins's agent for the sale of her husband's work after his death.

2. *Portrait of John McClure Hamilton* (1895). Oil on canvas, 79-1/16 x 49″.

3. *Portrait of Professor George F. Barker* (1886). Oil on canvas, 24 x 20″.

4. *Portrait of J. Laurie Wallace* (c. 1885). Oil on canvas, 50 1/4 x 32 1/2″.

MORGAN & CO. 14 PLACE VENDOME
PARIS, MARCH 6, 1931

Dear Mrs. Eakins,

I have three letters of yours to acknowledge: the very friendly and interesting one written on receipt of my news from the Louvre, the one accompanying the photographs and the one announcing the withdrawal of the Hamilton picture. I also have a letter from Mr. Cranmer telling me that the Buffalo art gallery wants that work,—for which I am glad.

I took the photographs to M. Guiffrey, the curator of paintings at the Louvre and, though he was greatly interested in them, he said that those catalogue reproductions did not do the pictures sufficient justice (in the absence of an original work to show the quality), so he begged me to try to get him real photographs which should render the clearness, tone, and detail that he remembered from the picture which I was so happy to be able to show him. Such matters always have to come before a committee of the museum, some members of which are administrative men, others are archaeologists, Orientalists, etc.—at all events not the specialists of painting who are accustomed to distinguish the essential qualities of a work even from a half-tone reproduction, (which is not an easy matter, even so).

So, in order to facilitate matters, I wrote in a letter to Bryson Burroughs (to whom I had to send some lines today on another matter)—that I should be obliged if he sent you (or me) good photographs of the Professor Barker and the J. Laurie Wallace [paintings].

Another matter that M. Guiffrey discussed was the size of the work. Although the Louvre is so big it is not unlimited and is pretty well filled. Many pictures are off the walls for lack of space, though gradual reorganization will provide more. But, as a general principle, a smaller picture can more readily be placed in a desirable position than a large one. He had seen only the one work by Mr. Eakins which I have, and, remembering its size, was not quite prepared for canvases as large as these. Of course the Hamilton picture now withdrawn, was the biggest one, and you will understand that he does not at all put large ones out of consideration, but said that it was always easier to give a good place to works of smaller size. Even so, I want the representation to be by an important canvas, like the ones which you suggest.

And perhaps I should have said at the outset that M. Guiffrey, as also one of the other curators, were deeply appreciative of your good feeling toward the Louvre and want me to thank you most heartily for your offer. M. Guiffrey looked at the photograph of Mr. Eakins at the time when he was with Gerome,[1] and said—"Yes, that brings back the whole period, doesn't it?" The period, so rich in great men, is one that is constantly gaining in people's esteem. I cannot forbear adding that my own personal favorite, Barye,[2] grows more splendid the more I see of him—and I have discovered several admirable judges and collectors who think the same. And the French people I have known are always strongly moved by the loyalty of those who have worked with them. So you can see how pleasant it is for me,—after having M. Guiffrey express such admiration for the painting—to hear him speak with such appreciation of your willingness to present a work by Mr. Eakins. I repeat that both he and M. Koechlin were ready to purchase a picture—their only doubt being as to its price in relation to their limited budget which (I am certain) American admirers of the artist would have been ready to supplement.

I think the best plan would be for you to drop a line to Mr. Burroughs[3] saying which photographs you want. The elimination of the Hamilton might suggest some other to replace it. There was an admirable photograph of the Linford made by Mr. Brummer's photographer, Carl Klein, and I am sure he could furnish a print of it. Or Mr. Burroughs might have some favorite which would still be available. With his long-standing and deep admiration for the work of Mr. Eakins, I am sure that his opinion would be worth consulting—especially as he has the type of judgment on desirability for a museum which would be especially useful here. He might have a photograph of Mrs. Macdowell's portrait of her father-in-law or Carl Klein, again, may have one. I am still strong for the Linford and am glad Mr. Bregler[4] likes it too. Thank you for your cordial support of my idea.[5]

We are all well and working hard and happily. My wife joins me in sending you our best wishes.

Always faithfully yours

Walter Pach

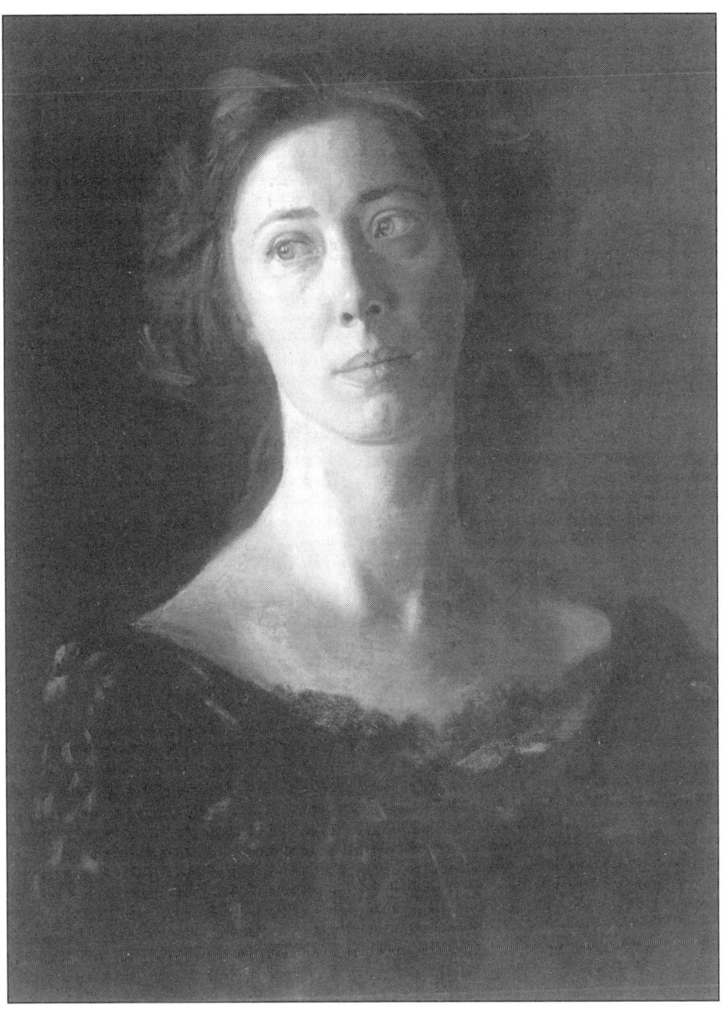

Thomas Eakins, *Clara* (Clara J. Mather), ca. 1900. Oil on canvas, 24 x 20 in. Musée d'Orsay, Paris.

1. Jean-Léon Gérôme (1824–1904), with whom Eakins studied at the École des Beaux-Arts.

2. Antoine-Louis Barye (1796–1875), France's premier sculptor-painter of animals.

3. Bryson Burroughs (1869–1934), curator of painting at the Metropolitan Museum of Art and a friend of Pach's (see Pach-Burroughs letters, p. 126).

4. Charles Bregler (1864–1958), a student of Thomas Eakins who, following Eakins's death in 1916, preserved his art and memorabilia, and became a friend of Susan Eakins.

5. The painting ultimately accepted for the Louvre collection was *Clara* (Clara J. Mather), c.1900. Oil on canvas. It measures 24 x 20″ and is currently in the Pompidou Center in Paris.

PHILADELPHIA, MARCH 28, 1931

Dear Mr. Pach

I received your letter and acted on your advice to consult Mr. Burroughs and Mr. Brummer. I have not heard from Mr. B. I think probably he may not write me until he has found it possible to send better photographs.

A note from Mr. Brummer, tells me he will find if Klein has negatives, will get him to make some prints and send them to you. . . .

I would think the portrait of J. Carroll Beckwith[1] would be interesting—The head I have always felt a great lesson in good construction and color. If I can find a photograph I will send it, the size framed, 54 x 90. . . .

I appreciate very much your kind interest about the picture for the Louvre

With kindest wishes for Mrs. Pach & yourself

Very sincerely, Susan M. Eakins

1. Beckwith (1852–1917) had taught at the New York School of Art and been a member of the Society of American Artists.

PHILADELPHIA, JUNE 27, 1931

Dear Mr. Pach

Your letter announcing the choice of pictures for the Louvre arrived to me a few days ago. The choice pleases me, the others thought of are just as fine. The Eakins work has all the same quality, so it is which one, happens to please best.

You have given your consideration and time to this matter and written me careful interested letters, which I do appreciate very much, Mrs. Pach and you [are] both so kind and thoughtful for my sake. . . .

Wishing every happiness & success for Mrs. Pach and yourself and best wishes for your boy.

Sincerely yours, Susan M. Eakins

Source of Letters: Archives of the Pennsylvania Academy of the Fine Arts. Also available through the Archives of American Art, Smithsonian Institution, Mrs. Susan M. Eakins Papers, reels 4218, 4235.

ARTHUR BURDETT FROST JR. (1887–1917)

The son of Arthur Burdett Frost, the well-known illustrator of the *Uncle Remus* and *Br'er Rabbit* stories and a painter of realistic hunting and fishing scenes. Arthur Jr. studied at the New York School of Art, where he was a fellow student with Walter Pach under William Merritt Chase and Robert Henri. (Pach once told me how George Bellows, also in the Henri class, helped set a fire under Frost's chair in order to "thaw his name.")[1] Frost accompanied his parents to Paris in 1906 and enrolled in the Académie Julian at his father's urging; however, after renewing friendships with Patrick Henri Bruce, who had also studied at the New York school, the two of them came under progressively avant-garde influences, first in a class taught by Henri Matisse and then through meeting Robert Delaunay, who encouraged their experimentation with colorful abstractions. These latter associations caused the elder Frost to complain with increasing bitterness that his son had degraded his talent and that when he eventually came to his senses, it would be too late.

All but one of the accompanying letters were written to Pach by the elder Frost after the death of his son, which occurred four days before his thirtieth birthday. While his demise has been attributed to a life of dissipation which proved fatal, the January 5, 1918 letter by Frost to Pach implies that the father was responsible for killing his own offspring.

1. Interview with Walter Pach, September 5, 1952.

Hotel National
Davos-Platz, Switzerland, May 5, 1912

Dear Pach

I am very glad to hear from you: I haven't written to you because my eyes are in a bad way and I have been obliged to cut my writing down to answering only letters of necessity. . . .

Arthur[1] is pronounced cured and goes away from here next Wednesday, the 8th. He is going to Munich to stay a few days but will be in Paris on the 13th. He has an apartment in the same house as the Bruces,[2] their old apartment, 6 Rue Furstenberg. He will be there till they go to the country, which will be soon. He is in better health than for a long time, his year up here has been a good thing for him. . . .

Sincerely always, Arthur B. Frost

1. Frost's son, Arthur Burdett Frost Jr.

2. Patrick Henry Bruce, formerly a fellow student in Henri's class; and his wife.

---

32 Crescent Road
Madison, N.J., Jan. 5, 1918

Dear Pach

I thank you sincerely for your sympathy and for your very kind letter.

You say in your letter that it was senseless and wrong to take my boys life, you never said anything truer.[1] Senseless wrong and cruel, hard and cruel, he loved life and had everything to live for and it is cruel.

I can't believe that he is gone. I can't realize it, it seems to me he *must* come back to me.

He is buried at the little Church of St James the Less near Philadelphia, where we were married.

I would like to see you very much: I would like to talk to you about my boy's work. I was not in sympathy with it as you know, but it was his and I have great respect for it.

Do you think, if you wrote a short appreciation of his work and what he was trying to do that Scribner's would publish it in the Field of Art?[2] Mr. Scribner is one of my dearest and most intimate friends and I know he would put it in the Magazine, but I do not want to do it in that way, I would rather it went in on its merits I have read all your articles . . . and they are very good. . . . Would you like to do it? It would give me a great deal of gratification if you would. Just a short little article. Please tell me what you think of it and be *perfectly frank* with me. I know you are a true friend to both my dear boy and me.

Thank you again for your very kind true letter

Very sincerely yours always, Arthur Burdett Frost

1. Arthur Jr. died on December 7, 1917; the terse announcement in the next day's *New York Times* simply referred to the death as sudden, which would seem to contradict a theory that he died of dissipation.

2. Pach did write the article, which appeared in *Scribner's Magazine* the following May (vol. 63, pages 637–639) under the title "Some Reflections on Modern Art Suggested by the Career of Arthur B. Frost, Jr." The photograph of the young Frost taken by his father, which is referred to in the following letters, did not accompany it.

Feb. 1, 1918

My dear Pach

Mrs. Frost and I like your second article *very* much. I want Jack[1] to read it, he will be home this evening and I will return it to you tomorrow.

I think it is very remarkable how well you remember the different stages of Arthurs progress. it shows a great interest in him and a fondness for him for which Mrs Frost and I are very grateful to you.

I have a very good negative I made of him about eighteen months ago. do you think Carington would use a print of it if you showed it to him? I am going to print some from it tomorrow and will send you one for yourself and another to show Carington, for if he uses it the engraver will spoil the print. they always have done so in my experience.

I will return the article to you tomorrow.

Very gratefully and faithfully yours, Arthur Burdett Frost

1. Jack was the Frosts' surviving son.

Undated [February 1918]

Dear Pach

Thank you for the M.S. [manuscript] I am very glad to have it. I was afraid the photograph of Arthur would be too much for the Magazine as I know they do not want to give too much space to him. I am very glad indeed that they will publish the article. I will take very good care of the M.S. and put it away with Arthurs things.

I am sending you the pictures of him which I took in Wayne[1] about eighteen months ago. They are not as handsome as my boy but they are very like him and to me are the best I have of him. He was very much sunburned and his skin was shiny making the pictures hard . . .

Very sincerely yours always, Arthur Burdett Frost

1. Wayne, Pennsylvania, outside of Philadelphia. Frost's parents had moved there in 1914.

Source of Letters: Archives of American Art, Smithsonian Institution, Arthur B. Frost Letters, reel 4217, which contains additional Frost/ Pach letters.

CHILDE HASSAM (1859–1935)

A painter and etcher, and a leading exponent of American Impressionism. Born in Dorchester, Massachusetts, he began his art career as a book illustrator, but by the time he was in his mid-twenties he was producing academic oils of Boston streetscapes, mostly depicted in inclement weather. Hassam traveled to Paris in 1887, enrolled briefly at the Académie Julian, and during a two-year stay became enamored of Impressionism; upon returning to the United States those early, gray city scenes were replaced by a lighter, brighter palette and increasingly short, deft brushstrokes.

A decade after his initial trip to Paris, Childe Hassam returned to France, on this occasion to Pont-Aven in Brittany, where a number of painters among The Nabis, followers of Gauguin, had worked in an Impressionist manner. Back in New York, it was Hassam who conceived the idea of forming a group of American Impressionists to protest the patronage by American collectors of French artists of that style. Through Childe Hassam's efforts such a group, labeled Ten American Painters, was brought into existence. Their first of twenty annual exhibitions was held in New York's Durand-Ruel Gallery during April 1898.

Hassam painted Manhattan for three decades, eventually concentrating on the cityscapes of Fifth Avenue. During this time it was his practice to paint out-of-doors in the French Impressionist manner, either at street level or from a bird's eye perch on a balcony.

Hassam's initial, extant letter to Pach expresses thanks for reminding him to submit work to the First Annual Exhibition of The Society of Independent Artists.

March 21, 1917

Dear Mr. Pach

Thanks for taking the time to write me—I thought I was late for the exhibition[1] and I told Milch[2] to call you up and see about time limit. With good luck to you I am sincerely

Childe Hassam

1. The First Annual Exhibition of The Society of Independent Artists, held in the Grand Central Palace, Lexington Ave. and 46th St., from April 10 to May 6, 1917. Hassam's entries were *Diana's Pool*, *Appledore*, and *The Country Fair, Still Life*. Pach served as the Society's treasurer.

2. Albert Milch, gallery owner who was Hassam's art dealer.

---

130 West 57th Street
New York, Nov. 30, 1929

Dear Mr. Pach:

I did not disclose to Miss Watts of Harpers a slight slip in the book "Art in America" that I read with interest—It is a blend of the Walkers—there is no "Johnny Walker" in it to be sure—but you have Horatio and Henry Oliver well mixed—H.O. made the decorations in the Congressional Library and Horatio never made a decoration in his life—not even for that amuseing [*sic*] "old woman" N. E. Montross.[1]

I had just read the ebullitions of that other old women in Washington D.C. that he wishes the artists to support—to pay for the publication of in fact—he so ingenuous as to ask them each a dollar for it. Then there is the squawking old hen on the Evening Sun who writes about the collecting and exportrining (?) of Marie Sterner[2] who has gotten together some of the worst things I have seen yet. She is now literally an old lady. I have known her myself for a long lifetime—Verily Art in America is run by old women but most of them wear trousers—

Yours sincerely, Childe Hassam

1. Newton Emerson Montross, a New York gallery owner.

2. A gallery owner in Manhattan.

New York, March 24, 1931

Dear Mr. Pach:

Your exhibition looks well[1]—the best things that I have seen of yours—I was there twice and talked to John Sloan and to Miss Kraushaar on the two occasions—you have the time I take it to do what you want to do.

I shall send you a plate of Helen Wills a portrait of her made at East Hampton in 1928 and a second state just completed—some added work with the burin. It is I think a very complete small plate and the burin work was added over the steel facing—which gives a pretty clean line without the burr that the copper gives—All these things are worth knowing—Part of the background is my garden—and part the tennis court of the Maidstone Club—where she has played a great deal—the tree is an American tulip tree (Liriodendron tulipifera) on[e] of the most beautiful of our American forest trees commonly known as the tulip poplar

I shall inscribe a proof to you when you return here as I have no intention of getting tangled up in French tarifs [*sic*]—they have a tarif on art now—the very thing that the[y] abused us so much for—Am I right—I shall send it along as soon as I have had printed the number of my edition.

Very glad to hear from you

Sincerely yours, Childe Hassam

1. It was held at the Kraushaar Gallery March 11–28.

New York, March 8, 1932

Dear Mr. Pach:

The copper plate—steel faced (as that was the only way that the final fine lines of burin work could be done on the mask) was sent to you today care of Morgan & Co.

The subject is "Helen Wills at Easthampton" There are two other plates of her, same title 2nd and 3rd in my catalogue of plates—I have a proof for you here when you return to New York—if M. Angoulvent (?) has some proofs pulled he will I hope give you one. It is (not the important thing to us I know) a good likeness of perhaps the best ambassador that America sent to Europe since Benjamin Franklin I hope that it may please some of the French people.

I am sure that you are enjoying your sojourn next door to that vast storehouse (The Louvre) of the Fine Arts.

Our own Metropolitan Museum made a record of me last summer at work at East-hampton, and at play too, going through the Long Island breakers, also playing golf on the Maidstone Club links ending up with the artist looking at his own pictures (these are four oils and two water colors) hung in the Museum—It occured [*sic*] to me that this was the first time that such a thing had ever been recorded in the long history of the Fine Arts—A painter looking at his own works bought by and exhibited in his own lifetime by what must be now accounted one of the great Art Museums of the world.

That is the only news that I think of that may interest you. of course there will be others. The Boston Museum has had one made of Benson[1] making an etching—done by some Film Co. Mine was made by the Metropolitan's own operators.

John Sloan whom I have not seen since he had his prostate gland removed is I hear allright again—I proposed his name twice to the Academy of Arts and Letters but he was outdone by literary candidates—both good—James Truslow Adams whose remarkable book "The Adams Family" you have perhaps seen. The other possibly you know him is Wm Lyon Phelps who holds the chair of English Literature at Yale University—elected at the last election—

With kindest regards to you—and your family I am allways [*sic*]

Most sincerely yours, Childe Hassam

1. Frank W. Benson (1862–1951) was, like Hassam, a member of "The Ten American Painters" who exhibited annually at the Durand-Ruel and Montross galleries in New York from 1898 to 1918.

Source of Letters: Archives of American Art, Smithsonian Institution, Childe Hassam Papers, reel 4217.

ROBERT HENRI
(1865–1929)

Painter, teacher, and leader of insurgent artists who challenged the conservative, taste-making exhibitions of the day. Born Robert Henry Cozad, Henri studied at the Pennsylvania Academy of the Fine Arts, where he influenced such younger students as John Sloan, William J. Glackens, George Luks, and Everett Shinn; they, together with Henri, became members of The Eight (the others were Arthur B. Davies, Ernest Lawson, and Maurice B. Prendergast).

Henri urged his associates at the Pennsylvania Academy, and from 1902 to 1908, his students at the New York School of Art, to paint the seamy side of everyday life rather than that which was elegant and fashionable. Among his coterie of pupils at the New York school were Edward Hopper, George Bellows, Rockwell Kent, Guy Pène du Bois, and Walter Pach.

Pach soon surpassed his mentor's comprehension and taste for modern art. Pach's letters to Henri from 1906 express interest in such artists as Rembrandt, Frans Hals, and Manet—Henri's favorites—but by the time the two met in Paris in 1912 and viewed the Autumn Salon, Henri had serious reservations about the Fauves and Cubists, while Pach was already envisioning their inclusion in the Armory Show of the following year.

Henri was a member of the Association of American Painters and Sculptors which would sponsor the show, but the organization's president, Arthur B. Davies, intentionally eliminated him from any decision-making role, considering his taste in art too limited. As a result, Henri's letter to Pach of January 3, 1913, written just two weeks prior to the Armory Show's opening, sought to elicit information from Pach about the event that was being widely publicized in the press. The line Henri quotes from Horace Traubel's poem, "For I was the open door to you," left little to Pach's imagination as to what his former teacher sought.

Pension Leder
Zijlweg 21 F
Haarlem, Aug. 27, 1906

Dear Mr. Henri,

At length arrived in this happy land of Rembrandt and Frans Hals and one-cent cigars galore—. . .

The week in Paris was a wild and hurried one. There is so much—like Versailles and the monuments—that people have to be shown on a first visit (never to see again), that pictures cut less of a figure than would have been to my personal liking. Still, that had to be, and Mr. Monte[1] in some well-directed talks has kept it before the minds of the people that we are here on an art-tour and should only do a sufficient quantity of sight-seeing; and they have taken it all right. A number are sketching quite steadily—myself, I have done no more than make a couple of unsatisfactory goes at it but promise myself great things when I come back. They don't allow copying here now over the summer; as one friend of mine said—I thought cleverly—it interferes with the tourist trade. Maybe I shall do something in Amsterdam—Hals "Jester," for example. . . . My great disappointment in Paris was missing the Durand-Ruel private collection. But I saw some beautiful things: Manet's "Absinthe drinker" etc. some Courbet, Puvis and Monet at the store. Bruce[2] said Guy du Bois was going to take up his father's work on the paper. . . .[3] To-day we saw the Rembrandt "homage-exhibition" in Leiden. There are some most glorious things there. I really am coming to paint here after the rest go. With very good wishes to you all, I am—

Sincerely yours, Walter Pach

1. Louis Gaspard Monté, of Columbia University's Teachers College, gave lectures to the Henri students while the mentor remained in Madrid.

2. Patrick Henry Bruce (1881–1936), a member of the Henri class.

3. Guy Pène du Bois (1884–1958), also a Henri student; his father, Henri Pène du Bois, who had been art critic for the *New York American*, died on a ship back to America shortly before this letter was written.

Haarlem, Sept. 14, 1906

My dear Mr. Henri,

. . . On Saturday, every one except Mrs. Stevens[1] left London—Mrs. Ward[2] to go to Edinburgh and the remaining nine to sail on the "Etruria" which I saw them do. Everyone, including Miss Mansfield was in good health and spirits, and it seemed as if every detail—the various boxes of class paintings and copies as well—was in order. I came back to London, had a good look at the National Gallery, had a visit to the A. B. Frost family[3] and then a very pleasant passage over to Holland arriving Wednesday. I have a place to work (the studio over Brinkman's Cafe that Miss Pope[4] and Miss Niles[5] will know) and have started in, out-doors as well. . . .

With best wishes to you all I am

Very respectfully, Walter Pach

1. Esther Stevens (1885– ?).

2. Hilda Ward (1878–1950).

3. Arthur Burdett Frost Jr. (1887–1917) had studied with Henri at the New York School of Art; his father, Arthur Burdett Frost Sr., was an illustrator of children's books, including *Uncle Remus* and *Br'er Rabbit* (see Frost Sr./Pach letters).

4. Louise Pope (n.d.)

5. Helen Niles (n.d.)

Haarlem, Sept. 30, 1906

My dear Mr. Henri,

I know that time will be getting scarce in these, your last few days in Madrid . . .

It was with pleasure that I heard that you had gotten so much fine work done.[1] Your old friend Potter (John B.—of Boston) was here and is going to Madrid, in which place I recommended him to your address. I have been at work a little too—finishing a copy of Hals' "Jester" this week. I wanted to orient myself in Dutch atmosphere a little before painting the country—since I cant get back to Spain. Will you give the girls[2] my best regards and remember me kindly to the Carmona family, believing me

Very truly yours, Walter Pach

1. The following March, Henri was a member of the thirty-man jury for the National Academy of Design's Spring Annual, where two of his three entries were subjects he had painted in Madrid: *El Matador* and *Spanish Gypsy—Mother and Child.* When they failed to receive unanimous approval from the other jurors, Henri, as a protest against the rejection of paintings by his associates Glackens, Luks, and Shinn, and his students Rockwell Kent and Carl Sprinchorn, removed his pair of canvases from further consideration. This sparked his formation of "The Eight," which artists exhibited together in an independent gallery show in February 1908.

2. Henri's female students who were then with him in Madrid.

---

10 Gramercy Park
New York, Jan. 3, 1913

Dear Pach:

Its a long time between my letters—first I want to thank you for the magazine with the Besnards[1] and the excellent photographs—the latter forming a contrast rather strong for the Besnards The photographs I enjoyed and continue to enjoy. I have known Besnard in better times—he was younger, did not know so much but knew more. It seems as though he took a flight from the Beaux Arts and enjoyed his freedom and he made record of it in those College of Pharmacie decorations (remember the time and the conditions of the time) I remember the day I wandered from the protection of Julians[2] and found them—then very much neglected in the College of Pharmacie. —no matter where they rank in the art of that day—the best of which we know was being produced quite without our knowledge which the school and the Salon screened[3]—The note that was of his personal emotions has its value and is part of our constructive force. great part or lesser part every record of personal evidence counts in the whole. —and so, with so much said to his credit I may now freely say I think these of the magazine article seem little more than skillful illustrations. —and later came the magazine with your article about Winslow Homer[4] wh[ich] I think very fine, very simply said and all good meaty saying all the way through. I hope you will write a lot more that will be equal to that. Some one told me that there was talk of your coming over soon—and in connection with the AAP&S exhibition[5]—I have not heard directly as I have seen few times the members and then with such business afoot that many informations were passed unmentioned. Maybe this letter will not find you there—if not then I'll tell it in words and much more—if there's time. How busy one gets in New York! I have been hard at work—hard enough in the daylight to want to spend all the night light in rest. There is a growing state of expectancy about the "armory" exhibition. and there is little doubt but that it will make a great stir. —and do a great deal of good in a great variety of directions.

and now in addition to thanking you for the magazines, the photographs, the satisfaction I had in your article about Winslow Homer I want to thank you again for your excellent hospitality in Paris.[6]

Sincerely Yours, Robert Henri

P.S.—news items.

Geo Bellows has been having by invitation one man shows in Toledo Columbus and Detroit. He is now glued fast at Columbus where he has had a number of portrait commissions—those finished very successful.

Guy de Bois is writing most of the Arts & Decoration articles (N.Y.) and painting his small character subjects—I have not seen any of this years—but they say well of them.

Boss[7] continues with the school[8]—the School is now known as "Independent Sch of Art"

Golz[9] still director of Columbus Sch of Art. Col. Ohio. Bellows wrote fine of him and spoke of a philosophic evening & discourse with him.

Kent[10] is out in Minnesota.

I havent seen Coleman[11] he's a good man I wish he had a better chance.

Sprinchorn[12] doing fine work

The Dressers[13] spent an evening here but I dont know just what they are doing now—I'm counting on seeing them soon.

Sloan doing some etching, a great deal of drawing and more painting than ever before—good stuff.

I have heard reports wh[ich] show that Van Sloan [*sic*][14] & Bohnen[15] stirred things up on the California Coast.

The news items run out here but turn over———

I received the following on a card from Horace Traubel.[16]

> "I feel good about the day I was born:
> The day I was born was the greatest of all
> days: Theres nothing to compare it with:
> Nothing to compare it with but the day
> you were born: or any one was born
> nothing to compare it with:
> For the day I was born to myself that day
> you were born to me: you whom I love;
> Just as the day you were born to yourself
> that day I was born to you: you who
> love me:
> For I was the open door to you: for you
> were the open door to me: we are the
> life and death of each other:
> I feel good about the day I was born.

1. Paul-Albert Besnard, who became one of Henri's favorite artists during his student days in Paris.

2. Académie Julian, the art school where Henri and many Americans enrolled.

3. Henri attributed his failure to be aware of the French Post-Impressionists and more contemporary artists to these institutions' rigid adherence to academicism.

4. "Winslow Homer," *Gazette des beaux-arts* (November 1912), 73–79.

5. The Association of American Painters and Sculptors, the group of artists who organized the International Exhibition of Modern Art in 1913, the so-called Armory Show.

6. Henri and Pach met by coincidence in Paris in 1912 and viewed the Autumn Salon together, where Henri was taken aback upon initially seeing art by the fauves and cubists. Pach was in the French capital at the time to meet Arthur B. Davies and Walt Kuhn, and aid them in choosing avant-garde works for the Armory Show.

7. Homer Boss.

8. In 1912 Henri turned his art school over to Boss.

9. Julius Golz. All of the artists mentioned in the postscript, with the exception of John Sloan, had been Henri students and were known to Pach.

10. Rockwell Kent.

11. Glenn O. Coleman, who worked as an usher at Carnegie Hall and at other employment in order to support himself as an artist.

12. Carl Sprinchorn.

13. Lawrence and Aileen Dresser.

14. Frank Van Sloun Jr.

15. Aloys Bohnen.

16. Traubel, Walt Whitman's biographer, founded a Philadelphia monthly called *The Conservator*.

Source of Letters: Yale Collection of American Literature, Beinecke Rare Book and Manuscript Library, Yale University, which contains one additional letter.

Also available through the Archives of American Art, Smithsonian Institution, Walter Pach Papers, reel 4217.

FISKE KIMBALL
(1888–1955)

Architect, teacher, and museum director. Recipient of Bachelor of Arts and Bachelor of Architecture degrees from Harvard and a Ph.D. from the University of Michigan, he taught art and architecture at the universities of Illinois, Michigan, and Virginia, and established the Institute of Fine Arts at New York University. Dr. Kimball was at one time a practicing architect, aided in the restoration of Colonial Williamsburg and Thomas Jefferson's home, Monticello, and was a fellow of the American Institute of Architects. He served as director of the Philadelphia Museum of Art from 1925 to 1955. His several books include *Domestic Architecture of the American Colonies* (1922), *American Architecture* (1928), and *The Creation of the Rococo* (1943).

The correspondence between Pach and Kimball began the year he assumed the museum directorship and continued to 1949.

13 EAST 14TH ST.,
NEW YORK, MAY 6, 1925

Dear Kimball,

Thanks very much for having the Architectural Record with your article on Sullivan[1] sent to me. I read it with pleasure and with interest. And though I am going to renew, at least in part, my old objection, I am glad to say I think we are not as far apart as may at first appear.

For I do believe in formalism, if I use the word accurately; at all events in an abstract harmony of proportion. And to attempt to make the evidence of the system of construction replace that is, in my opinion, to abdicate all title to artistry. That does not mean, however, that the proportions of a Greek building will hold good for a Gothic, a Renaissance or a modern building. Even where the systems of construction are sufficiently similar, there will be difference of genius in the periods that will give any valid work a difference of aspect from those of the earlier time. And where a difference of construction occurs, as with the steel skeleton, there must be difference of aspect. I do not see it, in any essential degree, in the work of Wells[2] and his School.

That may be my insensitiveness. But where I feel sure of my objection is in respect to your comparison with the painters. Monet is, in reality, only at the slightest of removes from his immediate predecessors. His color analysis is a very slight disguise—only the academic simpletons of the '80s and '90s could have failed to see that, and we know what nonentities they were. Sullivan and the steel-frame men, on the other hand, made a real break with the past. As the immediate past was mostly bad, I believe, their relative position, as regards it, is different from that of Monet as regards the Corots, Rousseaus, Daubignys, etc. of his youth.

But what I fall foul of entirely is calling Wells the Cézanne of architecture. Leaving out the question of their greatness, (and I cannot believe myself *so* insensitive as to fail to see something of the grandeur of Cézanne in Wells—if he has it), Cézanne simply carries classical balance and proportion into the vision of the Impressionists (his own in his early days). If something more than an Impressionist in his later period, his last work in no wise contradicts his first. Matisse said to me once that Cézanne added nothing to his earlier work but merely developed what he had at the start. In contradistinction to this, Wells et al. seem to me a revulsion from Sullivan, attempting a return to forms once vital but no longer so in their handling of them. But I repeat that I am in an accord with the idea of art that they are trying to keep alive.

So, there!

Now, and it isn't quite by the way—for I've been wanting to write you this for some time—you kindly consented, some time ago, to let me have a line that my publisher could use about my book: that it was recommended reading or required reading (or you would like it to be) or whatever you could say. A professor at Leland Stanford and one at Smith wrote me spontaneously that they were using it with classes; Sachs[3] at Harvard told me he was recommending it, and, together, that started me off. Don't strain any point if your conditions do not warrant such a statement as I have suggested—I could quite understand that they might not, but if the thing is not too troublesome, I should be glad of it.

We are hoping to see you here very soon.

Yours cordially, Walter Pach

1. "Louis Sullivan—An Old Master," *Architectural Record* 57 (April 1925), 289–304.

2. Joseph Morrill Wells, chief designer for McKim, Mead and White who espoused the classical ideal.

3. Paul Sachs (1878–1965), assistant director of the Fogg Museum of Art at Harvard University.

May 8, 1925

Dear Pach:

I am delighted to have a good long letter from you, in the same mail as one from Paul Cret[1] who is to my mind far the most intelligent of the architects. It is very pleasant at all events to have you take the Sullivan article seriously enough to write me so fully. It would not be any fun if we all agreed exactly. It is amusing to see how different still Cret's point of view is. I do not think we are really very far apart. Of course, just as you say that Monet was only slightly removed from his immediate predecessors, I would emphasize that the same was true of Sullivan. All the long historical part of my article at the beginning was designed to point this out. By emphasizing his continuity with the thought of Ruskin, Semper[2] and Viollet-le-Duc[3] when I spoke of Wells as the Cézanne, I myself left aside the question of their greatness. What I wish to emphasize is that it was Wells who first reacted against the prevailing realistic or scientific theory that the merit of architecture is to be found in truth to structure, as Cézanne was the first to react against the realistic theory that the merit of painting was to be found in "truth to nature."

I would quite agree that "there will be a difference of genius in the periods that will give any valid work a difference of aspect from those of the earlier time." I think this is true of the work of Bramante[4] as compared with the work of the Romans, and I think it is true of the work of Wells and McKim as compared with the work of Rome and of the Renaissance. But I think this difference comes rather from the inevitable difference of requirements rather than from a conscious effort to invent a new alphabet of forms. Naturally it will appear most where the requirements are most different and thus the most notable work of today is in the steel-frame buildings where the essential problem of the moment is the composition of mass. As I recently saw it expressed by a Dutch critic, their merit lies "nicht so viel in ihron [ihrer] Wahrheit, als in ihren [ihrer] Klarheit,"[5] but this clarity of organization of form could never have been attained without the reaffirmation of the principle by Wells in buildings of traditional type.

When you write "Where a difference of construction occurs, as with the steel skeleton, there must be a difference of aspect," I think that (so far as this difference of construction does not itself bring new types of mass, space, etc.) you are still unconsciously tinged with the old nineteenth century scientific theory of functionalism. We are all together on what Harvey Corbett[6] said to me the other day: "I have only one God, beauty of form."

I am delighted to send you the enclosure.

We have moved out to the country and I am only commuting in the daytime two or three times a week, but hope I shall run into you.

Faithfully yours, Fiske Kimball

1. Cret (1876–1945) was a French-born architect who designed the Folger Shakespeare Library in Washington and the Detroit Institute of Arts.

2. Gottfried Semper (1803–1879), a German architect.

3. Eugène Emanuel Viollet-le-Duc (1874–1879), considered the leading restorer of medieval monuments in France, including Notre Dame Cathedral.

4. Donato Bramante (1444–1514), renowned architect of the High Renaissance in Italy.

5. "Not as much in its Truth, as in its Clarity."

6. Harvey Wiley Corbett (1873–1954), who was appointed an associate architect for Rockefeller Center.

Jan. 24, 1929

My dear Pach:

It was very kind of you to have your "Ananias" sent to me by the publishers, and I have already expressed to them my admiration of it, but I want to add a special word directly to you.

All you write about the Museum strikes a sympathetic chord, and it is not because I have not read the entire book that it is on page 8 that I feel this particularly. We dream here of a museum which would not exclude the art of any race, but would include all that is ordinarily called ethnology. Within each school we know we *must* select for what we call the display collection, only we don't intend to select by the standards of Ananias.

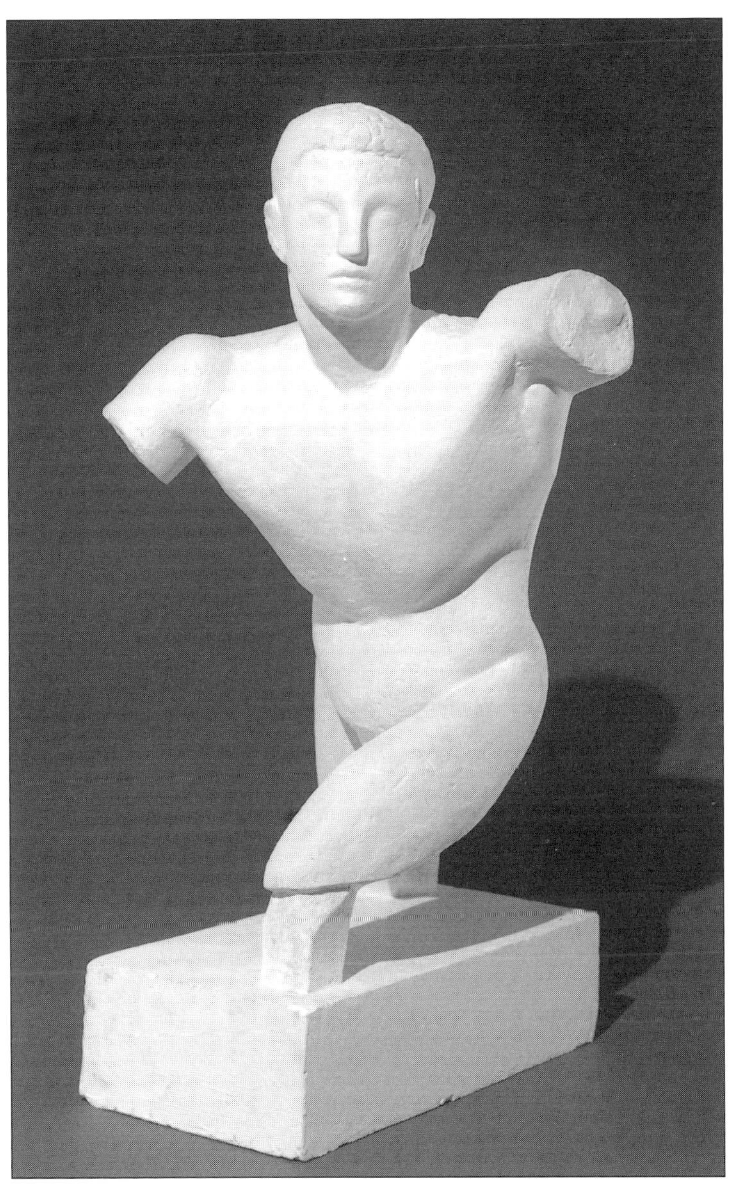

Raymond Duchamp-Villon, *Torso of a Young Man*, 1910-11. Plaster, 23 3/4 x 13 1/16 x 12 1/4 in. Hirshhorn Museum and Sculpture Garden, Smithsonian Institution, Gift of Joseph H. Hirshhorn, 1966. Acc. HMSG 66.1460. Photograph by Lee Stalsworth.

I note where you speak of the etchings of Delacroix, which I had not known he made, and which you say may be bought for $12. or $15. 1 would value your judgment enormously (knowing the whole range of these) if you would pick out one or two for me, at Weyhe's or elsewhere. There is $50 at your disposal, if needed.

With cordial regards,

Ever faithfully yours, [Fiske Kimball]

NEW YORK, JAN. 27, 1929

Dear Kimball

Thanks ever so much for your letter and your good words about the book. I do think I've said some true words about museum problems in it, and I'm glad you approve.

I'll go to Weyhe's and have some Delacroix things sent you the first chance I get.

Don't by any chance miss the Duchamp-Villon show now on at Brummer's (almost his complete work). I think it's a thunderbolt, and several people who considered that I was speaking too strongly of him have quite come around to my way of thinking. If you have not yet a definitive feature for the head of your staircase you could here see the figure of the young man (not merely the torso) in full size. I had forgotten that it was so large: perhaps it would be big enough. But you must see the show.

Yours cordially, Walter Pach

WALTER PACH
3 WASHINGTON SQUARE
NEW YORK 3, N.Y.
SEPT. 22, 1958

To whom it may concern,

I was present at the studio of Duchamp-Villon, at Puteaux, near Paris, when in the fall of 1912, he made the plaster cast of the *Torso of a Young Man* for the Armory Show. It was exhibited there in 1913 at its three showings—in New York (at the 69th Regiment Armory), in Chicago (at the Art Institute), and in Boston (at Copley Hall). It then was acquired by me and has remained in my collection till the present day.

A distinguishing feature of this version of the work is the squarish block under the left knee. As far as I know there is no other example in which this appears. In later versions such as one which was cast for me, after the sculptor's death, by his brother

Jacques Villon (a work I shall retain permanently, since it has my name in the bronze) the block under the knee is absent, as it is in the cast—in bronze—belonging to Mr. Alexander M. Bing. I know a terra cotta of the figure and am practically certain that the small block does not exist there either. While [I] can not say the total number of casts that have been made, my belief is that they are all of the later state (without the block). In that case the plaster I own would be unique; it certainly has a certain delicacy of modelling—in the head, particularly—which has disappeared in the bronze version which I retain. It was Mr. Bing's bronze which was shown at the big exhibition of works by the three brothers which was held at the S. Guggenheim Museum about 1957.

I am relatively sure that I have never lent my plaster to any exhibition in the last forty-five years.

Walter Pach

Collection of the Hirshhorn Museum & Sculpture Garden Archives, Smithsonian Institution.

New York, Jan. 30, 1929

Dear Kimball,

I have directed Weyhe to send you two fine Delacroix etchings which I selected. They cost $15.00 each. Also I set aside Delacroix's etching "Jewess of Algiers" and "Lion devouring a Horse"—the latter a lithograph and one of the very finest by the artist—at the gallery of J. B. Neumann, 9 East 57th St. Will you write him whether you want them—one way or the other, as he is reserving them against my orders. Please mention that it was for you that I asked him to hold them. They are $18 each and very desirable.

Yours cordially, Walter Pach

Feb. 4, 1929

My dear Pach:

It was very kind indeed of you to select the Delacroix etchings for me. The two from Weyhe's have come, and I am greatly delighted with them. It was kind of you to reserve the pieces at Neumann's also. I expect to be up in New York very briefly next Wednesday, and will try to drop in to Neumann's to see them to make my decision.

I never look to you for help in vain.

Faithfully yours, [Fiske Kimball]

Feb. 11, 1929

My dear Pach:

I was in New York Wednesday a little while and went first to Neumann's, but he was out, so I asked the little girl there, who did not know anything about the matter, to send me down the two lithographs on approval also.

Then I went to Brummer's to see the show of Duchamp-Villon. The figure is indeed very fine and powerful. As the large studies for the "Castorale" show, the conception of the pose is such as not to be really suited for the place we have in mind, but I asked Brummer for the photograph, which he promised. I am at my wit's end over the whole matter.

I don't know whether I told you that I went to Despiau's[1] studio in Paris, and saw everything there. In spite of the Eve and Diane "c'est plutot pour la tête,"[2] as a friend of mine expresses it. Then, why do they insist on nothing but women, women, women? There was one very fine male figure, in plaster model, in half scale, abandoned. In any case, from all I hear, it is perfectly hopeless to expect a commission to be executed by any of these fellows within a lifetime.

There we stand.

Faithfully yours, [Fiske Kimball]

1. Charles Despiau (1874–1946) created small bronze portraits.

2. "It's rather for the head."

New York, May 24, 1929

Dear Kimball,

Thanks very much for the pages from the Architectural Record. I am glad to have this interesting material, which had not come to my notice before.

We sail for Europe in two weeks or a little less, to stay a year or two. All the address I have is c/o Morgan & Co., 14 place Vendome, Paris.

Good wishes to you.

As always, Walter Pach

Nov. 17, 1933

Dear Mr. Pach:

This will serve to remind you that we are looking forward to your lecture at the [Philadelphia] Museum on Wednesday, November the 29th, at 3.30.

I wish very much that I could have the pleasure of having you to lunch with me again as last year. But it happens, this being the day before Thanksgiving, I expect to be out of town. Will you, accordingly, feel free to make use of my office before the lecture. My secretary, Miss Toomey, will look out for you. This year, not having Howard to look after these things, we are making a practice of not having any introduction. The lecturer just takes the stand as he does at the Metropolitan. You, at least, need no introduction to our audience.

I shall be sorry not to see you.

Faithfully yours, [Fiske Kimball]

Source of Letters: Philadelphia Museum of Art Archives, which contains additional Kimball/Pach correspondence.

ALICE KLAUBER
(1871–1951)

A painter who was active in art, music, and literary circles in her native San Diego. Ms. Klauber was in her thirties when she wrote to Walter Pach about initially enrolling in William Merritt Chase's Summer 1907 class in Italy (Pach served as a manager and lecturer for his former instructor, as he had done the two previous summers). When she went to Spain during the summer of 1912 with a class led by Robert Henri, another of Pach's teachers at the New York School of Art, she enthusiastically filled ten sketchbooks with observations of city life in Madrid.

Two summers later she arranged for Henri and his sister-in-law to come to La Jolla, near San Diego; this led to his providing names of artists to be invited to the forthcoming Panama-California Exposition of 1915, San Diego's way of celebrating the completion of the Panama Canal (Alice Klauber was in charge of furnishing the Women's Headquarters at the exposition). She was also one of the founders of the local Art Association, which later became the San Diego Fine Arts Society and ultimately the San Diego Museum of Art.

The Pach letters to Ms. Klauber reveal a restrained but growing affection for her—from an initial, businesslike "Dear madam" to "Dear Alice Klauber" and "Dear Alice." Any prospect of marriage was probably thwarted by his lack of a steady income and the fact that she was a dozen years his senior. Though Pach retained virtually all of the missives sent to him by other correspondents, none exist from Alice Klauber. He may have destroyed them prior to his own marriage in February 1914.

Wm. M. Chase
Art Classes in Italy
Summer of 1907

Louis G. Monté
High School of Commerce
Brooklyn

Walter Pach
935 Broadway
New York

March 4, 1907

Miss Alice Klauber,
San Diego,
California.

Dear madam,

Some few days ago, I sent you a prospectus of Mr. Chase's summer trip, in response to your valued request for the same. But it occurs to me that since you were so interested as to write, a few additional details might not be amiss.

Mr. Chase, as our most eminent painter and teacher needs no further introduction. Mr. Monté has been some seven times to Europe—by himself and as director of parties covering Italy thoroughly three times. He is a specialist on art-theory, history and pedagogics, and during his tenure of office at Teachers' College, Columbia University and other institutions, he has lectured before many important classes. He is recognized as one of the leading authorities on his subject.

This will be, for me, the sixth season with classes of this order. Should you care for references as to my work with them in painting and art-knowledge, languages and European management, I think even a random selection from the couple of hundred students with whom I have been associated, would satisfy you.

We have arranged the trip to afford the maximum of profit and enjoyment to the party, while bearing in mind the character of its personelle where possible, and economizing its means where in no wise interferes with the comfort to which Americans in Europe are accustomed. Trusting confidently that you will be able to be with us, I am

Cordially yours, Walter Pach

[Same letterhead as the previous letter]
April 22, 1907

My dear Miss Klauber,

I have the pleasure to acknowledge your note of April 7th, your telegrams of April 18th and 20th, and now this morning your note of April 12th and Mr. Klauber's of April 16 and his check for $75. . . .

I, personally, shall not have the pleasure of meeting you (if you go right to Boston) until you get to Naples, as I leave before the rest of the party to take a final look over the places we have written for in Italy and arrange for those that could not be so obtained. If you were to be in New York though, I should be glad to see you in my studio (above address), where I shall probably be till the last week in May. . . .

If you have a good palette and box, I think you would do well to take them with you—providing the trunk is not too full. I would not take paint etc. as it is heavy and in the past, Devoe and Reynolds have always sent a full stock with us, at American prices. We furnish easels for the studio. . . . I have made careful note of the character of locations desired. They would cost $20. (each) more, for we pay $80. for our "minimum first-class accommodation" mentioned in our prospectus. If I find that we can allow more than the $80. I will tell you when I get the saloon-deck berths, and this extra payment can wait till then. But the balance of the $500 (or $460) I must ask for by the time fixed for the rest of the party. I understand that Mr. Klauber is not a student, but have not yet heard of Miss Epstein's intentions. This would make a difference in the total sum still due—either $1385 if she means to take instruction or $1345, if she does not. I am

Very cordially yours, Walter Pach

---

9 rue Campagne Première
Paris, Nov. 16, 1907

Dear friend Alice Klauber.

I have two cards from you—the Velasquez and the Hals—both will look fine on the walls of my studio. When Mr. Henri saw a photograph of my portrait by Mr. Chase, he exclaimed—"He couldn't resist that Velasquez mouth while he was in Madrid." The portrait is one of the things they can show you in my studio, which is in Father's place, you know. . . . I was thinking of going up to Belgium as there are, in the

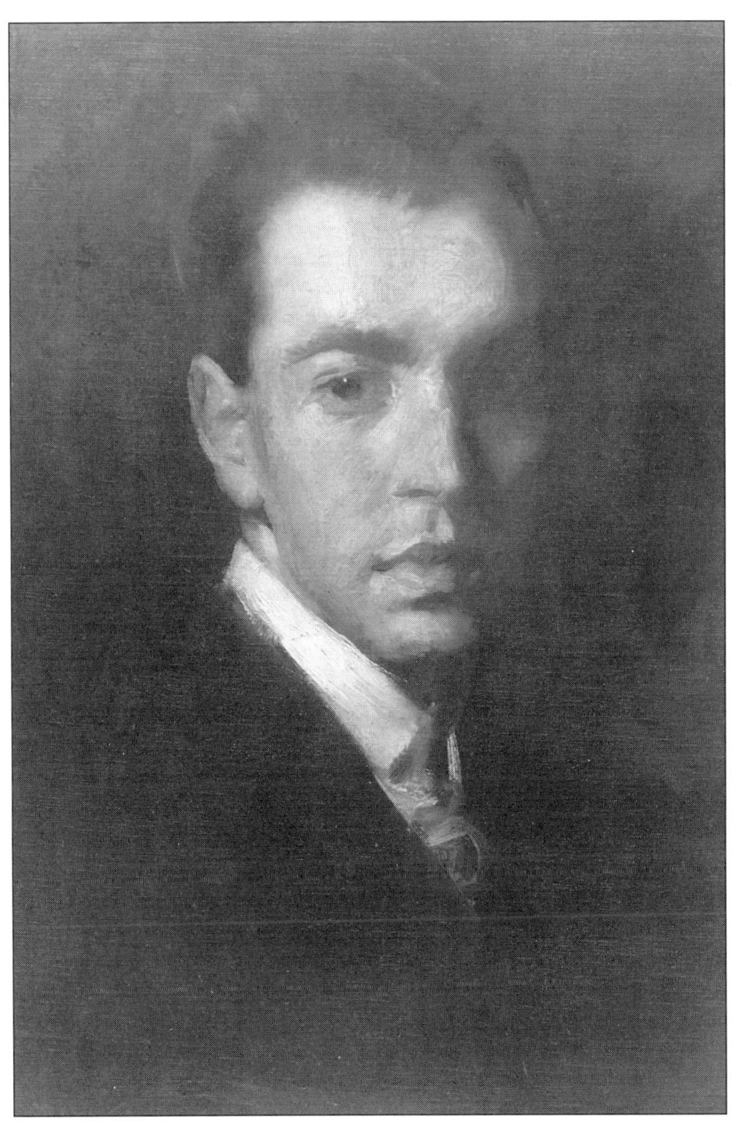

Williams Merritt Chase, *Portrait of Walter Pach*, 1905. Oil on canvas, 16 x 20 in. North Carolina Museum of Art, Purchased with funds from the State of North Carolina. Acc. 70.36.1.

museum of Tournai (France—but near Belgium) two great pictures by Manet. This will give me a chance to see Amiens after all as they have great things there and I hurried away—partly because I didn't want to waste another day there,—mostly to see you once more. . . .

I did see Monet, and a splendid two hours with him. He doesn't contemplate going to America—preferring to paint the country he knows. He looks the part: his ruddy face and bright brown eyes set off by a big white beard, his sturdy frame clothed in very simple plain clothes despite his earnings and the famous three automobiles. He showed me numberless pictures of all his career nearly, the "Salon des Réfusés" canvas amongst them. He was painting solidly then, and it seems so simple and unmistakable that you simply marvel why it should have been rejected. He told me most interesting things about the old days and the great artists. Sometime perhaps you'll hear in full. Finally I came to the great question, giving him all freedom to decline answering it if he liked. I said what was the opinion of some people on Matisse, and then asked "Do you see those qualities?" There was not an instant's hesitation in his reply of "Nullement" [Not at all]. *French has no stronger* (polite) negation. He went on to say, quite fully, that he had been told that Matisse had remarkable intelligence and so he had studied the pictures attentively with a friend and distinguished critic. With all desire not to see another mistake added to the list of which his own misjudgment forms so prominent a part, he said he had made up his mind that there was nothing there. I felt easier—even about the big still-life in Rue Madame. . . .

I wrote Mr. Chase about Cézanne. His one pupil Bernard, and Monet (a great admirer of his) protest against such exhibitions as that which Mr. Chase saw (unfinished, unrepresentative things which he (Cézanne) threw aside) and I think Mr. Chase will give him another consideration. . . . I'm painting a café-interior with peasant-workmen enjoying themselves—from memory of course. My staying here will depend on circumstances. My brother writes that I can most likely have a position in my old college[1] if I want it,—in February. But it would be lots better for my work to stay here and if I can put some articles through and nothing turns up at home, I may do so. Don't know—as the Steins say. I've been to Mr. Leo Stein's and the Matisses haven't gained any. I've about given it up. . . .

Now I'll say au revoir and bon voyage. I hope you really did find Monté and myself "as represented" and that you had the pleasure from it that I did in meeting you. With remembrance to your brother, I am, as *we* say in Spanish

Suyo, ato y afmo,[2] Walter Pach

1. City College of New York.

2. "Yours, sincerely and affectionately."

c/o Thos. Cook & Sons
Brussels, Feb. 8, 1908

Dear Alice Klauber,

I *have* a lot of correspondence of yours to answer . . .

That's certainly a fine suggestion of yours that I get up a book on Vermeer. There ought to be one and I know of none save a German work that costs either 500 or 1000 marks. I fear there's little to be done in the way of new facts about his history. I asked Roger Marx of the "Gazette des Beaux-Arts" about it and he said the archives had been pretty well ransacked in the search for traces of him. . . . I've sent my story of Monet to Scribner's (on a venture) and asked at the same time for the commission to write a Cézanne article.[1] Better than that will be (if it succeeds) a descent I made lately on that same "Gazette." I can't tell yet, but I try & hope that I'm to have a series of articles on American painters in that impressive journal. Pray for me. . . . Do you know, I've not seen hide nor hair of that Matisse article yet—nor of the check for it, which is even more annoying. Every mail is a likely one for it now. As you can imagine, the Steins' eagerness for it is only second to my own. I shall never have to reproach myself with having given the Matisse pictures an insufficient trial. I've gone to see them, thought over them and the arguments intended to uphold them, studied the masters they're supposed to descend from . . . but my progress has been small. The drawings remain fine—I see a certain color and a certain possibility in some of the still-lifes (principally) that I didn't at first but otherwise I've not changed much. Meanwhile I like Cézanne better in seeing more of him, and two big exhibitions of van Gogh impressed me very much. Picasso's latest are still incomprehensible, but I expect to make the connection between them and his earlier and wonderful things. . . .

I don't know Pater's "Marius the Epicurean" at all—only one book of his, the "Greek Studies." Your reference, with what I re-read in George Moore last summer and Oscar Wilde's speaking of him (in "De Profundis," that charming German girl in Florence gave me) renews my wish to read it, and I shall—sooner or later. Also that Browning you mention. Did you make a note [of] George Borrow's name—for "Lavengro," "The Bible in Spain" etc. He's fine. . . .

My work went on tolerably in Paris; some of it will be shown at the Indépendants.[2] I interrupted it pretty much with picture-seeing for which I had a sudden desire and with teaching in a school there which was a waste of time (artistically) but gives me a job to fall back on here if other things don't pan out. I shall paint now. Au revoir, my good friend.

Good luck, Walter Pach

1. Pach's 'At the Studio of Claude Monet,' "The Field of Art," was published in the June 1908 issue of *Scribner's Magazine*, pages 765–767; his "Cézanne—An Introduction" appeared in *Scribner's* the following December on pages 765–768.

2. The Paris Indépendants.

---

9 rue Campagne Première
Paris, March 9, 1908

Dear Alice Klauber,

Your letter of Jan. 23rd reached me in Brussels . . . I think I must have known of my order for an article on American painting in the "Gazette des Beaux-Arts" when I wrote.[1] That's the best news (of its kind) I've had in ages for I hear, in a round-about way that my Matisse article was not used (though my orders were positive and explicit), I've no word from my Monet article yet (it's a bit early) and the mother of my friend in Haarlem was still too scared of being painted to let me have that job. So I'm hoping W.[inslow] Homer Esq. and the rest of the worthies to whom I've written for repros of their work will hurry up, for I'm anxious to get to the "Gazette" job—with most excellent reason. . . .

This morning I shall take your little copy [of a Hals painting] to the American consul's, swear some "strange oaths" that it was I who did it etc. and then deliver it to a steamship company. . . . I'm extremely anxious to know how my little "Willem van Heythuysen" will strike you. . . . The face I went over till I feel pretty much that it's what it should be, the red in the chair may be just a little too-too, but I'm not sure,—it can't be much more red than it should be anyhow. The photos I have seen change the values very much. My friends like it, except Arthur Frost who says it's a mud-pie both for form and color and not at all like Matisse (heavings!). I believe I'm ready to let that matter drop. Since Matisse has been teaching, the bunch is worse than ever,[2] they now *all* claim that they don't know anything, especially before making statements like the above. Frost thinks it's because he hasn't had any opportunity to see pictures, being just back from a six-weeks' stay in Italy. —I got some more frames from the Venetian lady and have six things at the Indépendents—to open Mar. 21st. . . .

Your description of the San Diego country was fine. Sometime I must surely come out there.

With my best—Walter Pach

1. Pach's article, "Quelques notes sur les peintres américains," appeared in the *Gazette des beaux-arts*, volume 2, 1909, on pages 324–335.

2. Arthur Burdett Frost Jr. and Patrick Henry Bruce, both then enrolled in the Henri Matisse class in Paris, had been fellow classmates of Pach when they studied with Robert Henri in New York.

Pension Innocenti
Florence, Aug. 19, 1908

Dear Miss Klauber,

. . . Here is the big burden of my news: I'm going home. My family were in Paris last month and Father offered to take me into his business with him.[1] I saw nothing in it but a quietus on everything I was working toward and practically declined; but just after the folks left, Chase came through Paris from Florence (Uffizi portrait all done [it looks like one sitting, but is fine in many ways anyhow] villa arranged, etc.) and he said 'No, that's not the way to look at it. You need not be extinguished at all, in fact I don't think it's in your disposition to be thrown out by such a change. You'll come back and with a free mind.' And as the Old Man put it that way, with lots more and stronger talk, I thought it seemed right probable and so wrote Father I'd come, and in ten days I sail. It will be no cinch at first, but I guess the thing really is to clinch with the twisty old $ dollar—mark at once and finish him—rather than have the trail of the serpent over the rest of my days. . . .

The Steins send you their love, which I need not tell *you* is no small thing, even though they do extend its warmth to many people. The Bardi villa which they have is fine and the whole family seems to be very well.

Did not know how it would be—telling you I was going into business, but the Steins said it was all right. . . . You know my N.Y. address: 935 Broadway or my home—either one: Maybe I shall write again soon and anyhow I shall be glad to hear from you. As always—

Heartily, Walter Pach

1. Pach Photographer, at 935 Broadway, New York.

1135 Park Avenue (or 935 Broadway)
New York, Nov. 2, 1908

Dear Alice Klauber,

. . . Excuse me for the handwrite in this letter and amount which I fear is going to be illegible; . . . I should have to tag on to say something of my feelings on being back in New York. I fear they are not very good feelings. I don't believe I like much here except a few people. The family is fine, and the old friends,—The painter bunch—is the same—only too much so, for the year abroad has made me different and while personally they are as fine as ever (the best I've met) we look at things differently now that there is not the old agreement of thought. Perhaps we shall come together more. I am not settled in my mind. I have not got the business-thoughts and the art-thoughts to hold their places—so to speak, to keep out of one another's way and confusion is sometimes the result. I dropped rather easily into the business—it is not new to me, only this time I must get into it thoroughly and I don't feel quite sure that I shall, though I try. Now that Father has me here he finds me rather a problem. I think I am making pretty good progress and shall be able to say later as to the success of the plan. One fellow said the tone of a letter of mine, written shortly after my return, was doleful. I don't quite think it was (in fact I am blamed sure it wasn't) there was surely no reason for it to be so. I have been very very busy: the Cézanne article, the "Gazette" article and a pretty good dose of translating scientific German—an essay on deep-sea creatures. Yesterday it was just a year since I missed you on my return from Amiens. Gee, I wish there were another opportunity to see you. I wouldn't let any chances get mixed with it.

Good wishes—Walter Pach

1135 Park Avenue
New York, June 9, 1909

Miss Alice Klauber
Box BB, San Diego, California

Dear Alice,

Your letter of May 27th came last week, the same day as the card from Tia-Juana. . . . I am painting the portrait of a beautiful little girl cousin which I hope will finish up shortly as the best thing I have done. Lord knows, I need something to make me feel I can paint a little yet, for I have not done a good thing since I left the business. —But you don't know of that: it simply transpired that I could not possibly keep on with the photography if I had any notion of being a painter. We had never fixed it up how I was to do my own work while in the business,—while I was learning I was willing to let it lay over a while. But when it came to my taking the place of an important employee who was leaving, I "enquired to know" and found it was a matter of fifty six-business-day weeks per year. No painting to be done in that state of affairs—hence my exit,—everything smooth and unruffled. Since then I have sold my copy of Hals' "Jester" to Smith College Museum and have found quite some literary work. I need lots. Write me soon, won't you? As ever,

Most cordially yours, Walter Pach

New York, Aug. 31, 1909

My dear Alice,

This evening I received your letter of the 25th . . . I have been no good after the day's doings; a rather small number I have put in with the fiddle (which is beginning to give forth sounds which a practised ear can recognize as tunes—it has been at rest for almost three years) or else with books. There has not been much done in that way,—I read the easier kind on the street-cars—Turgenev's "Father's and Children" ["Fathers and Sons"] (great), Geo. Moore's "Evelyn Inness" (bully) de Wyzewa's "Les Maîtres Italiens d'Autrefois" (mostly very good), two of Berenson's, Henry James' "The Ambassadors" (my first—I liked it), Lord Redesdales "Tales of Old Japan" Okakura's "Ideals of the East" (simply great) some Ibsen dramas and now "Marius the Epicurean" which I am reading slowly, as it is too beautiful to let any of it go half-understood. I ought to read it at home, but for there I have Rood's "Modern Chromatics," a very important book which a friend lent me in January(!) (he has since re-affirmed that I should keep it till finished). I have started several times and now seem to be sticking to it. But often I feel as if I just can't work on that, and take up some poetry—a matter I am awfully deficient in appreciating. My Walt Whitman always stands by me firmly and the few Verlaine and Mallarmé things that I read and re-read, not very frequently taking up new pieces. Lately, on Mr. Arthur B. Davies' recommendation, I got "A Lute of Jade"—selections from the classic poetry of China,—a little book (published by Dutton) with things in it—everything I've read in it—that are a revelation—most wonderful. If you don't write me that you have gotten it, I shall take up my next letter by copying a piece or two from it and then you will have to get it. . . . My Davies paper is not yet published: I hope you will see that as one of my friends thinks it the best I have done. I have two other articles commissioned, and to-day turned in the Mss. for a little guide-book sort of *machine* which was ordered. . . .

I jog along fairly well, and keep up quite a bit of interest in things and get not too little enjoyment from them.

With best wishes

Always sincerely yours, Walter Pach

New York, Nov. 13, 1909

My dear Alice,

It was Saturday, a week ago to night, that I got your note, and I should have answered it and sent the things before this; but the frame-maker has not kept his word and so I will write first and send the things afterward. I think beside the sketches I can find some Goya etchings and some photos or something. Also if you want more sketches I know lots of men (or several anyhow) who would doubtless be willing to send. You must use your discretion somewhat as to prices: for the two things I have picked out and also for the two I got from my good friend, Joe Garvey the minimum is $15. each. I always put $35. for this size on the card when I have them in the exhibitions here and it is a fair price though not an exorbitant one. If you can sell them for enough to give us more than the $15—so much the better. I think I will include my Tintoretto copy of an "Unknown Man"—price $75. I asked $125 when it was exhibited at Smith College Museum, which bought one of my things—Perhaps by sending time I shall have something else and shall put an inventory and price-list in the box. No need to ask if you've written Wheeler.

I am enthusiastic over the idea of the shop. It will give you an employment that I should think would prove fascinating, and such places—not just commercial and (what is more dangerous and even more to be avoided) not "arty"—are exactly what this country needs. And I should imagine there was a good field for you out there. Not long ago, Mr. Davies was telling me that they wanted to have a Prendergast show in 'Frisco—a swell thing. When you get things going, I feel pretty sure I could get a number of the big men to send you things. Meanwhile please write me without hesitation about anything you want, even if you're not sure I can get it.

With wishes for a booming success

Yours cordially, Walter Pach

---

13 East 14th St.
New York, May 6, 1925

Dear Alice Klauber,

On receipt of your letter, I at once called up Pierre Matisse,[1] and think you must have received the prints from him before this. I turned over to him the check for $60. and he was to write you the prices of the prints he sent, in case you or your friends wanted to take others than the ones included in that payment. The prices you found in Paris must have owed their lowness to the exchange, for the prints have increased in price very much since 1915.

Lately I had the visit of Mr. Wm. Templeton Johnson of San Diego.[2] He was, as you doubtless know, here to secure a director for your new museum, and he consulted me about it. I am too much bound up with things here to consider it for myself, though I know we should both be glad to have you as a neighbor.

You must really help with the Museum—as it is of the first importance that your director be a man who knows art. There is too much of a tendency all through the country to put in administrative men, or men who are "pretty good" on art—and a vast miseducation is resulting everywhere, or almost everywhere. It is while people's minds are open that the harm is done: when they have closed on something bad, or mediocre, it is hard to change the direction of a museum.

I recommended Mr. Block of the Omaha Society of Fine Arts (without knowing whether he would accept). Mr. Johnson was afraid he would not be the one to handle the crowd (if that is the right word) at San Diego; I am not afraid of that—I have seen him do it at Omaha where I have lectured for three years now, on tours. And he does know art. Mr. Wehle,[3] at the Metropolitan, is also an admirable man. I said these things to Mr. Johnson, but our time having been very limited, I shall write him, to repeat them.

You asked about myself: just now I am trying to dispose of a lot of work—a great collection I have been cataloguing (it is very varied and requires a lot of research-work), some articles, and the last lectures of the season. Then we go to some quiet place to paint. My show was a success.[4] The first and most important thing to say in justifying that statement was that *I* liked it; but the newspapers were favorable, as a rule, and—for a first show—the sales were not bad. Now I must paint a lot and keep up with the start I have made.

I hope things are well with you and that you like the prints. I think they're ripping. . . .

With remembrances from the wife,

Yours cordially, Walter Pach

1. Pierre Matisse (1900–1989), son of Henri Matisse, came to the United States in 1924 and established an art gallery in his name in New York.

2. William Templeton Johnson (1877–1957), a well-known architect in Southern California who designed the San Diego Museum.

3. Harry B. Wehle, assistant curator of paintings at the Metropolitan Museum of Art.

4. In February 1925 at the Brummer Gallery in New York City.

Source of Letters: San Diego Museum of Art Library, which contains additional Klauber/Pach correspondence.

Also available through the Archives of American Art, Smithsonian Institution, Alice Klauber Papers, reel 583.

LEWIS MUMFORD (1895–1990)

Author and critic. After early expectations of becoming an electrical engineer, in 1912 he anticipated a career as a newspaper reporter or playwright. During the next seven years he studied at the City College of New York, Columbia University, New York University, and the New School of Social Research, and came in contact with Thorstein Veblen at the latter institution. After a brief stint in the navy during World War I, Mumford accepted the position of editor on *The Dial*, a literary and art magazine, and commenced a career as a freelance writer as well. His first book, *The Story of Utopias*, appeared in 1922, followed by *Sticks and Stones* (1924), *The Golden Day* (1926), *Herman Melville* (1929), *The Brown Decades* (1931), *Technics and Civilization* (1934), and *The Culture of Cities* (1938), among others. He served as a professor of humanities at Stanford University from 1942 to 1944, as a visiting professor of architecture at North Carolina State College from 1948 to 1952, and as a visiting professor of land and city planning at the University of Pennsylvania in the 1950s.

Correspondence between Pach and Lewis Mumford began in 1922, and Mumford's first letter, written the following year, refers to Pach's article on modern art as "far & away the best piece of criticism we've had in America to my knowledge. . . ."[1] Letters between them spanned the next thirty-five years.

1. "Art. Modern Art. The Modern Period," *The Freeman* 7 (July 4, 1923), 398, 399.

7 Clinton St.
Brooklyn, July 5, 1923

Dear Walter:

Just a breathless note to congratulate you on the opening article on Modern Art.[1] It is far & away the best piece of criticism we've had in America to my knowledge—a really profound analysis. If the rest of the series goes on at this level you'll have left nothing for the rest of us to say! I am delighted—and other people are too.

My fond respects to Mrs. Pach

Lewis

1. "Art. Modern Art. The Modern Period." The article dealt with art produced between the French Revolution and World War I, and made reference to such innovators as Delacroix, Courbet, Daumier, and Cézanne.

---

c/o Mrs. A. Draves
Route 12
Westport, Conn., July 6, 1923

Dear Lewis,

I don't think you can know quite how kind it was to write that note that came to me to-day. You would have to know the cords and cords of pen-holders I chew up in writing an article and the special anxiety I have felt about this series, seeing that it is on the subject on which I feel most of all desirous of acquitting myself something like creditably.

In 1911 William C. Brownell[1] asked me to write it for Scribner's (the book house, not the magazine) and I have had a couple of other good offers to publish it. . . . Now I have taken the plunge, thanks to the Freeman's hospitality, . . . Miss La Follette and Brooks[2] have bucked me up about the articles, but yours is the first word written or spoken (if I except my wife's) to come to me from outside the editorial staff of the paper and give me the welcome idea that the work has good in it . . . and while I am at it, I might say thanks again for your help on the Mexican article.[3] It went through like a breeze . . . Mr. Wells said specifically that your suggestion, which I told him you had made and which—as you advised—involved the only considerable change, helped the thing immensely. We shall have to celebrate that when we're all near together again.

Despite this place's being favorable to long hours of work—which I need to finish the last volume of Faure—I still have some hankering for the city. Perhaps it would be different—I'm sure it would from the way you told of it—if I were tramping through those Tyrolese Alps or the Appalachians . . . I know the country is good for me physically if I *am* such a city man. And it is certainly fine to be able to run in and see Brooks.

I don't know if your week-ending would ever lead you up this way, but it *is* a very nice place and while this house is full until July 17th there would be a room after that, probably. Or if you would ever run up for a day (it is only an hour and a quarter or so from New York) we should be so glad to see you and Mrs. Mumford and could doubtless get up a nice party with the Brooks'. With kind regards to Mrs. Mumford and thanks again for your letter, I am

Yours cordially, Walter Pach

1. William Crary Brownell (1851–1928) was editor-in-chief of Charles Scribner's & Sons.

2. Suzanne La Follette and Van Wyck Brooks were among the five editors of *The Freeman*.

3. "Art. The Popular Arts of Mexico," *The Freeman* 6 (January 31, 1923), 496–497.

4. Elie Faure's *History of Art*, which Pach was translating from the French.

---

13 East 14th St.
New York, Dec. 12, 1924

Dear Lewis,

It is only to-day that I have been able to get the *New Republic*, (it was not on the news-stands hereabout yesterday), and now—with some people coming in to see me shortly—I have to choose between this very hasty word to you and postponing an acknowledgment—which I have it so much at heart to make that I hope you will pardon its insufficiency.

Your review[1] gave me the greatest pleasure I have had from any word about my book—spoken or written. I can't say that it is the correct judgment—being still (and probably for very long too near the writing of it), but it is what I would have hoped for if I had ventured to set my hopes very high.

Mr. Huebsch[2] must have thought me pretty nearly posing when I expressed discontent with one review that was praise from end to end. The reason was that it seemed to me undiscerning, that I felt the writer's next article would be all wrong. So that it is not only for what you say here, but for what you have written elsewhere that I rejoice in what you have written—and I fear you know only too well, from my indiscreet questioning in these last weeks, how eagerly I have been awaiting the appearance of your article.

By the way—to give this letter a little more substantial content than my thanks—which I do offer you most cordially—do you know a passage in van Gogh's letters, (Vollard edition, page 104), where he says of the prostitute "Etre exilé, rebut de la société, comme moi et toi artistes le sommes, elle est certes notre amie et soeur."[3] I have often quoted that in lectures (though not in print) as the most terrific indictment of the nineteenth century's attitude toward the masters. Perhaps you can use it, since you treat the question more often than I.

Herewith is Kimball's article,[4] which I should call merely lamentable (for his sake) if it were not one of the best proofs of the power of your book.[5] Only a work which could end up with that great envoi, lead up to it, justify it and demand it, could bring forth the angry outcry of Kimball's review. I think that even among readers of the Herald, it must have defeated its purpose.

I have been thinking about the Duchamp-Villon book[6] you have, and have decided that you really must keep it, if you will do me the favor to. Only the fact that, out of the limited edition, I have been unable to get my share so far (because of the printer's holding out on us) has made me parsimonious with the copies; but I don't know how one could be better employed than in your hands, so please do retain it. There is something of my own work in it, and you have said the kindest word about that.

With renewed thanks

Yours most cordially, Walter Pach

1. Of Pach's *Masters of Modern Art*.

2. Benjamin W. Huebsch (1876–1964), publisher of the Pach volume.

3. "To be exiled, rejected by society, like me and you artists that we are, she certainly is our friend and sister."

4. Fiske Kimball, a one-time practicing architect who would be appointed director of the Philadelphia Museum of Art in 1925.

5. *Sticks and Stones*.

6. Pach's *Raymond Duchamp-Villon, Sculpteur, 1876–1918* (Paris: Presses de l'Imprimerie Crozatier, 1924).

---

135 Hicks St.
Brooklyn, Dec. 15, 1924

Dear Walter:

Your letter gives me keen pleasure; and I, in turn, am almost at [a] loss to thank *you*. You are the only person who has so much as mentioned the Envoi, and yet, as you saw, that is the nub of the book. As for the gift, I accept it with deep gratitude, on condition that you treat me as *custodian*, with the privilege of surrendering it to you when better need or occasion calls. I agree completely with Duchamp-Villon's views on architecture in our time: he distinguishes clearly between using mechanistic forms, as Erich Mendellsohn [*sic*][1] uses electric lamps in the shape of insulators, and creating new forms which shall be *analogous* to those in a power plant or a factory, but necessarily *different*. A hundred thanks for this. If ever I have a chance to revise Sticks & Stones[2] I shall call upon D-Villon's words to bolster up my own imperfectly expressed meaning.

Devotedly yours, Lewis

P.S. I treasure that passage from Van Gogh. I only know the probably expurgated American edition of the letters.

1. Erich Mendelsohn (1887–1953), a German architect who designed the Einstein Tower in Potsdam in 1920.

2. Mumford's book *Sticks and Stones* was published earlier in 1924; its initial chapter was derived from five articles on American architecture written by him for *The Freeman*.

New York, Feb. 15, 1925

Dear Lewis,

Your letter about my show[1] is the first I have had about it, just as the one about my *Freeman* articles (the ones that went into the book) was the first I had about them. Both came most opportunely and I am grateful to you this time as I was before. It is not because "me hated rival," Forbes Watson,[2] roasted the show in the *World* this morning that the letter is opportune, although your underlining of the words 'emotional *suggestion*' is as if an anticipation of his chief complaint that my work lacks just that quality. Cortissoz,[3] on the other hand, is friendly and speaks of careful drawing and a couple of other things he finds good, though at the end his recollection of my critical heresies makes him take back some of his approval.

But I had discounted those articles before the pictures were hung, and what was, and still am eager for is the opinion of some half a dozen persons like yourself and Bryson Burroughs[4] and Ivins[5] who can see the work in comparison with other things of our time. That it should even have suggested Seurat to you is the best thing I could have hoped for. . . . Seurat was a genius, and he "realized" his art which is more than I have done. But I think some of my liking for him must have to do with my trying to think through to the reasons of things, which he certainly did. I saw his picture of the *Circus* again this week and it was immense—like an Italian fresco, so in rejoicing over the fact that his name came to your mind in writing me or in seeing the show, I hope I am not losing all sense of proportion. . . .

I am sure the Duchamp is the best portrait I have done, and I don't mind its being ten years old. I have not had such a personality to deal with since, but even so, it is better to have that work so far back because I can look at it more impersonally myself, and I think that some of the character-portrayal I was insisting on then is in the later heads. . . .

With greetin[g]s to you both,

Your always, Walter Pach

1. Held at the Brummer Galleries in New York.

2. Forbes Watson (1879–1960), Editor of *The Arts* Magazine.

3. Royal Cortissoz (1869–1948), art critic for the *New York Tribune*.

4. Bryson Burroughs (1869–1934), painter and curator of paintings at The Metropolitan Museum of Art.

5. William M. Ivins Jr. (1881–1961), curator of prints at the Metropolitan Museum.

BEI HERRN A. W. FROHBERG
PERMOSER STR. 4,
DRESDEN A., AUG. 6, 1929

Dear Lewis,

. . . I am sure that your run over to Europe, as short as it is, will give you a fresh start, mentally, and that your work next winter will benefit by it. When you are in the Hague, try to see the Kroller (Croller?) collection: one of the finest groups of modern things, including a great Seurat. London, Samuel Courtauld has wonderful things. . . . At the Tate Gallery you could doubtless learn how to get to see the collection.

We were so glad to have news of Van Wyck. I have not heard from Eleanor since we sailed. I sent her a few lines quite recently, for the most part because I wanted personal news, but also because I am anxious to get through with the Elie Faure book. I have had only half the translation from her and, as it is promised to Harper's and long over-due, I must translate the rest myself, if it is too much for her at present.[1] I should have taken the whole job off her shoulders ere now if she had not written me in March or April that the first draft was entirely finished by Van Wyck: she was to correct the mistakes in rendering the French. —Well nothing matters as compared with knowing that Van Wyck will regain his health, even if it does take years. . . .

Always cordially—Walter

1. Faure's fourth volume, *History of Art, Modern*, was not published by Harper & Bros. until 1937; the first three of the series, also translated from the French by Pach, appear in 1921, 1922, and 1923.

4002 Locust St.
Long Island City, Oct. 23, 1929

Dear Walter:

I have been dilatory and dumb, as Whitman says: and that is a poor return for the very generous and happy letter you wrote me in the beginning of August: but an inertia hung over me all summer, and it did not blow away until finally we came back to the city—when it did so so vigorously in a perfect whirlwind of engagements, teas, dinners, exhibitions, and so forth, that the will to write letters was effectually counterbalanced by the fact that I was, from moment to moment, peremptorily doing something else. Life is in balance again now; so I proceed: and to begin at the beginning, let us go back to the Middle of July. Sophie[1] had, even then, not fully recovered from the winter. So I cancelled my steamer reservation for the next week in order that she might have a week by herself in Martha[']s Vineyard, for the sake of the change and refreshment and absence of responsibility. I then sailed the following week on the Ile de France, and arrived in Europe just two days before my lectures were to begin. No time to rest. Worse than that: swollen tonsils and a last day of seasickness on board: also a feeling of despair, occasioned largely I suppose by the tonsils, at the fact that I had made the trip at all. My heart wasn't in it: things were too uncertain at home, and the winter had even then not worn off sufficiently. Well, thanks to Eva Goldbeck[2] in Paris I got through a day there and went on to Geneva; and thanks to Zimmern's[3] hospitality—I lived with them in Baron Necker's ancient house—and to the stimulus of the students and the good wine and everything, I got through the week very decently, improving lecture by lecture, until I finished fortissimo with as good a lecture as I had ever given. Meanwhile, I had decided to cut my trip short and return home. I was not in the mood for travel in the quick fashion I had planned; the prospect of it irritated me in the state I then was; and I knew that my observations and my contacts would all b[e] falsified by my internal state. So I came back, after spending twelve days on the continent; and when I reached New York decided that I had made a damned wise decision. Sophie had not had a happy time fending for herself; and the truth was that I should not have gone in the first place. Once this unhappy episode was over, everything began to knit together again. I waxed fat; we all improved. Our courage returned, too: we bought one of the pair of houses beyond Juckett's new place, from Spingarn.[4] A month ago we returned to the city. Now I have caught up with the calendar! This winter I shall be working on a little book on the arts in America since 1870;[5] arts in capital letters, America in lower case: hence philosophic rather than descriptive. Engineering: architecture: city design: perhaps painting, if I am sufficiently foolhardy.

I have not seen Suzanne LaFollette's book yet,[6] but doubt if they will conflict. If she has left nothing for me to say, I shall of course gracefully withdraw and not say it! As for gossip, though I have seen many people, there is little to give, or little that is worth broadcasting over the Atlantic. You know of course about the new Modern Gallery,[7] formed under the suspicious, or rather, in auspicious guidance of Frank Crowninshield:[8] I trust his coadjutants and supporters are nicer people! Irita Van Doren has been or is being divorced from the revered Carl.[9] Jimmy Walker[10] is about to flimflam the five million idiots who compose the city into submitting to have their pockets picked by his gang for another term. The New American Caravan[11] has just appeared and is being damned with faint praise in positively the dullest reviews it has ever been my bad luck to read: but since the book pleases the booksellers, it is doing very nicely from the publishers standpoint. Should you see any young Americans in Paris who have mss. that are unprinted, especially if they are experimental, fresh, or otherwise worthy of notice, please tell them to send them on direct to me. As for Brooks, I haven't heard a word from Eleanor[12] all summer and have been loath to make a direct approach; but I expect to hear tomorrow, through Zinsser,[13] what has been happening to him. Eleanor, I fear, was pretty well done up by the winter's experience; so I haven't really even hoped to hear directly from her. Did I tell you about the Dutton incident. (Secret.) Macrae[14] wrote to ask if I would edit the Emerson.[15] Eleanor had told him that I would. I decided to take a chance with Macrae's intelligence and generosity—I had no particular reason to believe he had much of either—and tell him the whole story of the mss., alluding of course only in the vaguest terms to Van Wyck's illness and indisposition.[16] He rose to the occasion splendidly: saw my point: agreed that he had no moral right to publish the Emerson under these circumstance: and wrote accordingly to Eleanor. I don't think she will have any fault to find with my proceeding when she has had time to think over things calmly; but in the meanwhile, she may well feel that I have been working against her—as of course I have: against her bad judgement. We saw little of the Robinsons[17] and less of Miss La Follette during the summer; but the Spingarns have been very nice, and since we have bought the house and certified our intentions of staying, as it were, they seem even more hearty in their cordiality than before. This may be an illusion on our part; since often enough one mistakes accident for design in human relationships. I have gossiped on like an octogenarian: it is time for you to I take the cue! I wish we could sit down together and talk over some of the hard parts in my new book.[18] I have been going, for the sake of mental calisthenics, through the whole literature of philosophic aesthetics; and I have dug up one or two mid-nineteenth century writers, one an Englishman named Dallas[19] and another an American named Bascom,[20] who made some very pertinent contributions to esthetic analysis—in the midst of much rubbish. Bascom states the Crocean doctrine of art as expression admirably, and Dallas had a very valid conception of the role of the unconscious in art: the essence of art, for him, is to reveal that which cannot be told: a profound truth, it seems to me, if one grasps its implications.

How goes your painting? Sophie joins me in affectionate greetings to you & Magda—not forgetting Raymond!

Lewis

1. Sophie Mumford, Lewis's wife.

2. The Mumfords released their apartment to her several years earlier.

3. Sir Alfred Zimmern (1879–1957), an Oxford University Fellow, had arranged for Mumford to lecture at his school for international education in Geneva.

4. Joel Elias Spingarn (1875–1939), an American publisher and literary critic.

5. *The Brown Decades: A Study of the Arts in America 1865–1895*, published in 1931.

6. Suzanne La Follette (1893–1983), an editor for *The Freeman*; her book was *Art in America*.

7. Reference is to the Museum of Modern Art; its formation was announced the previous month.

8. Frank Crowninshield (1872–1947), editor of *Vanity Fair* and a founding member of the museum board.

9. Carl Van Doren (1885–1950), author and editor of The Literary Guild.

10. James John ("Jimmy") Walker (1881–1946), mayor of New York City from 1926 to 1932.

11. The 1929 edition of a yearbook featuring new American writing. Mumford was one of its editors.

12. Van Wyck Brooks's wife.

13. Dr. Hans Zinsser (1878–1940), a professor at Harvard Medical School who was one of Van Wyck Brooks's doctors.

14. Elliott Beach Macrae (1900–1967), president of E. P. Dutton and Co., publisher of most of Brooks's books.

15. Brooks's manuscript for "The Life of Emerson," which was published in 1932.

16. Brooks had been receiving treatment for a psychiatric disorder.

17. Geroid T. Robinson and his wife; he was an editor of *The Freeman*.

18. *The Brown Decades*.

19. E. S. [Eneas Sweetland] Dallas (1828–1879).

20. John Bascom (1827–1911), author of *The Aesthetics or the Science of Beauty* (1862).

---

c/o Morgan & Co., 14 place Vendôme
Paris, Jan. 16, 1930

Dear Lewis,

Your letter of October 23rd began with observations on the way time goes, and I must speak of the same thing as I take up my pen (I've used it precious little of late). Elie Faure[1] was saying the same thing about time again, the other day, and remarked that there was some deep cause—in the nature of our period—for the phenomenon. I hope it will skip a cog now—for I'd so much like to hear from you.

Well, as to ourselves and Paris: It's just a marriage made in Heaven (if only Paris could know it!) We are as happy as the day is long, and we begrudge the time to sleep, though we do sleep long and well. I am even patient about my work, though goodness knows it doesn't justify patience any too much. And this week I had a grand visit at the studio of the most impatient man in the world. That is Picasso, and it was awe-inspiring to see the lengths that that passion of his has carried him. I have seen thirty-five years of painting from him (he will be 49, this year) and he simply keeps springing back to his work like a tiger attacking. Not but that he does not do very calm things too. Lately I got a recent etching of his (by luck—for they cost $60 in the shops. That's *some* price for contemporary work—without the fictitious boosting of the things in New York galleries)—and the print is just a piece of well-sustained perfection. The next day he may do a piece of breath-taking experiment, but even that will have something definitive about it. And there's so much that's exciting here. I've confidence that it will get under my hide—which I felt getting flabby in New York. What a shame that your own visit to Europe didn't net you more!

By mistake Suzanne La Follette's book was not sent me on publication; I've not seen it yet. I've written to ask for it. I'm not sure it's well done, but she had a heavy proposition to deal with, and there's undoubtedly room for all sorts of further discussion from you of the subject. I wish to goodness we could have an evening on the thing—though my own thoughts are pretty far from it. They are mostly around some variant of the opposition between the Classical and the Romantic points of view. Should we work for perfection or for a wider vision? The latter may carry with it the former and just possibly but not probably, perfectionism may induce a new grasp of things (the two go together in Delacroix—who obsesses me more and more).

Did you read the two editorials (especially the latter one of Dec. 21st[)], which The Art News had on the American show at the Modern Museum.[2] It would be worthwhile to look them up at a library. As I am one of the men omitted from the show, it might seem envious had I written the article, but I should have been astounded had they included me in the show—and I don't think they could have made a good show without the most drastic cuts. We've just got to work—and not expect too much in a hurry.

I'm positive you did the right thing about Van Wyck's mss. Though I've heard quite a number of times from Eleanor, I know only in general about Van Wyck—no details, but his condition seems to give her less of acute distress than last spring.

I know nothing of the two writers on aesthetics you mention—Bascom and Dallas. If you can get hold of *Formes*, a beautiful new magazine of which two issues have appeared here, you will find stuff in it which ought to interest you. It has an edition in English. Waldemar George, the editor, is continually more interested in the philosophy of art and is getting brilliant men to contribute. If ever you chanced to feel like publishing anything with them, I am sure you would be welcomed.

I mentioned your "Caravan" proposition to Francis Steegmuller (Byron Steele, author of "O Rare Ben Jonson!"). He is the only young writer I've seen; he was interested. We see very few people, really, and almost no Americans. It isn't exclusiveness on our part, but a desire to retain our energy and enjoy our quiet and our work. We do think of Americans though; there are lots of fine people in New York. But the big sweep of things is still here, as far as my line of work is concerned. After the years when we had to look to the Matisse-Derain generation for the continuance of things (and they keep up and go ahead quite marvelously) new men are coming forth again as in the days before the war. I look forward to the Independants next week with impatience; the Salon d'Automne, while still in existence, has gone the way of all flesh—it even smells that way. The Louvre is the quintessence of excitement—if you only get past the crust of it. The dealers are wonders: half-pirate, half-poet. Magda is getting much from her stay, and enjoying it. Raymond is at an excellent American boarding school just outside Paris. He likes it. We go to see him at the end of one fortnight in the month, the other he spends the weekend with us (Our studio is a corker—but too small for the three of us).

Best regards to Sophie. All good wishes to the three of you.

Walter

1. Elie Faure (1873–1937), a French art critic and essayist, whose five-volume *History of Art* was translated into English by Pach. The final book in the nine-year long project was published in 1930. Pach had also translated Faure's essay on *Cézanne*, which was produced as a pamphlet available for sale at the 1913 Armory Show.

2. The editorial contended that "the problems presented by the exhibition . . . are too serious to be dismissed casually. . . . [T]he attempt to include all types [of art] seemed to result in a confusion which did justice to none. . . . The depression which the exhibition causes arises from the whole rather than from the mixture."

Long Island City, March 12, 1930

Dear Walter:

It was a great joy to get your letter. The winter has been, on the whole, a happy one for all of us—although Sophie spent five weeks of misery with a carbuncle on her neck, after Thanksgiving, & at the present moment I am laid up and confined to the house by the same kind of sweet visitor—in my case due, I think, to an infected tooth. But we've had fun in the spaces in between, meeting people again, going to theaters & concerts & parties & exhibitions, and, in general, raising hell. I have done precious little work, except by way of preparation. My Dartmouth lectures were a success, or so it seemed; but I find my mind brooding, not over my next book, or the arts, but over one that looms up directly after, an attempt to put together in a clean tangible form a modern philosophy of life. I resent a little the writing of the present book, but I lack the year or two of further seasoning that's necessary before the bigger work will be ready; so in the meanwhile, I mark time & gather energy for the big ordeal! Suzanne La Follette's book was altogether a happy surprise: I hadn't believed, till I saw it, that anyone could have done such a good job. Harper's approached me about it four years ago, and I refused because it seemed to me that the spadework hadn't been done: but she bravely surmounted that handicap & despite occasional lapses, she has made a real contribution. My own book is on quite different lines; for one thing, it will not be historical. At the end of the week The New Freeman will be out. Everyone is curious about it: Curious & a little doubtful. I am glad to see, judging by the typography alone—I have an article in the first no.—that she is not trying to resurrect the old bones: so far good. On the other hand, she has taken on George Jean Nathan as dramatic critic; and that seems to me definitely a stale touch. . . . Doubtless you've read & heard about the Modern Museum developments. The director *began* by making compromises, & I doubt if there is any chance that the museum will ever get properly on its feet. Not merely did they make a ridiculous selection of American artists—fancy including Walt Kuhn & Kent, to say nothing of an *American* like Feininger!—but they attempt to get, not the best pictures available, but those that are owned by their patrons. It smells, despite one's gratitude for all the magnificent Cézannes they assembled for the opening show. I liked the Derains & the Dufresnes at their French show: but Valentine showed better Matisse's [*sic*] this winter, & some of the French work seemed very skimpy & thin, Leger & Laurencin for example; & I cannot share Faure's admiration for Bonnard. Do you? I hope your own work is thriving, & I wish I could run over this spring to embrace it & you: but what with my book & a tonsil operation for Geddes, and making our new home in Leedsville livable, I doubt if there'll be any chance of that, till next Fall at earliest—if then. Remember us all warmly to Raymond & Magda—

Ever yours, Lewis

PARIS, DEC. 26, 1930

Dear Lewis,

Your letter of September is before me. We were glad to hear that Sophie's trip to Europe was such a success and that you had gone ahead with your book. I shall be deeply interested in it, as you know already. Just lately I had a new light on the subject myself. It is in the shape of a study by Thomas Eakins[1] that I saw in an exhibition a number of years ago and that I had been trying to track down to its hiding place ever since. Now it has come to its surface again, the surface—if one can mention the word in reference to so deep a thing—being the wall of our studio where it hangs with works by the greatest men of the Nineteenth Century. And it holds its own with them! So much for any question of an inferiority complex in my mind as regards American art. Prendergast would stand up too, with the best men of his generation—which isn't saying that either American is the equal of his greatest French contemporaries . . . lately I got Weyhe's advertisement[2] of Rockwell Kent's new book in which Lawrence Stallings couples the name of our blatant boob with that of Leonardo da Vinci. And then people wonder why I am not anxious to get back to a place where such things are possible. They are not here: rotten men go into the Luxembourg, to be sure,[3] (not as rotten or as frequently as in the past), but no well-known playwright would compare them with supreme masters or if he did, no bookseller of Weyhe's position would broadcast the jackassery. However, there is good in America, in the quiet places, and I shall have pleasant times and pleasant associations, especially when we go back. . . .

We have just had a letter from Eleanor Brooks, the first in a long time. She says there is not much change in Van Wyck, which is sad. Do you get to see him?

I have had only three of four copies of The New Freeman since it was started, and did not get much of a thrill from it. There were good features—and I was willing to blame myself and my interest in things here for my not liking the rest; but perhaps it is part of the general depression in America. After the war, when the franc was down, Marcel Duchamp made the excellent remark that the output of the painters could be called "*de mauvaises emissions*,"[4] like the government paper. I see only the Nation here (no dailies)—and the Art News, which has gone away off since Fulton left it, so I don't know what is doing in America. There is *some* fine work here in the preposterous welter at the big salons, or rather, outside of them. Hardly any good men send there any more and I guess I shall never go again. Paris needs quiet, just as New York does—and I do; and it knows how to get it. My show at Kraushaar's is during the first fortnight of March. I shall be working up to the last moment before sending, as usual. I have just done a portrait which is, I am sure, my best. Did you hear that four of my Paris water colors have been accepted by the Metropolitan? . . .

. . . good luck to you all.

Walter

1. The untitled work, a gift to Pach from Mrs. Eakins, is referred to in her letter to him of September 25, 1930.

2. Erhard Weyhe owned a bookshop and print gallery on Lexington Avenue in New York.

3. After a notable French artist died, it was traditional for his or her work to remain in the government's Luxembourg Museum for ten years before any could be transferred to the Louvre.

4. "bad emissions."

Tangier, Aug. 23, 1931

Dear Lewis,

It was good to get your letter of the early Summer and to know you are steadily at work. . . . I shall certainly look forward to your book on the Brown Decades. Is it from the brownstone used in building the old private houses?[1] They were my ideal of opulence when I was a boy and lived in a "railroad flat," and "Irish flat," as one of our friends called it in disparagement. . . . I know a certain amount of work by Robert L. Newman[2] and think him a sympathetic artist, but not a great one. I suppose no one does compare him with Ryder—and I don't put Ryder on very great heights, as Childe Hassam does, for example. Of course it's nothing new for me to talk Prendergast, but I don't think enough people realize, as yet, what a beautiful painter he was. I didn't see the catalogue of the "50 Prints"; there *is* some creditable black-and-white work being done in America. Did you hear that I had caused a picture by Eakins to be acquired by the Louvre? Probably not; I don't think it's been in the papers. In fact, I don't know that the picture has reached Paris yet. I got the photograph, on which it was accepted, from Bryson Burroughs, who engineered the obtaining of the painting from the Pennsylvania Museum, the recipient of what remained to Mrs. Eakins of her husband's work. I'm awfully pleased for her sake, as well as for the cause of that art-recognition in America that I spoke of before. One thing that holds you back on doing anything for *American* art is that one sees in it with special clearness that "patriotism is the last resort of Scoundrels". . . .

Morocco is a sort of a dream place—only that it's so real. We have just come to it as a place to pass the summer in, but it's stupendously beautiful, very cool (here at Tangier—the interior is hot), and the interest and mystery of the Moors are inexhaustible. What I like best are the story tellers, especially one venerable blind man, whom one sees at evening in the market place surrounded by a crowd of simple people who hear the Thousand and One Nights for the millionth time. I wish I spoke Arabic so that I could fit the speaker's gestures and tone with his words, but the former are unmistak[ab]le. What I really needed Arabic for was to talk to a model we had. She is one of the most beautiful creatures I've ever seen, not only through her face and figure, but in her way of wearing her gorgeous clothes. And she lives with complete abandon to the sun and the air, though hemmed in by Moslem ideas about women, who are really just animals here—like fawns, doves, etc. Magda was probably right in saying that I should be disappointed if I could speak to her.

We go to Spain in another week, shall be there about two weeks, and then back to Paris—always the best place in the world, even after Morocco! Many people would snicker over my saying that; but they haven't spent the time in Paris necessary for them to appreciate its superiorities. Good luck to you all.

Cordially—Walter

1. Lewis Mumford explains in *The Brown Decades*, published in the year this letter was written, that the term he coined refers to the period between 1865 and 1895. He describes the seventeenth century of American history as a long winter, the eighteenth as a slow spring, and the period that began with the Civil War as a "violent stormy summer" that "shook down the blossoms and blasted the promise of spring. . . . By the time the war was over, browns had spread everywhere: mediocre drabs, dingy chocolate browns, sooty browns that merged into black. Autumn had come" (p. 5).

2. Robert Loftin Newman (1827–1912), an American who sought to express subjective feelings through pigment and color.

PARIS, FEB. 17, 1932

Dear Lewis,

I have just finished The Brown Decades, and it's a fine book. The parts on [H. H.] Richardson, [Louis] Sullivan, and [Frank Lloyd) Wright set their figures in an exact place for me, though I knew about them in a general way, and I think that for many people those solid pages on architecture (airy and luminous, beside being solid) will give the work a special value. I can say with a shade more confidence that the estimates of Homer, Eakins, and Ryder are weighty and just—and again with an element of beauty that does away with any prosaic tinge that might attach to those other words. But it is not the individual portraits and interpretations that leave the main impression on my mind: it really is the period that is portrayed—I might almost say created, for no one I know has isolated those decades before, and I am sure that the future will more than confirm your seeing of them. There are minor differences in appreciation that I should make, as regards Prendergast, for example; you use some excellent words about him but I think he deserves a larger space and, yes, even more recognition as *the* man who brought American achievement in painting nearest to that of the great Frenchmen of his day.

Thank you for giving me a place similar to that of La Farge[1] (who really was a great influence), and I should be glad to think I had done what I could in bringing the vastly important ideas of the later time to our artists and public. . . .

I made a couple of notes as I went along. Doubtless you have caught the typographical errors like Nath for Nast (P. 19), Edouard for Edgar Degas (P. 210), C. W. for C. D. Warner (P. 252). 1 put them down anyhow for later printings, against the chance that they have slipped so far; there are some that do that for years.

I was especially impressed with the section ending on Page 159 with the words "The only kind of tower the architect must deny himself the privilege of building is a Tower of Ivory." . . .

I have the notion that when Ryder spoke the words you quote—that the galleries of Europe meant nothing to him (as it wasn't to you personally, I'm almost wondering if he really said that), he was speaking on a moment's impulse, an isolated one. Once when I called to say good-bye, when about to go abroad, I was just reaching the front door when I heard his heavey shoes clattering excitedly down the stairs after me, and when he saw me waiting he said "Oh, I'm so glad I caught you yet. I wanted to ask you to give my love to that Rembrandt in the Pitti [Palace]!" I believe that was more typical of him. . . .

Yours cordially, Walter Pach

1. Mumford wrote: "La Farge did in America what only an eclectic artist could do: he placed the American artist on a footing with his contemporaries in Europe, and overcame . . . the touch of provincialism that would in the long run have proved a serious handicap to American art. Mr. Walter Pach has performed a similar function in our own day, with equal vigour and understanding; . . ." (p. 208).

---

39 West 67th St.
New York, March 13, 1934

Dear Lewis,

I thought last night that you were the guest of the Whitney Museum people and that I ought not to take time that belonged to them by starting a conversation, when I had so much to say. It must wait for a better time.

But I want to write this line the first thing this morning to tell you I liked immensely what you told that audience, especially about the two New Englands. . . . I think it was useful, too, that you put in some words about the narrower type of nationalism. Not that that audience is particularly afflicted with it, but that a large part of the country is. One other point that struck me, and I think I have never heard it said in so accurate a way before, was your explaining that painting formulates a new idea in the world while it is still in the image state that has not yet reduced itself to words.

I hope I can some time follow the "Go to see the Terburgs" advice, for I am not altogether sure how much I shall like the Orozcos.[1] In 1922, in Mexico, before he had begun to paint—in the true sense (I remember some water colors, but they were more drawings in wash) I was struck with the power of his draftsmanship, and that seems to me his main asset still, though he has tried to add to it. Unless he has succeeded more than in the (very few) paintings I have seen, it would seem too limited an equipment for the literary content of his work—which latter I like. Perhaps, as with [Diego] Rivera—whose easel pictures I think far less successful than his murals—Orozco has to be seen in large-scale works. The one time I saw those at the New School,[2] in 12th St., I did not like them.

I certainly did take the strongest interest in the lecture.

Best wishes again to Sophie.

Yours, Walter Pach

1. José Clemente Orozco (1883–1949), the Mexican muralist whose subject matter often deals with the smoldering unhappiness of mankind. He had attended Pach's lectures on art at the University of Mexico in 1922.

2. Orozco's mural at the New School for Social Research was a fresco.

WESTPORT, AUG. 20, 1934

Dear Lewis,

We came out here a little over two weeks ago. . . .

I had been reading the *Technics* book[1] pretty steadily, a little at a time, before we came out here—where I finished it soon after our arrival. . . .

As people so much better qualified than I have told how good the book is, I want to speak of one place that I believe I do know something about and where I disagree. It is in the matter of photography, which you speak of as one of the arts of the machine. I don't think it is an art, except in that wide sense in which numberless activities are called arts—all too-loosely, I believe. I do not "disdain it because it cannot do what Rembrandt or Tintoretto did," and for the reason you give in the same sentence, I think: that it is Science or rather you say that to disdain it is to disdain Science because—(etc). Its function is reproduction, the contrary of art. As you say, all photographs are essentially snapshots; they reproduce what is before the lens and (this time to quote exactly what you have on Page 241)—"As with all instruments of multiplication the critical question is as to the function and quality of the object one is multiplying." The photograph is essentially that object—in a mirror whose image chemistry renders permanent. Stieglitz says that he will make a photograph and let some one else make one of the same subject, with the same camera, under the same light, etc., etc.—and that the two pictures will be different. The difference will be no more important than that which permits workmen to distinguish one from the other two apparently identical products of their factory. Their practised eyes *do* see some infinitesimal distinction. But that does not make the thing a work of art—which, like a Rembrandt etching, *can* be "multiplied" without loss of the genius in it.

. . . I do want to add a line on the excellence of your *New Yorker* article on the Modern Museum and its shortcomings. I really think the Metropolitan is incomparably the more hopeful place. Best wishes to Sophy and to you. As always

Cordially, Walter Pach

1. Mumford's volume, *Technics and Civilization*, published by Harcourt, Brace & Co. in 1934.

---

148 West 72nd St.
New York, May 2, 1935

Dear Lewis,

We are happy at your news, and thank you for the letter that brought it. May the life of Alison Jane be long and happy—like the ones so well deserved by her parents.

. . . I wanted to add a word about the [Bryson] Burroughs matter, a friend just now having given me the *New Yorker* of April 20th.[1] I think your rejoiner was very convincing, especially as neither Mrs. Force nor Goodrich[2] answered you on the point which you raised and which you now repeat in italics. I told them, when declining their request to join in their protest, that I had still a warm regard for Burroughs and that I thought your criticism went too far (more exactly, it was one that could in all fairness be levelled at the trustees—who deserve far more, especially for what they did to Burroughs); but I would not, as I said consent to anything that would tend to impair the usefulness that you have given to your column. As I told you on the phone, the motive behind the protest was spite over another of your articles,—the instigator of the protest keeping out of it after egging the rest of us on. Mrs. Force and Goodrich did, however, feel warmly toward Burroughs, who was lovable beside being learned. His weakness was the result (in part, at least) of his job and the men who rode him in it.

Once more, all good wishes to you and Sophie and the new little girl. I have just been at Dartmouth. The Orozco things are very impressive, despite deep-rooted faults.

As always, cordially, Walter Pach

My fresco will be on view at Knoedler's, on May 20th.

1. Lewis Mumford, "In the Galleries: Mirrors and the Metropolitan," *The New Yorker* 11 (April 6 [not the 20th], 1935), 79–80. The article reviews a retrospective exhibit by the late Bryson Burroughs, an artist as well as the museum's curator of paintings. Mumford's italicized portion reads: "[O]ne has to see his work *en masse* to realize what a jugful of tasteless syrup it was."

2. Juliana Force and Lloyd Goodrich were manager and curator, respectively, at the Whitney Museum of American Art.

New York, Nov. 12, 1936

Dear Lewis,

Thank you very much for the paragraph in the *New Yorker*. It ought to help a great deal with the public and I know it has already helped with Kleemann—who is sensitive to recognition. He was enormously bucked up by what you wrote on Ryder last year.

It is good to have some one puncture that old superstition about "pure" water color. (Frank Alvah Parsons,[1] when I once accidentally heard a few words of his lecture at the Metropolitan, defended a Cabanel[2] picture by saying it represented a pure woman—even if her draperies were transparent, like the water color of the classicist "masters" of the medium). But I guess we shall have to wait a bit till we see the people who fuss about purities or impurities get down to essentials in pictures. You must have felt there were some in mine or you could not have used the convincing tone you did—and that is the main thing.

The Picasso article is strong—and recalls the article you did on the Abstract Show at the Modern Museum last year. I thought then as now that you were breaking through to some very genuine considerations and that "the world do move."

Best wishes to Sophie and the still younger folks, and good luck with your own work. I'm sure your article will make mine more acceptable to many people—which I need it to be.

As always

Cordially, Walter

1. Frank Alvah Parsons (1866–1930), President of the New York School of Art (the former Chase School), which later became the New York School of Fine and Applied Arts.

2. Alexandre Cabanal (1823–1889), a popular academic painter of historic and classical subjects.

---

65 rue des Saints Peres
Paris, April 29, 1957

Dear Walter:

Even before I came over here I had many occasions to think of you this winter: for, in preparation for a book I've begun, I went through my rich files of correspondence, since 1920; and your letters to me were among the real treasures of that collection. (Unless you have made some other disposition of your own papers, they will remain with mine, for some future young historian to pore through,—I hope not just paw through!—eagerly.) Every time I walk through this quarter I think back to all your friendliness and hospitality in 1932, the first time I really *took in* Paris; or was ready, rather, to let Paris take in me! I write you now after ten days of quite blissful solitude—Sophy joins me tomorrow, I'm glad to say—for all my French friends here are by some queer chance either ill or in some other part of the world. Never has the city spoken so lovingly to me as this time, or said so much. At the Louvre I was amused to find how one's tastes mature with age. Ingres, whom I couldn't bear when I was young and rebellious against all he stood for, now seems to me worthy to stand beside any of the other masters; and his

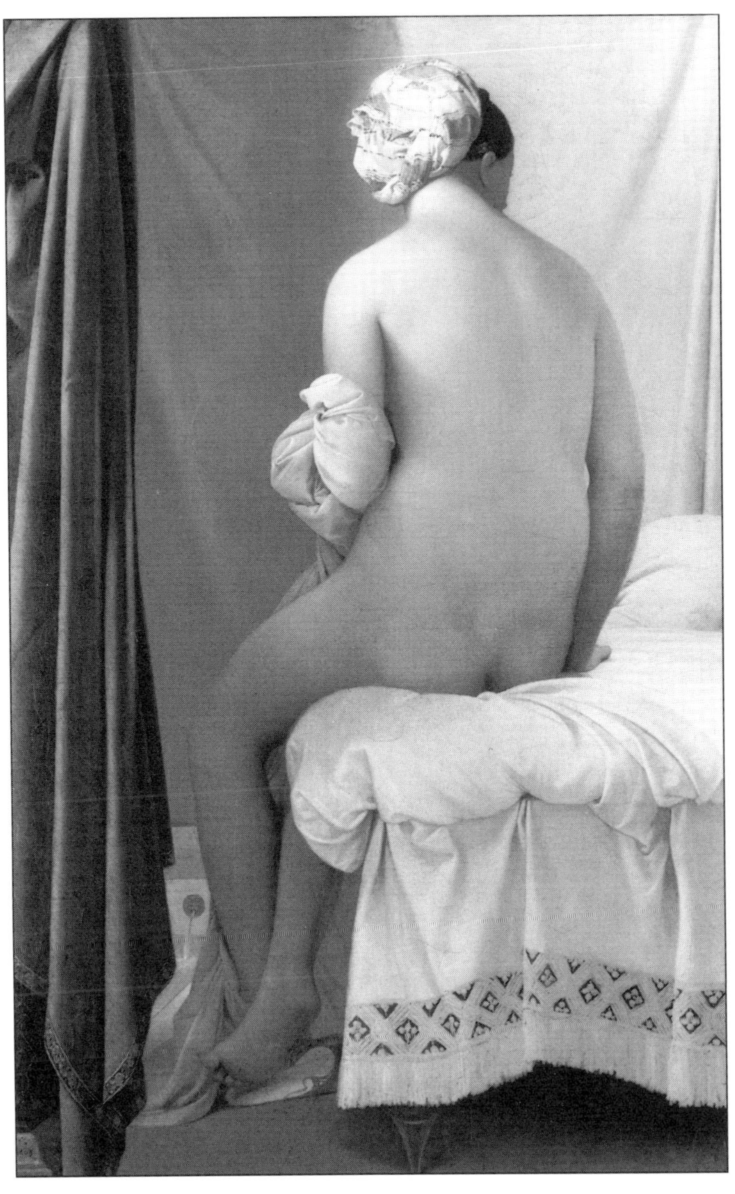

Jean-Auguste-Dominique Ingres, *The Valpinçon Bather*, 1808. Oil on canvas, 56 5/8 x 38 1/4 in. Louvre, Paris, France. Réunion des Musées Nationaux/ Art Resource, NY.

Baigneuse, which I never noted before, seemed to me as close to perfection as Veronese's Susanne. As for your Géricault, I found The Raft of the Medusa so powerful it was almost painful. But these are doubtless old thoughts with you. . . . We have three months ahead of us, on my Guggenheim, before coming back to America: but I could not stay in this second home of yours, dear Walter, without sending you at least this brief salute.

Warmly & affectionately, Lewis

New York, June 2, 1957

Dear Lewis,

Your quite unexpected but so *very* welcome letter has been in my hands for over two weeks, as I regret to say . . . what a satisfaction it was, and is, to me that our talks of 1932 recurred to you on seeing the Louvre again. Yes, Ingres does stand with the giants, even if that last word is hardly one that one would think of for him at the first moment. Cézanne spoke of "l'humble et colossal Pissarro," and *there* is a pair of words that scarcely go together. With all the strong feeling I have for Pissarro, I should not have thought of "colossal" for him (though Cézanne had a right to). Anyway, Ingres does keep on growing in stature, despite many works that are below his best, even far below. But that *Bather* you speak of (undoubtedly the large canvas of 1808, *la Baigneuse de Valpinçon*) is such a marvel! And *Mlle Rivière!* and M. *Bertin!* and the *Stratonice* at Chantilly! I take it you've been there—if only for the little pictures by or near to Fouquet; they are among the miracles of painting. If by any chance you've not seen them (and other great things there) do go at once—first informing yourself about the days for visits (it's closed on racing days); and on Sundays one used to be herded through with a mob by an attendant who allowed only four or five minutes, perhaps, for the "Fouquet" (or Pol de Limbourg) paintings, a maddening business.

You are so right, too, about Géricault. The *Raft of the Medusa* may well be the greatest picture of the century, though I prefer Delacroix, myself. . . .

When the Van Wyck Brookses were in town for a month or so, this spring, I had several good talks with him and wondered at his capacity for suffering fools—if not gladly—at least with equanimity. I can't do it. Lately James Rorimer published an article containing these words: "Best-loved pictures nowadays include such different types as Leutze's *Washington Crossing the Delaware*, El Greco's *View of Toledo*, Dali's *Crucifixion*, and Van Gogh's *L'Arlésienne*." The Dali is a particularly offensive picture, and to string together those names makes me think he could just as well go on with Ella Wheeler Wilcox, Walt Whitman, a pimp, and Abraham Lincoln. No wonder the public is always more badly confused, when the head of the Metropolitan Museum refuses to discriminate between good and bad. . . .

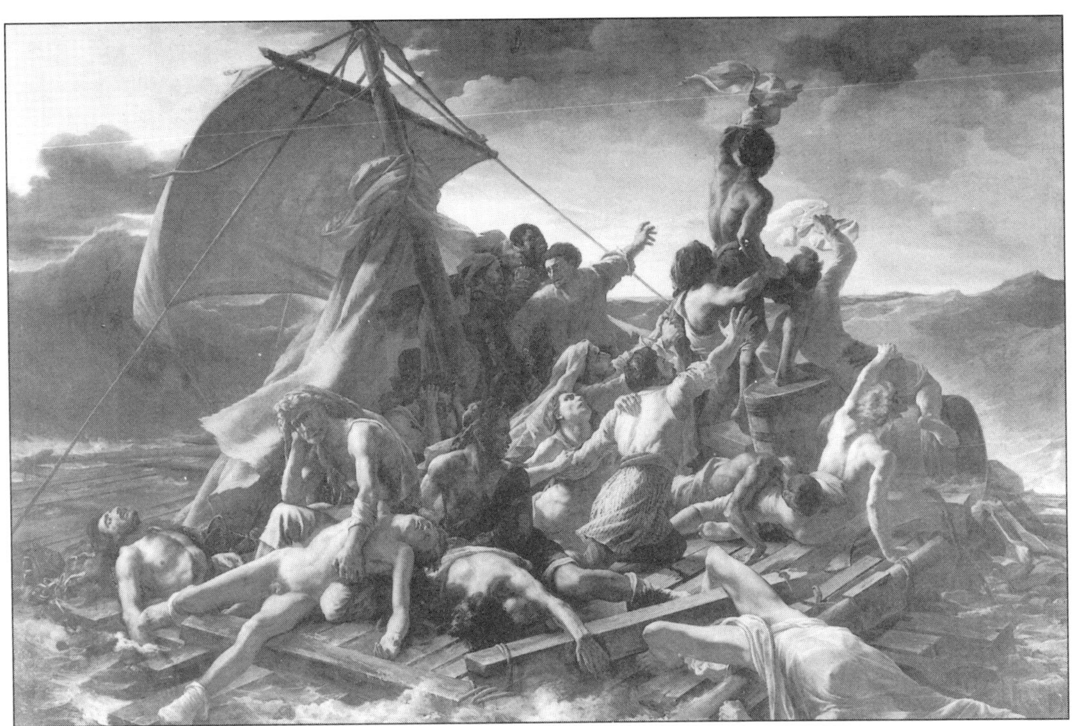

Théodore Géricault, *The Raft of the Medusa*, 1819. Oil on canvas, 16 ft. 1 in. x 22 ft. 11 1/4 in. Louvre, Paris, France. Réunion des Musées Nationaux/Art Resource, NY.

I'm so glad you are living in the rue des Saints Pères and are enjoying that blessed quarter of Paris. Do you sometimes walk to the Place des Innocents for the Jean Goujon figures[1] that so affected Renoir when he was a small boy? It is one of my favorite spots.

All good wishes to you and Sophie. I do hope for a get-together on your return.

Cordially—Walter

1. Goujon (active 1540–1562) created his *Fountain of the Innocents* there.

Source of Letters: Lewis Mumford Papers, Rare Book and Manuscript Library, University of Pennsylvania, which contains additional Mumford/Pach correspondence.

Also available through the Archives of American Art, reels 4217, 4218.

DUNCAN PHILLIPS
(1886–1966)

Art collector and author. He was the grandson of the co-founder of Jones and Laughlin Steel Company in Pittsburgh. In 1921 he opened The Phillips Memorial Art Gallery, now The Phillips Collection, in his home in Washington, D.C. Although heralded as the country's first public museum of modern art, the Phillips contained precious few works of the most contemporary twentieth-century art during its early years; its first canvas by a French Cubist, purchased in 1928, was Jacques Villon's *L'Atelier Mecanique* (*Machine Shop*), painted in 1913 and acquired from the artist by Walter Pach the following year. On January 27, 1913, Mr. Phillips recorded this comment made to him by Pach: "Speaking to Diego Rivera in Detroit last week of the work of Villon, he [Rivera] said 'the best picture that Jacques ever painted was the *atelier de mechanique*.' As I got the picture from Villon's studio during the war and brought it to America then, Rivera had not seen it in nearly twenty years; it is significant that he should retain the work so clearly in his memory."[1]

Correspondence with Duncan Phillips was initiated by Pach in 1926.

1. Handwritten note, Accessions Folder, Registrar's Office, The Phillips Collection.

48 WEST 56TH ST.
NEW YORK, MAY 15, 1926

Dear Mr. Phillips,

I enjoyed my visit to your gallery very much indeed and want to thank you again for your friendly reception. I spent some time among the pictures after you left and found them even better than they had appeared at first. I hope I may come back in a year or two, for at the rate you are going I am sure you will have one of the finest modern collections.

Do you know the Ingres in the Quinn Collection?[1] It was not shown at the Art Center,[2] as Mrs. Anderson[3] did not want to part with it at the time. But she is now willing to—for $25,000, though I know that the Bank (which handles the estate) sometimes accepts offers, having successfully made one myself.[4]

The picture is one of unusual quality, even for Ingres. I remember Mr. Quinn's pride when he got it, and his showing me the illustrations in the Ingres book to prove how the painter had surpassed his earlier version of the subject.[5]

I sail for Europe on June 1st, to be gone until September 1st. If you some time have a spare hour in New York, it would be a pleasure for Mrs. Pach and myself to see you here.

With regards,

Yours very sincerely, Walter Pach

1. *Raphael et la Fornarina*. Oil, 10 1/2 x 21 1/2″.

2. In the *Memorial Exhibition of Representative Works Selected from the John Quinn Collection* at the Art Center in New York City, January 7 to 30, 1926.

3. Julia Quinn Anderson.

4. For Raymond Duchamp-Villon's *The Horse*, 1914. Bronze, 15 3/8″ high.

5. Despite Pach's enthusiasm for the work, Phillips did not purchase it. Twenty-two years later the collector acquired his first Ingres painting, titled *The Bather*.

---

39 WEST 67TH ST.
NEW YORK, JAN. 5, 1933

Dear Mr. Phillips,

Thank you for your letter.

I go to-morrow to Worcester to speak at the opening of the new museum building and of the International Exhibition. From Worcester I go to Chicago where I have four

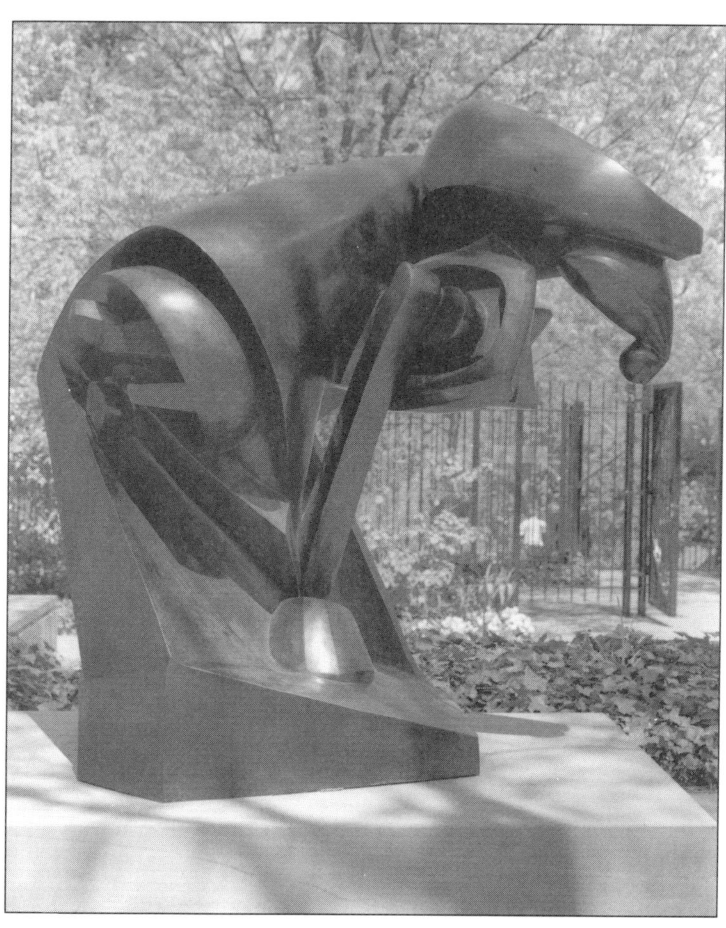

Raymond Duchamp-Villon, *The Horse*, 1919 (15 in. plaster models, 1914). Bronze, 59 in. high. The Baltimore Museum of Art: Alan and Janet Wurtzburger Collection. BMA 1974.62.5.

lectures at various times before the 17th when I leave for a stay in Detroit—first having made a run to Milwaukee. So that I shall not have much of a rest here before starting out again for Washington and I don't think I should try to get there before the 26th—on the *evening* of which date I give my lecture. . . . I should hope to have the pleasure of seeing you— . . . I certainly count very much on another sight of your beautiful things and on a good talk with you and Mrs. Phillips.

With regards from us both,

Yours cordially, Walter Pach

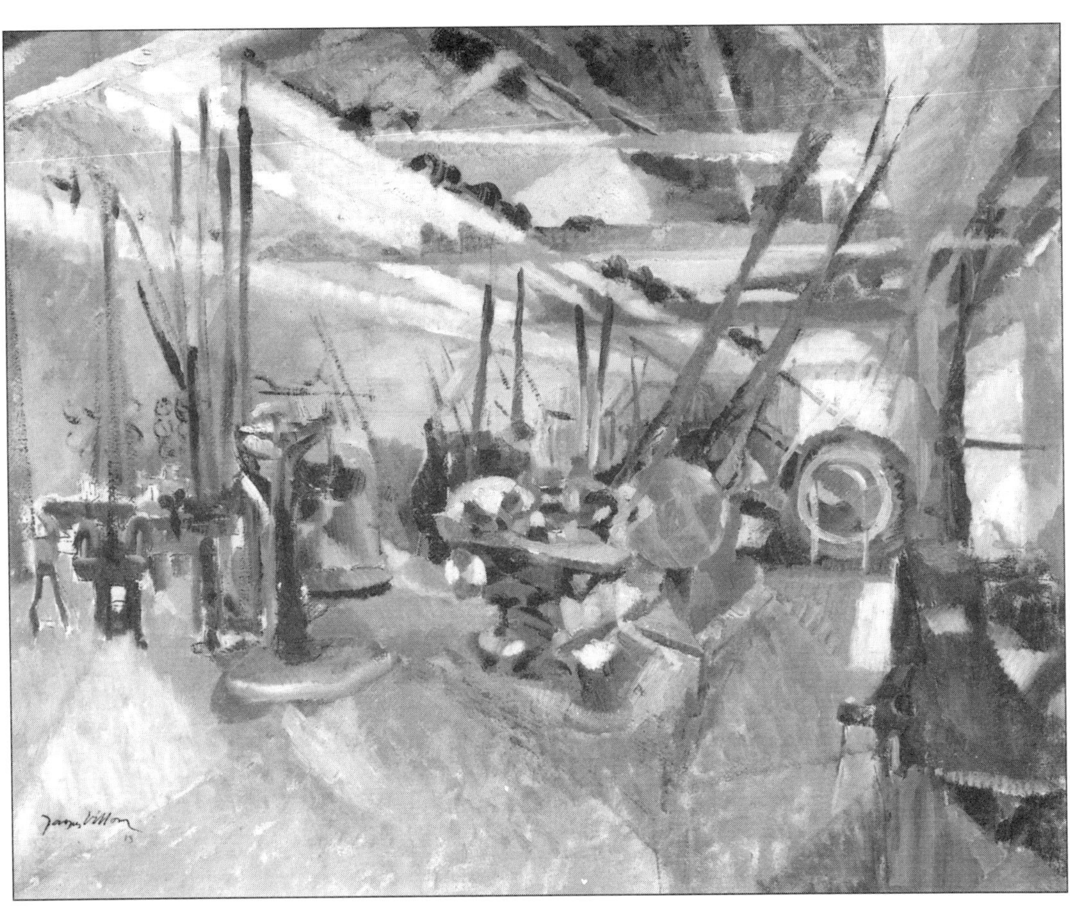

Jacques Villon, *Machine Shop*, 1913. Oil on canvas, 29 x 36 1/2 in. The Phillips Collection, Washington, D.C. Acquired 1928.

New York, Feb. 2, 1933

Dear Mr. Phillips,

This is mainly to say thanks once more for the good time I had at your house. . . .

There *is* one tiny emendation to my report on your Villon picture[1] which I should like to add for the record, for the sake of the artist who, I believe, has made important developments since 1913. It is to say "Rivera had seen nothing of Villon's work since the war (had he done so he might modify his statement that the *Atelier de Mécanique* is the best thing in *all* of Villon's work."

With kind regards to Mrs. Phillips, and with the hope to see you both here soon, I am

Yours very sincerely, Walter Pach

1. The report referred to was in the form of the following note written by Pach while at the Phillips Memorial Gallery five days earlier.

WASHINGTON, JAN. 27, 1933

Speaking to Diego Rivera in Detroit last week of the work of Villon, he said "the best picture that Jacques ever painted was the *atelier de mechanique*." As I got the picture from Villon's studio during the war and brought it to America then, Rivera had not seen it in nearly twenty years; it is significant that he should retain the work so clearly in his memory.—Walter Pach

---

OCT. 2, 1933

Dear Mr. Pach:

I have only been here a few days and our plans for the season are really still unsettled, consequently I have delayed answering your letter of June until we could decide whether there would be any lectures at all in connection with our season of exhibitions. Our financial prospects for the year are very bad indeed and we are not justified in doing any more than we did last year. We may open the Gallery daily instead of three times a week and charge the public for admission, the first time we have had to do so. I hope that we can have one or two paid lectures later in the season in addition to such talks as are given by myself and other members of the staff. I wish therefore that you were coming down to Norfolk at a later date for then there would be a better prospect of our being able to have you speak under our auspices. If we were to send out word that you are lecturing at our Gallery even before our opening date, November first, it would indicate to the public that we are starting an unusually active season when as a matter of fact the exact opposite will have to be the truth. We have thought of selling tickets for your lecture but have immediately vetoed that idea as contrary to our policy and our ideals for the Gallery which desires to continue to carry on its educational program as it has done in the past.

Our late opening this year is due to the fact that our greatest things are still at the Art Institute of Chicago and at one or two other exhibitions. The Gallery will be open through October but we shall make no public announcements of exhibitions until we open every day, except Monday, November first. It will be open to out of town visitors by request during October. I hope you will let me know if it would be possible for you to come back later in the year, in other words if your schedule would permit a special lecture in our Gallery after January first, 1934, in case we find that we can afford to have one or two speakers. Also I would like to know the lowest charge you could make, with expenses, and I would like to see again a list of your various subjects.

I hope that you and Mrs. Pach have had a pleasant summer. I did a lot of reading and some writing on art. Mrs. Phillips and I included in our reading The Spirit of Forms by Eli Faure in your admirable translation. With best regards,

Sincerely, [Duncan Phillips]

FEB. 26, 1940

Mr. Walter Pach, Director General
[Masterpieces of Art Exhibition] New York World's Fair 1940
56 East 68th St., New York

Dear Mr. Pach:

I have your letter of February 17th suggesting that we lend to the 1940 Fair four pictures by Daumier, Corot, Renoir and Cézanne. I have thought over your choices from our Collection and wish I could talk over with you my reasons for proposing an alternative loan. Our Renoir of the Canotiers[1] has been shown so often in New York and also throughout the country that I feel we should not send it again. I have made plans to have it relined this spring in Washington and Mr. Gaston Levi is coming for the purpose. I am sure you can get a more important Daumier than our "Mountebanks Resting." Were you to invite our "Uprising" it would be a contribution for the Collection to be proud of but this little picture is certainly not an outstanding example.[2] As for the "Mt. St. Victoire" of Cézanne, as you know it is now at the Museum of Modern Art where the usual thousands who throng that Gallery are becoming familiar with it. And now I have promised the great Cézanne Self Portrait to Miss Morgan's American Friends of France for a benefit exhibition she is arranging at Duran[d] Ruel's. That leaves of the pictures you suggested only the Corot Landscape which I will be very glad to lend. May I suggest that instead of the other three we could lend Van Gogh's "Public Gardens at Arles," a marvelous masterpiece which has not been shown in New York since the first exhibition of the Museum of Modern Art with the exception of a brief visit at the time of the return engagement of the Van Goghs at the same institution. My choices for the World's Fair this summer would be the Van Gogh Garden, and second the Self Portrait, third the Corot La Grande Metaire.[3] I am glad that you are selecting the pictures for the exhibition for that insures it will be important. With best wishes,

Sincerely yours, Duncan Phillips

1. *The Luncheon of the Boating Party* [*Le Déjeuner des Canotiers*], 1881. Oil on canvas, 51 x 68 in. Phillips finally agreed to lend it.

2. *Mountebanks Resting* measures only 12 x 14 3/4 inches; it was deaccessioned from the Phillips Collection.

3. Phillips loaned the Renoir, van Gogh's *Public Gardens at Arles*, and Corot's *La Grande Metairie* (the latter exhibited under the alternate title, *Farm, Early Morning*).

---

3 Washington Square
New York, Nov. 24, 1944

Dear Mr. Phillips,

I shall be very glad indeed to have our *Tiger* in your exhibition of Delacroix.

I first saw the *Hercules and Alcestis* when it was sold in Paris, and admired it then—in 1908. Since that time, it has seemed finer each time I have seen it and, when I was at your place a little over a year ago, I saw again that it was of the really great quality.

Thank you for what you say of my article,—and good luck to the show.

With remembrances to Mrs. Phillips, I am

Your very sincerely, Walter Pach

New York, Feb. 7, 1945

Dear Duncan,

You don't need to fear that every time you open your hospitable doors to me, a barrage of letters will result. But, just this time, I find I need to send you a postscript to yesterday's letter.

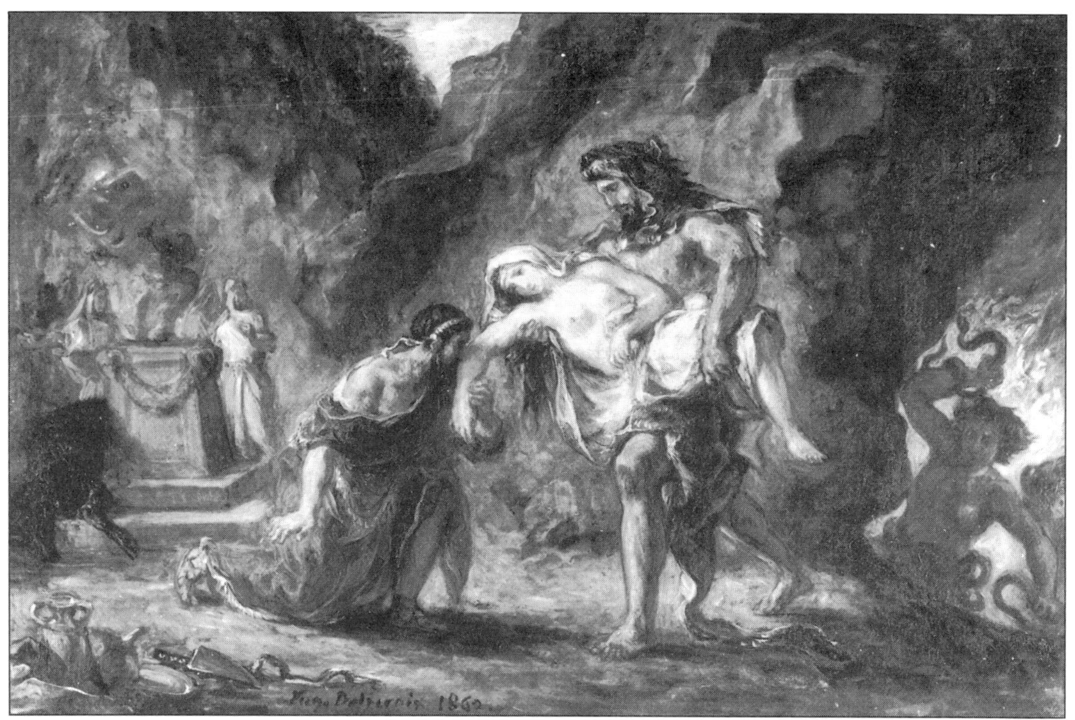

Eugène Delacroix, *Hercules and Alcestis*, 1862. Oil on cardboard set in wood panel, 12 3/4 x 19 1/4 in. The Phillips Collection, Washington, D.C. Acquired 1940.

For one thing, I thought it might really be worth while, yet, to recall one famous coupling of the names of the two artists we discussed. Baudelaire, in his reply to the critics of Delacroix's drawing, said he knew only two men in Paris who drew as well as Delacroix: they were Daumier and Ingres. There is indeed a relationship between the drawing of Delacroix and that of Daumier,—indeed an important one. But, as I said yesterday, time prevented me from going into such matters.-

Then, having a strong memory of your new Géricault, I should like to reproduce it with an article I am publishing on that master in the Gazette des Beaux-Arts. May I then so far tax your kindness as to ask that you have a photograph of the "Two Horses" sent to Mme. Assia R. Visson, 2715–36th Place, N.W., Washington. I shall write her that I have asked you for it.

With regards to you and Mrs. Phillips, I am

Yours very sincerely, Walter Pach

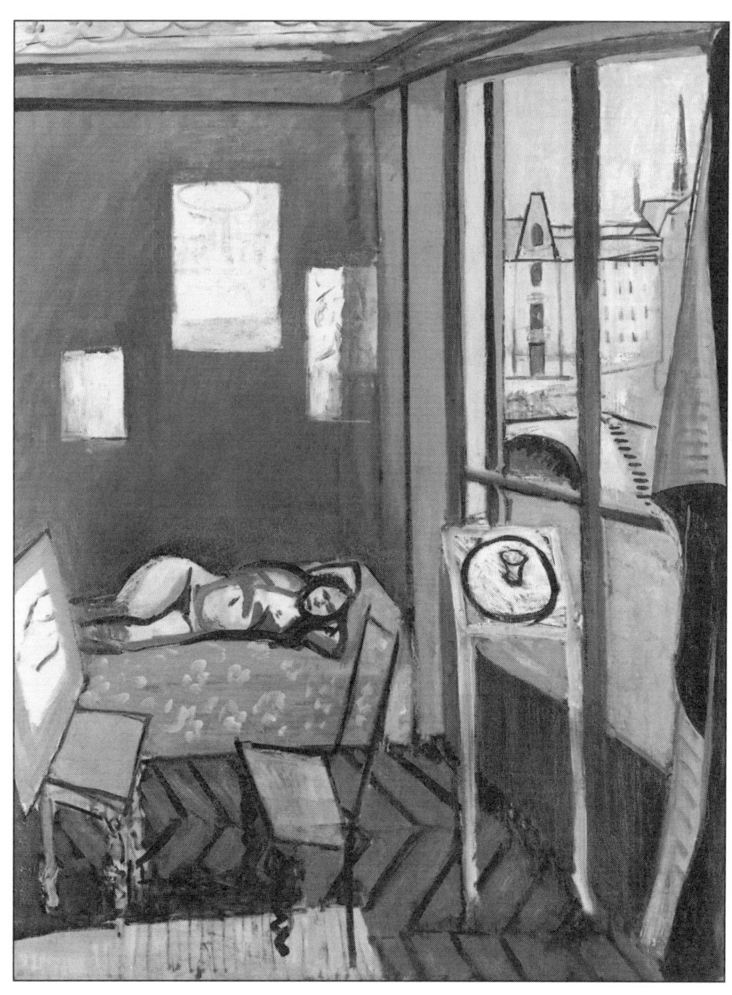

Henri Matisse, *Studio, Quai St. Michel*, 1916. Oil on canvas, 58 1/4 x 46 in. The Phillips Collection, Washington, D.C. Acquired 1940.

New York, Feb. 12, 1948

Dear Mr. Phillips,

For some years I have been working at a book on American museums, for the Rockefeller Foundation. It is now going to press, and I am assembling the illustrations. It would be a great pleasure if I could represent your Gallery by the splendid Matisse

Interior (please give me the title more exactly, if that is not correct).[1] I have always thought of it as one of his real masterpieces, and hope you will be so kind as to let me have a glossy print of it.

Thanking you in advance, if you will, and hoping to see you before too long, I am

Yours very sincerely, Walter Pach

1. The book, *The Art Museum in America: Its History and Achievement*, was published in 1948 by Pantheon Books. The Phillips Memorial Gallery's Matisse, *Studio, Quai St. Michel*, appears on page 195.

March 12, 1948

Dear Mr. Pach:

I have recovered from a bad cold which I must have had when your notes about the photographs arrived. I note in your letter of March 10th to Miss Bier[1] you say that your publisher now permits more illustrations and you ask for Ryder's "Resurrection" in addition to the "Atelier, Quai St. Michele [*sic*] by Matisse. I wish, if you are writing on American Collections, that you could at least have five or six to represent us instead of two. Of course the great Renoir, Daumier and Van Gogh masterpieces should be included and at least one of our group of works by Degas and Cezanne. Did you see the marvelous Portrait of Mme. Cezanne which was acquired last year? And the new masterpiece by Rouault which is entitled Verlaine? I do wish you could come to Washington more frequently for it [is] always a pleasure to see you.

Please let us know whenever you come our way.

Sincerely yours, [Duncan Phillips]

1. Elmira Bier was assistant to the director of the Phillips Gallery.

New York, March 18, 1948

Dear Mr. Phillips,

Thank you for your letter of the 12th, and for your unfailing interest in my work.

I should love to reproduce more of the magnificent things in your collection, but what am I to do, when I have to cover the whole world's art and all the collections of our museums in a limited number of illustrations? As it is, places as important as Yale, Providence, Cincinnati and many others are totally unrepresented, and one plate must

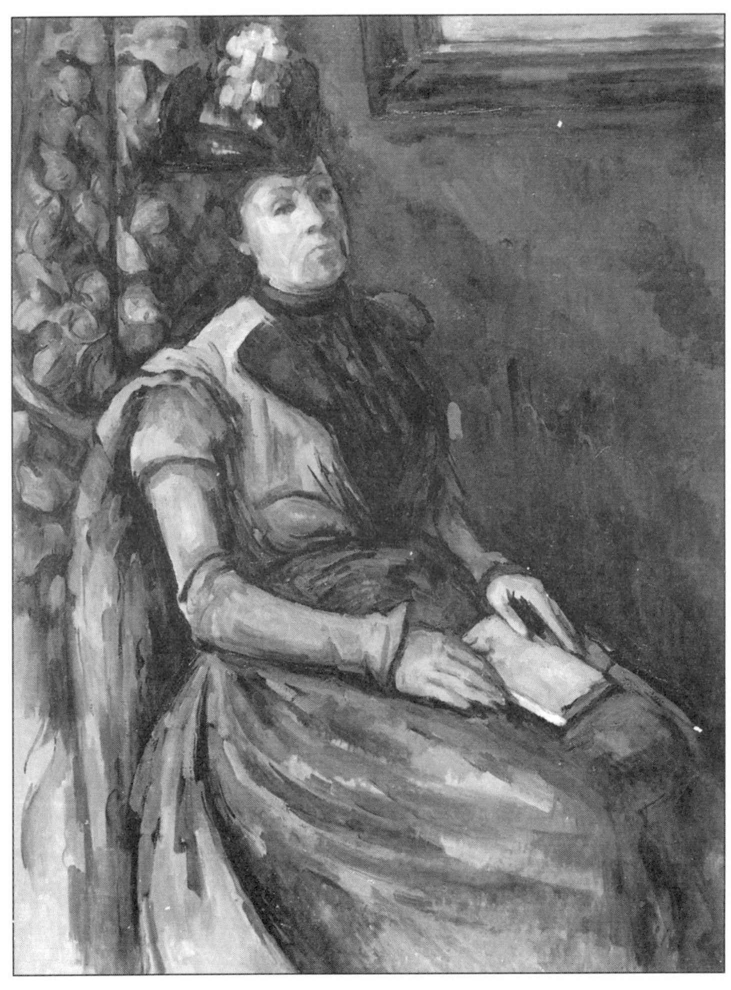

Paul Cézanne, *Seated Woman in Blue*, 1902-04. Oil on canvas, 26 x 19 3/4 in. The Phillips Collection, Washington, D.C. Acquired 1946.

do for the whole great art of China. There is no end to the problem.

I am glad also to see by your letter that my request for the Ryder is in hand; Miss Bier wrote me that the Matisse was to reach me by March 13th, but neither print has come yet. I know they will, . . .

With kind regards to Mrs. Phillips,

Yours most sincerely, Walter Pach

New York, March 22, 1948

Dear Miss Bier,

The photographs have just come and I thank you for attending to them for me—only, it was Ryder's *Resurrection* that I wanted, not the *Moonlit Cove*, which I return under separate cover. The Matisse is fine; and now may I have the *Resurrection*?[1] It might yet be in time for Easter.

Yours very sincerely, Walter Pach

1. The correct Ryder photograph was sent, for it appears on page 239 of the Pach book.

Source of Letters: The Phillips Collection Archives, Washington, D. C., which contains additional Phillips/Pach correspondence.

Also available through the Archives of American Art, Smithsonian Institution, The Phillips Gallery, reels 1933, 1945, 1954, 1968.

MAURICE PRENDERGAST (1858–1924)

Painter, printmaker, illustrator, and member of The Eight. Born in St. John's, Newfoundland, he immigrated with his family to Boston at the age of eleven. After working as a designer of show cards, he and his younger brother Charles (1863–1948) spent three years in Paris, where they studied at the Académie Julian under Jean-Paul Laurens and Joseph-Paul Blanc, and with Gustave Coutois at the Atelier Colarossi. Returning to Boston in 1894, Maurice began exhibiting watercolors in the Boston Art Club shows, followed by inclusion in Philadelphia and New York annuals. In 1895 he produced 142 illustrations for Sir James M. Barrie's My *Lady Nicotine*, and between 1891 and 1902 Prendergast created approximately 200 monotype prints. He visited Paris again in 1907 and upon his return spoke in glowing terms of Paul Cézanne with fellow members of The Eight, who were unfamiliar with Cézanne's work. Prendergast exhibited with The Eight in 1908 and in the 1913 Armory Show, becoming president of the Association of American Painters and Sculptors, the Armory Show's sponsoring group, in 1914.

Walter Pach and Prendergast found a common ground in their admiration of Paul Cézanne, Prendergast being acknowledged as the first American artist to appreciate the Frenchman and Pach having written the initial article about Cézanne to appear in an American magazine.[1] Prendergast's first letter to Pach was written in 1909; his last one is dated February 2, 1922, two months before Pach's article about him appeared in print.[2]

1. "Cézanne—An Introduction," *Scribner's* 44 (December 1908), 765–768.
2. "Maurice Prendergast," *Shadowland* 6 (April 1922), 10–11, 74– 75.

56 Mt Vernon St.
Boston, Dec. 6, 1909

My dear Pach.

you will think it strange I have not replied to your nice letter before

but it is just now we saw the Cezanne

my brother telephoned to Mr Sumner[1] after you left and he told [us] not to come until his house was in good shape

the Cezanne interested me extremely

it look[ed like] one of those Pochards[2] he done when he was [with] Pissaro[*sic*][3] you are right about the beauty of the canvass   it is conscientious and absolutely sincere   he seems to be very careful with the quality of his canvass and lets the canvass show when it would give lightness to his colour. I noticed the same with some of the canvasses in his exhibition

this sketch is done at the first wack and it made me jealous of his beautiful greys

I wish Mr Sumner secure one of his "nature mortes"[4] Fruit pieces where he painted one thin coat over the other

I am glad we have this Cezanne in Boston and it was such a pleasure for me to see his work again and you cannot realize my gratitude for giving me this opportunity to see it.

both Charley and [I] enjoyed Mr Sumner we found him the right sort.

I wrote Davies after you left and have had no letter   I sincerly hope he is coming out all right and be himself again[5]   it would be a great loss if anything happened to him he is one of the few my sympathetic friends I am fortunate to possess   we both send many cordial thanks to you and hope we will meet again soon.

keep yourself in good trim and become strong is the word of the artist Cezanne with a heavy handshake

Maurice Prendergast

1. John Osborne Sumner (1863–1938), professor of history at the Massachusetts Institute of Technology, who owned the Cézanne oil, *Harvesters* (ca. 1880). Pach had introduced him to Maurice Prendergast and his brother Charles (1863–1948).

2. Pochades are small wooden panel paintings.

3. Camille Pissarro (1830–1903), whose influence was crucial to Cézanne's development.

4. Still-lifes.

5. Arthur B. Davies (1862–1928) had contracted typhoid fever in the fall of 1909 and remained ill for months.

CITY HOSPITAL
BOSTON, JUNE 25, 1913

My dear Pach

Your postcard found me in this Hospital where I am fully recovering from a delicate operation. had the postrate [*sic*] gland removed. charley brought your card to me this morning and it give[s] me great pleasure to tell you I am leaving this cut and dried place to morrow.
Friday—

I have been confined here for three weeks and I have suffered a lot of pain but on the [whole] I feel as if I am going out a better man.

When I came in I receive[d] your other postcard also with the portrait of the old man he suffered also. I have it stuck in the mirrow [*sic*] frame and he followed all through my sickness. with his benevenolent [*sic*] eyes. my dear old [Pach] I am grateful for the interest you have shown in me and I am sending you the best of all wishes for your self good health and hope you are going to show us some corking good canvasses soon.

Give my best wishes to Davies and I hope he is in good trim. and don't forget the rest of the boys. I have not seen Miss Haskell[1] since you left she call[ed] at the Studio when [*sic*] I was in the Hospital and Charley returned his visit

Yours Sincerely, Maurice B. Prendergast

1. Mary Elizabeth Haskell (1873–1964) was in the process of moving from Boston to New York with her lover, the Lebanese writer and artist Kahlil Gibran.

MT VERNON ST.
BOSTON, [JULY 11, 1913]

My dear friend Pach

I am sending you back the interesting post cards. it was a treat looking at them—they all had something in them "Quelque chose là."[1] Ingres especially his drawings and painting of the Nudes.

I am coming along after my Hospital experience and getting my strength back again I am thankful to say. both Charley and I leave for Brookville a little place on the Maine coast to stay three or four weeks. Cutler[2] makes it his summer residence and it is partly through his invitation we are going.

We had a letter from Miss Haskell telling us about a delightful time she had in New York Meeting the Boys and admiring the New work of Monsieur la President[3] and she had nothing but good words for you Davies Gregg Kuhn & MacRae.[4]

I have not started to do any work yet Just crawling around still I am looking darn hard at the skies I hope everything is going on well with you and scraping up interest in your surroundings. charley sends you best wishes and good luck to you with a thousand thanks for your thoughtfulness in sending the Post cards and hope they will arrive without mishap.

With good wishes from your friend

Maurice Prendergast

P.S. if you hear of any thing half studio half workshop let us know there is trouble about renewing the lease of the studio here and it looks as if they are going to build. if we leave here it is New York for us.[5]

M. B. P.

1. "Something there."

2. Carl Gordon Cutler (1873–1945), an artist who exhibited in the Armory Show.

3. Arthur B. Davies, who was president of the Association of American Painters and Sculptors, sponsors of the recently-concluded Armory Show.

4. Frederick James Gregg (1865–1928), Walt Kuhn (1880–1949), and Elmer Livingston MacRae (1875–1955) were, respectively, publicist for the Armory Show; secretary; and treasurer of the association.

5. It has generally been assumed that the Armory Show in New York was the catalyst for the Prendergasts' move to Manhattan. By the fall of 1914 they resided at 50 Washington Square South, the same New York building that housed William Glackens's studio.

Chez Mme Paul Souffleux
15 Rue des Hautes Saler
St Malo, June 12, 1914

My dear Pack [*sic*]

Your letter of May the 16th has reached me at St Malo acknowledging my check for and a catalogue of the Modern Departures. It was a pleasure reading your letter in my preceding letter to you I forgot to mention about your article and the reproduction of one of my pictures in the Century[1] my pictures looked immense and I am sending you my most hearty thanks for doing me so much honor some of the fellows on the boat coming over with me Leonard also had a number they liked it very much but barred Cox I have changed my mind about staying here and am going home by the Middle of August. I have been here since the 22nd of april the weather has been so bad I have been unable to get out with my [paint] box there is a new collection opening at the Louvre the [Isaac] Camondo and I notice by the papers they contain 3 or 4 Cezannes and several Degas among them

Renoir is creating quite a stir he is doing some small Panels down at Cassis which are most delightful in color a way ahead of his former lan[d]scapes.

I am glad everything is going along in good style and I am hoping to see some good things of yours. with cordial thanks for your letters

yours faithfully, Maurice Prendergast

1. "The Point of View of the Moderns," *Century Magazine* 87 (April 1914), 851–864.

Boston, July 7, 1915

My dear Pack

I was deeply touched when I received from you Dufy's little book on the Soldiers please tell Monsieur Dufy when you write him I feel more pleased than if I got a gold medal and I shall always treasure it in rememberance of him and his work it brough[t], up that nice dinner we had at the Romano and the pleasant evening at your friends studio and both charlie and I look forward to seeing you all again when we get back we have been here for a week or so before going to Ogunquit Maine I must say Boston is an interesting place in summer and it is delightfully rainy and cool I dont think I should care about living here again it has a local side the same as Quebec and Halifax they lack the great stimulus of New York.

I hope you and Mrs Pack and the baby are all fine.

and charley joins with me sending you and Mrs Pack the best of all good wishes.

always your

faithfully, Maurice B Prendergast

---

50 Washington Sq. S.
March 23, 1916

My dear Pack

I put the letter for you in the box at 9:00 A.M. and received yours in reply at 5.45 P.M. so we cannot say the mail delivery is backwards in N Y. your names for the catalogue is right

2 oils
Lan[d]scape with figures
The Beach

3 pastels
man on Hors[e]back 1
________________ 2
Lan[d]scape with figures

they say there is no God. but I still have the habit of saying my prayers so I will pray for the exhibition[1]

You spoke about photographs yesterday & I have a good one to give you when you need it for your book

Yours faithfully, Maurice B Prendergast

1. "Exhibition of Modern Art Arranged by a Group of European and American Artists in New York" was organized by Pach for the Bourgeois Galleries.

Feb. 28, 1921

My dear Pach

First and foremost I want to tell you how much I enjoyed your visit with Mr & Mrs Brummer Both charlie [and I] found the Brummer[s] extremely interesting and I am glad we have [them] in New York he is going to give us an exhibition of our works between March 15 and April 4th[1] which I think is a good time. and I hope the exhibition will be successful both for his sake and ours and we want to thank you for bringing this meeting about.

I am not going to write much about Matisse when I read your F[2] since I have lost it if I recollect there was a good many points I agreed with you

charlie likes the exhibition and says they are numerous good things.

I will try and get up some afternoon this week and see it.

I press your hand and wish you the best of all good luck

Maurice B. P.

1. Joseph Brummer offered the Prendergast brothers an exhibition to inaugurate his new gallery at 43 East Fifty-seventh Street.

2. A reference to Pach's article, "Art. A Modern Artist," *The Freeman* 2 (December 8, 1920), 302–303. While Matisse is mentioned, the article is primarily about van Gogh.

Jan. 26, 1922

My dear Pach.

The Shadow land[1] man brought the two pictures back this morning and showed us two reproductions I was curious and I must say they exceeded my expectations they were perfectly charming in color. for this pleasure to me I want to thank you! if you are going to write an article I will give you all the assistance I can. I think those reproductions are worth backing up.

I want to join my thanks with charley['s] for your fine book.[2] [i]t was a pleasure to read it the english was so well written and you get all the spirit of the writer

I take off my hat to any thing "*that is first class*"

I hope every thing is going along satisfactor[il]y to you

give my regards to Madame and a hearty handshake.

as ever yours, Maurice B Prendergast

1. Pach's article, titled "Maurice Prendergast," appeared in *Shadowland* 6 (April 1922), 11, 74–75.

2. The second volume of Elie Faure's *History of Art*, which was translated from French into English by Pach.

Feb. 2, 1922

My dear Pach

I am sending you back the Manuscript[1] with cordial thanks

it was a pleasure reading it and you expressed a lot which I feel. and you are right about Cezanne his work strengthened and fortified me to pursue my own course.

I was much influenced by Pissar[r]o but with water colors it was nature pure and simple that influence[d] me some effects I would see would really drive me frantic

"shadowland" is going to be a good art magazine I have not look[ed] at it much but I shall look at the next issue with great interest

I send you all a happy handshake and good luck and good wishes.

Maurice B. Prendergast

1. Pach's article about him in *Shadowland*, which would appear two months later.

Source of Letters: Archives of American Art, Smithsonian Institution, Maurice B. Prendergast Papers, reels 4216, 4217.

JOHN QUINN
(1870–1924)

New York attorney who served as the pro bono lawyer for the Association of American Painters and Sculptors, organizers of the 1913 Armory Show. A law school graduate of Georgetown University and Harvard, he established his own law firm in New York in 1906. Quinn was one of the earliest American collectors of modern art, purchasing a Fauve painting by Alfred Maurer in 1911 and oils by Gauguin, van Gogh, and Cézanne the following year. In 1912 he helped to incorporate the Armory Show association, then loaned seventy-nine works to the exhibition and subsequently purchased forty-nine from it. Soon after the Armory Show, Quinn and Walter Pach joined forces in promoting modern European and American art through various exhibits in Manhattan and beyond. Because of Pach's continuing contact with the leading French artists of the day, he played a major role in the formation of the John Quinn art collection: Writing to the Frenchmen on Quinn's behalf, translating their letters for him, and informing Quinn of various drawings, paintings, sculptures, and prints by them available through his, Pach's, efforts or those of others.

Correspondence between the two began in 1914; Pach's last letter to Quinn was written on July 15, 1924, thirteen days before the latter's death.

John Quinn
Attorney and Counsellor at Law
31 Nassau St.
New York, May 10, 1913

My dear Pach:

I received yours of the 8th yesterday. I had no time yesterday to write to you. I have just telegraphed you as follows:

> "Walter Pach, Esq.,
> Copley Society,
> Copley Hall,
> Boston, Mass.
>
> Please reserve definitely two [Augustus] Johns referred to your letter eighth. Kind regards to Gregg.
>
> John Quinn"

I think the one that he calls "The Orange Frock" and the one that he calls "The Yellow Dress" have a little more vigor than the third one of the figure which he calls, I think, "The Red Shawl."[1]

If there are any notices in the papers especially referring to the John things, I should be glad if you would send me duplicates, so that I can send one set to John.

I was sure that you would all like Boston better than Chicago.

If I can run up toward the end of the show, I shall do so. Kuhn got a promise out of me which I shall fulfill if I have physically the time to do it.

With kind regards to Gregg, I am,

Sincerely yours, John Quinn

Walter Pach, Esq.
Thorndike Hotel
Boston, Mass.

1. Augustus John was represented in the Armory Show by forty-six works; of that number Quinn loaned twenty-one oils, twelve drawings, three gouaches, and a watercolor. The three paintings referred to in his letter, all oils, were loaned by the artist.

1135 Park Ave.
New York, Feb. 16, 1914

Dear Mr. Quinn,

As we arranged over the phone I directed the Packing and Shipping Co. to send a van at 10 A.M. tomorrow and have written to give them the exact names and titles for the order.

"Here are the three cards. For the collection of Auguste Pellerin (about eighty Cezannes!) Mrs. Thursby has only to write him a line at his office—57 Bd. Haussmann mentioning who would accompany her and the (visiting) day she wanted to go. If she cares for oriental art, she should call at the shop of Brummer 3 Bd. Raspail. He is not at all well known but has really wonderful things and would show them to her if she asks, and not make her feel that she was being invited to buy, as he is a very old friend of mine—more art-lover than dealer.

No previous appointment with the Steins is needed. They are at home every Saturday night—quite informally. It would be better to drop a line to Brancusi as he is a great worker and is embarrassed to have visitors come in suddenly. The Duchamp-Villons (and Villons, who live across the garden) used to be at home on Sunday afternoons but I don't know if it's still so. You get to Puteaux by taking the Métro to Porte Maillot and then a tram—generally the one that goes to St. Germain en Laye. The rue Lemaître is near the place de la Défense, which is a tram-stop."

Always cordially yours

Walter Pach

I took out an insurance policy as we said.

Feb. 17, 1914

My dear Pach:

Thanks for yours of the 16th, which was received this morning. It was awfully good of you to take so much trouble regarding Mrs. Alice Thursby . . . she is interested in modern art and knows French and has lived in Paris and has written me that she expected to stay in Paris for some months and to go "to all the exhibitions and look up talent" . . .

Can you let me know how long the things are to be in St. Paul? The reason I ask is that I promised to send the [Auguste Elisée] Chabaud and the Redon to [Charles] Prendergast, in Boston, with some other pictures, to have frames made. I put off sending them for one reason or another, and now it will delay him longer. So that I am anxious to have them back as soon as possible.

Again thanking you for your courtesy in regard to the cards for Mrs. Thursby, I am

Sincerely yours, [John Quinn]

NEW YORK, FEB. 24, 1914

Dear Mr. Quinn,

When I talked over with Mr. Montross[1] adding the works sold to the collection for Detroit,[2] he thought it was going to too much trouble for those people and today when I mentioned the matter to Mr. Davies,[3] he concurred. So I shall not have to keep your new acquisitions on the road. You will understand that I thank you just as much for the cordial manner in which you acceded to my request,—it was just that I was told that as long as we were making the out-of-town at all, it should be as strong and complete as possible. I am glad now, that you are going to have your new pictures around you as I think you'll like them.

Yours faithfully,

Walter Pach

1. Newton Emerson Montross, New York gallery owner, who displayed a selection of works by French and American artists represented in the Armory Show on the first anniversary of that event.

2. The possibility of adding to the exhibit certain works purchased by John Quinn and others, when the show moved on to the Detroit Institute of Arts, Cincinnati Art Museum, and the Peabody Institute in Baltimore.

3. Arthur B. Davies, president of the Armory Show's organizing society.

AUG. 25, 1914

My dear Pach:

. . . I had a letter from Jacob Epstein[1] this morning. He is working down at a place called Pett Level near Hastings. He wrote me that he had just heard that the Oscar Wilde monument had been unveiled and could be seen.

He writes:

"I can feel only bitterness that the work to which I gave ten months of hard labor, after being hid for so long, mutilated and made a scandal of, should at last be surreptitiously unveiled."

As to Brancusi, he says:

"I can without reserve say that Brancusi is indeed a fine sculptor. I have the greatest admiration for his work. The good sculptors now in the world are few at the most—only three or four I think."

I thought you would be glad to know that.

Yours very truly, [John Quinn]

Walter Pach, Esq.
33Beekman Place
New York City

1. Jacob Epstein (1880–1959), an American-born British sculptor who created colossal stone sculptures and expressionistic bronzes.

[Translated from the French]
Hôtel de L'Univers & du Portugal
Paris, Nov. 14, 1914

Received from Mrs. Elié Faure two paintings by Mr. Jean-Paul Lafitte ("Landscape" and "Sketch for a Composition"). These works will be shipped to the Carroll Galleries, 9 East 44th St. New York. It is understood that the galleries cover all costs of transportation, insurance and return shipping to the artist if the works are not sold.

Walter Pach, Representative of the Carroll Galleries

New York, Feb. 2, 1915

Dear Mr. Quinn,

Here is the translation of Jean Le Roy's[1] letter . . . I skip certain passages that are of no interest to his thoughts on the war:—

"I never knew whether I had missed one of your letters and whether you had read the other poems in my 'Prisonnier des Mondes'. Perhaps it is ridiculous to ask you what you thought of them, but I am so isolated, and my existence before the war seems the story of the age of fable. We are all, we young men of France, men condemned to death, and we cannot look forward. Only the past exists. That is the state of mind I used to hate the most violently. It will surely last for a short time only.

These last ten days I have been a soldier in a little city in the midst of the Loire, on an island. There is the shore, the two arms of the river and two canals. I am becoming acquainted with many things only half-seen before: the French countryside in winter, for example. In the morning we go out into the country, to the marching tune of our cadenced steps. I march in the first rank and a great strength carries along. And then I mingle, naturally, with a great deal of human life. We are all very young—from nineteen to twenty-years old, at our mess we sing and play with an intense abandon. So I forget the sadnesses of the time: my friends on the firing line, Kohler who has been in an icy hole for three months, Romanet who has been wounded (I do not know for certain whether it is our comrade Romanet),—the poor ravaged towns—Senlis, destroyed. It was a delicious little city that I came to know a short time since.

I was so happy to learn that you were getting up an exhibition. It reminds me that our great religion of art does not cease to live night or day, and that we need have no regret if we do not realize the works we have dreamed, for others 'will see what we thought we saw'.

I could not go to see Marcel Duchamp in Paris. What is each of the three brothers doing? . . .

Write me, please. Soldiers watch for letters quite nervously, when the corporal calls out the names of the fortunate ones. Always yours, my dear old Pach,—Jean Le Roy."

"He is a tall, manly lad,"—reserved with people, till he knows them pretty well because he is modest and always gives others credit for knowing much more than he does—when the reverse is often the case. I know it is not funk that makes him talk so in his letter; it is that he really feels he has something better to do than the brutal business he is in,—when his period of training is over and he gets to more active service he will have more equanimity. If only nothing happens to him; one English lady I saw in London was almost more concerned about him than about her own son, who was going out shortly.

I saw Gregg today and made sure he no longer thought of writing the book on the modern artists. There was no reference to you in what we said.

Cordially yours, Walter Pach

1. Jean Le Roy was a talented young French poet. He was killed during World War I, in April 1918, at the age of twenty-three.

Feb. 3, 1915

My dear Pach:

I received yours of the 2d this morning. I have read it with interest. Thanks very much for translating Le Roy's letter. . . .

I think I get a little glimpse of this young chap from the phrase of yours that "one English lady you saw in London was almost more concerned about him than about her own son, who was going out shortly." That is the eternal poet for you. There are lots of chaps who are only happy when some woman is petting them or is "concerned about them." They get away with it under different names—some melancholia, some pessimism, the more clever ones as geniuses. But the largest number march successfully to the conquest of ladies, young and old, under the banner of the artistic temperament. And how the ladies, young and old, do fall for it! A damned pity it is that a good many of the other near geniuses or fake geniuses aren't put to the good solid work that this young, perhaps real, genius is.

You are quite right. He hit the nail on the head when he says that he and his friends are "like men condemned to death and can't look forward."

Thanks again for sending me the letter.

I wish you success with the Kennerley[1] venture. If I can help you in that direction, don't hesitate to let me know.

Sincerely yours, [John Quinn]

1. Mr. Kennerley, who worked for a New York publisher, had proposed that Pach do a series of essays on various modern artists.

New York, March 9, 1915

Dear Mr. Quinn,

I want to give you a note of the offer I made for you to Dufy.[1] The four pictures you selected were the "Still-Life" ($200) "Promenade" ($200) "The Studio" ($400) and "The Belfry of St. Vincent" ($200): The prices noted above after each picture are those which he asked; they total $1000. Your offer was $700 for the four works, to be paid as follows: $300 down and $200 a month later and the other $200 a month after that. Last week I had a cable from Dufy consisting of the one word 'accept:' So you are now the owner of the four pictures—and they are, all four, things that I like, and believe you will care for permanently.

After reading Barnes'[2] letters, I can only repeat the word 'incredible' I used on hearing the first one. Only it ought to be stronger, in proportion as he gets himself deeper and deeper into the mud that he attempts to throw. The word 'cad' that ends the last letter to him is the most satisfactory that *could* be used, and while there were moments during my reading of the letters to him when I thought it almost a pity to dirty one's hands with the lashing of such a fellow, yet he deserved it so richly and it has so plainly flicked him on the raw, that I guess it was worth while to do the job. Also I had some good laughs over the letters to him,—what a pity *he* couldn't have taken them with a laugh, and mended his ways. What I am most interested in, in connection with my present work at the Galleries, is seeing whether there isn't some man of means who will take ahold and help put the good art of today where it belongs. To me Barnes' calling our men weaklings is almost his lowest drop.

Yours cordially

Walter Pach

1. Raoul Dufy (1877–1953), French artist.

2. Dr. Albert C. Barnes (1872–1951) was, like John Quinn, an early collector of modern art. The letters were prompted by the first major one-man show by Maurice Prendergast, held the previous month at New York's Carroll Galleries. Barnes sought to circumvent the gallery by purchasing works directly from the artist, whereupon letters signed by the gallery director but written by Quinn (who had helped bring the establishment into existence) served as a well-mannered response to Barnes's rancorous missives.

New York, April 15, 1915

Dear Mr. Quinn,

The last couple of days I have been quite rich in letters from Paris, and as there are a number of things in them that you will be interested in, I take my pen in hand to write you—after many days.

Véra writes that he has good news of deSegonzac[1] and of de la Fresnaye.[2]

Madame Villon says her husband[3] is some distance away from the trenches again. He is very happy over his sales. Madame Derain finally got her money, she says her husband[4] is driving an auto-truck at the front.

Rouault writes me a very grateful letter which really belongs to you. It is quite curious so you must at least read it some time. Matisse has sent the etchings, including a new series he has done since I was there. He says he is preparing a new series of lithographs.

The best letter—with a piece of surprising news—was from Marcel Duchamp. He has got ahold of three pictures of his that were at a dealer's and unobtainable when I was there and has sent them for me to choose one in place of the sketch he gave me. Of course if you preferred these new ones to mine you would just take your pick of these new ones, in fact—on a chance—I hope you will. He says I should keep mine if I like it better than the others but I guess I can find one to take among the new ones if you wanted mine.

Now, the surprising thing is that he wants to leave France, in fact is quite decided to. He has been dissatisfied there for some time, and I imagine his not serving in the war makes his position less pleasant.

He says he would be glad to come to New York, provided he can earn his living there. He has the University diploma of Bachelor of Letters and his experience as librarian at Ste. Genevieve. He reads German very well and speaks it somewhat; he is less strong on English.

I shall write him of what I think are uncongenial conditions for him here, but shall look about at various institutions where there could be a place for him, as I should be really happy to see him here, if he finally decided to come. He is one of the finest young men I know, with one of the most brilliant minds. Do you think of any institution that might have room for him? My wife is quite sure that Brentano's would take him but I should not like to see him in a position that gave him no time at all for work.

Your copies of "l'Art Décoratif" (the big collection) will be shipped.

I am

Yours cordially, Walter Pach

1. André Dunoyer de Segonzac (1884–1974). French artist; three of his drawings of nudes were purchased by Quinn from the Armory Show.

2. Roger de la Fresnaye (1885–1925), a French cubist.

3. Jacques Villon (1875–1963), French painter and brother of Marcel Duchamp and Raymond Duchamp-Villon.

4. André Derain (1880–1954), French fauve.

April 30, 1915

Allan Dawson
The Globe and Commercial Advertiser
New York City

Dear Mr. Dawson:[1]

This will introduce to you my friend Mr. Walter Pach of 33 Beekman Place, this city. Mr. Pach is a gentleman of cultivation and learning and is an artist of fastidiousness and great cultivation. I know most of the art critics in this town and know or know of the work of contemporary art critics abroad. The crying need of art criticism in this country is someone who not only knows the classics and the old masters of art but who is familiar with the work of the men of today, the men who may be the classics of tomorrow.

Mr. Pach is a learned man in art. He knows the literature of the subject, both of early art, the great masters of art, and the men of today. He knows the great traditions. He has the feel of the subject. He has all the learning of the subject at his finger ends and I state that of my own knowledge.

Besides being an artist he is an expert critic of paintings and knows how to judge and appraise a picture. Besides being an artist and learned in the history of art, he has a personal knowledge of many of the leading artists of today both here and abroad. He has perhaps a more intimate knowledge of foreign living artists than any man in this country. In addition to this he is an excellent writer and has contributed articles to such magazines as the Gazette des Beaux-Arts, The Century, Scribners, Harpers, the International Encyclopedia and other important publications.

Mr. Pach is a facile writer and has had much experience with newspaper work. He is a man of agreeable personality, absolutely incapable of writing an unfair or biased criticism, and equally incapable of depreciating a good work because of any personal reason, or of over-praising a poor work. In short I think he would make an ideal critic.

I am rather surprised that he is willing to think of taking the place but I hope that he may take it because his work would be not only distinctive but would outshine that of any other art critic in the city. The thing that I have regretted for some years is that we have no really modern art critic. As I told you, we have men who discuss personalities and what may be called the minor politics of art. But art criticism—it is very rare.

I believe that Mr. Pach would make the art criticism in The Globe notable; in fact I believe that before very long his contributions would come to be regarded as the best art criticism that we would have.

For the sake of people like myself who are disinterestedly interested in art, if I may use that phrase, I hope that the artists and the public may have the benefit of Mr. Pach's services.

Yours very truly, [John Quinn]

1. Quinn wrote this letter on Pach's behalf to the chief editorial writer for *The Globe and Commercial Advertiser* the day after the death of its long-time art critic, Arthur Hoeber. Pach was either not offered the job or did not accept its terms.

May 12, 1915

Dear Mr. Pach:

With this I send you my check to your order for $200.00, being the second installment on the four oil paintings by Raoul Dufy purchased by me. As you will remember, the special price for the four was $700.00. I sent Miss Bryant a check on March 13, for $300.00. This payment to you of $200.00 leaves a balance due of $200.00, which I will send you in a month from date. Will you please get a money order for the $200.00 now sent and forward it to Dufy.

Yours very truly, John Quinn

I send this to you but if you prefer it may go through the Carroll Gal[lery] Inc as I understand the other payment did. But I do not want to give Miss B. unnecessary trouble. Arrange it as seems best & endorse the check accordingly

JQ

May 29, 1915

My dear Pach:

Referring to the eight water colors by Derain, the artists price of which was $30. each, making a total of $240, and referring to my talk with you on the telephone this morning, I send you herewith $100 in cash for you to send by postal order or postal money order or any way that you determine to Madame Derain. I hadn't intended to buy all those paintings and I was largely influenced in doing it by what you said of Madame Derain's condition. In writing to her therefore you might state that I have bought heavily this winter in art and state as tactfully as you can that I cannot pay the whole price at once and you can state that the other $100 will be paid in a month and the $40 at the end of the next month.

I suggest that you write such a letter as will make it clear that these eight are taken *out of the Gallery accounts*.

In regard to the painting by Marcel Duchamp "Study of a Girl," as he is on the way here there will be no letter necessary for you to send regarding that. But I am instructing the Gallery to state that I will be responsible to him directly for the payment of this $120 through you, so that they can credit themselves with that item in their books as well as crediting themselves with the eight Derain items in their books.

Sincerely yours, [John Quinn]

NEW YORK, MAY 29, 1915

My dear Mr. Quinn,

. . . Repeating what I said over the phone this morning, my friend Arensberg (who bought a Gleizes[,] a de la Fresnaye and a Picasso etching from the [Carroll] Gallery) is willing to buy one of the new small pictures by Duchamp; so that if you felt you had enough, or if your main idea was to have the artist sell two pictures because I was willing to exchange mine,—here is the chance.

Let me say again how glad I am for Mme. Derain that you took the water-colors;—also sending her the $100, which will look quite big as five hundred francs, made it a pleasure to write her the letter.

I am

Yours cordially, Walter Pach

NEW YORK, JUNE 30, 1915

Dear Mr. Quinn,

I had a letter this afternoon from Duchamp-Villon (the sculptor) regarding the various questions I asked him at your suggestion, and I give his answers, as follows:—

"What you propose about the wooden panels (the 'Cat' and the 'Parrot') will be all right, since Mr. Quinn is keeping the two casts of them. That will be $150 for each—which is quite a reduction, but I accept the reasoning you submit of Mr. Quinn's support of our movement. As to the terra-cotta ('The Lovers') and the bronze ('Woman Seated'), I propose, in order that the matter may be agreable [*sic*] to all—the Gallery, Mr. Quinn and myself—to set as a price the lump-sum of $500 from which is to be subtracted the expense of casting, chiselling, giving the patina, stand and mounting. The cost of this must be higher in America than here by about one third; so I estimate this at $80 to $100. If I reduce the terra-cotta to $280, I want to keep the right of casting another one—for I was considering this one as unique before, which will explain the price I asked at first. I must tell you that the expenses I had with it, in the way of moulds, baking etc. etc., came to about $100, which would leave me $180 profit. You can see that that does not make this a big sale for me. The same is to be said of the bronze of the woman seated,—I shall get $120 from that out of which I shall pay myself back the expenses of my model, of casting etc., which were about $60.

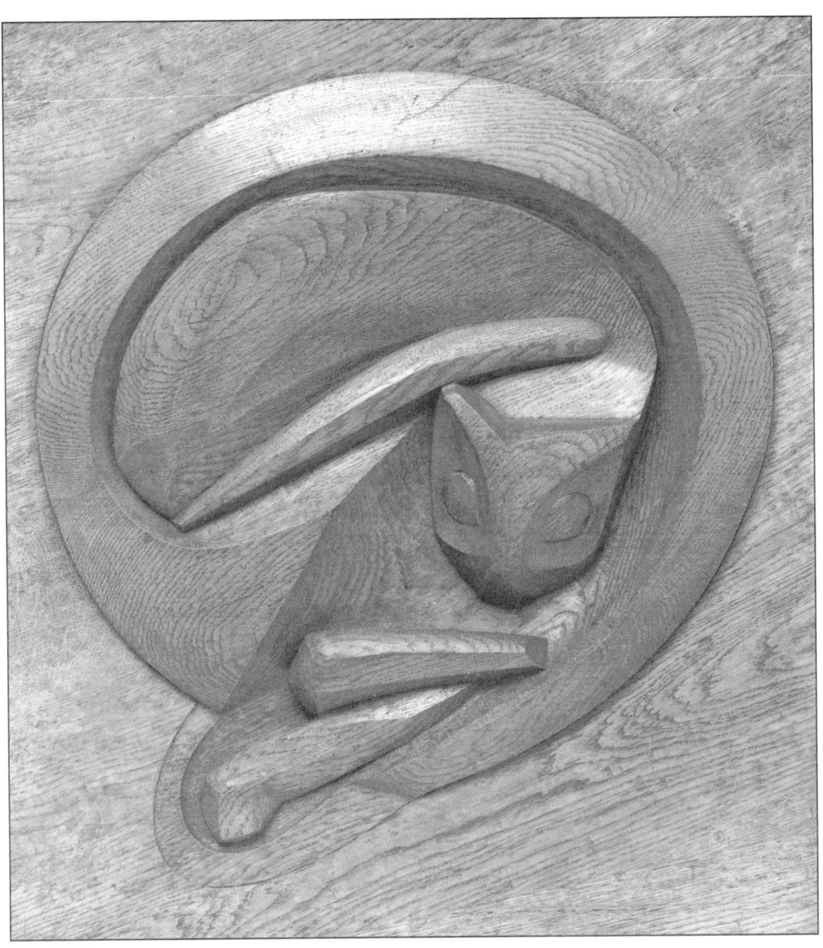

Raymond Duchamp-Villon, *Cat*, 1913. Carved oak, stained walnut, 68.6 x 63.2 cm

To sum up: I should get $400 for the two works, since $100 will be spent on the execution of the bronze. I don't think that will seem exorbitant; I will add that the reduction comes to nearly half the price I first asked, and I only make so important a reduction because of the abnormal situation in which the art-business is at present.

I want also to avoid the exaggerated expense of returning the big piece (the terra-cotta). There is no hurry for the present; see first if the solution above may work out . . ."

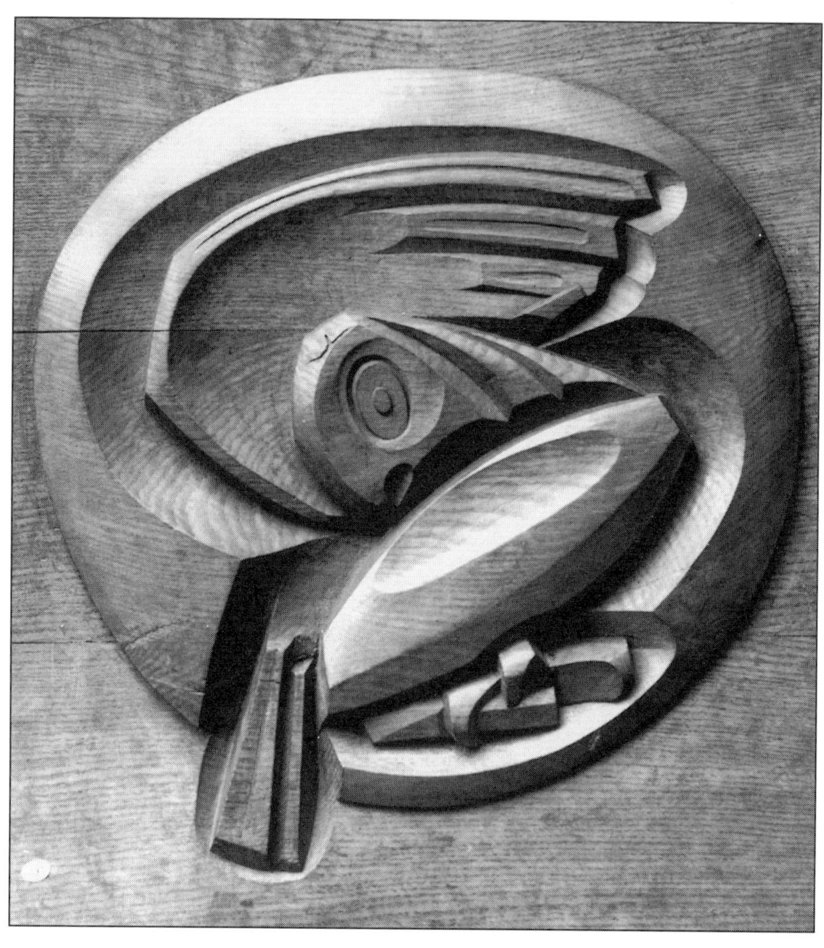

Raymond Duchamp-Villon, *Parrot*, 1913-14. Wood bas-relief, 25 3/4 x 23 11/16 in. Yale University Art Gallery, Gift of Collection Société Anonyme.

The rest of his letter is cheerful as usual; nothing new since Duchamp sailed, only he is rather hoping for more active service.

I also had a delightful letter from my friend Jean Le Roy the poet. He is under fire now—sends me a poem and is thoroughly worth your hearing sometime.

Yours cordially, Walter Pach

July 12, 1915

My dear Pach:

I received yours of June 30th. You know the amount that I have bought and paid for in the way of art this winter running into thousands of dollars and confidentially far far more I think than any other man in New York City in comparison with my means and more than many very rich men. But I am inclined to accept the proposition contained in Duchamp-Villon's letter which will amount in total payments to the sum of $700 provided I can have the privilege of paying that sum in two or three payments in the autumn as I have done for the other things. I doubt if any one else would buy them this summer. It would be expensive to return them and pay insurance and freight and expressage. I could not think of buying on any other basis.

I understand the sculptor is to reserve the right of casting another copy of the terra cotta panel "The Lovers" from the clay model. When I made the suggestion to you I thought that was and would remain unique but in the circumstances I am willing to agree that he should have the right of casting another one from the model.

As to the bronze figure (Woman Seated) I understood from you that the clay figure was the only one but you now tell me that there is a bronze in Berlin. I should like to have it understood that that bronze in Berlin and the bronze that I am to have cast here would be the only ones made. I assume that is agreeable to the sculptor for he does not make that a condition in his letter as he does regarding the large panel.

Yours very truly, [John Quinn]

P.S. I am notifying Miss Bryant that by an arrangement with the artist through you I am acquiring the four items in question, namely the two woodcarvings, the large panel entitled "The Lovers" and the seated figure, and that I will remit for them direct and that hence the Gallery should credit itself with those four figures just as though they were returned. When you advise me regarding the drawing of the seated figure also I will give similar advice to the Gallery.

Please let it be understood that these payments to Duchamp-Villon are to be made by me direct through you. . . .

New York, July 12, 1915

Dear Mr. Quinn,

. . . When I spoke to Duchamp about the drawing, he said he was sure his brother would not want you to pay more than $30.00 for it, considering the number of his works in your collection. He also said his brother would be quite satisfied not to make another bronze of the "Seated Woman" but he thought he might possibly like to make a marble of it. This would be of course quite another matter than a bronze,—anyhow will write Duchamp-Villon and get his personal statement on the subject.

To give you a note of our conversation over the 'phone:—I am writing Rouault that if he made a 25% reduction on the ceramic panel of the woman, the round picture of the woman and the group of poor people you *might* take the things—making payment in the fall. The same to Segonzac on the five remaining drawings and the oil study of a recumbent model.

With very good wishes I am

Yours sincerely, Walter Pach

New York, July 14, 1915

Dear Mr. Quinn,

I have your letters of July 12th and 13th. I am quite sure that nothing can be done about the French works in Berlin, so we had better consider the matter closed for the present anyhow. I shall have no further use for the correspondence from Mr. Jones of Donald Harper's office. He was very kind in his reception of me,—accompanying me to Ambassador Herrick and doing all he could to get the things from Berlin, subsequently. It is almost a pity not to have followed his suggestion of reporting the conduct of the people at the embassies to the State Department here,—but doubtless that would have been without result. . . .

I saw a little of the work of Gaudier Bzerska[1] in London, and John Cournos showed me photos of several other pieces when he was here last year. The work was certainly that of a man very much in earnest and going in the right direction, the sort of artist England (or any other country) needed. It is indeed a shock to hear of his being shot down and adds one more count to the score of those who are responsible for the criminal horror of this war. Italy has shown her wisdom and civilization in keeping her artists of all kinds out of her armies; it would be well if the other nations followed her example before we have any more such tragedies. Dufy wrote me—I don't think I told you—that Braque is in the hospital with a wound in the head. I have asked Madame Derain in my letter if she has news of him,—Braque being a friend of her husband's.

Today I spoke with Bryson Burroughs about the possibility of your considering the loan of Duchamp-Villon's bas-relief to the museum. He said that sculpture came outside of his authority altogether, which I knew—and said I was simply asking his friendly advice as to how they would feel about it in Mr. Robinson's department. He said Mr. Robinson's personal feeling toward the school was not a sympathetic one, but that his principle was to obtain good examples of all worthy efforts,—irregardless of his individual preferences. So the best way was to write him a preliminary letter before directly making an offer of a loan. If the matter were laid before Mr. French (Daniel C.)[2] who has had the say about the *American* sculpture, he would, quite surely, be opposed. Mr. Burroughs said this to me confidentially.

I have been thinking of the matter of my remitting to the French artists in the fall. After the letters I have had to write this week (Rouault, Segonzac, Dufy, Derain, Duchamp-Villon and various others resulting from my work for the exhibitions), I hesitate about going in for another bunch. . . . While I don't want to shirk anything that is for a good cause if there is no one else to attend to it, I do think that Miss Bryant's interest in the matter—since you intend her to have a commission, aside from what she has done in the way of sales this past season—might bring this correspondence within her province. . . .

I do not announce this as a final decision at all: if you had any special reason for desiring me to attend to the affair, I should do it. . . .

Yours cordially, Walter Pach

1. Gaudier Bzerska (1891–1915) was a Frenchman who went to London in 1911 to study sculpture; with the outbreak of World War I he enlisted in the French army.

2. Daniel Chester French (1850–1931), a traditionalist sculptor who generally created conservative, idealized figures.

---

c/o Gape Clark, Harriman, N.Y., Aug. 18, 1915

Dear Mr. Quinn,

I have had replies from Rouault and de Segonzac lately and want to give you a note of them. In substance, they would both accept the offers proposed . . .

Duchamp has written me about having seen you several times, about the excursion to Coney Island and a good talk he had with you at Delmonico's. I am ever so glad you could have him come, as I like him very much and feel quite grateful myself for your having made him feel that he was among friends.

Hoping the summer has been a pleasant one for you, I am

Yours cordially, Walter Pach

Aug. 20, 1915

My dear Pach:

. . . I will write Rouault accepting his proposition and taking the following:

Large porcelain panel	$120.
Poor People (group)	90.
Head of Woman (round)	100.
Total	$310.

. . . As to de Segonzac you give the figures "francs 1200 instead of francs 1600." The prices are:

Painting of Woman Reclining	$80
Drawings—Trees in Springtime	40.
Repose	60.
Church	40.
Isadora Duncan A	60.
Isadora Duncan B	60.
Total	$340.

Or in francs total 1700, deducting 25% leaves a balance of francs 1275. 1 will send a Paris draft direct to de Segonzac for this amount very soon, that is in the course of the next week or two.

I have asked Miss Bryant to send me those items.

You may be interested to know that I am about to write to Dufy making him an offer to purchase his remaining water colors and oil paintings. I am going to suggest a reduction to him of one-third in price, which considering the other things that I purchased is fair.

Miss Bryant got a very sweet letter from Madame Chabaud suggesting that an offer be made for some of her son's things. I am going to make her an offer on two of the landscapes and on one painting of The Clown, but I won't bother you with either the Dufy or Chabaud matter. I am obliged to you for writing to Rouault and de Segonzac.

Miss Bryant has paid Marcel Duchamp in full for the things of his which she sold. . . . I had Duchamp in to dine with me one night this week with Storck and Miss Bryant and after which we went to his studio. I like him very much. . . .

With regards to Mrs. Pach and hoping that the youngster is flourishing, I am

Yours very truly, [John Quinn]

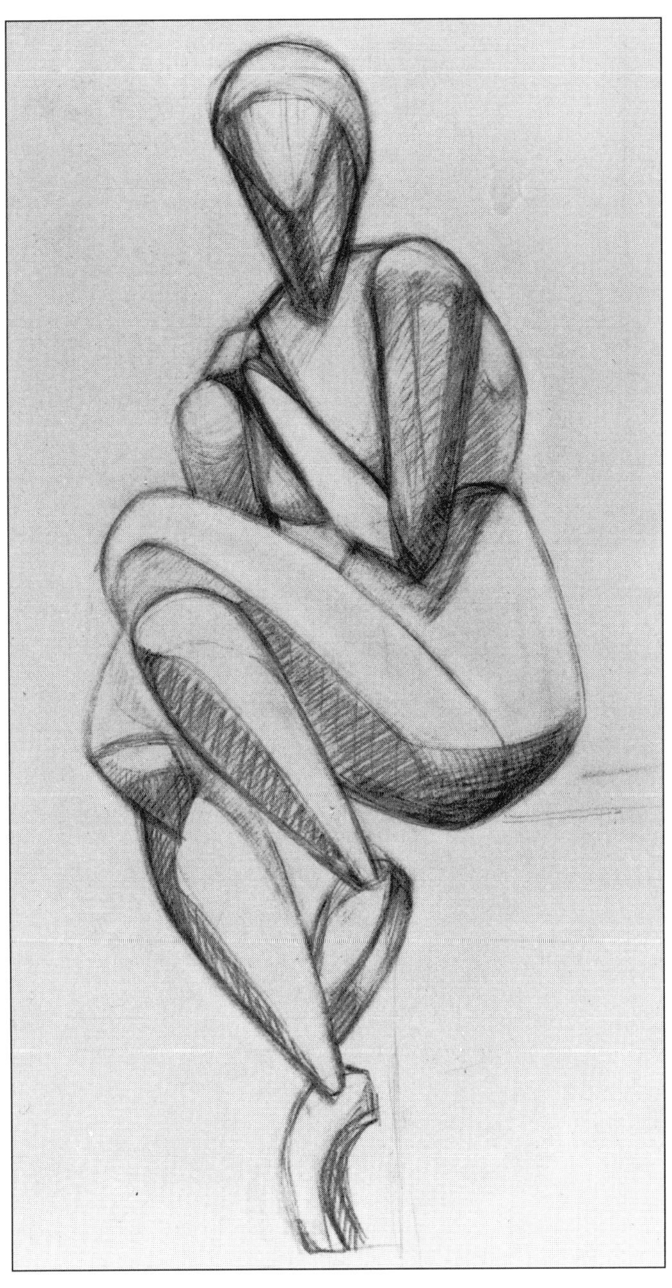

Raymond Duchamp-Villon, *Seated Female*, 1914. Charcoal, 17 11/16 x 10 in. Museum of Art, Rhode Island School of Design, Mary B. Jackson Fund and Membership Dues.

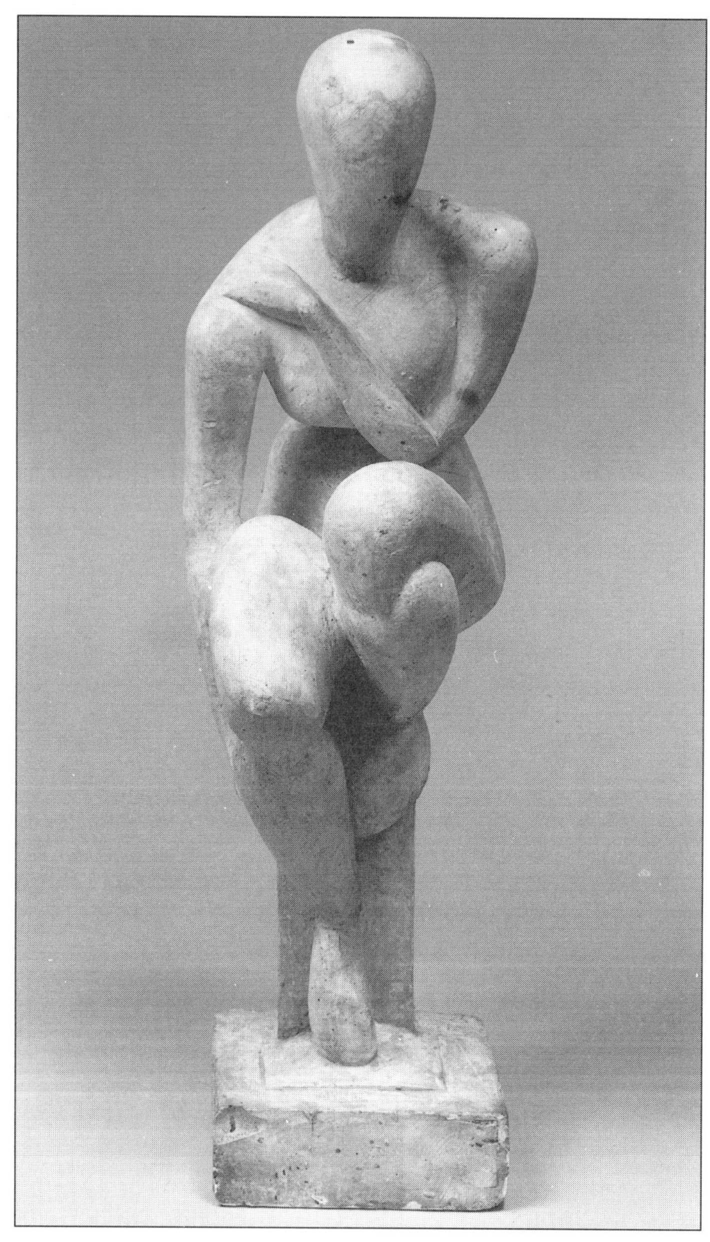

Raymond Ducahmp-Villon, *Seated Female Nude*, 1914. Plaster, 28 x 8 1/2 x 12 in. Philadelphia Museum of Art: Gift of the Family of the Artist. Acc. 1978-15-2. Photograph by Will Brown, 1980.

Harriman, N.Y., Aug. 22, 1915

Dear Mr. Quinn,

. . . received one [letter] from Duchamp-Villon last night, and as it is mostly about your sculpture of the "Woman seated" I will give you a translation of that, with one or two other things of interest that he writes. . . .

Duchamp-Villon encloses the sketch which I forward, and says:

"The matter of further castings of the two sculptures is perfectly understood,—the bronze is to be the only one outside of the example in Berlin, of the terra-cotta, there are also to be only two casts. . . . As to the bronze to be executed in America, the pedestal should be of black marble, and the patina should be gilt. Putting on gold makes it a little more expensive but it gives the piece its definitive appearance as I conceive it. As to the form and dimensions of the pedestal, the plaster model will be found to have tracings to indicate where the surfaces of the copper end. I enclose an explanatory sketch however. . . .

"You know what is going on here: an immobile tragedy, in which activity is no longer to be distinguished from torpor, and we all suffer from it—without knowing for how long.

"Villon is relatively at rest; we are expecting him on a four-days furlough. After a year, it is more than deserved. —I have tried to work a little, but it is more difficult than usual; the little I do is not lost, as an effort anyhow. And then I do not expect to be at St. Germain throughout the war, for it is a miracle that I am here yet. So the modeling of some little figures gives me patience for the months to come when I shall go further into this hell.

"I get but a little news of our scattered comrades: Gleizes has returned, to be with the General Staff at Paris. I have not seen him yet and do not know if this new post is to be permanent. Remember me to my friends in America, please. . . . When we have reached our goal of establishing life on a definitive basis of peace, I hope the occasion may present itself for me to go and see you and to work for your free America. When? Let us say six months so as to have patience. Yours (etc.) R. Duchamp-Villon."

I wish it could be over in six months but I fear it won't.

We have made up our minds to come back to New York the end of this week. I shall be glad to—and to see you, I hope, soon afterward.

Yours cordially, Walter Pach

33 Beekman Place
New York, Aug. 30, 1915

Dear Mr. Quinn,

. . . I send you the enclosed receipt from Mme. [Alice] Derain that came the other day. It is for the last $140. you sent by me, and she adds that it closes the whole account. She also wrote a friendly note thanking warmly for the aid she has received, so I pass that on to you. Derain is at the front in the automobile artillery. He is in good health. . . .

With good wishes

Yours sincerely, Walter Pach

(Translation of a letter from Elie Faure, the well-known art critic, author of a work on Velasquez, a "History of Art," the brochure on Cézanne, etc., etc. M. Faure is a physician with a large practice in Paris. In view of his referring to the possibility of his death, it seems only just to note that from the beginning of the war his work has been constantly attended with the greatest danger, as he is now a surgeon with the army and has had to succor the wounded as they fall, on the firing line itself.)

Paris, August 26, 1915

Dear Mr. Pach,

Your letter finds me in Paris where I have been for the last few days, on furlough because of illness brought on by a state of overstrain and fatigue. I am going to the Midi for a month and then return to the front, which I have not left for a year, and I hope to remain there until the end of the war or until my own end. That life has an irresistible attraction for one who has once tasted it, everything behind the front seems to you mean and miserable, and the nearness of death gives life a powerful flavor which makes you enjoy it in all its aspects.

The farther I go, the more I look on civilization—or rather one civilization—not as a moral phenomenon but as an aesthetic phenomenon, in which war may play a necessary rôle in exalting the taste for life, the energy to realize and the sweep onward to the unknown. "The happy peoples have no history" because it is in tragedy that the great peoples have gathered their strength to mold history. History is a picture where the blood, the flesh, the sensibility and the enthusiasm of man are the materials of the artist who paints it. All the great art-epochs have come out of a time of tragic trial and of exceptional expansion of energy: the great century of Greece, after the Median wars, the only century of art in Spain after its maritime and military expansion, the only century of art in Holland after its revolutionary emancipation, French Romanticism after the Revolution. Europe will come out of this drama definitively broken, or with its youth renewed for a thousand years. Everything depends on the energy it still contains.

So let us speak no more for the present of the translation of my book. It is a little thing by the side of the formidable genesis that we are living. I, also, shall find in it renewal or death. And in the one case or the other, what do my past works matter in comparison with my works to come,—or with the eternal night? I have a most friendly gratitude for your having taken up the matter with so much affectionate ardor and I hope you may succeed with it one day, but I look on your probable non-success with no disquietude. My fourth volume now lacks only one chapter to be complete. As it is, it is by far the best thing I have written and I think you will have some pleasure in reading it. But when will it appear? Not before the end of the war certainly. In any case, I continue to write and prepare for the future as if nothing was taking place. This war did not surprise me, and if it deals me painful blows in some of my affections, it does not throw me out of the path my instinct traces for me. I was never more master of my brain nor more prodigal of my heart.

I am happy that Lafitte's painting had a success, but it is a bitter happiness and one in which the terrible irony of life reveals itself. Lafitte was killed some months ago in an assault on a German trench,—without enthusiasm and without fear. Like myself, he had no hatred for Germany, but he had the feeling that France and we ourselves could find, in this formidable contact, sources of new energy—of which our victory on the Marne revealed the existence with supernatural splendor. That day, David, weakened, covered with blood and dust, struck Goliath on the forehead and since then, despite his marvelous vitality, in spite of his strength and his mass, the colossus trembles on his knees and will end by falling. I saw that miracle from within, I took part in it with a million other Frenchmen; it is one of the great memories of my life, and I think, since that day, that France will not perish. If she dies, she will have revealed in her last gesture what lightning can still flash from the soul of a great dying people.

Mme. Faure and I send our regards etc.

Eli Faure

P.S. I congratulate you on being a father. It is the highest reason for living.

Aug. 30, 1915

My dear Pach:

. . . I am thinking of making an offer to Duchamp for that study of the Nude Descending the Stairs with the black margins on either side, provided he is willing to take off 25% for cash. I think the money may come in all right for him. . . .

Yours very truly, [John Quinn]

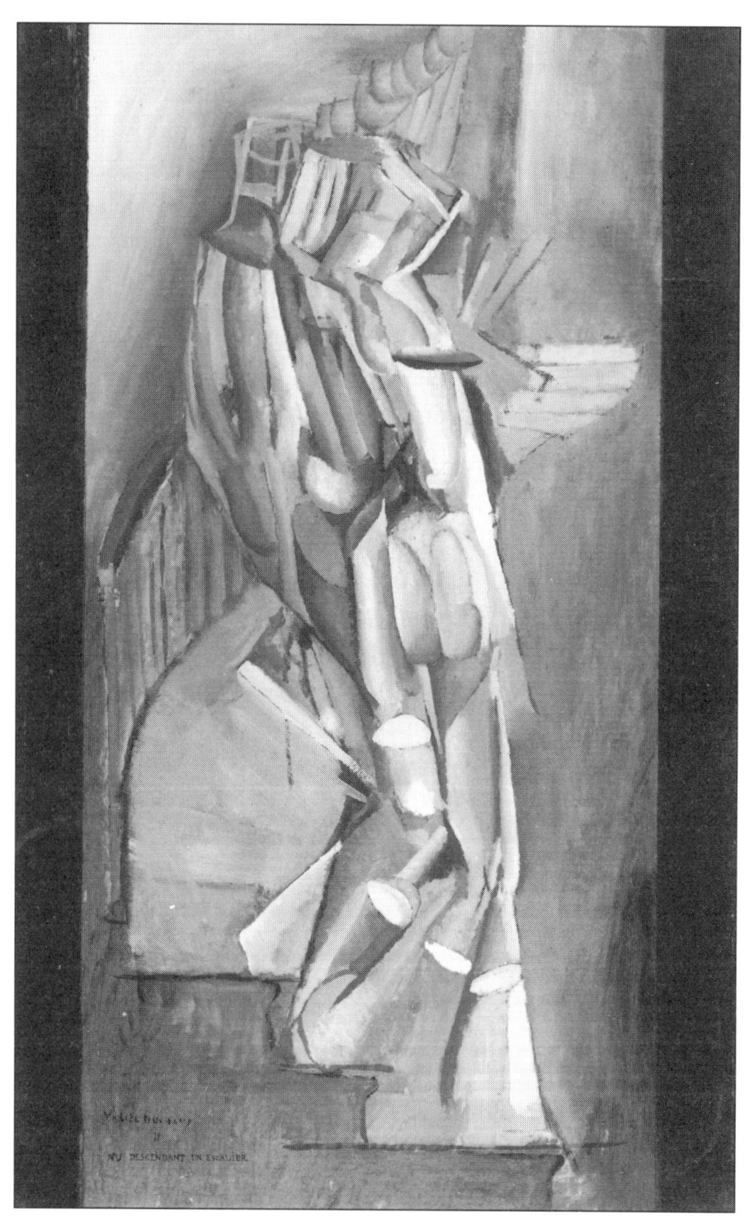

Marcel Duchamp, *Nude Descending a Staricase No. 1*, 1911. Oil on cardboard, 37 3/4 x 23 1/2 in. Philadelphia Museum of Art: The Louise and Walter Arensberg Collection. Acc. 1950-134-58. Photograph by Graydon Wood, 1994.

New York, Sept. 27, 1915

Dear Mr. Quinn,

I wrote to Brancusi, covering the points you mentioned,—about the various works, about your purchases and making a reasonable price on the sculpture. . . . Duchamp is really quite determined to do some sort of work that will save him from the necessity of living by the sale of his pictures and I was wondering whether it would do any good to speak to Miss Belle Greene for him again. She did not know of anything in the spring. I will bring the study for the "Nude descending a Staircase," and the Rouault, the first time I am over near your place.

Cordially yours, Walter Pach

New York, Oct. 4, 1915

Dear Mr. Quinn,

Last Saturday, my friend Arensberg, at whose house Duchamp has been living, called me up on the long-distance telephone from the place he is at in Connecticut . . . to let me know that he would buy Duchamp's sketch for the "Nude Descending the Staircase." I told him of course that it was too late,— . . .

Yours cordially, Walter Pach

New York, Oct. 5, 1915

Dear Mr. Quinn,

I thought you might want a note on the three sums of $120.00 each we spoke of this morning.

One is for Miss Bryant: twelve etchings at $10.00 each (I only hope Matisse will remember that he wrote me that,—he asked $15.00 for them at first.)

The second is for three monotypes at $40.00 each, to be sent me, since Matisse simply sent the monotypes to me. The third $120.00 is for Marcel Duchamp whose address is now *34 Beekman Place*, just across the street from me. There is a phone under the name "Orient and Occident"—Plaza 4771.

I have just had a letter from Dufy in which he says he got the $100. I sent him for you in July, also $100. from you due on the first purchase, and a part payment on the purchase of his remaining works. He is in the arsenal at Vincennes near Paris, writes in his usual charming way and seems in good spirits.

Yours cordially, Walter Pach

Oct. 8, 1915

My dear Pach,

. . . I want also to acknowledge yours of the 4th regarding the "Nude Descending the Stairs". . . . I am glad to have it first, because it is interesting as a specimen of Duchamp's work; secondly, because I know and like the "Nude" and thirdly, because it is to me a personal souvenir of the Armory Exhibition. . . . I am to remit of Marcel Duchamp $120 for the sketch of the "Nude Descending the Stairs" . . .

I doubt very much whether Belle Green would be able to place Marcel Duchamp. Would you like to have me speak to her? If you would I shall gladly do so. . . .

With kind regards, I am

Yours very truly, [John Quinn]

New York, Oct. 10, 1915

Dear Mr. Quinn,

I have your letter of the 8th . . .

When I wrote to you about Miss Greene's possibly helping Marcel Duchamp to a position it was simply with a general idea of her being acquainted with librarians. Since then, however, a particular case has come up in which she could in all probability give assistance. Duchamp has been again to the French Museum (Institut Français) 599 Fifth Avenue, where I introduced him in June. The director, (if that is his title) Mr. Juen, was very well impressed with Duchamp at that time and said he should come again. He now informs Duchamp that there is probably need for a person to catalogue, arrange and otherwise look after the growing library of the Museum; also that the president of the institution recently died and that Miss Greene—who is at present the secretary, I believe—is likely to be made president. The place would be an exceptionally suitable one for Duchamp, from every standpoint. And if I take the liberty of adding one more to the list of requests you have received, to help men to positions, it is with a clear conscience as to the entire fitness of the man for the place. Also Duchamp is very serious in his wish to earn his living at something outside of his painting; and in view of the character of his work, I am in complete sympathy with his desire to keep his mind free of any consideration of money in thinking about his painting. He has always made his living at other employment and while neither he nor I have any idea that he would grow commercial if he were to rely on his art for a livelihood, he would not have the sense of independence he has thus far,—and it has been of great importance to him. So if, as you say, you would not mind speaking to Miss Greene for him, I am convinced it would be a good thing. At my request, she tried to find a place for him before he came to America, but was unable to do. I would speak to her again myself (and will, if you say to) but I had just met her once through a note of introduction from my father.

With good wishes—

Yours cordially—Walter Pach

Oct. 15, 1915

My dear Pach:

. . . I will write to Miss Belle Greene along the lines of your letter, in favor of Duchamp. . . . I hope it will result in something. I will let you know as soon as I hear from her.

Yours very truly, [John Quinn]

New York, Oct. 18, 1915

Dear Mr. Quinn,

I suppose you have seen the new "Modern Gallery" at 500 Fifth Avenue, the offshoot of Stieglitz's place.[1] I think it is a good thing to have it up there, and am glad it is to be run as a business and not as a club-lecture room-laboratory, the way the other place was.

With good wishes

Yours very sincerely, Walter Pach

1. Although Alfred Stieglitz's Little Galleries of the Photo-Secession (the 291 Gallery, at 291 Fifth Avenue), which opened in 1905, continued exhibitions through 1917, shows were inaugurated at his Modern Gallery on October 7, 1915.

New York, Feb. 27, 1916

Dear Mr. Quinn,

I did not have Brancusi's letter just at hand this morning and as I only got it a day or two ago and had only read it once, I wanted to write you just what he said, so here it is. He didn't write me before because he has had a fierce job getting all his things to a new studio. In the old one it was impossible to photograph the big door, but he can and will have it done in the new place and will send me that photograph "and others," (subjects not specified). The "Kiss" is sold—he does not say to whom,—he is happy that I get so much pleasure from it, and says if I care enough about it he will make me another one in stone so that it may be durable. I will either write him that he should make that one for you or tell him you are having my copy cast in bronze,—just as you decide. Let me submit, though, that as my plaster has not quite the identical quality of his original in the "Lorraine stone," and as he is so extremely sensitive about the appearance of his things (you remember that he was really upset at the idea of exhibiting casts at the International),[1] I think it would be a better plan, both for his interests *and* your own to write and ask him about the idea of casting from my plaster . . . .

With good wishes, I am

Yours cordially, Walter Pach

1. The Armory Show.

New York, May 7, 1916

Dear Mr. Quinn,

By this mail I am sending you the four photographs of Brancusi's architectural pieces; here is the translation of his letter. (He has been further delayed by trouble about moving.)

"There is the gate, the bench and the cariatide—I have made the bench as a pendant to the gate and the cariatide   it is about a pedestal that Mr. Quinn spoke to Mr. Steichen[1]—the whole three belong together   If they should interest Mr. Quinn, he could have them for 12,000 francs, the "Kiss" included—I have not been able to photograph the "Kiss" as it is unfinished—It is quite a bit larger than the other and, I think, much finer—as for the pedestal, I shall do my best, and if I am to send them, please tell me to what address—I have put the two largest dimensions on the back of each photograph."

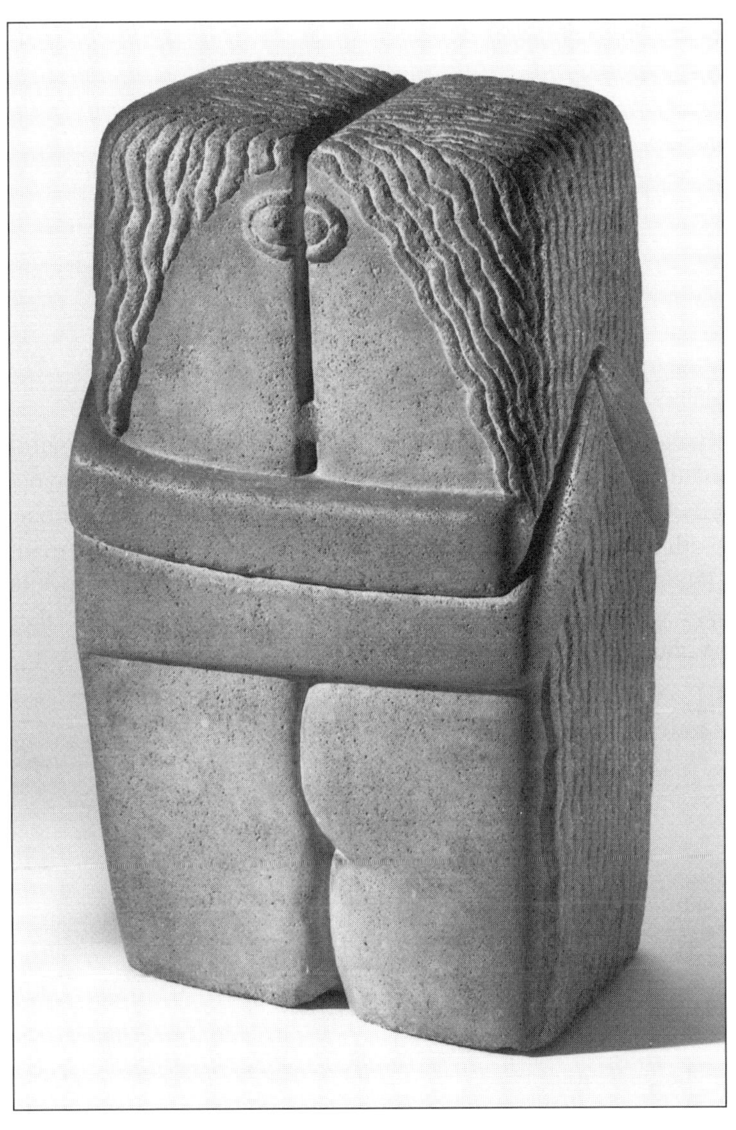

Constantin Brancusi, *The Kiss*, ca. 1912. Limestone, 23 x 13 x 10 in. Philadelphia Museum of Art: The Louise and Walter Arensberg Collection. Acc. 1950-134-4. Photograph by Graydon Wood, 1994.

I seem to have some recollection about writing him about a pedestal. Was it not perhaps for the "Kiss"? If so, I don't see why he speaks about Steichen unless he confuses this pedestal with the one for the "Golden Bird."

Hoping to see you soon, I am, with good wishes,

Yours cordially, Walter Pach

1. Photographer Edward Steichen (1879–1973) had viewed Brancusi's sculpture in Paris as early as 1911; at one point two sculpted heads by the Frenchman had been placed in Steichen's custody.

New York, May 15, 1916

Dear Mr. Quinn,

[Albert] Gleizes telephoned me this afternoon that he was going to sail this coming Saturday and that he would take his pictures along,—also that he had arranged with the Artists Packing and Shipping Co. to have the pictures put on view if one telephoned over there in advance—perhaps in the morning for an afternoon visit or the day before if one went in the morning. You will find the name I give above in the telephone book, if you wanted to go by yourself, or I should be pleased to go along if you let me know ahead.

Yours very cordially, Walter Pach

New York, May 15, 1916

Dear Mr. Quinn,

Here is the memorandum of your purchase of Gleizes' pictures:

Title	*Dealer's price*	*Price to you*
The Brooklyn Bridge	$400.	$200.
Landscape at Toul	$400.	$200.
The Houses among the Trees	$200.	$100.
	Total—	$500.

His address for the first payment of $100. that he would like to have before his departure on Saturday is as follows:

Albert Gleizes 302 West 73rd St.

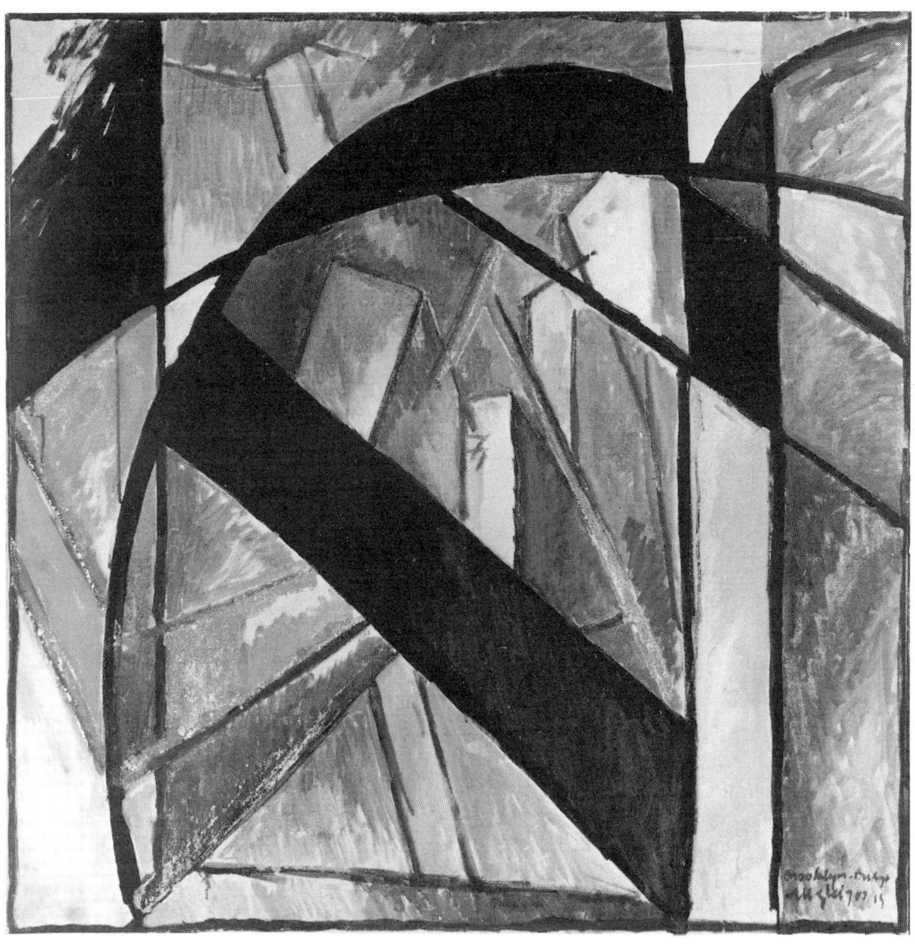

Albert Gleizes, *Brooklyn Bridge*, 1915. Oil and gouache on canvas, 40 1/8 x 40 1/8 in. Solomon R. Guggenheim Museum, New York. 44.942.

The "Houses among the Trees" was, according to his statement, at the Exposition Universelle of Lyons, the first such exposition to accept the work of the Cubists. The ticket on the canvas is from that occasion. I will find out from Gleizes where the remainder of the money is to be sent. I have his father's address in Paris anyhow, where he can always be reached.

With regards, I am

Yours very sincerely, Walter Pach

I just happened to think that Rouault's "Superman" of which you are now the owner is reproduced in Harper's Weekly as one of the illustrations to my very short article on modern art. Did you say you had not seen it? If so I will send you a copy.

W. P.

MAY 19, 1916

My dear Pach:

Thanks for yours of the 18th with the titles, prices and information.

I should be very glad if you would ask Gleizes to send me his Barcelona address. If I sell my place in the country I will be able to pay him up by midsummer. If not the balance would have to go over until the early autumn.

Again I want to thank you for the trouble and time you have taken in the matter.

I did not know that the Rouault "Superman" had been reproduced in Harper's Weekly. If you will kindly let me know the date[1] I will get two or three copies of it. You need not bother to send me a copy.

I am sending the $100 in currency to Gleizes by hand.

Sincerely yours, [John Quinn]

1. The April 29, 1916 issue.

NEW YORK, MAY 19, 1916

Dear Mr. Quinn,

I telephoned to Gleizes your offer for his picture "Women at a Window," ($200 to be paid in the summer sometime), and he accepted and assured me that it was entirely satisfactory to him,—you having purchased a number of his pictures. For my own part, I will repeat that I think it a very good picture, of an interesting moment in Gleizes' development and, in general, well worth a place in your collection. . . .

With good wishes,

Yours very sincerely, Walter Pach

New York, June 22, 1916

Dear Mr. Quinn,

I wanted to give you a memorandum before this that I had written Brancusi last week confirming the commission for the "Kiss," asking the price of the "Cariatide" and saying that you could not make any decision at present as to the other two pieces. . . .

Yours cordially, Walter Pach

New York, July 17, 1916

Dear Mr. Quinn,

Following our conversation over the telephone, I sent the cable to Brancusi,—conceived as follows:

"Quinn willing to pay your price twelve thousand francs for Cariatide, bench, gate and Kiss on condition that he have option on your next important marble. Letter follows." . . .

I shall probably see Duchamp tomorrow and shall speak to him about the three paintings by Villon that he still has; I know that he will be delighted for his brother's sake that you are considering them.

With good wishes,

Yours very sincerely, Walter Pach

New York, July 23, 1916

Dear Mr. Quinn,

. . . I spoke to Marcel Duchamp about the three pictures he still has by his brother, saying that you might consider them if a reduction of 25% in the price were made,—those being the terms you had made with the other artists. He said that he could answer for Villon and that such an arrangement would be entirely satisfactory. . . .

With good wishes,

Yours sincerely, Walter Pach

P.O. Box 333
Ashokan, N.Y., Sept. 2, 1916

Dear Mr. Quinn,

. . . This week the spell was broken by a fine mail from Paris. Le Roy is at Verdun and is proposed for the *croix de guerre* for having defended his machine gun under two severe attacks during which he volunteered on dangerous missions. (It is his aunt who writes me this). He speaks of the Germans becoming demoralized.

Then Rouault wrote me a nice note. He is happily installed in his new house in Paris and is working. I had explained to him that it would be better to participate in group exhibitions for a year or two yet, until he has gained more of a public here, after which he could risk a one-man show, and he sees the point.

Finally—and here is what will interest you most—I have a letter from Brancusi, as follows:

"It is understood. Mr. Quinn shall have the preference as to the purchase of my next important marble, and the payment for the sculptures he buys now shall be according to his wishes as you indicate them to me. I have made arrangements to ship the sculptures and as soon as the packing is finished and I know the name and date of the ship for insurance, I shall telegraph you and I shall write a word to Mr. Quinn." I hope he [Brancusi] is not summoned to Rumania for the war. He was called three years ago in the war with Bulgaria, but as the French would not have him on account of rheumatism, he may not be called on to go all the way home. . . .

With good wishes, I am

Yours cordially, Walter Pach

---

33 Beekman Place,
New York, Oct. 9, 1916

Dear Mr. Quinn,

I have just thought of another person who would be a valuable member of the Paris commission of the French gallery. That is our good friend Georges Rouault. As Conservateur of the Musée Gustave Moreau, he is already in Government employ—so one would not be suggesting an (apparently) radical man,—and he would be a hard fighter for his convictions and the better kind of art. . . .

I hope to hear, by the end of the week anyhow, whether we can get the building I saw, for the Independents.[1] It would be a great step if we could as there are few places in New York that would do.

I am

Yours very sincerely, Walter Pach

I am writing Mme. Redon to ask whether she would agree to quarterly payments for a choice of her pictures.

1. The First Annual Exhibition of The Society of Independent Artists would be held from April 10 to May 6, 1917, at the Grand Central Palace, Lexington Avenue and 46th Street. Pach was its treasurer.

New York, Oct. 11, 1916

Dear Mr. Quinn,

. . . Have you seen a new art magazine called "The Art World"? It is published at 10 E. 43rd St. After one gets over one's first irritation with it, one has to admit that for solid fun there is no such thirty-five cents' worth to be had elsewhere. The little analyses of the Titian and the Degas give the keynote. My wife says Billy Sunday is the editor.[1]

Yours cordially, Walter Pach

1. William Ashley "Billy" Sunday (1862–1935) was a professional baseball player who became a flamboyant evangelist.

New York, Jan. 30, 1917

Dear Mr. Quinn,

I feel guilty at not having given you any more news about the Independents after all your interest in the work. . . . I will wait no more and say that in two weeks over six hundred applications have come in. We are going to have a good many of the known men and, I believe, some worth-while stuff from the unknown men . . . as is shown by the response to our circular. . . .

I had a letter from Duchamp-Villon a couple of days ago, and one from his wife. He wrote from the hospital where he had been for over a month with typhoid. It was very bad at times. Twice, as he said, he nearly "left his skin there." It was a heavy trial for his wife who is a nurse in a hospital quite a way from him, so that she could not see him but three times. The danger seems to be over, but she writes that he is very weak and worn. I am grateful that he is spared and hope there is no doubt that he is really convalescing.

With kind regards

Yours cordially, Walter Pach

Jan. 31, 1917

Personal

My dear Pach:

I received yours of the 30th this morning.

I am glad to know that the membership of the Independents is going along so well. Six hundred so far is very good indeed. Of course there will be a lot of very poor and very bad and very rotten stuff. But there ought to be *some* good things. You know that I am disgusted with missionary efforts, attempts to bring "art to the masses," university settlement applied to art, exhibitions in mission houses, and so forth. Why don't the uplifters confine themselves to the poor, the populace, and the prostitutes? If the uplifters succeed in bettering the physical and financial and economic condition of the poor, their interest in art will take care of itself. The uplifters had better look to the sewers and to the ventilating facilities and the hours of employment, the number sleeping in a room, plumbing, and so forth, of the submerged, rather than attempt to bring art to them. The next thing you know we will have some of the highbrow uplifters wanting to develop a sense of art in the whore-houses. Whether it will be new art or old art remains to be seen. Of course nude art would be out of the question because that would be too direct a competition with the business object of the place.

I am interested in art and not in whether certain asses have a knowledge of art or not. I applaud the missionary spirit as to plumbing, ventilation, hours of labor, wages, sanitation, taxes, and so on. But damn the missionary spirit as applied to art. . . .

Sincerely yours, [John Quinn]

New York, Feb. 11, 1917

Dear Mr. Quinn,

I have just had a line from Mme. Redon to say that she accepts your proposition of quarterly payments to apply on the price of such examples of her late husband's work as you select. She says the price of it in Paris is going up rapidly and she is holding on to what she has. . . .

Yours very sincerely, Walter Pach

Feb. 16, 1917

My dear Pach:

I stopped in at Miss Bryant's[1] this morning and picked out six Redons as follows:

Title	*Artist's price*
"Illumined Flower" (pastel)	francs 2,000
"Vase of Flowers" (gray background)	2,500
"Vase of Flowers" (pink background)	2,000
Etruscan Vase (tempera)	1,800
Pandora (panel)	4,000
Orpheus	4,000
Total	francs 16,300

Miss Bryant has the remaining four out of the ten, namely: "The White Bo[u]quet," "St. John," "Apollo" and Stained Glass Sketch.

In accordance with your understanding with Mme. Redon, I am to pay the 16,300 francs for the five examples selected in quarterly amounts, which will be 4,075 francs each quarter. . . .

I am very greatly obliged to you for writing Mme. Redon for me. I hope you will tell Mme. Redon when you write to her how glad I am to have these examples of her husband's work. I wish you would also tell her that I bought one of his things at the armory exhibition, the Roger and Angelica painting in oil, so that I now have six of his important things. . . .

With kind regards, I am

Yours very truly, [John Quinn]

1. Miss H. C. Bryant was director of the Carroll Galleries.

THE SOCIETY OF
INDEPENDENT ARTISTS, INC.

20 West 31st Street, New York City
Telephone Madison Square 7079

WILLIAM J. GLACKENS
President
CHARLES E. PRENDERGAST
Vice-President
WALTER PACH
Treasurer
JOHN R. COVERT
Secretary

DIRECTORS
Walter Conrad Arensberg, Managing Director

George W. Bellows
Homer Boss
John R. Covert
Katherine S. Dreier
Marcel Duchamp
Regina A. Farrelly
Arnold Friedman
William J. Glackens
Ray Greenleaf
Charles W. Hawthorne
Rockwell Kent
John Marin
Walter Pach
Charles E. Prendergast
Maurice B. Prendergast
Man Ray
Mary C. Rogers
Morton L. Schamberg
Joseph Stella
Maurice Stern

33 BEEKMAN PLACE,
APRIL 18, 1917

Dear Mr. Quinn,

I have finally found out prices for the pictures by Delaunay that you looked at here at the exhibition. Gleizes did not receive any word from Delaunay—just the paintings, and he did not want to set a price till he was sure he could not find out from other people here. He now says—$400 for the "St. Séverin"[1] and $300 for the "Landscape." He would have liked to have said less but wanted to make sure Delauney [sic] would be satisfied.

A lady who declines to give her name has enquired twice about the price of the Delaunays. Everyone seems right interested who sees the show. I like it better as I see more of it, but wish I was not so tied down by it.[2]

With regards,

Yours very sincerely, Walter Pach

I will reserve the Delaunays for a day or two if you 'phone me,—my number at the Palace is Vanderbilt 2597.

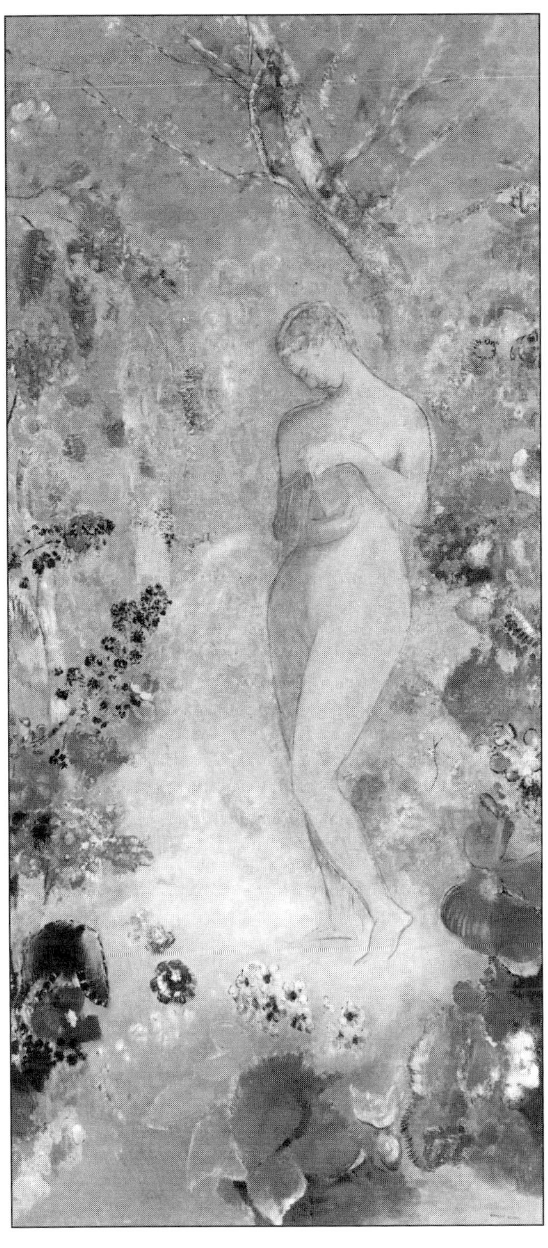

Odilon Redon, *Pandora*, n.d. Oil on canvas, 56 1/2 x 24 1/2 in. The Metropolitan Museum of Art, Bequest of Alexander M. Bing, 1959 (60.19.1).

1. Quinn purchased Robert Delaunay's oil, *Saint-Séverin* (1909), from the Society of Independent Artists Exhibition, through Pach, for $350.

2. Pach was chief salesman for the Independents Exhibit, the same position he had filled at the Armory Show four years before.

THE SOCIETY OF
INDEPENDENT ARTISTS, INC.
NEW YORK, APRIL 24, 1917

Dear Mr. Quinn,

After another delay, in which time he has seen Picabia and other friends again, Gleizes tells me that there is no address at which one might be reasonably sure of reaching Delaunay with a cable. The latter simply sent over the paintings without the least message, and Gleizes considers that it would probably be a waste of money to cable him at the hotel in Barcelona where he was last heard of, as he has probably moved several times since being there. So I can only repeat that he [Gleizes] will take the responsibility of selling the pictures at $300 and $400.

As to Madame Redon, I will translate the lines in her letter of January 27th to me regarding your offer to buy certain of M. Redon's works at the original prices, to be paid for in quarterly remittances.

"—It would be bad grace on my part to refuse to sell to an admirer of Redon three (or four) of his pictures at the prices that Redon had fixed during his lifetime; therefore I consent. But for the pictures that remain I will ask you to return them to me as soon as the war is over. They are unknown here; it was Redon's production of 1914 and they must be in his great exhibition where his work will be represented from the time when he was eighteen years old. Beside the prices of Redon's works are between four and twelve thousand francs . . . and they are going up rapidly now. . . ."

On receipt of this letter I informed you of Mme. Redon's consent and you wrote me that you had selected some at the Carroll Galleries.[1] I think they were:

	francs		*francs*
Orpheus	4000	Vase of Flowers (pink background)	2000
Illumined Flower	2000	Etruscan Vase (tempera)	1800
Vase of Flowers (gray background)	2500	Pandora	4000

. . . Yours very sincerely, Walter Pach

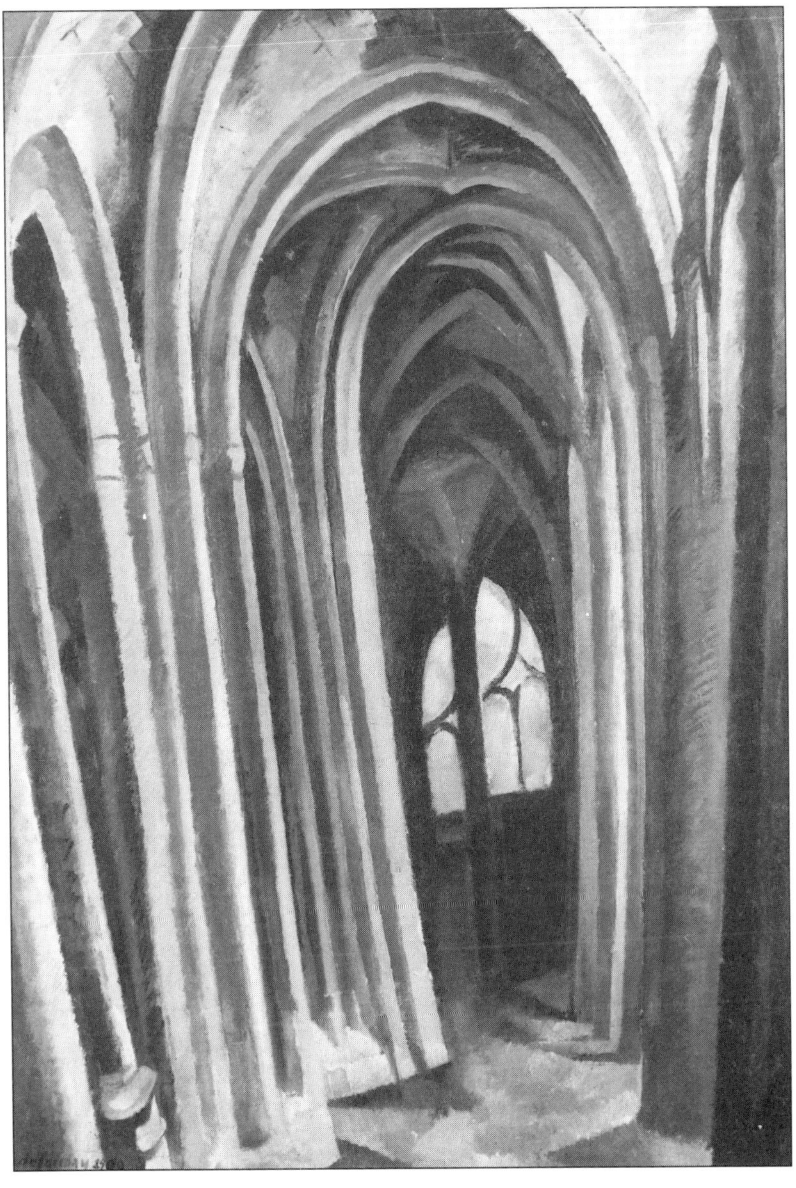

Robert Delaunay, *Saint-Séverin*, 1909. Oil on canvas, 38 x 27 3/4 in. Philadelphia Museum of Art: The Louise and Walter Arensberg Collection. Acc. 1950-134-42a. Photograph by Graydon Wood, 1997. © L & M Services B. V. Amsterdam 20010305.

1. Quinn purchased all six of the works through the Carroll Galleries as follows, with the cost indicated in dollars:

Orpheus (1903), pastel	$702
Illuminated Flower (1900), pastel	351
Flowers in Chinese Vase (1912), oil	351
Poppies and Daisies (1905), oil	438
Etruscan Vase (1912), tempera	315
Pandora (ca. 1910), oil	702

Walter Pach, Esq.,
Care The Society of Independent Artists, Inc.,
20 West 31st Street, New York City

May 1, 1917

My dear Pach:

. . . I am glad to know the two Delaunay pictures will come to me. . . .[1] I hope to get in to see the exhibition several times before it closes.

Yours very truly, [John Quinn]

Wednesday, May 3,1917

P.S. As there will be six purchases coming to me, as well as the one I loaned to be returned, I wish you would have them all sent to my apartment, 58 Central Park West . . . the two Delaunays, the two Sheelers,[2] and the two small ones of your friend [Raymond Duchamp-Villon],[3] as well as the returned one which I loaned. . . .

1. In addition to *Saint-Séverin*, Quinn purchased Delaunay's *Landscape* from the show.

2. Charles Sheeler's *Landscape No. 1* (1916), an oil, for $150; and a crayon drawing titled *Barns* (1917) for $50.

3. Duchamp-Villon's *Torso* and *Architectural Sculpture*.

Aug. 1, 1917

re French pictures consigned to Carroll Galleries, Inc.

My dear Pach:

. . . Miss Bryant . . . inquired whether it would be agreeable for her to "have the French pictures which she still has sent to the Artists Packing & Shipping Company and packed there". . . .

Now I do not think that is the way it ought to be done. . . . If she were to have these packed up and sent to the Artists Packing & Shipping Company, there would be no way of protecting yourself by receipting for just what you got. . . .

What I suggest therefore is that you come down to New York arrange by appointment with her when you shall come there, and have the Artists Packing & Shipping men come there at the same time, and then that she certify to you all of the works that she has on hand, by name of artist or consigner, by title or subject-matter of work, and price in francs, and that you receipt to her for those works respectively. . . . Miss Bryant has closed the gallery. . . .[1]

She raised, but in a very nice way, the question of your possible sale of the things and of her commission. I told her that I would suggest to you that, without any obligation on your part as to an accounting, when the war was over and you came to return the things, if you had been able to dispose of any in the meantime, and if there was any net profit, you would be willing to allow her fifteen per cent of the net profit. I think that this phraseology in your receipt to her will fully protect you. . . .

Her address is, as you doubtless know, care of Carroll Galleries, Inc., 67 Fifth Avenue. Her telephone number is Stuyvesant 1288.

With kind regards, I am

Your very truly, [John Quinn]

Walter Pach, Esq.,
c/o Mountain House,
Valhalla, New York

1. The Carroll Galleries.

Valhalla, N.Y., Aug. 16, 1917

Dear Mr. Quinn,

Following our conversation on the 'phone, I have written to Miss Bryant and am sending the letter by this mail.

I have said that it seems to me that I ought to take over the pictures now instead of later,—that I will come to town any time and that it will not cost her much over half an hour to get the things out as we can have the men from the Artists Packing and Shipping Co. there to help.

I said that I had called you up on the 'phone and that it was your opinion that I had made myself responsible to the French artists and dealers by writing them about the transfer and that I should therefore have the works in my actual possession.

Yours very sincerely, Walter Pach

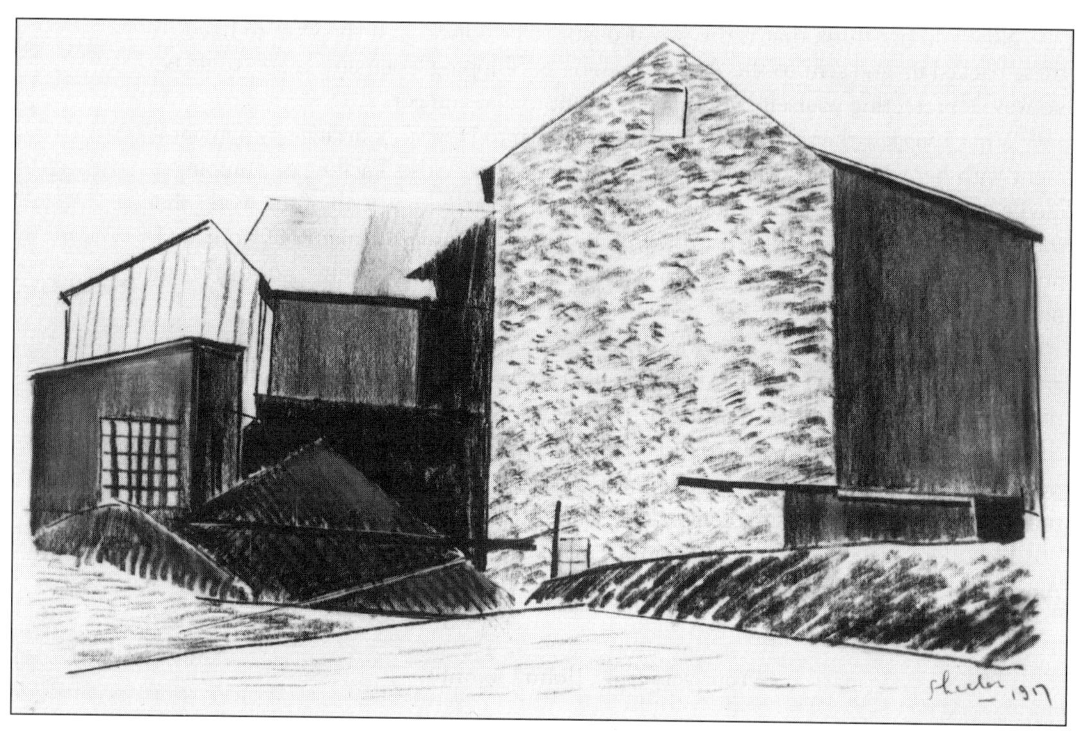

Charles Sheeler, *Barns*, 1917. Conté crayon on paper, 6 x 9 in. Albright-Knox Art Gallery, Buffalo, New York, Gift of A. Conger Goodyear to The Room of Contemporary, 1940. Photograph by Biff Henrich.

VALHALLA, N.Y., AUG. 26, 1917

Dear Mr. Quinn,

. . . I have not heard from Miss Bryant since writing her last time,—of which I informed you at the time. I was in town one day this week and 'phoned to her but could get no reply. I shall be coming to the city in a day or two again and shall try once more in case I have not had a letter from her. As soon as I do get an appointment I will let you know.

This week I had a letter from Dufy,—just a few lines to say he was well, and working on the plates for the book of which he sent me the prospectus that I enclose.

Yours very sincerely, Walter Pach

Valhalla, N.Y., Sept. 3, 1917

Dear Mr. Quinn,

. . . I note that you are holding Redon's "St. John" at my disposal.

I have just consulted the letter from de la Fresnaye[1] in which he says that he has not received the balance due him on the pictures sold at the Carroll Galleries' exhibitions of 1914–'15. This letter is dated Feb. 21st, 1917.

I was in town on Friday and tried to get Miss Bryant on the 'phone three times, but there was no reply. I have not had any answer to my letter of about two weeks ago saying that my responsibility to the artists and dealers made it necessary for me [to] take over the works at once. . . .

With good wishes

Yours sincerely, Walter Pach

1. Robert de la Fresnaye (1885–1925) was a cubist who had adopted that style of painting in 1911.

Valhalla, N.Y., Sept. 7, 1917

Dear Mr. Quinn,

I will come to my main news at once: the pictures left the Carroll Galleries today and are at the Artists Packing and Shipping Co., being boxed.

I got the lists from Miss Thompson and Mr. Curtin[1] and found that everything at 67 Fifth Avenue was right according to the lists, except for the [André] Mare "blotter" which Miss Bryant says she must pay for if it cannot be traced and the Dufy book which she had put away in another place for safekeeping and will send me presently. A gallery in Washington, to which she sent the Matisse etchings, sold four of them but has not yet remitted the $40, so that remains outstanding. . . .

With kind regards

Yours sincerely, Walter Pach

1. Thomas Curtin, Quinn's assistant.

13 East 14th St.
New York, Feb. 12, 1918

Dear Mr. Quinn,

I called on Miss Anderson last week and found her correcting the final proof of the French number of the Little Review. That is to say of the number (February, I am pretty sure it is) which will be on the newsstands tomorrow. So it was out of the question to have either the Cock[1] or the poems[2] in this French number, but there is to be another one in May or June and so we have leisure to arrange about that and make sure that we get the best possible result with the medallion.

I understand thoroughly your idea of the type of photograph that should be made. Sheeler's[3] delicate work, as fine as it is in many ways, would not be in keeping with the vigorous, spirited even strident note of this piece. I shall see to the photographing of it myself and shall send you a copy of the plate.

The Derain water-color used for the catalogue of the first Carroll Galleries exhibition was reproduced in half tone from a photograph. The Cock would certainly make a fine effect that way, but I want to see how the color of the sun and the violet background reproduces before we decide to go ahead with the half-tone plate. It is good that we are not to be hurried with it.

I wrote to [Ezra] Pound[4] and sent him a copy of my letter to you and one of each of the two Le Roy poems, which I got with your letter of February 4th.

Yours cordially, Walter Pach

1. A painted plaster, medallion-shaped sculpture by Raymond Duchamp-Villon; it had just been purchased by Quinn through Pach for 800 francs (about $160).

2. Two poems by Jean Le Roy.

3. Charles Sheeler (1883–1965) had taken up photography about 1910, and within a few years he was in demand as a photographer of art. In 1919 Quinn would commission him to photograph the Jacob Epstein sculptures that Quinn owned.

4. Pach had initially met Ezra Pound in 1906 in Madrid; Quinn first met Pound when the writer had returned from England for a brief stay in America.

New York, March 24, 1918

Dear Mr. Curtin,

Mr. Quinn asked me to give you a memorandum of some etchings etc. by Jacques Villon that I brought him this afternoon. He bought the following:

2 large etchings at $30. . . . . $60.
3 small [etchings] at $20. . . . . 60.
3 water-colors at $15. . . . . 45.
$165.[1]

Yours sincerely, Walter Pach

1. See Pach's letter to Quinn of April 19, 1918, for additional data regarding these works.

New York, April 8, 1918

Dear Mr. Quinn,

. . . We have been obliged to give up the tent idea for the Independent show. I think you will be rather glad of that and—considering the splendid location we have found—I am too. Still the tent had enormous attractions, it seemed almost symbolic—making one think of Esau and Ishmael and Barnum and such people (the circus men are fine fellows) and we only gave it up when all the Arabs had folded their tents and stolen away. Despite promises and assurances, no tent is to be had.

Now that I know you're coming back soon, I needn't worry about getting the Duchamp-Villon medallion [for the Independent]: you can give orders for my getting it when you come.

But I want to ask for another man's work,—if you don't mind. That is Picasso; de Zayas has not one to give us, though he is sending us other things. Would you mind letting us have two Picassos? We are in a big store—42nd St. between Broadway and Sixth Avenue,—so it's quite safe now. I shouldn't have liked to have asked before, though with a new tent, the danger would have been small.

I don't know whether we are going to have a greater or smaller percentage of bad stuff this year, but we shall have some good pictures and I'm feeling so strong for the idea of the show that I'm not regretting that I went into it again. I'm not working like last year—nor anywhere near as hard.

With many good wishes

Yours sincerely, Walter Pach

Please don't lend the Picassos unless you'd care to.

New York, April 19, 1918

Dear Mr. Quinn,

Replying to your inquiry received through Mr. Curtin,—I do not think the Villons have any special titles, at least there are none on the list Duchamp gave me. We can distinguish them roughly by size and subjects,—thus:

One large watercolor of street musicians (almost monochrome) Two smaller watercolors,—women (I think), brighter colors	$15 each
3 etchings on China paper, nudes, about 6 3/4 x 10 inches (size of plate), early works—perhaps 1903	$20 each
larger nude, standing full-length three quarters back view about 1911 and very large nude, standing, front view arms raised, paper about 20 x 26 inches	$30 each

Hoping to see you soon at the Independents,

Yours cordially, Walter Pach

New York, May 19, 1918

Dear Mr. Quinn,

Gleizes was at my house last night. He has had some unpleasant money-experience, having trusted some one in a business venture with a sum of money which has disappeared,—leaving him very short. He asked me if I could sell the little water-color by Marie Laurencin that he had at Bourgeois' [Gallery] a year or two ago. It is, I should think, about nine by twelve inches in size (I speak from recollection) and showed two or three lightly sketched female figures and a swan, I think. He asked either $125. or $100. for it at the time but would now be glad of $50. for it, to carry him along.

You understand that I do not suggest your buying the picture unless you really want it; I am just in my usual rôle of passing along the information as it has come to me. . . .

Yours sincerely, Walter Pach

May 22, 1918

Personal and confidential

My dear Pach:

As I said when you called me on the telephone this morning, I am not interested in the little Marie Laurencin oil painting [sic] offered by Gleizes to me at $50. It had been twice offered to me before, and I did not care for it. I have done my share of buying work from young artists "to encourage them" or "to help them," and I hope I am through with it. Too often when I buy things "to help an artist" or "to encourage him"or "because he needs it," I regret it later on. I have done my share of that and I am through with it. And I feel just the same way about buying this Marie Laurencin. If a work of art doesn't appeal to one, one shouldn't put it in one's collection. . . .

Very truly yours, [John Quinn]

1637 Euclid Avenue,
Berkeley, Calif., Aug. 4, 1918

Dear Mr. Quinn,

. . . Duchamp-Villon wrote me that he is better again, though still in a hospital. He said he would send you, on approval, a drawing he made for his medallion of the Gallic Cock. I wrote I was sure you would like to see it. . . .

With regards

Yours cordially, Walter Pach

New York, Oct. 4, 1918

Dear Mr. Quinn,

. . . It certainly was a victory, at this time, and with the public mind as it is today, to have kept the tax off of the sale of works of art by their producers. The brief covered the matter in an interesting and conclusive way and ought to have prevented an art-tax of any kind; but if I were to hear nowadays that all sales of art works were prohibited for fifty years I should think the story only a little improbable. . . .

With regards

Yours sincerely, Walter Pach

Duchamp-Villon sent me a one-act play, a "bouffonnerie" he calls it, that he wrote in collaboration with another fellow, in a hospital. It is perfectly delightful.

New York, Oct. 29, 1918

Dear Mr. Quinn,

. . . I have had a great deal of bad news to give you lately and a letter I received from Mme. Raymond Duchamp-Villon brings me the most dreadful message that I think I could have received: her husband is dead "of a crisis of anaemia following an urgent operation." He had been suffering ever since his typhoid fever of about two years ago and had gone from one trouble and one operation to another. I knew that he was in a bad state, but the blow is a grievous one none the less. You liked him as an artist from the first days you saw his work, and it is, I hope, a satisfaction to you that in adding so many of his splendid things to your collection you gave him support which he held in great esteem. I wish, even now, that you could have known the man—so simple and earnest and cordial,—and such a man! I can not say what his loss means to me—I had so counted on being with him again after the war. . . .

Yours very sincerely, Walter Pach

New York, Dec. 6, 1918

Dear Mr. Quinn,

Bourgeois[1] asked me to come and see him yesterday about the picture by van Gogh formerly at the Carroll Galleries, for which he thinks he has a customer. He had heard indirectly from Duret (the owner) about my having it. In conversation I said that I had other things of the Carroll Galleries, and he would like to try his hand at selling those also. He is getting up a show for Boston and would probably place some there; also he might show some in his own place, though not in public exhibition. It seems to me that the thing to do is to let him go ahead, but I have not said that I would as I felt I ought to mention the matter to you first. . . .

Yours very sincerely, Walter Pach

1. Stephan Bourgeois, owner of the Bourgeois Gallery.

New York, Jan. 13, 1919

Dear Mr. Quinn,

I have just had a letter from Mr. Torrey in San Francisco who says that in view of the present high price of gasoline he would be willing to reconsider a refusal he made a year or more ago to sell Duchamp's 'Nude descending a Staircase.'[1] At the time, Arensberg[2] wrote to him about selling it, but he did not want to. He puts it in my hands and as he does not say I should speak to Arensberg about it first, I write to you of it. The price he sets on it is one thousand dollars.

I could have waited with this till you call me up, but thought I would give it to you like this as a memorandum.

The figure he names is of course a big advance on what he paid, but that was six years ago, when he got the picture at the studio price,—or almost that, and we have all come to feel more strongly about Duchamp's work since then. I wished at the time that I could have bought one or more of his things at the International,[3] but I was no more able to do so then than now.

Yours sincerely, Walter Pach

1. Frederic C. Torrey, a San Francisco art dealer who purchased the painting from the Armory Show for $324.

2. Walter Arensberg would ultimately acquire the canvas.

3. The Armory Show was officially named the International Exhibition of Modern Art.

New York, May 23, 1919

Dear Mr. Quinn,

. . . since you are always interested in Elie Faure, I thought I would give you some lines from a letter I just had from him.

He says:

"Here the groupings of painters are re-forming, but I do not have the impression that the war has as yet produced a great change in the ideas of the artists. That will doubtless be for the generation that will follow.

Political affairs are sad, no choice is being made either for or against Bolshevism, and the moment is so dramatic that perhaps they are right to act so. It is evidently a question of completely abandoning an ancient order for a new one, a phenomenon that has not occurred in 2000 years. I can pretty well see a St. Paul in Wilson,[1] a Julian the Apostate in Orlando.[2] And I confess that for the former I do not share the enthusiasm of the revolutionaries of the whole world, for he seems to me to have more character than intelligence. From another standpoint, a new faith is preparing, and Wilson is doubtless designated to rally to certain elementary ideas a sort of intellectual slavery which is necessary for the formation of that faith. Between the two orders there are various Stoics,—always like twenty centuries ago; it seems to me that I am of this class. The dilemma is a terrible one: culture must be destroyed to feed the faith. It is quite evident that the faith will triumph, and, at bottom, I wish it to. But I can not abdicate my judgment. So then, I suffer, I observe and I try to objectify. You will find the résumé of the spiritual drama that the Stoics of my sort are living, in 'The Wheel' and especially in 'The Dance on the Water and the Fire.'"

The former is a novel he recently published and which I have just read,—a strong work; the latter book is a series of essays now running serially in "L'Europe Nouvelle,"—a weekly.

That shows that Paris is still alive and thinking. Another proof of it is the big Matisse portrait that de Zayas just brought over. It is a dream,—to me, one of his very big things.

Now I will stop,—with good wishes

Yours sincerely, Walter Pach

1. President Woodrow Wilson.

2. Vittorio Emanuele Orlando, who served as prime minister of Italy from 1917 to 1919. In the latter year he led the Italian delegation to the Versailles Peace Conference.

New York, June 8, 1919

Dear Mr. Quinn,

I'm glad you said there was no hurry about the letters to Matisse, Derain and Picasso, as I have had a deluge of orders for translation since then which ate up my whole small stock of leisure . . .

In thinking how I would write them, it occurred to me that the best plan might be to write two letters: one from you making the offer to take works from them from time to time,—the other from me coming as a more or less independent introduction which should say what I knew of you and your collection. . . .

. . . I know Matisse very well indeed, Picasso not so well and Derain not at all—personally.

With good wishes

Yours sincerely, Walter Pach

New York, June 15, 1919

Dear Mr. Quinn,

Enclosed is a copy of my letter to Matisse, Derain and Picasso in its final form,—i.e., the one I wrote plus and minus your suggestions, literally included. According to our conversation on the 'phone this morning it probably answers the points you brought up in the letter you said you had written me. So if there is nothing further in that I shall not answer it when I get it. I have written to Matisse but shall not post the letter till I get yours and see if there is anything else to be included.

Since speaking to you this morning I have been able to get Picasso's address: It is Pablo Picasso, chez Mme. Clovis Sagot, 46 rue Laffitte, Paris. My Spanish friend tells me that that is always the best address for Picasso as she is a very old friend of his who has always looked after his affairs to some extent and sends him mail at once wherever he is.

That brings me to a point connected with matters I meant to speak to you about when I saw you personally. I am in some doubt whether any of the three artists will be able to sell to you direct as all are or have been under contract with dealers to dispose of their entire production through the latter. That was, of course, not the case with Rouault, Dufy and the rest. I don't know if those contracts are still in force, and I shall be interested to know how the artists reply.

With good wishes,

Yours very sincerely, Walter Pach

[Letter from Walter Pach to Matisse, Derain, and Picasso—final form.]

My dear . . .

(Personal and introductory).

I have just heard from Mr. John Quinn that he is about to write you regarding an arrangement whereby he could see more of your work, with a view to adding more examples of it to his collection, and I write especially to tell you that I think his offer is one that would be of very real interest to you. Mr. Quinn is not a rich man and is a busy practising attorney who has given a great deal of his leisure time to the cause of art. It was due solely to his efforts and at his own cost that the fifteen per cent United States customs duty was taken off modern art in 1913. And again in the late Revenue Act taxing art sales, Mr. Quinn on behalf of the artists, and at his own expense, made the briefs and a trip to Washington and the arguments there which resulted in sales by living artists of their own work being exempted from the ten per cent tax which was imposed upon all other art sales. Mr. Quinn has been able to buy a certain number of works of art each year for quite a long time, and as his interest as a collector is entirely in modern work, his collection of artists since Cézanne is by far the most extensive and important in this country. When I speak of your interest in being adequately represented in it, I am not thinking of the period of the works so much as the importance of the artists who appear there, for, beginning with pictures by Chavannes, Cézanne, Redon, Gauguin and van Gogh, he has worked ahead consistently and logically with Matisse, Rouault, Dufy, Derain, Picasso, Braque, Metzinger, Gleizes, the brothers Duchamp-Villon, Brancusi and others. Add to this the fact that he has been able to secure a considerable number of examples of these artists which must rank with their best works, and I think you will agree with me that I have not exaggerated in saying that it is important for you to be represented in such a collection by a suitable number of works and by a quality of works which will give the true bearing of your art and its place in the movement of our time.

In addition to Mr. Quinn's general desire to add good examples of work by living men to his collection, there is the great advantage of sales direct by artist to Mr. Quinn being exempted from the ten per cent tax which, in the case of important examples is not a negligible thing.

Our opportunities for seeing the best modern work are very limited over here, and it is on this account that he makes the suggestion, of which he has told me, that you send him photographs. I am sure that the financial side of the matter would be agreeable to you, for several of the artists I have named above have had dealings with Mr. Quinn and will tell you that he has always been willing to pay for their work in a way they found quite satisfactory.[1]

1. The number of Matisse, Derain, and Picasso works acquired by Quinn in this manner is unknown; however, the collector did purchase four of André Derain's views of London at some time during 1919.

New York, Aug. 4, 1919

Dear Mr. Quinn,

. . . I wanted to speak to you about a letter from Bernheim's in Paris, I had some weeks ago. They asked me to use my efforts to obtain payment from Miss Bryant of the amount of the Seurat drawing she had and which Bourgeois sold in 1916. She wrote in 1917 asking for more time. I have 62 Murray Ave., Port Washington as my last address for Miss Bryant, and wrote her there at once. I have had no reply. This is just the thing we hoped to avoid when I took over the pictures two years ago, And now it comes about anyhow. Can you give me any advice as to how to proceed?

I have taken the remaining things out of storage and am having them re-packed for shipment to Paris, as Mr. Bourgeois is going there, a little later and will take the case with him. He has a few of the things at his gallery and wants to try to sell them. The small Redon is still at Ehrich's where I lent it for the exhibition this season, and I have a few etchings and wood-cuts. Otherwise this shipment will finish up the Carroll Galleries stock.

Hoping you have had a pleasant time I remain

Yours sincerely, Walter Pach

Schroon Lake, N.Y., Aug. 20, 1919

Dear Mr. Quinn,

I don't believe the enclosed letter from Miss Bryant can be of much interest to you,—it certainly is of no help to me in writing to Bernheim's. Still I thought it might be worth while to forward it to you for the sake of the suggestion in the postscript:—I shall certainly *not* follow it, i.e. have Bernheim's write you. There is nothing left save to write them that it is a hopeless case. . . .

Yours cordially, Walter Pach

[Copy]

Aug. 14, 1919

My dear Mr. Pach:

In reply to your letter in reference to the Bernheim Jeune matter, I greatly fear it is going to be difficult to adjust it. However you may see a way clear. Frankly I do not.

When the Carroll Galleries was discontinued I made a list of all the monies that were owing to firms and artists abroad and sent the list to Mr. Quinn and he deducted the amount from commissions owing to the Galleries from pictures sold to Mr. Quinn. Everything was cleared up at that time and that closed the accounts payable in full. I should not like to write Mr. Quinn about the matter at this late day so I do not know just what to do. Can you suggest anything?

Sincerely yours, (Sgd) H. C. Bryant

Would it not be as well to have Bernheim Jeune send Mr. Quinn the account direct? I really am at a loss as to the best way to handle the matter.

H.C.B.

---

13 East 14th St.,
New York, Sept. 11th, 1919

Dear Mr. Quinn,

Thank you for thinking of me with the newspaper-cuttings about your having received the red ribbon.[1] It will make a very nice note in your color scheme and I'm delighted to learn that the distinction so highly esteemed in France should have come to you.

I saw Gregg's[2] article first, and with his mention of art, my first thought—before I read it through—was that the award was made for what you have done for French art. It might well have been. And yet the day is still so far off when the painters you care for will have become "official" successes that you may have, for a long time yet, the better kind of pleasure that comes of collecting for the sheer love of it.

As testimony to your devotion to the great cause of France, the Légion d'Honneur is really a thing to be happy over, and, as I said, I am glad with you. It is much better to receive it so than for anything concerning art. I remember you once said in a letter to one of the artists that it was a great regret to you that your duties here prevented your going to the war. I think that the red ribbon, coming at this time and for this reason, must be more than a recompense,—it must be a proof that your presence here meant as much in usefulness to the issue you had at heart as anything, perhaps, you might have done had you gone abroad. When you do go, and see how your decoration is prized over there, you will have, I think, even an added pride [in] it. With good wishes, I am

Yours sincerely, Walter Pach

1. A red rosette worn in the lapel designated the wearer as a recipient of the French Legion of Honor.

2. Frederick James Gregg, art critic for the New York *Herald*.

NEW YORK, SEPT. 25, 1919

Dear Mr. Quinn,

. . . I was grieved when you told me he [Robert de la Fresnaye] was tubercular. He was exempt from military service in 1914, went as a volunteer, was wounded and discharged from the army and enlisted again. . . .

Duchamp's address is c/o Francis Picabia, 32 Avenue Charles Floquet, Paris. I had a very pleasant letter from him the other day. He had been to visit Madame Duchamp-Villon at Laon, where she is still in the service as a nurse. He expects to return to New York in December.

Yours very sincerely, Walter Pach

NEW YORK, OCT. 19, 1919

Dear Mr. Quinn,

. . . [Charles] Sheeler brought from Philadelphia the rest of the [Morton] Schamberg[1] pictures that we decided to keep, and turned them over to me this week. Beside what was left from the exhibition, I have now about ten paintings that were not shown at Knoedler's. I shall be glad to show them to you any day, if you would like to see them.

Yours very sincerely, Walter Pach

1. Morton Schamberg (1881–1918), an early American modern, had discovered Fauvism and Cubism when he and Sheeler visited Paris beginning in 1909. Schamberg died during the influenza epidemic of 1918.

NEW YORK, JAN. 28, 1920

Dear Mr. Quinn,

. . . I imagine [Ambroise] Vollard is publishing his Renoir book himself. It will not be out for a while yet. He has promised to send me one to show publishers here with a view to an American edition. I at once got an American publisher for him[1] and wrote back for a copy of the text so that I could translate that and have it ready. Elie Faure was with Renoir shortly before he died and writes me that I can not imagine the splendor of his last paintings! . . .

With good wishes

Yours sincerely, Walter Pach

1. Ambroise Vollard's *Renoir: An Intimate Record* was published in New York in 1925 by Alfred A. Knopf.

NEW YORK, FEB. 10, 1920

Dear Mr. Quinn,

I received today a catalogue from Kessel in Paris of a sale in which he is interested. It is the "S.S. Collection" to be sold on March 22nd, so there would be time to send in bids on things there if you wanted to. There are fifteen Toulouse-Lautrecs, four Marie Laurencins and three Cézannes—one that was in the International—all illustrated. You ask Vollard about Toulouse-Lautrec so I mention this as against your not having got the catalogue. If that should be so, and if you want it, I will send it to you. . . .

. . . if you have no objection on any ground, and if it will not be robbing you of too much time to get these pictures out, I should be very happy indeed if we could have, for the Independents, the loan of the two Matisses you got last spring, two of the Rouaults and two of the Dufys. There,—that is a pretty tall request if you have any sentiment against the things going out, in which case, please dismiss the matter forthwith—or it is a benefaction to the artists and a few others who will enjoy those works for three weeks, if the thing appeals to you that way. . . . We should want the pictures from March 8th or 9th till April 2nd but if you care to let them go[1] I should be obliged if you would inform me (with titles) by February 17th so as to put them in the catalogue.

With good wishes

Yours sincerely, Walter Pach

1. Quinn did lend the works to the Fourth Annual Exhibition of The Society of Independent Artists.

NEW YORK, FEB. 16, 1920

Dear Mr. Quinn,

In the enjoyment of seeing those pictures yesterday, I forgot one point I meant to speak of. In 1917 and 1918, when you lent pictures for the Independents you preferred not to have a mention of your name in the catalogue as the owner of them. I shall assume that the same holds true this year unless I hear from you to the contrary . . .

Yours very sincerely, Walter Pach

New York, March 3, 1920

Dear Mr. Quinn,

. . . I have had your six pictures insured during their stay at the Waldorf,[1] the policy covering all risks and being in the amounts you gave me for each picture, the total being $11,000. 1 enclose a member's card which I have made a season ticket for the exhibition. . . .

With good wishes

Yours sincerely, Walter Pach

1. The location for that year's Independent.

New York, March 23, 1920

Dear Mr. Quinn,

. . . I am glad you got the [Jean] Metzingers, as they are surely of the best of his work and will, I believe, rank very high in the art of their decade. Perhaps I should give you a temporary memorandum that they cost for the Landscape—$300.
"Head of a Woman" 150.

These are the prices that Gleizes put on them in 1915 or '16.

Yours very sincerely, Walter Pach

New York, April 4, 1920

Dear Mr. Quinn,

. . . Mr. Durand-Ruel told me yesterday that Pierre Renoir, the son of the artist, had come out in print with a statement that the collection of small pictures sold as his father's at the Anderson Galleries this season were fakes.

I'm so glad you see progress in the Independent shows. The work has been slow and arduous but it is only by long-continued effort that anything in art can be done over here, or anywhere. . . .

Yours sincerely, Walter Pach

New York, April 6, 1920

Dear Mr. Quinn,

When you first asked me about translating letters for you, you spoke of paying me for the work. I did not say yes or no on that point because I felt I would rather not have any payment for it unless it ran to a good deal of time and trouble and I feel so now. The work has come in comparatively small quantities from time to time and I have, as a rule, been able to get it in at odd moments, so that it has not been burdensome. . . .

On the other hand, from your standpoint, it occurs to me that you might really feel freer if you paid me . . . I *have* kept track, roughly, of the work done because I thought you might ask me about it and I mention the matter now because the Roché[1] letter which I am enclosing (with the original), the amount runs to more than 10,000 words, all told,—French to English and English to French.

If you want to make a payment for this work now or when there has been more,—do so. . . . Otherwise I should be very glad to let all question of remuneration drop here . . .

Yours very sincerely, Walter Pach

1. Henri Pierre Roché (1879–1959) was a writer by profession who met Quinn in 1917; two years later he agreed to serve as Quinn's European art agent.

New York, April 29, 1920

Dear Mr. Quinn,

. . . Madame Picabia called here the other day bringing two drawings by Rodin that she wants to sell as she needs money. She wants $200 for each. They are the type of drawing one is familiar with—such as those in the Rodin gallery at the museum. One is in lead pencil,—a nude, the other has some strokes of brown water color. It represents a Cambodian dancer and is signed, the other is not. I do not know if this is of any interest to you, but I thought I would mention it.

Marcel Duchamp showed me two water colors by Villon, the other day, which I had not seen before. They are small and might be considered studies by some people, but I think they are complete, and very beautiful. I asked him if they were purchasable and at what price, if so. He named thirty dollars each. . . .

With kind regards I am

Yours sincerely, Walter Pach

New York, May 18, 1920

Dear Mr. Quinn,

I have been looking into the prices paid to translators. For workers of a better order than the commercial agencies employ, the price paid the translator averages $4.00 per thousand words . . . the ten thousand words I have done so far would come, at $4.00 per thousand, to $40.00 and if that amount is satisfactory to you, it will be to me also.

I telephoned Duchamp at once about leaving the Villon water-colors at your apartment with his address and telephone number and I imagine he has done so before this.

With friendly regards, I am

Yours sincerely, Walter Pach

New York, May 23, 1920

Dear Mr. Quinn,

. . . The exhibition at the Museum is quite staggering,—and of course it's only a part of what is here.[1]

You have put a good many of my friends in your debt again by lending those things—and they look great. I thought I knew your portrait of Madame Cézanne, but I simply did not realize that it was so beautiful. It holds its splendid place right next to that prodigious thing of Mrs. Meyer's.

What I was particularly interested to see were the Redons. The years that have passed since I brought them over exclude any chance of my judging on anything other than the merits of the pictures, which I see with a fresh eye. They are exquisite, great, important things.

With kind regards, I am

Yours sincerely, Walter Pach

1. The Metropolitan Museum of Art's 50th Anniversary Exhibition, held from May through October 1920; Quinn had loaned a large number of works to the show.

New York, May 31, 1920

Dear Mr. Quinn,

Sheeler[1] and I have been planning to dispose of the remainder of Schamberg's[2] pictures as there is no sense in my holding them here indefinitely. We spoke to Mr. Daniel, the dealer, about it and he is inclined to make some sort of a deal. When I saw him, the end of last week he said he would come down to my place very shortly to see just what I have.

It just comes back to my mind that you wanted to add a couple to those you got last year,[3] so I thought I would let you know of the likelihood of their going out of my hands. Mr. Daniel did not say just when he would be down, but I think, if you still want the pictures, that it would be well to drop in soon.

With good wishes

Yours sincerely, Walter Pach

1. Charles Sheeler (1883–1965), known to Pach since their student days at the New York School of Art.

2. Morton L. Schamberg (1881–1918), a fellow art student of Sheeler's and Pach's. In 1908 Schamberg and Sheeler shared a studio; the following year they became reacquainted with Pach in Paris.

3. Quinn had purchased Schamberg's oils, *Landscape* (1915), *Telephone* (1916), and *Portrait of a White Rose* (n.d.), in June 1919 from the M. Knoedler & Co. exhibition, "Paintings and Drawings by Morton L. Schamberg."

New York, Sept. 18, 1920

Dear Mr. Quinn,

. . . For a long time I have wanted to write on Duchamp-Villon. In the spring I talked over the idea with Marcel and wrote to Madame Duchamp-Villon and to Villon for data.

Here is the part that I am sure will interest you: Villon sent me fifteen or twenty photographs of works by his brother dating from after my last visit to France. Or rather, if I should not say works, at least of sketches and studies and one thing that is perhaps the most important of his career, through being his last considerable effort. I am sure you will want to see these, whatever you think of the rest of my ideas.

Beside the photographs, Villon sent me a manuscript of Raymond's which he had found among the latter's paper after searching, as I requested him to do. . . . I find it a very interesting,—even remarkable—study of the psychology of the artist. I have trans-

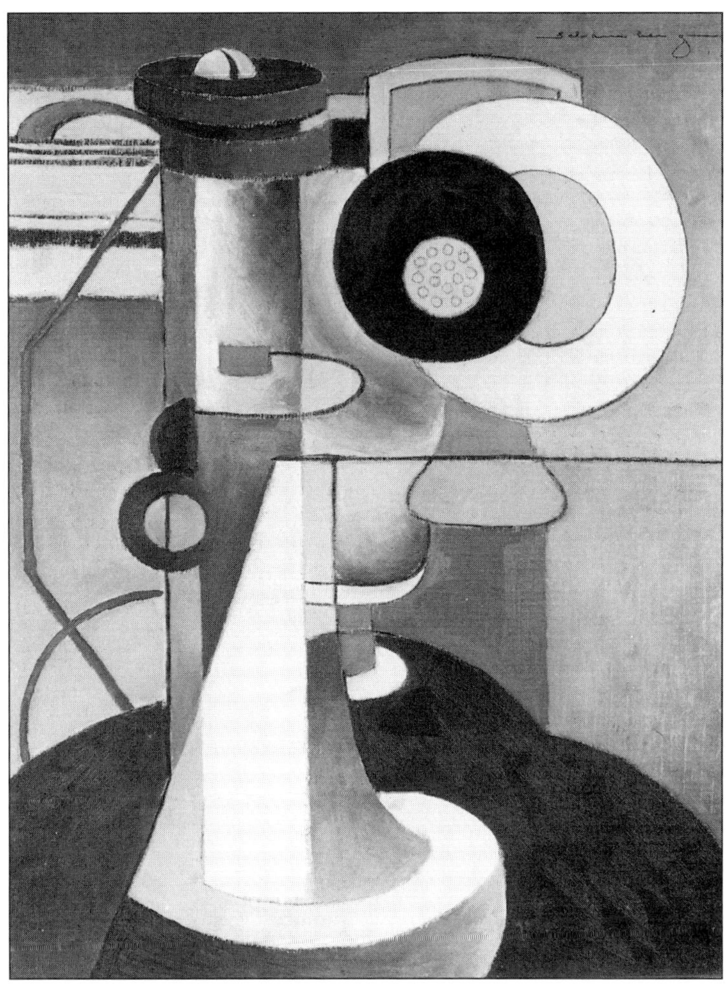

Morton Schamberg, *Telephone*, 1916. Oil on canvas, 24 x 20 in. Columbus Museum of Art, Ohio: Gift of Ferdinand Howald. 1931.263.

lated it . . . it seemed to me that a brochure of the various contents I have mentioned would be so fine to publish. . . . I thought you might care to be associated with the publishing of the brochure which would be the best testimonial of the art of our friend and a means of letting many interested people know it better. Mr. [Erhard] Weyhe the bookseller and publisher was in the country where I was and he at once said he would be glad to take an interest in it, guaranteeing the sale of a certain number of copies. . . .

If you would like to see the photographs and texts I should be glad to bring them at your convenience . . .

With good wishes, believe me

Yours very sincerely, Walter Pach

New York, Oct. 16, 1920

Dear Mr. Quinn:

I have the pleasure of giving you below a brief summary of the proposed contents of the book on Duchamp-Villon to transmit to Mr. Rodker.[1]

Text	*Number of words*
Article on Duchamp-Villon, his life and art, Walter Pach	6,700
Part of "A Sculptor's Architecture" (W.P.) published for the International Exhibition 1913	1,000
Manuscript found among Duchamp-Villon's papers: "Variations in Consciousness during the Work of the Artist"	2,900
Extracts from letters of Duchamp-Villon	3,400
Total	14,000

Illustrations: from 25 photographs

In addition, there is a drawing for the Gallic Cock which might possibly be used as a decoration for the cover or the title-page. . . .

I cannot say how delighted I am with your idea of the Ovid Press and I devoutly hope we are in time for it yet, as it would be the ideal solution of our problem. I am,

Cordially yours, Walter Pach

1. The book, which appeared in 1925, is titled *Raymond Duchamp-Villon, Sculpteur 1876–1918*. Pach authored the Introduction as well as the first half of the volume; it was published in Paris by J. Povolozky.

New York, May 8, 1921

Dear Mr. Quinn,

. . . I shall . . . let Mme. Duchamp-Villon know that the sculptures arrived. I have located her letter to me in which she states the prices, which are as follows:

The Horse	fr. 6000
Portrait of Dr. Gosset	1500
	total fr. 7500

there are also three other models of the horse, studies—of which she makes you a present.

Yours cordially, Walter Pach

Mme. D-V's address is:

Madame Raymond Duchamp-Villon, 7 rue Lemaître, Puteaux, Seine France

---

New York, May 18, 1921

Dear Mr. Quinn,

. . . I do hope you have a complete success with the question of the tariff on art. Just recently, in writing a study of American art and art-conditions, I spoke of our formerly having a tariff on art that tended to keep it out of the country. Then I used the proud phrase "That is a thing of the past," and went on to show what progress went with the change. I hope the thing is not to be reversed and I know that if any one can save the situation, you will. It would be a shame if we took that step back to barbarism.

With good wishes,

Yours sincerely, Walter Pach

On re-reading your letter to Madame Duchamp-Villon, I note that you say you will have the sculptures cast in bronze. It was his intention to have them in steel.

---

15 rue Louis Philippe
Neuilly, Aug. 3, 1921

Dear Mr. Quinn,

Marcel Duchamp told me of your conversation as to the brochure on Raymond [Duchamp-Villon] and said I was to look into the cost of it.

I got some addresses yesterday from a publisher who is a good friend of mine and today went to look into the matter of printing and plate-making. . . . The price for printing should not exceed 1500 francs (500 copies . . . The plates if they averaged 12 x 16 cm would come to about 60 fr. each or again 1500 francs for the twenty-five [illustrations]. That makes 3000 francs in all. . . .

Yours very sincerely, Walter Pach

---

13 East 14th St.,
New York, Dec. 10, 1921

Dear Mr. Quinn,

I have a request from Madame Redon to furnish her with a list of her late husband's pictures in this country and photographs of as many as I can secure.

I can make a pretty complete list from the records of sales at the International and the Carroll Galleries, so I do not need to trouble you in that respect. . . .

I omitted to say, above, that the list and photographs are for a big *Catalogue Raisonné* of Redon's painted work that is to be published by Floury to complement the catalogue of his engraved work,—. . . I take it that you would not object to my stating that the pictures are in your collection as this is a book of record and as quite a number of the pictures were loaned to last summer's exhibition over your name.

I am somewhat behind in my work for Harpers on the second volume of Elie Faure's History (the first volume appeared this week). Requests, that I could not well refuse, for articles and lectures have come in quite numerously . . .

With good wishes

Yours sincerely, Walter Pach

New York, Dec. 21, 1921

Dear Mr. Quinn,

I wrote to Mr. Burroughs at the Museum saying that you had given me permission to get photographs of the Redons you lent them,—. . .

I think you asked me on the telephone to let you know which ones the Museum could give me photos of; all they had were photographed there,—so I shall get from them the *Apollo*, *Etruscan Vase*, *Two Heads among Flowers* (old title The White Bouquet), *Vase of Flowers* (2), *Illumined Flower*, and *Orpheus*. . . .

With the season's greetings I am

Cordially yours, Walter Pach

New York, March 16, 1922

Dear Mr. Quinn,

. . . In the coming issue of "Shadowland" I shall have an article on Prendergast.[1] It is a curious magazine: the illustrations are mostly of chorus girls and the articles are all by serious men.

With good wishes

Yours sincerely, Walter Pach

1. "Maurice Prendergast," *Shadowland* 6 (April 1922), 11 and 74–75.

New York, May 23, 1922

Dear Mr. Quinn,

. . . You will be glad to hear, I hope, of the interesting summer we have before us. I am invited to give a long course of lectures in Mexico City, at the National University. My wife is as keen about the prospect as I—though I shall feel easier when the first lecture or two is safely over as I have never spoken publicly in a foreign language before. I am to lecture mostly on modern art. We leave in some three weeks . . .

With kind regards,

Yours cordially, Walter Pach

Universidad Nacional,
Mexico City, Sept. 20, 1922

Dear Mr. Quinn,

I had thought to write you long before this, and it is not negligence nor pressure of work that has made me postpone this letter, but simply the desire to have more than a negative report on works of art to be acquired here. . . . I wanted to get something for myself as well as for you. . . .

Enclosed is a photo of one piece, with the dimensions and weight on the back. It is a beautiful jade, bright green on the face turning to gray on the back. Such pieces are extremely rare: there is nothing equal to it in the museum here, in fact I never saw another so fine. The price asked is $500 (U.S. money), with a broad hint from the man who showed it to me (not the owner) that he could probably get it for $400. That probably means that they would take $250. To me the thing looked very fine and perfectly genuine. . . .

Item Number 2 is surely all right from the standpoint of authenticity but has another Mexican peculiarity in so far as price goes. After weeks of waiting I can't find out what the price is! My friend (who is away from the city) wants about $2000,—but that is more or less of a guess, based on what he knows the owner paid for the things, which he has been collecting for years. There are about one hundred and seventy three pieces, all small, the largest stone not over five inches long and some quite tiny; but all hard stone—the valuable kinds. We [Pach and his museum friend] went through them and made a provisional catalogue, as follows:

30 pieces of Oaxaca jade: heads, birds, flowers, ornaments, etc.
23 small objects of black obsidian (mostly ornaments)
6 pieces of gray-green Maya jade, including one very fine bas relief of the character of the other item (in the photo) which is Maya.
20 pieces of jade, diorite and obsidian from the Valley of Mexico including a really magnificent head with gold eyes. (Toltec and Aztec).
8 pieces of Totonaca sculpture (fine)
11 sculptures in calcareous or fossil material—animals, birds etc., very delicate and fine.
37 stone sculptures of various regions and of less interest
3 necklaces Oaxaca jade
2 " Valley of Mexico
1 " Tarasca green stone
3 " varied stones.

To get an idea of these things you would have to pay a visit to the Natural History Museum. . . . Many of them have more the quality of jewelry than sculpture in the monumental sense, but the average standard of the collection is very high. The owner will not break it up. . . .

I hope your summer has been a very pleasant one and that I may soon see you in very good health.

Yours cordially, Walter Pach

---

13 East 14th St.
New York, Dec. 4, 1922

Dear Mr. Quinn,

I have been home for some weeks and have been intending to give you word of my return in case you had anything to communicate to me.

Now I have a small matter to ask you about. Forbes Watson has taken over the editorship of "The Arts" which Hamilton [Easter] Field used to run (and which, I am assured, will have none of the character—or lack of character that he gave it). I am to write an article on Seurat for the first number[1] and in talking to Mr. Watson about illustrations he had a photograph of the "Poudreuse"[2] and asked me if I knew who now owned it. I said I should have to find out before answering. The question is, therefore, do you mind my saying you have it, and may we note your name as that of the owner, in the article. . . .

With good wishes

Yours very sincerely, Walter Pach

1. The article, "George Seurat (1859–1891)," appeared in *The Arts* 3 (March 1923), 160–174.

2. *The Powder*; currently titled *Jeune femme se poudrant* (*Young Woman Powdering Herself*), an oil painted in 1889–1890.

New York, Jan. 28, 1923

Dear Mr. Quinn,

In thinking over the matter of getting those Mexican idols (there are nine figure pieces, one decorated bowl or incense burner and one undecorated plate) it has occurred to me that it would be more prudent to send the money to Jean Charlot[1] instead of to Mr. Palaeios. The latter is very often away from the city on government expeditions . . . Mr. Charlot is a very good friend of mine and absolutely reliable. So if you will have the draft made out to Jean Charlot I will send it off at once.

Yours sincerely, Walter Pach

1. Charlot (1898–1979), who was born and trained in Paris, had emigrated to Mexico in 1921.

New York, March 5, 1923

Dear Mr. Quinn,

This morning I had a letter from my friend Charlot in Mexico City. It was largely in regard to matters connected with the Mexican group at the Independents[1] but also said that he had the $450 and was going ahead according to my instructions [to purchase the 11 Mexican idols for Quinn]. So I hope, in not too long a time, to hear that the objects have been shipped to you.

Also since seeing you on Friday, I had a letter from Jacques Villon to say that after certain extraordinary delays, the book on Duchamp-Villon is going ahead.

With kind regards

Yours cordially, Walter Pach

1. Pach was instrumental in having seven Mexican artists, including Diego Rivera, José Clemente Orozco, and Charlot, invited to exhibit in the 1923 Independents.

New York, May 31, 1923

Dear Mr. Quinn,

. . . I am disturbed to hear that you did not receive the letter from Rouault which you sent me on April 16th. On consulting my records I find that it was returned to you with translation on April 18th. . . . The main thing was that you might hear of a protest that was made in France over the organization of the French section of the International Exhibition at Pittsburg. He said he did not care to be mixed up with protests, although he considered it wrong that the exhibition committee should assume to represent French art while omitting, beside himself, such men as Matisse, Derain, Friesz, Puy and Signac. The last-named was then invited, but refused to take part.

Rouault said "I tell you this simply and without commentaries," the rest of the letter gave some minor details about his engraving. . . .

With kind regards, I am

Yours cordially, Walter Pach

New York, June 13, 1923

Dear Mr. Quinn,

I was down near your office on Monday and dropped in to bring you the proofs of the illustrations in the book on Duchamp-Villon which had arrived that morning. . . . I am more anxious than ever to see the book come out. I have had a long series of letters about it and the difficulty in the way of publication is not yet disposed of. It comes from the great rise in prices since I was in Paris. Each time that Villon has tried to get the book printed, the prices have jumped and—absurd as it seems to me—I have not yet, after a year, had a definite statement of the added amount needed. In my last letter to him I asked for it quite urgently as the thing has dragged so long, but he speaks of "making up the amount himself, if it is not too large". . . .

After worrying a bit over the Zapotec figures from Mexico, I have decided to be philosophical—as they are—and just wait for news. It took them five months to send a collection of old pottery I got together for a Western museum—and when I would write, they thought it was strange that I was impatient. . . .

I am going to a quiet country place [in Westport, Connecticut] where I can get out a number of articles I am to write and also can finish the last volume of Faure's History of Art which I must deliver by Aug. 1st. . . .

Hoping that your own summer will be a very pleasant one, I am

Yours cordially, Walter Pach

New York, Dec. 3, 1923

Dear Mr. Quinn,

Let me begin by acknowledging receipt of the catalogues, Parts I and II of your library, and thanking you for them. I want to say a word or two more of them but first I want to speak of my talk with the two Messrs. Bing.[1]

They 'phoned me on Saturday to put it off till yesterday, and when we got home last night, some people called who stayed till a late hour and so I have not got around to writing until today.

I had a long talk with the Bings, going back over the things that passed between us from our first interview, just before your return from Europe. The proposition then was for a permanent museum of modern art, though I said at the time that I had not the slightest idea what your intentions were regarding your collection, but that I knew that the suggestion had been made to you that you found an American Luxembourg.[2] When I told you of my talk with Mr. Bing, you at once put an end to that idea by saying that you were not going to give the collection and added "They don't mean to give the houses, do they?"[3] When I spoke to Mr. Bing about that, he said, as I reported a couple of weeks ago, that it *was* his intention to raise funds for giving the houses. But he had in mind all the time a permanent gift to the public. As I laid it before him yesterday, he was not willing to take over the matter of furnishing the houses, though both brothers said that they would be glad to make contributions to the fund, if one were raised, for having the long-term exhibition which should lead to a permanent museum of modern art. That keeps the result of my interview from being entirely nil, though it has not brought the houses which would have made the exhibition or museum much easier to realize. . . .

Matisse cabled me "We accept the offer of 20,000 Frs. for the Redons," so whenever you find it convenient, will you please get a draft to that amount for him, and I shall be glad to send it on. I had some $15 expenses with bringing the pictures over. Do you want to add that to your price for the pictures, or do you think I should write Matisse for it?

With kind regards,

Yours sincerely, Walter Pach

1. Alexander Bing and his brother, Leo, were financiers and developers; their firm of Bing and Bing was one of New York City's major developers of luxury residential buildings and houses for the middle class.

2. The Musée National du Luxembourg or Luxembourg Gallery in Paris was where art purchased by the French government was displayed until ten years after an artist's death, at which time it would be determined whether it could be accepted into the Louvre.

3. The Bings raised the capital and purchased the land on which was built Radburn, in Fair Lawn, New Jersey. It is considered the first planned community in the United States.

New York, Dec. 26, 1923

Dear Mr. Quinn,

Replying to Mr. Curtin's question over the telephone, the only sure address I have for Matisse is—

Henri Matisse, 92 route de Clamart, Issy-les-Moulineaux, Seine, France.

That is a bit long for a cable, but I reached him there a few weeks ago by cable, so I know that some one sends on messages if he is not there himself.

After writing twice to Mrs. [H. O.] Havemeyer for permission to reproduce one of her Manets in my book (Durand-Ruel's were ready to give me the photograph, so she needed only to say 'yes')—she had me come up this morning to explain what kind of a book it was. I saw all the great collection again but when it came to telling her about the book, with its David, Ingres, Delacroix, Corot etc., she said she would not like to let her Manet be made to sponsor the "modern art which certain people are trying to force down the public's throat."[1] I thought I might tell you this since her collection was mentioned as one which might furnish some pictures for a modern museum. . . .

Always cordially yours, Walter Pach

1. Pach's book, *The Masters of Modern Art*, was published in 1924 by B. W. Huebsch, Inc., New York.

NEW YORK, FEB. 21, 1924

Dear Mr. Quinn,

. . . Herewith is a photograph of a Corot which Elie Faure has sent me. He says it is one of the finest he knows—of "an amber-and-ashes" coloring, in perfect condition, and better than the photograph shows—(it loses the whites, for example). The work is for sale, the price being 125,000 francs. M. Faure thinks the owner would not make a reduction, unless it were a very small one, and he is in doubt about even that. I forgot to say that the picture is either twenty or twenty-four inches in height. It is "incontestable" as to authenticity, he says, the present owner either having gotten it from Corot or from the person who got it from the artist—I can't quite make out which from his phrase. It is in the big catalogue of Corot's work.

Would you be interested in the purchase of the work? If not, I should be obliged if you would send me back the photograph, as I have no other and there is a man to whom I should like to submit it if you did not care about going in for such a thing. . . .

With good wishes,

Yours sincerely, Walter Pach

New York, Feb. 25, 1924

Dear Mr. Quinn,

I received your letter today with the photograph of the Corot, and with news of your purchases, which naturally interested me very much.

I have been in at Brummer's and have seen the Matisses—whose effect is simply magnificent. The big still-life *is* a wonderful thing: I shall have to see it several times before I can say how great it is. At all events I am more glad than before to have it in my book. . . . The recent Braque (of the type shown in the photographs you sent me) which I saw in the Dial exhibition at Montross's also impressed me as an important development of his art, and it will bring the illustrations of my book up to the present to have that included.

What leads me to write you at this moment is that, a few hours after receiving your letter today, I had one from Mme. Duthuit, Matisse's daughter. I had written to Matisse in December that you preferred to keep the payment for the Redons out of your 1923 budget and would remit for them as soon or at *some time* after the first of January. I can not quite remember whether you or Mr. Curtin asked me to write him that, but I know it was the substance of the message I was asked to give him. Mme. Duthuit (who conducts her father's correspondence usually, especially when he is off in the south, as he is now) writes to say that because of their desire to get matters settled with the other heirs of the estate of which the pictures were a part, she wants to inform me that they have not yet received the payment. . . .

It is vexatious to me to have to come with this affair just after receiving the news of your going in for other purchases, but I can not choose but repeat the contents of Mme. Duthuit's letter, especially as she says she has not your address to write you direct. . . .

With good wishes

Yours very sincerely, Walter Pach

---

c/o Morgan, Harjes & Co.
14 place Vendôme, Paris, July 15, 1924

Dear Mr. Quinn,

I have your letter regarding the Mexican things and it was bad news to learn that they had arrived damaged. The photographs showed only one in a damaged condition when they left. The shipment reached New York about two days before I sailed, and I was so glad to think the business settled that I am especially sorry to have this disagreeable end to it.

I hope by this time you have seen the Duchamp-Villon book. Villon had just received a few copies of it before I reached Paris. He was going to send you one and expected the balance of the edition in a few days, when he would mail those to your friends. . . . I think the book will open the eyes of many people to his genius,—Elie Faure, who did not know Duchamp-Villon's work well, was greatly impressed by the illustrations and said he saw where [Jacques] Lipschitz [*sic*] and a number of others got their ideas. . . .

Yours very sincerely, Walter Pach

PARIS, AUG. 2, 1924

Dear Mr. Curtin,

I was on the very point of writing an acknowledgement of your letter of July 8th enclosing the copy of Mr. Quinn's letter to Hugo Brehme[1] of Mexico City when I chanced to see from the window Mr. Brancusi, the sculptor, who was spending the day in the small town here where I am working. I ran out to meet him and almost the first thing he told me was that Mr. Quinn had died.[2] Though I knew from Mr. Quinn's last letter to me and from Villon (who heard it from Roché) that Mr. Quinn was ill, I did not think it was so grave an illness, but more like his spells of weariness from work, as in other years. Today that I am stunned by the news is almost less than true, for I can hardly believe it now. However, Brancusi was so certain of it that I suppose there is no use fighting against the fact,—and it is a deep loss and grief to me. You know what it means to the artists—both those whose friend Mr. Quinn was in a personal way and those who simply had the encouragement of knowing that there was such an art-lover in the world. . . .

I do not know whether in the settlement of Mr. Quinn's affairs, especially in the matter of the collections,[3] I can be of any service, either in Paris or New York, but if I can, please feel free to call on me when there is occasion. I can not get it through my mind that Mr. Quinn is gone. It will be very long before any of us realizes what that means.

With good wishes to yourself

Yours sincerely, Walter Pach

1. A photographer who had done some work for Pach when he was at the University of Mexico; it was Brehme who ultimately sent the Mexican idols to Quinn.

2. John Quinn died on July 28, 1924.

3. Pach was one of many who sought in vain to have the John Quinn Collection, numbering over 2,000 works, retained as a unit. It was dispersed during two auctions, held on October 28, 1926, at the Hôtel Drouot in Paris, and on February 9, 10, and 11 of the following year at the American Art Association in New York. The fact that the collection had not been kept intact was a motivating force behind the establishment of The Museum of Modern Art in 1929 by Abby Aldrich (Mrs. John D. Jr.) Rockefeller, Lizzie Bliss, and Mary Sullivan.

St. Tropez, Aug. 30, 1924

Dear Mr. Curtin,

. . . I write at once to let you know I have your letter, but I can give you the title of only one of the Redon pictures: "The Death of Buddha." It is easily recognized. The other title was something like Mystic Head, but I can get it exactly from Matisse, whom I shall see when I go back to Paris. . . .

"The Death of Buddha" is an important work,—you might note that it was included in the retrospective showing of Redon's work after his death. Matisse bought the two pictures for his father and it was to settle up the latter's estate that they were sold. Matisse said he would have been glad to have kept them but it would have made difficulties with the other heirs. His price was 15,000 francs each; Mr. Quinn offered 20,000 for the pair and, to close up the matter, Matisse accepted, though 15,000 each was not high.

I feel sure the Mexican sculptures can be repaired, as one that I got was badly broken in getting it to New York and the repairs are hardly visible. Almost all ancient sculpture is repaired. I can have the work done at slight expense. It was on seeing a photo of the sculpture I own that Mr. Quinn asked me to send for the others, as I did not want to sell mine.

You ask for a "list" of the Redons: there were only the two, though of course there are many others in the collection. I know all of them but you doubtless have notes on them from the time of their purchase.

I shall drop you a line when I get back to New York. With good wishes,

Yours very sincerely, Walter Pach

---

13 East 14th St.
New York, Oct. 15, 1924

Dear Mr. Curtin,

Replying to your request of to-day for a statement for the executors of Mr. Quinn's estate, of what was said to me in Paris about the collection, I will outline the matter as follows:

A number of dealers of my acquaintance, having heard that the collection was to be sold, spoke to me of it, and all were of the opinion that the prices would be very low if the sale were held in New York. One said that the total would not be a quarter of what Mr. Quinn paid for the works. They were basing their judgments on their knowledge of American collectors, on the results of the Kelekian sale,[1] and those of the de Zayas and Léonee Rosenberg sales. All were of the opinion that the works would sell better in Paris, where, they said, the prices would be higher than those paid by Mr. Quinn, even after deducting expenses. I am not sure what these expenses would be: there are import and sales taxes. M. Fénéon of Bernheim-Jeune said he would see if the import tax could be paid after the sale. His firm would, if requested, give information about a sale in Paris and estimate the amount it might realize. M. Jos. Hessel also said that he would be interested to handle it, or that he would buy the collection as a whole and dispose of it himself. For the purposes of estimate or purchase, a complete catalogue with descriptions and photographs of important works would be needed. The Paris men said the state of the franc would have little or no bearing on the results, as it made no difference whether one said a picture was worth 20,000 francs or $1,000; what counted was the number of dealers and collectors who would be at the sale; in Paris,—the whole of Europe would attend—in New York, only Americans, and New York dealers with instructions from European colleagues to buy if very great bargains appeared.

I pass on the above information without modification or comment of my own, as I think it is for you to make the necessary investigation regarding it. Also, I think you might get information at the Metropolitan Museum. I had a brief conversation there regarding the collection, but was asked to regard it as private, so as to avoid criticism of persons concerned, who spoke in an unofficial way only.

Hoping that the above may be of service to you, I am

Yours very truly, Walter Pach

1. Dikran Kelekian was a Madison Avenue art and antique dealer whose collection included such diverse objects as Coptic textiles, an ancient Greek torso, and a Picasso drawing.

Source of Letters: John Quinn Memorial Collection, Manuscripts and Archives Division, The New York Public Library, Astor, Lenox, and Tilden Foundations, which contains additional Quinn/Pach correspondence.

Also available through the Archives of American Art, Smithsonian Institution, John Quinn Memorial Collection, reel 2017 L.

ABBY ALDRICH ROCKEFELLER (1874–1948)

Art patron, a co-founder of The Museum of Modern Art, and the wife of John D. Rockefeller Jr. Although Pach's initial correspondence with Mrs. Rockefeller in 1930–1932 deals with interesting her in the purchase of drawings by Delacroix, Géricault, and Corot, the letters that follow concern his recommendations for the Diego Rivera murals, which were originally commissioned for Rockefeller Center but ultimately removed from that complex. It was assumed that the reason for this action stemmed from the inclusion by Rivera of a portrait of Lenin and/or his depiction of syphilis germs in a scene of society folk playing bridge. But according to Pach: "I know that beneath both of the assigned reasons was the real one: quite simply, a dislike of Rivera's painting as art. What was wanted was the work of [José María] Sert, and that painter did, in fact, consent to replace the destroyed picture by one of his own."[1] Yet Pach felt compelled to add: "I believe that we may not place on the Rockefeller group all the blame for the destruction of the Rivera mural, some of it, I think, falling to the artist because of his provocative imagery."[2]

Letters between Mrs. Rockefeller and Pach were written from 1930 to 1940.

1. Pach, *Queer Thing, Painting*, 211.

2. Ibid., 292.

20 RUE JACOB,
PARIS, OCT. 10, 1930

My dear Mrs. Rockefeller,

Having read in the paper of your arrival here, I write as to what may prove to be quite a futile idea but one which, as you will see, interests me very greatly and which may quite possibly interest you . . . in the spring of 1929 we sailed for Paris in order to settle down and work in quiet—as I have too much difficulty in doing in New York.

It has been very largely what I might call a Delacroix year for me, climaxing with the exhibition at the Louvre (of almost a thousand works). But before that I had been constantly hunting for things by the master to add to our small collection. . . . And in seeing what there was, in the museums and private collections, I had the strongest confirmation of the idea that had been gathering force for many years—that he is the greatest painter since Rembrandt. At one time I thought that Cézanne loomed bigger in recent art, but on seeing works by the two painters in an exhibition, I found that it was Delacroix who had the more important thing to say.

(Let me put in that I have been following from this distance the career of The Modern Museum in New York, and I think it is doing a work whose importance no one can foresee. It may be the turning point of the development of art-appreciation in America—and in American art itself. I envy you your share of that work, of which I know something from my participation in the Armory Show of 1913 and many exhibitions since).

Twelve years ago I ran across a color print after a Delacroix which seemed to me, and still seems to me the finest easel picture of his whole life . . . a "Good Samaritan" that is not in any book that I know, mostly landscape, but with the human figures like those on the ceiling of the Sistine [Chapel].

I had twice tried to buy the picture before I saw it. The owner declined. I asked him again, personally, when I was at his house, and he again declined. But lately, I saw him in Paris and he spoke of getting on in years and of making some disposition of his collection . . .

Now, I don't know whether all this has been of any interest to you. To me it would be of real importance to know that the picture was in New York instead of in Berlin or Switzerland, or even Paris, for I shall be going home, probably in another year. If the matter does interest you . . . drop me a line, or you can telephone. . . . The number is Littré 51–52. . . .

Yours very sincerely, Walter Pach

Paris, Feb. 22, 1931

My dear Mrs. Rockefeller,

As I continue to be the lost soul haunting the picture shops here (though only after my painting day is done) I have kept in mind your own liking for the drawings of the modern masters. It is rare to come on one that I think you would greatly care for, but I am wondering if the Géricault which I send under separate cover is not such a one. You flatteringly spoke of wanting to see my "seconds" and this would most emphatically be among my "firsts" if I did not have to reserve the $500.00 it costs for other things. So I am glad to let you take it—in case you do care for it.

Géricault drawings are rarely to be found—though the imitators of his work, beginning right during his short life and coming down to contemporary forgeries (of which I have seen a number) have put forth numberless false Géricaults. The present drawing is incontestably authentic. The present owner has no proof that it was given by Delacroix to one of his friends, but it comes from that friend's collection, in which there was nothing of a similar type, so the legend that Delacroix (who owned any number of Géricaults) gave the drawing to this man stands a good chance of being correct.

The drawing is probably of an English subject; it is quite near to *The Coal Cart* which the master did in England. I have not the exact dimentions but think they are nearly if not quite those of the photograph. The medium is lead pencil; the effect is of a somewhat less black line than you see here,—otherwise the print gives a true idea of the work. It is of fine quality as you see. There are greater things by him—in the Louvre, but few outside of it. The price seems to me just about normal . . . I had the luck to get one of his paintings, a study and somewhat unfinished, but a superb thing.

I nearly forgot to say that the Géricault is at the gallery of Hector Brame 68 Boulevard Malesherbes,—or I should be very glad to arrange the purchase and to give the drawing to a hipp . . .

My wife joins me in remembrances to you and to Mr. Rockefeller.

Yours very sincerely, Walter Pach

Abeyton Lodge
Pocantico Hills
Tarrytown, N.Y., June 10 [1931]

Dear Mr. Pach:

Your letter of February 22d came when I was in the West. Upon my return I was ill and all my mail has been very much neglected.

Instead of buying the lovely drawing of which you sent me a picture, I decided to buy one of your paintings and am now the proud possessor of the painting of the anemone.[1] I am not sure of course, but it looks very much like the very anemone that I gave you the day we had the pleasure of having you and Mrs. Pach lunch with us. It is a lovely picture and I congratulate you upon being able to paint anemone so well.

I do very much appreciate all the trouble you have taken about the Géricault drawing I am going to keep the photograph of it. Perhaps it will still be there the next time we are all in Paris together.

Appreciating your thoughtfulness and with many pleasant memories of the times we saw you and Mrs. Pach in Paris,[2] I am

Very sincerely, Abby A. Rockefeller

1. Pach's oil, *Anemones*, had been included in his one-man show at the C.W. Kraushaar Art Galleries in New York from March 11 to 28, 1931.

2. The Rockefellers and Pachs had met in Paris in the fall of 1930.

Tangier, Aug. 26, 1931

Dear Mrs. Rockefeller,

Thank you for the friendly letter in answer to mine about the Géricault drawing. It was on loan, in an exhibition, when we were leaving Paris last month, so that perhaps, as you say, it may still be available when you come again. But if it has disappeared from the horizon, there will always be the incredible collection of drawings at the *conservation* in the Louvre, which we wanted to see and that you really must see, whether I am there or not. A telephone call will get you the information as to when those rooms are visible. Few people ever go there. . . . There must be some thirty or forty Géricault drawings, and those of Delacroix run into the hundreds. . . .

And it was *your* anemones that came back to you on canvas and—history repeating itself (save that I'm not Delacroix) I got a work by Géricault which the result of my exhibition made it possible for me to acquire. So thank you very much indeed, both for liking my work—which is the best thing there is for an artist—and for helping me to get a picture by a master. . . . One sees Delacroix everywhere here [in Morocco]. He painted the landscape, the people and the horses—and they are all just as he showed them. But even more, as I have just pointed out in my essay,[1] his glorious color is really to be dated from his contact with these Oriental masters of color, just a hundred years ago. It is only a thing in germ, in his works earlier than the Moroccan journey; perhaps without his seeing of this sunlight and the color it draws forth from the Moors, he might have continued with the blackish palette of his friends Géricault and Barye . . .

If you ever come over during that year, we shall be very happy indeed to see you. With regards, I am

Yours very cordially, Walter Pach

1. "Notes sur le classicisme de Delacroix," *L'amour de l'art* 6 (June 1930), 241–253.

PARIS, JAN. 19, 1932

My dear Mrs. Rockefeller,

Whenever I see anything especially fine in the way of nineteenth or twentieth century drawings, I think of the pleasant visits we had with you when you were in Paris. Just lately I came on one so extraordinarily—even uniquely fine that I am sending you a photograph of it—to keep, as a photograph. It gives *some* of the quality of the Corot it represents . . . I think, judging by my own experience and by some hundreds of Corot drawings that I have seen, that you will never come on one finer than this . . . the owner of the drawing is willing to sell it.

The man who has the great Delacroix of which I showed you the reproduction is still obstinately attached to it, so—as I wrote him when I bought something else—I have permanently dismissed it from my reckoning.

With good wishes to you and to Mr. Rockefeller, I am

Yours very sincerely, Walter Pach

---

39 WEST 67TH ST.
NEW YORK, MAY 10, 1933

My dear Mrs. Rockefeller,

All day long I have been having visits and 'phone calls about the Rivera matter,[1] and now at 9.30 at night a really good friend gives me the most sensible suggestion—that I write you and send the letter at once to ask to see you as early as possible for you to-morrow.

The point is that if the incident is not closed promptly, the professional trouble-makers who are always hungry for an opportunity to take up a "cause" will have an excuse for propaganda that will continue not only during the misunderstanding about the decoration but on every occasion when the Modern Museum or any other art-activity of yours or Mr. Rockefeller's is to the fore.[2] I am not an opponent of Communism, but I do object to the use of art as a pretext to further communistic interests, and so my one desire is to see this matter arranged and Rivera's fine work carried out as it deserves to be.

Since Mr. Rockefeller has not been quoted in the papers so far, the way is open for him to override the objections that have been made and simply deflate the whole business—which will then sink from notice as so many baseless things in the past have done. If the matter is embittered by controversy it will only increase the difficulty of getting rid of it—and that, I am sure, is the desire of people who are already planning protests of a disagreeable character which—as they are ostensibly in Rivera's interest—he can not easily disavow.

As an admirer of his art,[3] I said in my first talk with him on the 'phone this morning, that I should be glad to serve on a committee that would support his work. I *am* in favor of it, and so take this means to further his interest—which I believe to coincide exactly with your own. I shall be glad to come to you on receipt of a 'phone call tomorrow (Susquehanna 7–3417—the number is in the book) and I am sure that a dignified and satisfactory solution can be arrived at.

Yours very sincerely, Walter Pach

1. Diego Rivera had been commissioned to create a major mural for Rockefeller Center, but when he included a dominant figure of Lenin, Rivera was paid in full, then dismissed from the project. The day before Pach wrote this letter the mural was covered and boarded up (subsequently José María Sert was chosen to paint a replacement).

2. Mrs. Rockefeller helped found the Museum of Modern Art in 1929.

3. Pach and Rivera had become friends nearly a dozen years earlier, in 1922, when Pach spent a year lecturing on Modern Art at the University in Mexico City.

New York, May 11, 1933

Dear Mrs. Rockefeller,

When your secretary called up today she asked if she could telephone me in the evening to say what conclusion you had reached after talking the Rivera matter over with Mr. Rockefeller, I said I should be out. But it occurs to me that I could telephone to you in the evening. May I?

My own solution would be to have Rivera finish the decoration—one of the chief objections of the artists to the action of Tuesday night[1] being that it was too hard on a

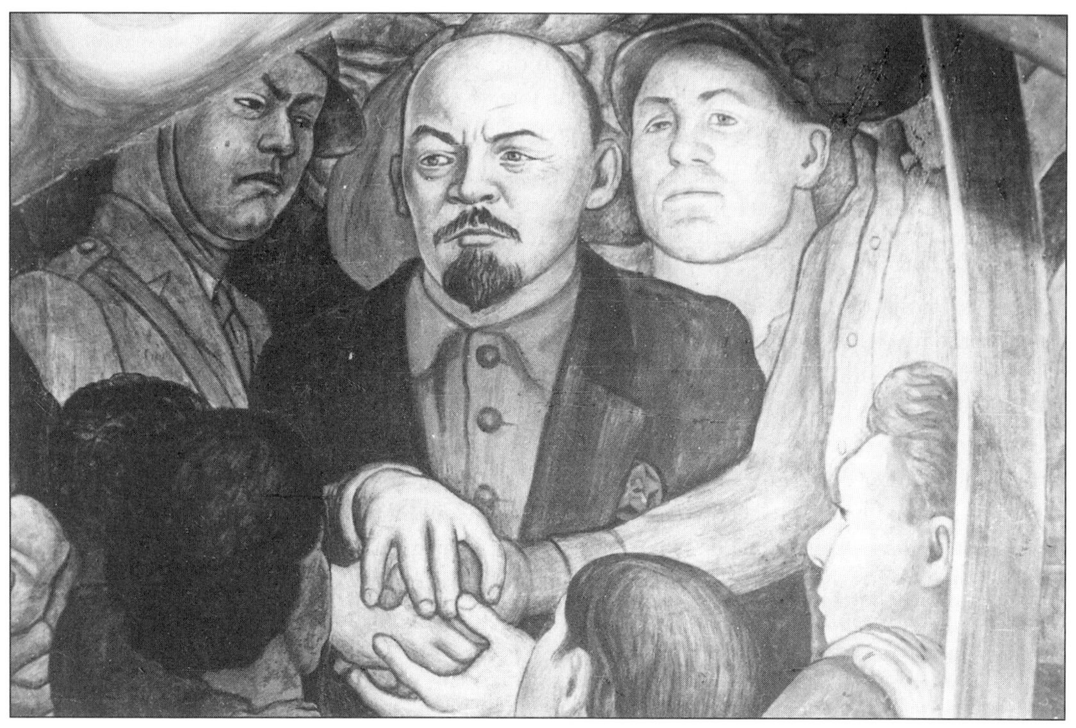

Diego Rivera, detail of Lenin (72 x 72 in.) in *Man at the Crossroads*, 1932-33. Unfinished fresco, RCA Building, Rockefeller Center, New York. Destroyed in 1934. Photograph by Lucienne Bloch, May 8, 1933, courtesy Old Stage Studios.

painter to be summarily stopped at his work, when it was nearing completion. Frankly—I quite share this view, whatever the difficulty of dealing with him as to treatment and subject. I think that in the articles which would appear in the serious papers, if the matter is not dismissed by friendly agreement, a serious objection may be made on this point. I understand that the decision to put the mural out of sight after sending Rivera away was largely the doing of the agents for the building. It seems to me that it is on this score that Mr. Rockefeller can step in to remedy a mistake—for I believe it to have been one.

If he could also see his way to permit the viewing of the mural—if only for a limited time—he would silence that part of the protest for which I myself care nothing (that of the element which merely wants disturbance), and perhaps even convince the managers of the building that the mural will not be a fatal obstacle to their success in their work. Without knowing much of such matters I should hazard the guess that it would do more good than harm.

I know that when Dr. Valentiner[2] sent me on a similarly pacifist mission to the architect of the Detroit Museum, who was disturbed by the Rivera murals there,[3] Dr. Valentiner made the point that Mr. Cret's building had gained by the painting of the decorations.

I had not meant to write at such length, but only to ask when I could telephone—in order to tell my friends this evening (the artists and writers) of your ideas.

Believe me

Yours very sincerely, Walter Pach

1. The dismissal of Rivera and concealment of his mural on May 9th.

2. Dr. William R. Valentiner, director of the Detroit Institute of Arts.

3. Valentiner persuaded his friend and patron, Edsel Ford, to commission two large Diego Rivera murals for the Institute of Art's courtyard.

[TELEGRAM]

NEW YORK, MAY 11, 1933

JOHN D ROCKEFELLER JR
26 BROADWAY NYK [*sic*]
WE WALTER PACH ALEXANDER BROOK JOHN SLOAN SUZANNE LAFOLLETTE AND PEGGY BACON HAVE BEEN NAMED A COMMITTEE REPRESENTING A GROUP OF ARTISTS AND WRITERS TO DISCUSS WITH YOU THE QUESTIONS RAISED BY THE DISMISSAL OF DIEGO RIVERA STOP WE WOULD APPRECIATE AN APPOINTMENT FOR THAT PURPOSE AT YOUR VERY EARLIEST CONVENIENCE STOP WILL YOU PLEASE REPLY TO MISS LAFOLLETTE AT HER HOME TWENTY TWO EAST TENTH STREET

WALTER PACH ALEXANDER BROOK JOHN SLOAN
SUSANNE LAFOLLETTE PEGGY BACON

1220A MAY 12

[A duplicate telegram, sent at 12:24 A.M., was addressed to Nelson A. Rockefeller, 115 East 67 St., New York.]

[The text of a telegram to be sent by Abby Rockefeller to Walter Pach was written in pencil on the back of Pach's letter of May 10, 1933].

Thank you for your letters of good will. Deeply regret incident stop Appreciate your suggestions course already determined & nothing can be done

[The telegram was not sent in this form].

Memo. for Mr. Nelson [Rockefeller]—from his Father [John D. Jr.]: The following is the message which Mr. Debevoise[1] and I agreed it was wisest for Mrs. Rockefeller to send to Pach who wrote her yesterday about Rivera:
"Your letters May tenth and eleventh to Mrs Rockefeller have been referred to the Managing Directors of Rockefeller Center"

Anna L Kelly, Secretary

1. Thomas DeBevoise, Mr. Rockefeller's legal adviser.

Mr. R. Jr. says this is the type of message which Mr. Nelson, Mrs. Rockefeller and he himself should send to anything that needs a reply. If any of the telegrams which Mr. R. gave to Mr. Nelson or which Mr. Nelson receives seem to require an answer, the above is the form of reply that Mr. Debevoise and Mr. R. Jr. think wisest.

AA [Abby Aldrich Rockefeller]?

May 12 [1933]

New York, Sept. 11, 1933

Dear Mrs. Rockefeller,

I can not tell whether it is right to write you again about the Rivera fresco at Rockefeller Center. It may be only an annoyance, if the matter is one that you want to leave in other hands; it may not be fair to suggest your taking it in hand if it could make complications with the managing directors, to whom your telegram referred me in May. But I did see them after that and have twice asked since for their decision—being told on all three occasions that none had been arrived at.

It is urgent, I believe, that one be reached now if the fresco is to be completed, for Rivera is going off to Mexico at the beginning of October, and I judge that it will be long before he returns here from the fact that when he first planned to go, he was going to leave unfinished the decorations at the New Workers' School, whereas he is now starting on the second half of the series and is making a great effort to complete it, instead of leaving it till his return—one that he evidently sees as so far off as not to count on it at all.

I have no appeal to make—but I do think it would be a thousand pities if the picture at Rockefeller Center were left in its present state. If circumstances ever made it advisable to unveil the work (which I am not suggesting—though of course I should be happy to have it shown) the blank space would be a constant reminder of the unfortunate controversy; and it is self evident that no other painter can complete it without vandalism.

Therefore if only in the interest of the building and its future, I feel that I must write you these lines. I offer my sincere regrets if I am troubling you, but the time is short and I so greatly fear that this letter, if sent to Rockefeller Center without a recommendation from you, would be delayed as to any action on it for such a time as it took before we had even the discussion with Mr. Robertson[1] this summer—and then it would be too late.

When I gave you my Delacroix article[2] in Paris, you asked if I did not have it in English. I have written little since then that would interest you, I think, the article in this month's Harper's being a big exception,[3] but you have probably heard of that whereas the paper on the Modern Museum might have escaped you, so I enclose it.

Two other matters that you have spoken of before,—seeing Mr. Gallatin's[4] great works by Delacroix and my own (very small) group of things may, I hope, be possible for you this season: I should enjoy both of them if you found free time for them.

With regards from my wife and myself, I am

Yours very sincerely, Walter Pach

1. Hugh Robertson, of the Rockefeller Center management company.

2. "Notes sur le Classicisme de Delacroix," *L'Amour de L'Art* (June 1930).

3. "Rockefeller, Rivera, and Art," *Harper's* (September 1933), 476–483.

4. Albert E. Gallatin (1881–1952), art collector, painter, and author.

Sept. 18, 1933

Dear Mr. Pach:

Mrs. Rockefeller wishes me to thank you for your letter, and also for your article on "Modern Art in Perspective," which she greatly enjoyed reading.

Mrs. Rockefeller has been not at all well for sometime [*sic*], and I am taking care of her mail for her. Mr. Rockefeller is most anxious that she should not become involved in any way in the controversial question mentioned in your letter, particularly as the whole matter is in the hands of Todd, Robertson, Todd Engineering Corporation, Managing Directors of Rockefeller Center, who have full data on the subject.

Mrs. Rockefeller hopes to be very much better by the latter part of the winter, when she trusts she can see you and Mrs. Pach.

Sincerely, Anna L. Kelly, Secretary

MASTERPIECES OF ART EXHIBITION
AT THE NEW YORK WORLD'S FAIR 1940
EXECUTIVE OFFICE: 56 EAST 68TH ST., NEW YORK, N.Y.
DIRECTOR GENERAL: WALTER PACH
FEB. 28, 1940

Mrs. John D. Rockefeller, Jr.
740 Park Avenue
New York, N.Y.

My dear Mrs. Rockefeller:

Following out the ideas set forth in the accompanying statement, I have the honor, on behalf of the Committee, to invite your participation in the work of the 1940 Exhibition of Masterpieces of Art, and hope you will be willing to lend the following paintings from your collection:

GOYA, Portrait of a Boy
CHARDIN, Serenade
HOPPNER, Miss Beresford
LAWRENCE, Lady Dysart

I realize that, in undertaking a work for the benefit of the country as a whole, the burden falls on individuals. But the country as a whole cannot furnish the works, we are cut off from the aid of Europe, and we, who are giving our time to this undertaking, hope that it may appeal to the generous spirit you have shown on other occasions.

Please feel assured that the help and instruction your pictures would offer to the hundreds of thousands of visitors to our Exhibition will be deeply appreciated not only by those direct recipients of your kindness but also by the group of public spirited persons who have subscribed the expenses of the showing.

Yours very sincerely, Walter Pach

Masterpieces of Art
56 East 68th St.
New York, May 13, 1940

Mr. John D. Rockefeller, Jr.,
30 Rockefeller Plaza

My dear Mr. Rockefeller,

I beg to acknowledge receipt of your check for $500.00 and to thank you for it on behalf of the officers and committee. Your generous donation will make the meaning of our exhibition more accessible to a great number of people through the help that our docent service is actively preparing to offer. I know that the plans for it are well advanced and that the one obstacle, that of our lack of an appropriation for it, is on its way to being overcome, thanks to you once more.

With warm appreciation, I beg to remain

Yours very sincerely, Walter Pach, Director General

Source of Letters: Rockefeller Archive Center, North Tarrytown, New York. Also available through the Archives of American Art, Smithsonian Institution, Abby A. Rockefeller Papers, reel 4218.

ALBERT PINKHAM RYDER (1847–1917)

A painter and poet who was born in New Bedford, Massachusetts, then the chief whaling port in the world. The sea played an important role in his art, not only because of his early proximity to it, but because of impaired sight he could paint large masses of a watery surface with a distant, generalized form more readily than subjects with minute detail.

By 1870 he moved to New York where he studied at the National Academy of Design, and between 1877 and 1896 he made four trips abroad, trips undertaken for the pleasure of the sea voyage rather than land travel or a concentrated study of art.

Ryder had no scheduled hours for painting. He is once said to have attended a Wagnerian opera and been so moved by it that he returned home about midnight and worked for two days without sleeping or eating, in order to produce his *Siegfried and the Rhine Maidens*. He lived the life of a hermit in one of the poorest neighborhoods on Manhatten's Lower West Side, and he resided in the back room of a tenement amid piles of trash and a heap of perhaps all the clothing he had ever owned. And yet his paintings, many of subjects he had personally experienced, were mystically romantic in an era of meticulous draftsmanship and joyous Impressionism.

Albert Pinkham Ryder had his advocates; at the 1913 Armory Show he was the only American artist to be allotted a "room" which allowed him to display ten oils.

He had initially met Pach in 1909 on an unrecorded occasion.

New York, May 26, 1910

My Dear Walter Pach:

Thank you for your kindly interest, and addressed envelope, which I received in time I hope for your answer to be delivered today.

I take it I'm not to write to Portland;[1] of course nothing could be better than the Temple of the Mind.

What a glorious summer you have before you

Best of all wishes, Bon Voyage and au Revoir.

"yours" faithfully, Albert P. Ryder

Nice of Davies; just like him.

1. The previous summer Ryder had shown seven oils at the Portland [Oregon] Art Association's "Loan Exhibition of Paintings."

The following printed poem was enclosed in an envelope, on which Pach had written "Poem by Albert P. Ryder"; across the top of the page are the words:

To: Walter Pach
Compliments of Albert P. Ryder

Reprinted in the Evening Sun on May 6th, 1909 from Mr. Macbeth's Art Notes under the title of

"The Voice of the Forest"

(These lines were inspired by a gale at Yarmouth Port, Mass., and the harmonies it tore from the trees.)

On ye beautiful trees of the forest;
Grandest and most eloquent daughters
Of fertile Mother Earth.
When first ye spring from her,
An infant's puny foot
Could spurn ye to the ground,
So insignificant ye are.
Yet ye spread your huge limbs,
Mightier than the brawny giants of Gath,
    How strong,
    How beautiful,
How wonderful ye are.
Yet ye talk only in whispers,
Uttering sighs continually

Like melancholy lovers,
x Yes, I understand thy language,
Oh voice of sympathy
I will draw near to thee
For thou canst not to me,
And embrace thy rugged stems
In all the transports of affection.
Stoop and kiss my brow
With thy cooling leaves
Oh ye beautiful creations of the forest.
x Yes I understand thy language
Oh voices of sympathy.

[The last two lines were handwritten by Ryder.]

NEW YORK, SEPT. 13, 1914

Dear Mr. Pach:

I am very pleased to get an intimation of your approaching visit which will have to be tomor[r]o[w] to fit Mr. Wheelers schedule.

Of course I shall be very pleased to visit Mr. Wheeler[1] and any friend of yours at any time.

I feel very flattered that Mrs. Pach is willing to take so much trouble over what I fear will be a small entertainment as I have nothing finished and only a few works here.

The hour has gotten late on me so I hope you will allow me to close with a cordial welcome and to say that I am asking you to be kind enough to come to 152 W 14th St. Large front room 2nd floor next to Gilsey Bldg corner of 7th ave

Very truly yours, Albert P. Ryder
Mail Address: 308 W. 16th St

Please come 3 oclock or after

"Adieuos"

1. Probably Clifton A. Wheeler (1883–1953), a painter and teacher on the staff of the John Herron Art Institute (now the Indianapolis Museum of Art).

Source of Letters: Archives of American Art, Smithsonian Institution, Albert Pinkham. Ryder Papers, reels 4216, 4217.

PAUL J. SACHS (1878–1965)

Art educator and museum director. After graduating from Harvard College, in 1904 he became a partner in the family business, the banking firm of Goldman, Sachs. However, in 1915 he left to return to his alma mater as assistant director of the Fogg Art Museum; two years later he was named assistant professor of fine arts at Harvard as well. During 1927–1928 Sachs was appointed director of the Fogg—a post he held for the next two decades—and full professor, which position he filled for the following thirty years. Paul Sachs became an internationally renowned authority on prints and drawings who helped educate a generation of future museum directors, curators, and professors. He was also one of the seven founders of the Museum of Modern Art.

The correspondence between Sachs and Walter Pach began in 1919 with an inquiry regarding two Ingres drawings that had been included in the Armory Show. In 1939 Sachs offered to aid Pach's effort to obtain a position at the soon-to-open National Gallery of Art in Washington. To this end, Pach forwarded to him, in his letter of October 26, 1939, the most complete biographical data he had compiled to date. The final correspondence between the two was written by Pach in 1958, just four months prior to his death.

Note: All of Paul J. Sach's letters are typed carbon copies, and therefore unsigned.

March 21, 1919

Mr. Walter Pach,
c-o Ehrich Galleries,
707 Fifth Ave.,
New York City, N.Y.

My dear Mr. Pach:

I was informed a few days ago that at the time of the Armory Show you exhibited two drawings by "Ingres."[1] Unfortunately I do not remember seeing them.

Now I ask you to let me know who owns these drawings, and whether you believe that the present owner would be inclined to lend them for two weeks in April for our "Retrospective Loan Exhibition of French Art; A Testimonial to the Devoted Service of French Officers at Harvard University during the War" or whether he would be inclined to sell them; if so, at what price.

Awaiting the favor of your kind reply, I am

Very truly yours, [Paul J. Sachs]

1. Both appear in the Armory Show catalogue listed simply as *Drawing* and "Lent by Egisto Fabbri. Not for sale."

---

13 East 14th St.
New York, March 24, 1919

My dear Mr. Sachs,

The drawings by Ingres you refer to were lent me for the International by a friend of mine in Paris, Mr. E. P. Fabbri.[1] He was in America for a time, about two years ago, but I think he has returned to Europe. However I have written to a brother of his here, and am enclosing your letter, so that if there is any chance of your getting the drawings by loan or purchase, you may. I doubt though whether they are in this country as I sent them back after the International. If I get any news to the contrary I shall let you know at once. I cannot think of any other Ingres drawings here. A friend of mine spoke of a painting being for sale some time ago but I don't know where just it is. I could ask him about it, if you wanted that.

Your very truly, Walter Pach

1. Egisto Paolo Fabbri (1866–1933), an Italian art collector, formerly of Florence.

March 25, 1919

Dear Mr. Pach:

Accept my thanks for your kind lines of the 24th, in answer to my inquiry regarding the "Ingres" drawings. I greatly appreciate your interest in this matter; and await further news.

I should certainly be interested to learn whether a painting by "Ingres" is for sale, although I confess that I think it highly unlikely that we could secure the necessary money to make such a purchase.

With kind regards, I am

Yours very truly, [Paul J. Sachs]

New York, Dec. 17, 1924

Dear Professor Sachs,

Although I should have wished to hear a good deal more fully your opinion as to my book,[1] I was greatly interested by what you did say, as was Mr. Huebsch, my publisher, to whom I related what you told me.

Not wanting to exaggerate, I am wondering if I might ask you to write me just a few lines—not to go into detail about the parts of the book that seemed right and the ones that were more debatable, as that would scarcely be put in a few lines—but to tell me just what you said of recommending the book to your students. That was a pleasure to me, and—I think I should say—Mr. Huebsch would like permission to quote it.

If you are in New York during your vacation, I should be very glad indeed to see you here—not that I could show you anything like what you have at the Museum (or hardly anything- I own a predella by Signorelli), but perhaps a few modern works I have would be of interest, since you fought out my pages. It may be that I shall be coming to Boston again, in which case I should hope for a less hurried look at your collections.

With regards,

Yours very sincerely, Walter Pach

1. Pach's *The Masters of Modern Art* (New York: B.W. Huebsch, 1924).

Dec. 19, 1924

Dear Mr. Pach:

Your letter of the 17th inst. reached Professor Sachs at the moment of his departure for town, so that he found no time to answer you in the way that he wished to do, but he requested me to send these few lines to acknowledge receipt of your welcome letter, and instructed me to say to you that if he can possibly find time during the Christmas recess he means to give himself the pleasure of paying you a visit in answer to your cordial invitation. He is not sure that he will be able to do this because he is taking a group of thirty-five students to New York and fears that his time may be too fully occupied, and yet he will try to see you if he possibly can.

Yours very truly, Secretary

---

48 West 56th St.
New York, March 24, 1926

My dear Professor Sachs,

While talking yesterday to Mr. C. de Hauke, of the de Hauke Gallery, 3 East 51st St., I happened to mention my lecture at Harvard in connection with two Cézanne pictures that I saw there. Mr. de Hauke said he would be willing to send them on for exhibition to the students a short time before my lecture, as also a collection of Lumière color transparencies after Cézanne which give the effect of the pictures to a quite remarkable extent. Both exhibits would be of value. The paintings (a landscape and a still-life) while fairly small, are of most beautiful quality.

I give you Mr. de Hauke's address above so that if you want to invite the works (which they are glad to place in educational institutions) you can write him a line direct.

I shall come out to the Museum early in the afternoon of April 7th so as to have a sight of it before my lecture. Looking forward to seeing you, I am

Yours very sincerely, Walter Pach

New York, Nov. 10, 1926

My dear Professor Sachs,

A friend in Paris has sent me two photographs which I am forwarding to you under separate cover. They represent a bas-relief in the Naples Museum and a painting made from it by Ribera.[1] I am told that the picture is one of the finest Riberas in existence, but the special interest of it is its showing of the Renaissance emerging directly from the antique in *painting*. In sculpture the thing is common enough, but I know no other such example in painting or any approaching it. And, fortunately, one could get a cast of the sculpture. The price of the picture is 300,000 francs (French). If you think there is a chance of your wanting the picture please let me know—or communicate with the person whose name is on the photograph. If the picture is outside your interests would you kindly send me back the two prints.

Yours very sincerely, Walter Pach

1. José de Ribera (1591–1652), the Spanish Baroque artist who emigrated to Naples early in his career and settled there.

Nov. 12, 1926

Dear Mr. Pach:

I beg to acknowledge with thanks receipt of your interesting letter of the 10th inst. At this writing the photographs have not arrived, but I have no doubt that they will come within a day or two. The matter you write about is of very real interest and I shall study the photographs with pleasure. Unfortunately, even prior to receipt of the material I am forced to say that there is no chance of our making such an acquisition at this time. We are not in a financial position to make any important acquisition just at present. Many thanks for your thinking of us in this connection.

I hope this winter to give myself the pleasure of calling on you on one of my New York trips. I shall be glad to greet you here whenever you are in the neighborhood.

Yours very sincerely, [Paul J. Sachs]

Dec. 23, 1926

My dear Mr. Pach:

I am very anxious that you should deliver a lecture, if you care to, at Harvard University, under the auspices of the Fogg Museum, and so I write to ask thus [*sic*] early whether you will do this on Thursday afternoon, April 7th, at 4.30. The honorarium that we are in a position to offer is, unfortunately, not very generous, but if fifty dollars does not seem too little I hope that you will find it worth while to make the trip and come and talk to us. I am very anxious that you should speak on any subject that you care to speak on, but if there are several lectures which it would give you pleasure to deliver here, perhaps it will suit you to let me make a choice.

Awaiting the favor of your kind reply, and wishing you the compliments of the season, believe me to be

Faithfully yours, [Paul J. Sachs]

New York, Dec. 28, 1926

My dear Mr. Sachs,

Thank you for your letter of December 23rd. I have only received it now—probably through a delay in forwarding it from my former address in 14th St. to which it was sent.

I shall be glad to speak at Harvard on April 7th and am noting the date in my calendar. My usual honorarium for out-of-town lectures is $100 (or more, depending on the distance from New York) and expenses. But as I know that budgets and appropriations are not easy to expand, please look on the $50 you mention as acceptable to me—and entirely so.

As to subject—I could speak on any phase of modern art covered in my book[1] (I have given lectures on single figures—Barye, Cézanne, Renoir and others,—as well as the period as a whole or parts of it).

Other subjects I have spoken on, in the courses at the Metropolitan Museum, have been Pompeiian Painting, Piero della Francesca and Signorelli—a Renaissance Master and Pupil; Three Great Americans—Eakins, Ryder, and Prendergast; and other matters less likely to be of use in your field. I shall be glad to have you select whatever topic fits in best with your programme. I don't doubt that your collection of lantern slides provides ample material for illustration, but I think it will be better for me to bring slides myself so as to be better prepared for my discussion of them.

Looking forward with pleasure to my visit, and wishing you a happy New Year, I am

Yours very sincerely, Walter Pach

1. *Masters of Modern Art*, published-in 1924.

New York, April 9, 1927

Dear Professor Sachs,

The visit to your Museum remains as a very pleasant memory, and I am glad that you are to be in Cambridge this summer (if it is not too hard on you) as I certainly hope for a trip to Boston sometime, with my wife. . . .

I enclose the photograph of the picture by Baron Gros[1] and find that the price is, as I thought, 50,000 francs. The picture is described as of the finest quality—and it looks it. The marks visible in the photograph are said to be due to old varnish and not to affect the paint. On my return to New York I found another letter from the owners who said again they needed money and therefore were offering the picture for so little. Bryson Burroughs said it *was* cheap. . . .

With thanks again for your kindness

Yours very sincerely, Walter Pach

1. Baron Antoine-Jean Gros (1771–1835), a follower of Neo-Classicism's Jacques-Louis David, created heroic epics combined with the romantic.

APRIL 15, 1927

Dear Mr. Pach:

On my return to Cambridge this morning I find your very kind lines of the 9th inst. enclosing photograph of the Baron Gros painting which does, indeed, look perfectly splendid. Unfortunately we have no funds at the moment. If I may, however, I should like to keep the photograph with your letter for future reference. . . .

With kind regards,

Sincerely yours, [Paul J. Sachs]

WALTER PACH
MORGAN & COMPANY
14 PLACE VENDÔME
PARIS, FEB. 19, 1932

Dear Professor Sachs,

About three years ago I felt that New York was taking too much of my time from my painting and thinking, and came over here for a fresh start at both. I had written so much and lectured so much without a period of withdrawal, to look anew at the sources of things, that I felt it was an injustice to my audiences as well as to myself. . . .

Certainly it was—in large part—to get a better grasp of it that I settled in Paris again. I had been here several whole summers since the war ended, but no winter—which is when one sees most,—especially people. Matisse, Derain, Picasso, Rouault, Villon and Dufy are all old friends whom I have taken up with again in these three years, and I have been seeing something of Braque lately. Of course all these men have lots of work in America—in a way it's easier to see shows of it there; but there's something too in getting the new crop here before it's been picked over, and then one sees the work in progress in the studios, hears what the men are aiming for, and gets the reaction of the other artists when the pictures go to the galleries. Above all one sees the effect on the younger generation (very fierce judges),—and then goes to the Louvre to check up on the way the moderns look after a backward glance at the unshakables . . .

I mention all this because I thought there was just such a *possible* chance of your seeing sufficient call for my services that you (or the secretary of one of the College or Museum Associations) might care to . . . arrange a programme of dates for me—or, let me say—might be willing to do so. . . .

When I have heard from you . . . I can write to the colleges and museums where I have been before or am to go to and that you do not cover, and tell them the dates I should have open.

With thanks in advance and good wishes, I am

Yours very sincerely, Walter Pach

New York University gave me the title of assistant professor when I directed their courses at the Ecole du Louvre in 1926. I had lectured for them since 1923 . . .

FEB. 29, 1932

My dear Mr. Pach:

I have your long and explicit letter of the 19th inst. and if I answer briefly it is only because I am exceedin[g]ly busy and asked by many people to do the very thing that you speak of in your letter of February 19th. . . .

Now what I propose to do and shall be very glad indeed to do is the following:

1. I expect a visit on Tuesday, March 8th, from Mr. Coleman, the Director of the American Association of Museums. I shall submit your letter to him and see whether he is in a position to undertake what you ask.

2. I shall be very glad to see that Mrs. McMahon gets a copy of your letter and see what she can suggest.

3. And I shall be very glad at the spring meeting of the Association of Museum Directors in May to submit your letter.

4. I shall be very glad to submit your letter to various people at the May meeting here at the Fogg Museum of the American Association of Museums.

While all this will not mean for you an unofficial agent for a lecture tour here, it will mean that your desires are clearly presented to those groups that can make your visit successful . . . much as I might like to be your agent for purely personal reasons, I cannot squeeze in this further work.

I sincerely hope that you understand the spirit in which these lines are written, and remain, with every good wish,

Sincerely yours, [Paul J. Sachs]

OCT. 24, 1939

Dr. Walter Pach, Esq.
148 West 72nd Street
New York City

Dear Dr. Pach:

Thank you for your lines of the 23rd inst., which I have read with real interest. I am glad you are impressed by the Giotto? of St. Francis, as Forbes[1] and I are. I tend to agree with you that if it is not by the master it is, at any rate, much closer to him than the Louvre picture.[2] We try to bear on the side of conservatism in the matter of attribution.

I am delighted to know that you are bringing out a book on Ingres.[3] It is much needed. It certainly is discouraging that so distinguished an effort as your Delacroix[4] should have brought with it no financial reward.

I come now to your problem, which you state very clearly. I have no snapshot solution to offer. On the other hand, I mean to address myself to the problem. The thing that occurs to me first of all is whether there might be a possibility at the National Gallery in Washington. It so happens that both Mr. Finley[5] and Mr. Walker[6] are spending the weekend with me and I shall discuss the matter with them, and I shall then communicate with you sometime next week. I may say now that only American citizens can be appointed at the National Gallery and only those who have passed the Civil Service examination. I suggest, therefore, that you get in touch with Mr. John Walker at the National Gallery, and in the meantime perhaps you will be good enough to send me a complete biography and a list of the places like the Metropolitan where you have frequently lectures [*sic*];—in short, a curriculum vitae.

Please understand that I have nothing definite in mind at present. I am very genuinely interested and shall explore various possibilities.

With kind regards, believe me

Sincerely yours, [Paul J. Sachs]

1. Edward W. Forbes (1873–1969), director of the Fogg Art Museum in Cambridge, Massachusetts.

2. Giotto's *Saint Francis of Assisi Receiving the Stigmata* (ca. 1295–1300?).

3. *Ingres* was published three weeks after this letter was written.

4. Eugène Delacroix's *The Journal of Eugène Delacroix* (1937) had been translated by Pach.

5. David E. Finley (1890–1977), director of the National Gallery of Art.

6. John Walker (1909–1995), the gallery's chief curator.

New York, Oct. 26, 1939

Dear Professor Sachs,

I doubt whether you can realize how much pleasure your letter gave to my wife and to myself. Even more than the possibility of work in which I could take satisfaction and at the same time make a living, I value the interest you express. Thank you for it. I am confident of making good in a suitable museum or university position (should one materialize). I should certainly feel that part of my task consisted in giving you cause to endorse what I was doing.

Let me hasten along to your suggestion of my sending you a "complete biography." Even keeping that to what I think the essential matters of my professional years, I am afraid I am again going to give you a pretty lengthy piece of reading. Perhaps, as you go through it, you can underscore the lines you would want to refer to if the occasion arose for use of them.

I was born in New York City in 1883, my parents and grandparents having been American citizens. Since the question of nationality is raised by the requirements of the National Gallery (I have, as you suggested, written Mr. Walker on the subject), I may say a word as to my family background: it is sometimes considered as affecting one's fitness for a place, and it had its effect on my doings.

My father, in 1867, joined his brother, who had started as a photographer; their firm has continued till this day and made pictures of all the presidents from General Grant to Franklin D. Roosevelt, besides innumerable other people of distinction.

When the Metropolitan Museum was founded, my father and uncle were its photographers, remaining so for many years. I have no memories farther back than those of being at the Museum. Observing the reproduction of the works there gave me a very early idea of their qualities and of the relationship between copies and originals. I have studied the latter subject from many angles, and think much should yet be done in clarifying its various issues. Not merely the question of processes (those of the hand and of the machine) arise, but also the matter of what makes an original work—what the creative element in art really is.

In 1903, I graduated from the College of the City of New York with a degree of B.S. Those are still the only initials of the kind I can write after my name, though I was made a member of Phi Beta Kappa this year. In 1926 N.Y.U. gave me the title of professor after I had lectured for three years at the institution. (Quite often I have been called Doctor, but that is, I suppose, because so many men in universities have the degree, and people assume that all have received it).

In 1902 I began professional art study with William M. Chase, continuing with him for four years; Robert Henri, in the old "Chase School," was also my teacher for three years, and later, in Paris I studied with Paul Sérusier and Maurice Denis, the former admirable theorist and teacher being particularly recommended to me by Henri Matisse, whom I had come to know.

In *Queer Thing, Painting* (a book written on the insistent recommendation of Mr. Henry W. Kent,[1] who felt that I must set down a lot of what he called "source material" on notable men I have known), I recount the evolution of ideas in my time as Americans became aware of the intense art activity of Paris—particularly in the years I was abroad. From 1903 to 1932 my time was about equally divided between America and Europe. From my return to this country in 1913 for the Armory Show (I had secured all the pictures from Paris for that exhibition), I found myself called on for elucidation of the absolutely unfamiliar "modern" art, and very numerous articles and lectures were the result. While I was convinced of the greatness of the best modern men and, above all, of the necessity of grasping the ideas that expressed so large a part of the essential character of the time, I went on with my studies in the older arts, and know that it was often because of my work in clarifying the relationship between the ancient and the modern that I was asked to write and speak. I know that this is particularly true of the Metropolitan where, for nineteen years (this will be the twentieth), I have been invited to speak in the Museum's special courses on Saturdays and Sundays. I am the only man who has been asked to take part in them every year during that time (save one, when I was given instead the portion of a course on modern art to cover, and then the years 1930 and 1931 when I was in Europe).

I can now stick closer to concrete data: In 1918, the University of California had me give two courses of lectures in its summer session, one on the history of art in general, the other on modern art. In 1922, the Universidad Nacional of Mexico, had me come to give its summer session lectures (in Spanish).

In 1923, with Fiske Kimball, Richard Offner[2] and others, I participated in reviving the art courses of N.Y.U.; I continued each year with them till the summer of 1929, having charge of the summer courses at the Ecole du Louvre in Paris, during the summer of 1926.

Omitting the large number of places throughout the United States where I have lectured once or a few times, I may add my work at Columbia. From 1932 till the present year, I have lectured there, either at the Institute of Arts and Sciences, or in the summer session. When the School of Architecture decided to give its work in drawing and modelling to an independent (but related) faculty and to add courses in painting, I was selected to found that studio, which I conducted during the two terms 1936–1937. I have for years taught painting and etching in my studio.

In 1936 I spent a month at Bowdoin College, taking over the classes in art history of Prof. Andrews, who was seriously ill.[3]

I am represented by painting and/or etching in the Metropolitan Museum, the Brooklyn Museum, the Whitney Museum of American Art, the Cleveland Museum, the Phillips Memorial Gallery of Washington, and other public collections. The Chalcographie du Louvre asked for one of my etched plates, from which prints are made for sale in the museum. M. Léon Rosenthal, the late director of the museums of Lyons, published an article in *Byblis* on all the etchings I had done till that date (1928).

My books are:

Georges Seurat, 1923
The Masters of Modern Art, 1924
R. Duchamp-Villon, 1924
Ananias or the False Artist, 1928
Modern Art in America, 1928
An Hour of Art, 1930
Vincent Van Gogh, 1936
Queer Thing, Painting, 1938
Ingres, 1939 (out November 15).

Besides, I have translated the five volumes of Elie Faure's History of Art (1921–1929) and the Journal of Eugène Delacroix (1937). For the latter the question was of editing, as much as translating. Also, I have published about a hundred and fifty magazine articles. Most frequently they have been on ph[a]ses of modern art. Thus the first magazine article on Cézanne in America (it appeared in 1908) was one that I wrote. I may say in passing that I now know it was not very good; that may permit me to add that Mrs. van Gogh-Bonger, the widow of Theodore van Gogh, wrote me (quite spontaneously) that two articles I published on her great brother-in-law were the only adequate ones to appear here at the time of his exhibition in New York in 1921 [actually in 1920].[4] At her death she bequeathed to me a drawing by Vincent. I have always, (when my means permitted) bought prints, drawings, and—on occasions—paintings and sculpture by men I admire, (ancient and modern). I regard such action as a means of sharpening one's observation as to qualities of art, genuineness, etc.; far more than one can do by merely "platonic" admiration, though the real motive has been my enjoyment from living with fine things.

The titles of the following articles, or lectures at the Metropolitan will give you an idea of the scope of my studies, outside the field of modern art: The Memoria of Velasquez; A Renaissance Master and Pupil—Piero della Francesca and Signorelli; Pompeiian Painting; Three Great Americans: Eakins, Ryder and Prendergast; John Singleton Copley; Odilon Redon; Classical and Romantic Art; Winslow Homer; The Greatest American

Artists: The Mayas and Aztecs; Mexican Ceramics in the Metropolitan Museum; Realism, the Art of the European Race; The Raphael from Russia on Mr. Mellon's acquiring the Alba Madonna; [Jacques] Louis David; Gericault; The Classicism of Delacroix; also quite a number in the *Gazette des Beaux-Arts, L'Art et les Artistes, Formes* etc., on American art, which I have been making known in France since 1909. Also encyclopedia articles (the Brittannica, the International, the Dictionary of American Biography, etc). Also cataloguing—for example the collection of Sir Edgar Speyer[5] (never published by him, but a big job—some 250 items, from ancient art through the Renaissance, Dutch and French Schools). Also contacts with collectors and museums—I found and secured David's *Death of Socrates* for the Metropolitan, works at Smith College, the two small Signorellis at Detroit, etc. Also newspaper work; also research work for works of reference.

You see—I have paid to paint (though I have also been paid for painting—on occasions).

Again I have run on to unconscionable lengths but, since you are so extremely kind as to express the interest you do, I thought I must write fully (suppressing much, however) and permitting you to be the judge of what is of consequence for any idea you may form or any statement you would find occasion to make.

Perhaps you think of my request as one to take in your stride, with the many problems that are turned over to you. For me, your willingness to give thought to the matter is—I must say—more than I had hoped. I thought you might have one or two "leads," like the one of the National Gallery, but since you are so good as to take up the matter in this more live and personal way, I can only say that I am deeply grateful for the kindness—an opportune one for me, even if no material result should follow from it. Please permit me to thank you again, though that is implied in my last lines.

Yours very sincerely, Walter Pach

1. Henry Watson Kent (1866–1948), secretary of the Metropolitan Museum of Art's board of trustees.

2. Offner (1889–1965), an educator and writer.

3. Henry Edwin Andrews (1872–1939), professor of art at Bowdoin College.

4. "Vincent Van Gogh," *International Studio* 74 (November 1920), xii–xx; and "Art. A Modern Artist [Vincent Van Gogh]," *The Freeman* 2 (December 8, 1920), 302, 303.

5. Speyer (1862–1932) was a British banking and railway magnate.

OCT. 28, 1939

Dear Mr. Pach:

Thank you for your very interesting and detailed letter of October 26th, which comes to me at an opportune moment because the authorities of the National Gallery are spending the weekend with me and I am submitting the facts to them.

I knew of your great activity, but I had no idea that it covered so wide a field and that you had accomplished so much. As soon as I have something to report I shall communicate with you again.

With kind regards,

Sincerely yours, [Paul J. Sachs]

New York, June 29, 1940

Dear Professor Sachs,

It would be such a pleasure to see the exhibition at the Fair[1] with you that I write in the hope that you will let me know when you are going to visit it. Also I want to say what deep pleasure I am having from the two Poussin pictures belonging to your mother.[2] I really feel that the *Birth of Bacchus* is the most beautiful picture in the whole exhibition,—and that is saying not a little. . . .

Yours very sincerely, Walter Pach

1. The 1940 New York World's Fair, for which Pach organized the "Masterpieces of Art" Exhibition.

2. Two of the six Poussins Pach borrowed for the exhibit were loaned by Mrs. Samuel Sachs: *The Birth of Bacchus* (1657), oil on canvas, 46 1/2 x 84 1/2"; and *Holy Family* (1651), oil on canvas, 39 x 52".

May 8, 1945

Dear Walter Pach:

Thank you for your friendly lines of the sixth inst. The package containing the two drawings by you and also the one by Bresdin has arrived safely.

First of all let me thank you for your very generous gift of the Bresdin which we accept with pleasure and gratitude. I am happy to have your two drawings, and I am framing them at once. Enclosed please find my check. . . .

Looking forward with pleasure to your visit and with thanks for your gift and your kind reception of me in New York, believe me,

Very cordially yours, [Paul J. Sachs]

1. Rodolphe Bresdin (1825–1885).

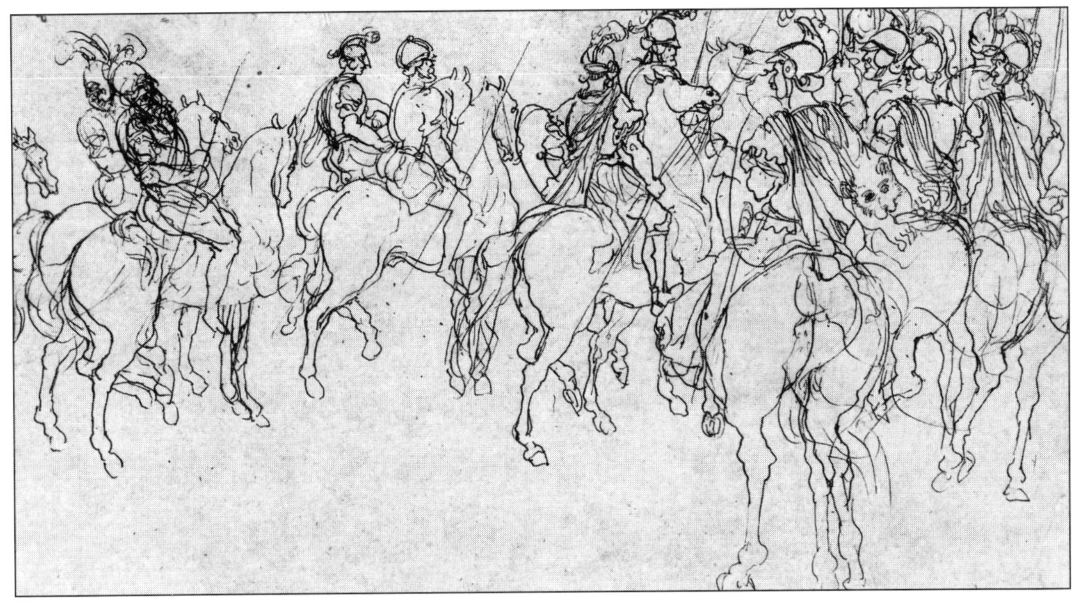

Rodolphe Bresdin, *Procession of Cavalry*, n.d. Black ink on tracing paper, 4 1/4 x 7 3/4 in. Courtesy of the Fogg Art Museum, Harvard University Art Museums, Gift of Walter Pach. © President and Fellows of Harvard College, Harvard University.

---

3 Washington Square
New York, Aug. 10, 1947

Dear Paul Sachs,

. . . I have been twice to the Century Club, and have taken my wife and some friends from Washington. We all enjoyed it so much that now I am in your debt again, and have to write to say thanks.

However, when an art collector who knows his possessions places them before the public, he scarcely needs to be told that they are giving pleasure. I remember that when I first was invited to the Havemeyer house, over forty years ago, I poured out my enthusiasm in what must have appeared to Mr. Havemeyer a perfectly interminable letter—which he apparently read through, since he commented in his reply on something I had said in it. Today I know better than to try to express my appreciation of the supreme things you have lent to New York. The Dürer of the Bavarian princess seems to me the foremost of them, and the Holbein is profoundly appealing, the Pollaiuolo and the Mantegna seem absolutely to demand mention even in a letter which says it will not go in for appreciations—and it will not, save to say that the great surprise of the showing was the pair of Millet drawings. He has been going up in my esteem for a number of years, and now those two drawings—unlike any I had seen before—send him upward once more. I guess you know about as well as anyone how much of delight drawings can give, so you will also know how grateful are the visitors to that exhibition. . . . I was reminded that you are in New York occasionally and, the point is, there might be a chance to return part of your hospitality. . . . Of course there is the question of whom to invite that you don't know. Across the Square from me lives Jacques Lipchitz, who loves drawings and for whom I got a card for the Century Club, just lately. He has a fine mind, and, on that score, Marcel Duchamp is still one of the very, very unusual people. Do you know him? He has been a friend since before the days of the Armory Show and still comes here when we ask him—though he is getting rather hermetical, otherwise. . . .

Hoping that you and Mrs. Sachs are having a pleasant summer, I am

Yours very sincerely, Walter Pach

New York, Dec. 28, 1947

Dear Paul Sachs,

I write to tell you of what I think of as a really great picture, one that I have here now since a son of the late owner has asked me to help him sell it, as part of the estate which he is engaged in closing up.

It is a van Gogh, probably of 1887, and I send you a photograph of it under separate cover. That will tell you more than any words of mine could do, except that I may describe the color as beautiful though reticent, and therefore unlike both the black, clumsily trowelled pictures of the Dutch period and the brilliantly colored pictures of the artist's last three years. . . . Jacques Lipchitz . . . saw the painting lately, and could scarcely find words strong enough to express his admiration. He kept repeating "C'est extraordinaire! c'est extraordinaire," and added "C'est déjà un tableau de l'école française,"[1] and it does have color and facture that van Gogh never reached in Holland. I think the work a masterpiece, unique (as far as I know) in van Gogh's production.

The price is $15,000, which is, of course, very low for a picture some 20 x 25 inches. I heard lately that a van Gogh was sold for $125,000. The reasons for the low price are: lack of a signature, lack of mention in the de la Faille catalogue, the period—before the explosion of violent colors during the last years. This seems to be the fashionable, popular aspect of van Gogh, for which people pay always increasing prices . . . what I should really like would be to see this work hanging beside a great Rembrandt. Both in humanity and in luminosity this work would show up well alongside a first rate work by the older Dutchman. . . . Have you any advice as to this picture and what to do with it? I'd be ever so obliged—as ever so often before. With regards,

Yours very cordially—Walter Pach

1. "That's extraordinary! That's extraordinary, that is already a picture of the French School."

Dec. 30, 1947

Dear Walter Pach:

Your very interesting letter of December 28th arrived, so it happened, just after I had finished writing a short prefatory note for an exhibition that will appear here this spring and in the course of that introduction, I ventured to quote a sentence from your writing. Now comes your exciting letter.

The photograph of the Van Gogh has not yet arrived but needless to say I am impatient to see it and I shall send you a brief note after I have studied the photograph you write about. If, as I am sure will be the case, I share your views and in view of what appears to be indeed a very low price, I shall ask Constable[1] to present the picture at our next meeting of the Committee of the Museum (the buying Committee) of which I happen to be a member. If for any reason he does not wish to do so or if because of the enormous purchases we have made at the last two meetings, it is impossible from a budgetary point of view to spend any more money at the Museum of Fine Arts, I shall then try to think of some other way that you might proceed.

With every good wish for the New Year and with kindest regards to you and Mrs. Pach in which my wife joins me, as always,

Yours very cordially, [Paul J. Sachs]

1. William George Constable (1887–1976), curator of paintings at the Boston Museum of Fine Arts.

New York, Dec. 29, 1948

Dear Paul Sachs,

. . . I won't wait longer about writing you—about the pictures I shall have in an auction at the Parke-Bernet Galleries. It will be on January 6th, the exhibition opening tomorrow.

There will be three by Delacroix, two by Eakins, a particularly fine water-color by Jongkind, a Matisse that I believe he esteemed highly, a very grand Aztec stone sculpture and a number of other such things. I just thought you might be rendering a service to some friend (or friends) who might like to know about it if you told them. I have hated, as you can imagine, to see the things go out of here, but I believe I am doing the best thing by letting them go. . . .

With good wishes of the season to Mrs. Sachs and yourself, I am

Yours very sincerely, Walter Pach

JAN. 4, 1949

Dear Walter Pach,

I do wish that I might have received your letter in time so as to write to the Parke-Bernet Galleries to send me a Catalogue of the pictures that you are putting up at auction at the Galleries on January 6th. Whether I could have done anything either for friends or for yourself, I do not know, but obviously it is pretty difficult to proceed intelligently without illustrations and at this late date I fear that I shall be hopelessly handicapped. . . .

We, ourselves, are in the throes of moving from "Shady Hill," which has been acquired by the University. We are happy that the property will permanently be in the hands of the University. . . .

With good wishes of the season to Mrs. Pach and yourself, I am,

Yours very sincerely, [Paul J. Sachs]

NEW YORK, JAN. 7, 1949

Dear Paul Sachs,

It was of course impossible to have a catalogue reach you before last night's sale, . . . When I wrote, it was under the assumption that you would be on Parke-Bernet's mailing list. The van Gogh drawing—which *was* illustrated in the catalogue—was the only one of my things which brought a really good price: $4,100. The Delacroix water color, not very much more than a sepia drawing, but complete and beautiful, sold for $1,500. Those were the two things nearest to your particular interests, I think, but there were other works, like the Aztec sculpture, which would have been bargains for any one. . . .

. . . I send you, under separate cover, a photograph of a Géricault drawing of a lady, and one of Redon's portrait of Vuillard. For the former I ask $400, for the latter—which

I selected from hundreds of Redon's drawings and which I consider to be in many respects, the finest drawing of his that I know, I ask $600.

I have three Constantin Guys that are good, though not important examples; and then two Delacroix pencil studies. One is almost pure outline, without his colorful shading, but it is one of his final steps in preparing what seems to me his greatest mural, the *Jacob and the Angel*, in the Church of St. Sulpice. For this I ask $700. Finally, there is a *Centauress*, a real masterpiece of color values obtained with a pale, silvery pencil. I hold this at $300.

Moreover, at a later sale at the Parke-Bernet Galleries two things might interest you: the only water color by Corot I have ever seen (and that Georges Wildenstein has ever seen); it is a figure study, not far from the stage of drawing. Then a Prud'hon which you saw here and which I felt you did not feel keen about. It is untypical in being very large and extremely finished. It is signed—which is unique save for one in the Louvre. M. Jean Guiffrey found the signatures to be identical, and was pleased, because Prud'hon wrote in a letter that he never signed his drawings, and M. Guiffrey—accepting my drawing as genuine—looked on its signature as authenticating the one on their own work. . . . With good wishes

Yours very sincerely, Walter Pach

New York, Oct. 17, 1954

Dear Paul Sachs,

Modern Prints and Drawings reached me the day before yesterday; . . . At first glance one sees that this is a beautiful book, studied (as I saw you studying it when I called on you last spring) from the standpoint of doing fullest justice to the marvelous things you reproduce (and I am glad of your discreet dig at color reproductions). In my memories of Vollard, I have told of scenes I witnessed several times when he went to endless trouble and expense to give just the right quality to the look of a text and the fullest nuances of an illustration. I said that was *his* form of art—and it is also yours in the presentation of your beloved prints and drawings (you have made them yours).

You will receive, I know, a quite limitless number of congratulatory letters, and this should be one of them—as I want to prove by putting in a word of discussion, such as I should not offer to one whose book everyone is bound to agree with throughout (and which is correspondingly dull).

I just can't find again your remark about some older critics who ought to have known better than to condemn recent tendencies they have not fully understood (it's something like that). But now I do locate the place once more where you quote Berenson's "destructive words" about what he calls "visual atheism."

Just lately I had a talk with a young critic who had written an article excoriating Berenson for that recent book of his in which, most probably, he uses the words you cite. I told that critic that I had reviewed the book from just the other standpoint: Berenson, the first man to mention Cézanne in English (I'm pretty positive), and a very early defender of Matisse, is still making progress when, in the same works, he calls Picasso the greatest living draughtsman after scepticism in earlier years. I wrote that one does not have to agree with him on every point, but that, condemning certain modern tendencies as he does, he is breaking through the constraint of too many people, like one museum official who said "Isn't it a pity that no one can tell the truth about modern art?" (for fear of being taken for a reactionary—the man in question being anything but that).

But a lot of modern art, so called, needs condemning—instead of purchase by museums, which thereby render more difficult the problem of laymen, who think every[th]ing [is] good if it's in a museum (temporary exhibition there is, of course, a different matter). I certainly think a lot of "abstract art" is what Matisse once called 'materialism'; I think it the decadence of what Picasso, Braque and, above all, Marcel Duchamp did about 1912—exactly as men like Henri Martin and Le Sidaner were the decadents of Monet, Pissarro and the rest.

I'm confident you'd rather have me say the above rather than pile up expressions of admiration for your book, which I could perfectly well do without departing from full sincerity, for I come back to saying it's a beautiful book—and not merely in its presentation. Thanking you for my repeated appearance in it, I am

Yours very cordially, Walter Pach

New York, Dec. 3, 1956

Dear Paul Sachs,

I am making free to send you herewith a review I wrote a month or two ago about a very bad book.[1]

I mention the time I wrote the piece (it may have been three months ago—the Herald-Tribune having delayed publication of it for so long) because several other reviews have appeared meanwhile and—though all that I have seen are unfavorable—I wrote my own lines without any knowledge of what other people would say. They devoted a great deal of their space to errors of detail, to telling whether this dealer or that one showed the "modern art" first, and other matters of the same kind.

To me, the important thing was to say whether the pictures this Mr. Blesh admires are good or bad. That is a much harder job, especially with the danger of seeming to think oneself a pontiff—and I do hope I've avoided that.

Please give kind remembrances from my wife and myself to Mrs. Sachs, and believe me

Yours cordially, Walter Pach

1. Pach's review of Rudi Blesh's book, *Modern Art, U.S.A.*, titled "Abstractionists Appraised," appeared in the *New York Herald Tribune* Book Review, November 25, 1956.

Dec. 10, 1956

Dear Walter Pach:

It always give me pleasure to receive an interesting letter from you like the one of December 3rd enclosing the review of Rudi Blesh's book "Modern Art, U.S.A." I had not read your review.

The thing that I like about your review is that you do not waste the time that others have done in devoting a great deal of their space to *errors of detail*. For me, as for you, the important thing was to say whether the pictures that Mr. Blesh admires are good or bad.

There are several sentences in your review that students and scribblers ought to keep well in mind, such as: "Art, whether ancient or modern, is a single thing," or "For the painter or sculptor, abstraction is simply an inner armature, a necessary one, differentiating a good picture or statue from mere representation," and finally, "We see that abstractionists have reached a dead end, indeed a very dead end, and we look forward with confidence to better things." Bravo!

Please give kind remembrances from Meta and from me to Mrs. Pach, and wishing you the compliments of the Season, believe me,

Yours cordially, [Paul J. Sachs]

Source of Letters: Harvard University Art Museums Archives, Paul J. Sachs files, which contain additional Sachs/Pach correspondence.

MORTON L. SCHAMBERG (1882–1918)

A pioneer abstractionist among American artists. Born in Philadelphia, he received a degree in architecture in 1903 from the University of Pennsylvania, but revealed an interest in art when he joined William Merritt Chase's summer class in Holland the previous year. The summer of 1903 he was with Chase in England, which was followed by three years at the Pennsylvania Academy, where Chase was a visiting instructor traveling from New York each week.

Schamberg met Pach, as well as Charles Sheeler, by 1905, when all three were with a Chase class in Europe (Pach served as a manager and lecturer to the group). Schamberg returned to Europe in 1908, settling in Paris where he studied the work of Cézanne, Matisse, Picasso, and Braque, and became further influenced by the orphism of Robert Delaunay. He exhibited five oils in the Armory Show, and was soon a part of the Arensberg circle, meeting Duchamp and Francis Picabia at the collector's apartment.

After painting pure abstractions based on mechanical images by 1914, Schamberg turned to Dada compositions; his plumber's pipe and trap, mounted in a carpenter's miter box, was titled *God*. He exhibited a drawing and painting in the initial 1917 Society of Independent Artists show, but died suddenly the next year as a result of the widespread Spanish influenza epidemic.

Morton Schamberg's last letter to Pach was written two weeks before his death.

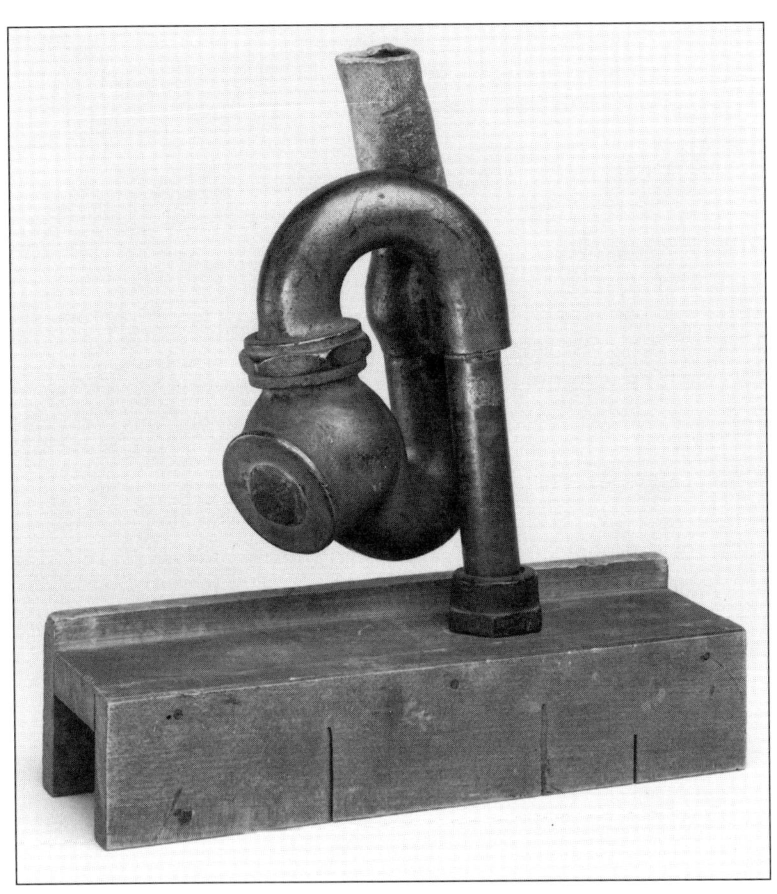

Morton Schamberg, *God*, ca. 1918, Wooden miter-box and cast iron plumbing trap, 10 1/2 in. high. Philadelphia Museum of Art: The Louise and Walter Arensberg Collection. Acc. 1950-134-182. Photograph by Graydon Wood, 1989.

Hôtel de l'Univers & du Portugal
10, Rue Croix-des-Petits-Champs
Paris, Nov. 5, 1908

Dear Pach,

Was so glad to get your letter that I'll answer it at once. I have planned to leave here on the 19th for Florence. Originally intending to remain here only about two months I came to this hotel which is a little more expensive than I can continue living and then I have no studio in which I can use models so I have had to work out of doors or memory things at a small scale in my room and I mostly want to paint people. Now I find that I would like to remain here a while yet as I find Paris so stimulating and delightful. Now I could hardly take a studio for less than three months more and that would cut down my time in Italy so much as unless I can manage to get ahold of some more money I don't see how I can stay over on this side after April or May. I would like to have about three months in Florence and two or three months in Rome, Venice and the rest of Italy. If I can possibly manage it I will come back to Paris for a while before going home.

I have been to the Autumn Salon three times and while I am, as you say, far from certainty, I have considered these things very seriously. The work of Matisse I find very beautiful at times, not always though it does not entirely satisfy me. I am inclined to consider it a very personal art rather than the part of a great movement. Such men rise frequently in the different fields of art and while I can like very much that which he has I cannot imagine myself being much influenced except so far as one must be more or less influenced by anything one cares for. Van Dongen[1] has some canvasses there too which I like pretty well but where I think the great trouble lies is in considering Matisse the leader, and the art doctrines evolved by the Steins (damn nice people as you say, and I continue to spend pleasant evenings there) and Bruce[2] and that outfit are to me the most awful nonsense. I think they as others have been completely upset by Matisse. I find myself antagonistic to their opinion at most every point. And I feel a good deal more certain on these things than on the pictures themselves. Their theories I don't like at all and know I don't—the pictures I like but don't know just how much. The visits to Steins are (as I wrote to Sheeler)[3] like pills for the Artistic liver. Bernheims[4] too always have something to see. I am more inclined toward Renoir than Cezanne. That is a superb canvass of Renoirs of the full length lady in Black in the Luxembourg and I am fond of the "Liseuse."[5] I am almost inclined to say that Renoir is the top notch of modern painting. But this trip has meant so much to me so far in the fuller appreciation of all sorts of intermediate men whom heretofore I hardly knew. I find myself less inclined to the worship of one or two great men who at the time seem to represent the best than toward a searching out of what is best in all the big men. By the way, yesterday by chance I went into the museum part of the Louvre and found about six or eight Egyptian portraits painted on wood. Had you seen them. Nothing has impressed me more than these since I've been here. I find them as fine as any portraits in the Louvre—marvellously beautiful and so convincing and subtle in character as to make them seem very modern. Oh, they are very, very, beautiful. Also an Egyptian bust portrait in stone which is almost alive, it fairly made me dance. The spirit has not moved me to do any copying. Perhaps I shall do some in Italy. I'll be very glad to hear of Garvey's coming and to meet him and I'm glad for Miss Wilson's address. I have done quite some work (about three dozen panels) a few of which I like pretty well though I don't understand that they are not better and also I'm very anxious to try some portraits. It is very good to hear from you so write me very soon again. More another time. As ever

Sincerely, Schamberg

1. Kees van Dongen (1877–1968), a Dutch-born member of the Fauves.

2. Patrick Henry Bruce (1881–1936) was the same age as Schamberg. Both had studied with William Merritt Chase at the New York School of Art, but Bruce was among a group of Americans in Matisse's class at about the time this letter was written.

3. Charles Sheeler (1883–1965), like Schamberg, had enrolled in Chase's summer classes in London and Holland.

4. Paris' Bernheim-Jeune Gallery specialized in showing works by contemporary French artists.

5. "The Reader."

Dec. 29, 1910

Dear Pach,

I intended writing you in time to wish you a Merry Christmas or at least a Happy New Year but don't seem to have gotten to it. I'm a little late—but good luck to you just the same.

I was very glad to get your letter of Nov. 10th and got great pleasure out of the papers you sent. Haven't had a chance to try and read them as yet as we passed them on to N.E.A. and they haven't come back as yet. Those Bonnards must have been wonders. During a visit to N.Y. several weeks ago I found in the Metropolitan three decorative panels of tiles done in Persia by imported Chinese Artists. I wonder if you know them. They are the finest things I've seen for some time. I managed to get photos of them. Had a card from A.M.D.[1] the other day. I certainly envy you seeing those Cezannes. How I would love to see a collection of them. I knew you would like A.M.D. Isn't she a great girl? I certainly have missed her: I did have an interview with Stieglitz while in N.Y. as you suggested. He was greatly interested but said he didn't feel qualified to come to any sort of judgement about my pictures after seeing them for only a few days. We quarreled a bit about a few things but on the whole I was well satisfied with his attitude. He hasn't the intelligence of a Leo Stein but he is sincerely interested and is getting into a position where he can do one lots of good. I feel that something may come of it later. I liked the few things of Weber's[2] I saw. I met Hartley[3] but have never seen anything of his. He saw my pictures for a few minutes and said about the same thing as S. that he didn't get them yet. He asked to come to my studio when he gets over here. Had a three hours visit to Henri's[4] studio. We couldn't get together at all. He only saw the photos of my things but he didn't like them. Both he and Stieglitz seem to have gotten the impression that I am too cock-sure of myself. If they only knew. The last month or so has not been very productive but I hope to get swinging again soon. The last year has been the best I've had and I have from twenty to twenty-five pictures from the year (canvasses and panels) that I like well enough to show. But I am never as much interested in the things I have done as the things I'm going to [d]o.

I saw the Russian Ballet a couple of weeks ago but the production was not a circumstance to the ones I saw in Paris. I wonder how you enjoyed Kreisler[5] To me he is one of the biggest musicians I have ever heard. Talk about luck. I have a dandy piano in my studio—Mrs Boyle—N.E.A.'s sister broke up housekeeping indefinitely and asked me to store the piano for her. She sent it around and then sent a man in to tune it and put it in condition. Of course I can't play but it is fine now and then when people come in who do. I am getting really acquainted with Bach, and he has spoiled my appetite for almost all other music, for the present at least.

I am enclosing some photos of some of my pictures. They are pretty successful photos but of course you know how much is necessarily lost in not being able to see the color. Please show them to A.M.D. when you get a chance, as I wrote her to ask for copies of any she may like.

Have not had a chance to show any pictures this year so far. Hope the Penna. Academy may take one or two.

How I wish I could read French. I've been enjoying Gautier so much but realize what I miss by translations. Just got Flaubert's Temptations of St. Anthony and look forward to reading it. The translation is by Lafcadio Hearn. More another time.

As always, M. L. S. [Morton Livingston Schamberg]

1. "A. M. D." is probably the Miss Dalgliesh referred to by Charles Sheeler in his letter to Pach dated October 26, 1910.

2. Max Weber (1881–1961) exhibited in the "Younger American Painters" Exhibit at Stieglitz's 291 Gallery during March, 1910; he also had a one-man show that opened there two weeks after this letter was written, so Schamberg may have viewed some of Weber's works in the gallery before they were framed and hung.

3. Hartley exhibited at, and regularly frequented, the 291 Gallery.

4. Robert Henri (1865–1929), inspirational teacher and the catalyst behind the Exhibition of Independent Artists, held in April, 1910, was receptive to counselling any young artist. Schamberg probably sought his advice at the suggestion of Pach, who had been a Henri student.

5. Fritz Kreisler was a renowned violinist.

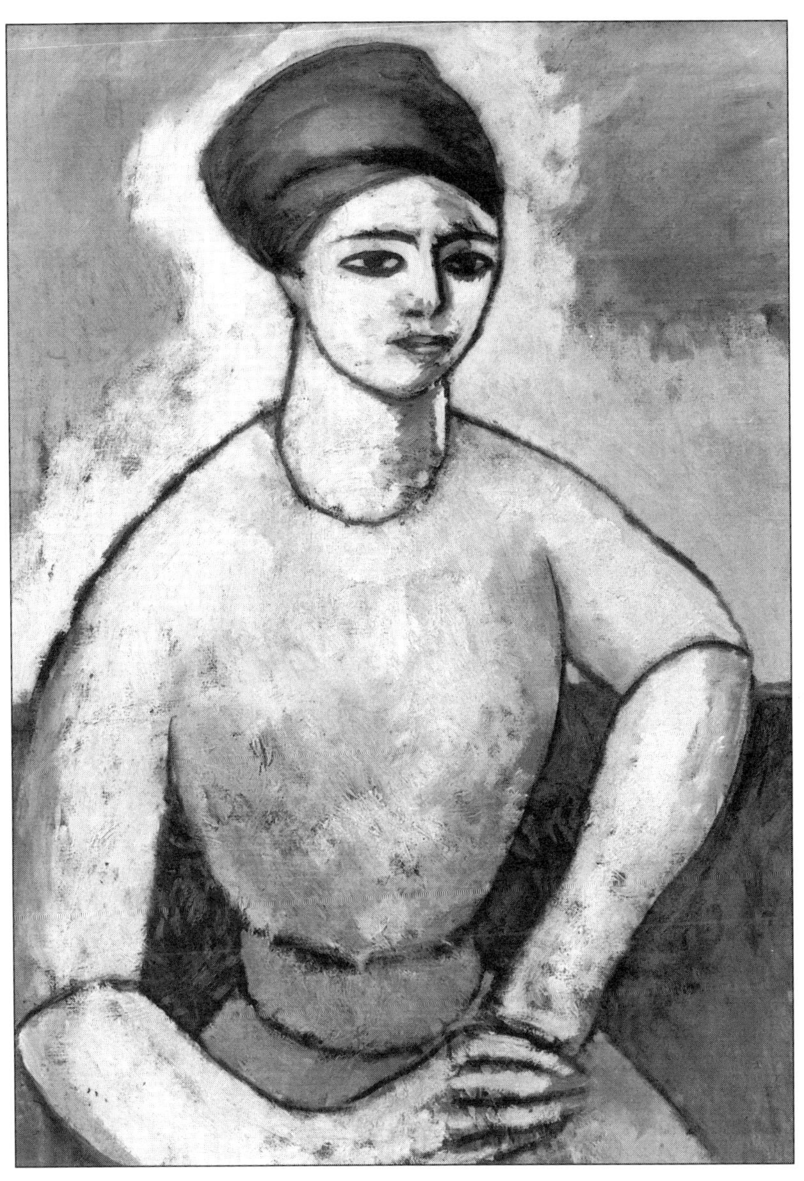

Morton Schamberg, *Fanette Reider*, 1910. Oil on canvas, 30 7/8 x 22 7/8 in. Williams College Museum of Art, Bequest of Lawrence H. Bloedel, Class of 1923. 77.9.11.

Aug. 23, 1912

Dear Pach,

Did you know there's to be an exhibition in N.Y. this winter of American painters and sculptors (a new organization as far as I know). The president is Arthur B. Davies. I got an invitation to exhibit with them the other day. It is rather funny as I have just gotten to the point where I don't care whether anyone sees my pictures for years to come. I don't expect to sell and don't need to if the photography goes and while I am glad to show them to anyone who is interested, I can say to hell with the exhibitions and dealers. However this thing sounds as though it might be worth while. We'll see. The MacDowell Club sounded fairly good at first too . . . [portion missing] . . . I'll surely get over during that show as they promise to have some Cézannes etc.

[Yours], [Schamberg]

[Reproduced from Milton W. Brown, *The Story of the Armory Show* (New York: The Joseph H. Hirshhorn Foundation, 1963), 45–46.]

Paris, June 30, 1914

[To Pach]

Many thanks for your letter. Have been to Vollards (did not see him) and will get there again to Kahnweilers, Bernheims etc. Am awaiting by the mail permits to see Pellerin collection tomorrow Would love to meet Brancusi and Duchamp-Villon but damn it, I can't speak French and besides, cannot leave my father for a minute. Have seen some great things but of course can't do all I want to. Best wishes to you and Magda—

Yours, Schamberg

Philadelphia, Sept. 30, 1918

Dear Walter,

I am thoroughly ashamed to write at this late date a thank you for that Indian tile which has given me so much pleasure. I selected the one with the big round face. Sheeler as I anticipated preferred the other one so it worked out beautifully—nothing has happened that I can find to write about though I would probably find much to talk about and I will be glad to hear all about your summer.

Hope I can arrange soon to make a trip to New York and then I will see you. I have just read a book which has made a tremendous impression on me. "The End of the War" by Walter E. Weyl. Always to you and Magda.

Yours, M. L. S. [Morton Livingston Schamberg]

Source of Letters: Archives of American Art, Smithsonian Institution, Morton Schamberg Papers, reels 4216, 4217.

CHARLES SHEELER (1883–1965)

A painter and photographer. Like fellow Philadelphian Morton Schamberg, Sheeler studied at The Pennsylvania Academy of the Fine Arts and accompanied William Merritt Chase and his summer art classes to Europe in 1904 and 1905. Sheeler and Schamberg shared a studio on Chestnut Street beginning in 1908, and both had their first one-man shows in Philadelphia's McClees Gallery. They also traveled together in Italy, where Sheeler was attracted by the work of Giotto, Masaccio, and Piero della Francesco, and the architectural order their compositions revealed.

Charles Sheeler exhibited six oils in the Armory Show of 1913, after which he, like Schamberg, met Duchamp and Picabia in the Arensbergs' apartment. Unable to earn a living solely from painting, Sheeler began a career as a photographer, accepting commercial assignments; in 1917 he exhibited photographs in a show at the Modern Gallery in New York, together with Schamberg and Paul Strand.

While many of his early photos were of simple, dramatically-lit interiors of a house he rented in Doylestown, Pennsylvania, and details of nearby barns, Sheeler, drawing on an attraction to Analytic Cubism, eventually superimposed two or more photographic negatives to achieve abstract compositions both in his photos and his paintings.

Like Morton Schamberg, Pach met Charles Sheeler by 1905, when they traveled together to Europe with the Chase summer class.

Oct. 26, 1910

Dear Walter

How's this for a prompt reply—received your letter about an hour ago—mighty glad to hear from you too, only do follow out your resolutions and write often, you know everything is happening at your end of the line now that your [*sic*] in Paris.

Here goes for my autobiography (covering the last six months). The summer for the most part is not a very happy memory, except as it made things that followed possible. The greater part of the time, I was sweating blood—you must know those times when you feel that whatever grip you have on things was slipping through your fingers like water, when even the process of putting paint on the canvas is awkward and you are overwhelmed with the impossibility of accomplishing anything, before you have painted a half hour. Well much was my experience, when suddenly I did a landscape that was the first tangible result from all of the agony that preceeded [*sic*] and from that [time] on work has been going very well and I feel that I have made quite a good bit of progress. After all it was the realization that I must add new elements to what I had, (the realization that the old was inadequate) that made matters so difficult. You ask what the direction of my work is now—that's hard, I wish I could show you a few things. For any attempt at explanation must necessarily be broad and cannot show the particular thing that I am trying to do. I feel its pretty much a result of my Italian trip and what little I know of Cezanne. I am greatly interested in the rendering of form and the elemental qualities of nature (rather than effect) and to accomplish it in the biggest and simplest way—then I am interested in design and in space composition and am trying to render things by the means of purer color. Schamberg[1] has said several times that he thinks my recent landscapes quite Cezanne like—as a matter of fact my knowledge of that master is limited to one canvas I have seen and to such reproductions as one finds from time to time in books & magazines. But he is one of the men that I am particularly anxious to know more of. I have been painting out of doors almost altogether with an occasional canvas in the studio, mostly imaginative and a still-life now and then. I enjoyed your account of some of the men in the Salon how I'd like to have a look. I had such fine opportunities to see the works of those men—only at the Steins and Bernheims[2]—so of course I have gotten very little from them—Matisse's work I see mostly and Picasso not at all. You can imagine how bewildering one visit to Steins' would be, but of course I have gotten somewhat straightened out by frequent talks with Schamberg and thinking about such things as I did see—I don't feel that they have anything directly that I want but I am open for anything that I may later decide that I have need of. This brings me up to the present—I am still hoping to get to N.Y. more than ever for in addition to the change in environment etc, they are to give a number of exhibitions at the

Photo-Secessionists Gallery that I feel are important for me to see, such as the ones' of Picasso, Cezanne (water colors) Matisse (sculpture) and some of the lesser men.[3] At present my only chance lies in the possibility of the sale of a picture out in Chicago (its about to be decided now). I am still hoping to get something to do over there but of course there's not much chance of learning of anything unless I am on the spot and I haven't the means to stay over there until I could locate something—unless Chicago comes up.

I sent my usual assortment of pictures over to Macbeth[4] this fall, never once thinking of the possibility of him turning them down, and a few days later received this brief note from him—"Alas! I do not like the direction of your new work the least little bit. It is such a departure from old time sound methods, that I would not care to exhibit it. I hope it is only an experiment." The amazing part is that it is not my recent work but very little different from the last he had—things that you saw when you were over, like "The Expulsion," small panel of two nude figures against a blue star lit sky, an Italian landscape with blue mountains and a clear blue sky, with cypress trees against it (one that you expressed a liking for) and several others. If he took exception to them I am afraid he would stand on his head if I had sent *really* recent ones—not that they are by an[y] means extreme. Well the point is I am out there (for the time being at least) and that was an other opportunity of showing things and I surely need every opportunity. Then I sent some pictures out to the Art Institute [of Chicago] (sent old ones, particularly so as to be sure of getting in for a friend was going to take a prospective buyer to see them) and didn't I get turned [down] there, in fact we both did—and that after such royal treatment the last three years, in fact last year they sent me a photograph of the wall showing my group. However the buyer is to have a chance to see them (that's the important part) for my friend has them at her studio now. The other day a man came into the studio and asked to see some work and he then explained that he was a Chicago dealer and had been in the east sometime looking at the works of the various painters with a view to showing some at his gallery. He was much interested with the work he saw in both of our studios and invited us to send some things for an exhibition of small pictures that he purposed [*sic*] holding in November. His entire attitude was different from any other dealer that I had met before—so much wider angle of vision than the rest of them, in fact than most painters—and the things he didn't understand he did believe to be the result of conviction and respected them accordingly—did you ever hear of one like that? We thought when he left it had been a god send—at least a satisfactory place to show things. Then I wrote to my Chicago friend inquiring about him and the two letters I have had in reply are not at all favorable—all of the dealers of whom she has inquired say they know lots about him but won't tell—only advise not to send pictures to him. So you see there is another fond hope, probably shattered. I am not sure that their prejudice against him may not be due to his radical views—they may be afraid of him.

I am glad to hear that things are going well with you, that you are at the painting and in Paris besides—I am glad your [*sic*] having your inning again its about time. I'd like to see what you have done. Glad you liked Miss Dalgliesh—I liked her much unfortunately I saw her only for about ten days, but she left a very pleasant impression with me—she's mighty appreciative.

With very best wishes to you

As ever, C. R. S. [Charles Rettew Sheeler]

Saw the Russian Ballet the other night for the first time—how I did enjoy them—aren't they marvellous. Did you see Mordkin do that dance with the bow & arrows? Superb!! Thanks for remembering my folks—they are always glad to hear any news of you.

1. Morton Schamberg (1881–1918), who had been a classmate of Sheeler's at the Pennsylvania Academy of the Fine Arts. They began sharing a studio in Philadelphia in 1908.

2. Sheeler had viewed works by Cézanne, Picasso, and Braque in the Paris apartment of Michael and Sarah Stein; he also saw modern art at the Bernheim-Jeune Gallery.

3. During 1911 and 1912, Alfred Stieglitz's Photo-Secession Gallery planned exhibits of eighty-three drawings and watercolors by Picasso, twenty Cézanne watercolors, and a dozen sculptures by Matisse.

4. William Macbeth, owner and director of the Fifth Avenue gallery that bore his name.

Source of Letter: Archives of American Art, Smithsonian Institution, Charles Sheeler Papers, reels 4216, 4217, which contain one additional letter.

JOHN SLOAN (1871–1951)

Artist and teacher. He began his career as a newspaper artist in Philadelphia while studying at the Pennsylvania Academy of the Fine Arts under Thomas Anshutz, and by 1897 had established himself as a serious painter, focusing on scenes of everyday life. After moving to New York in 1904, Sloan created his ten "New York City Life" etchings, then participated in the landmark exhibits of The Eight in 1908 and the Independent Exhibition two years later. He was represented by both oils and etchings in the Armory Show. As a teacher, Sloan began instructing at The Art Students League in 1916 and continued there for the next fifteen years.

John Sloan initially met Walter Pach in March 1906 when Robert Henri requested that Sloan teach his classes at The New York School of Art in which Pach was enrolled (the student was just two years younger than Sloan). During the ensuing years Sloan and Pach found themselves to be kindred spirits: They were among the six artists attending the preliminary meeting for the 1910 Independent Show; supported the formation of the Society of Independent Artists by becoming president and treasurer, respectively; and circulated petitions to save the Diego Rivera murals in Rockefeller Center. When both men were in their late sixties and seventies they also worked together to administer The Shilling Fund, established through the will of the artist Alexander Shilling, which directed that money from his estate be used to purchase works by American artists that would then be donated to U.S. museums.

Pach initiated his correspondence with John Sloan in 1910. His final letter, written in 1951 to Helen Sloan, the artist's widow, just two months after Sloan's death, concerns an article by Pach about his long-time friend.[1]

1. "John Sloan." *The Atlantic* 194 (August 1954), 68–72. Pach had inadvertently made the article eleven pages too long; what with deletions and revisions, it did not appear in print until three years later.

105 Johnson St.
Santa Fe, N.M., June 9, 1920

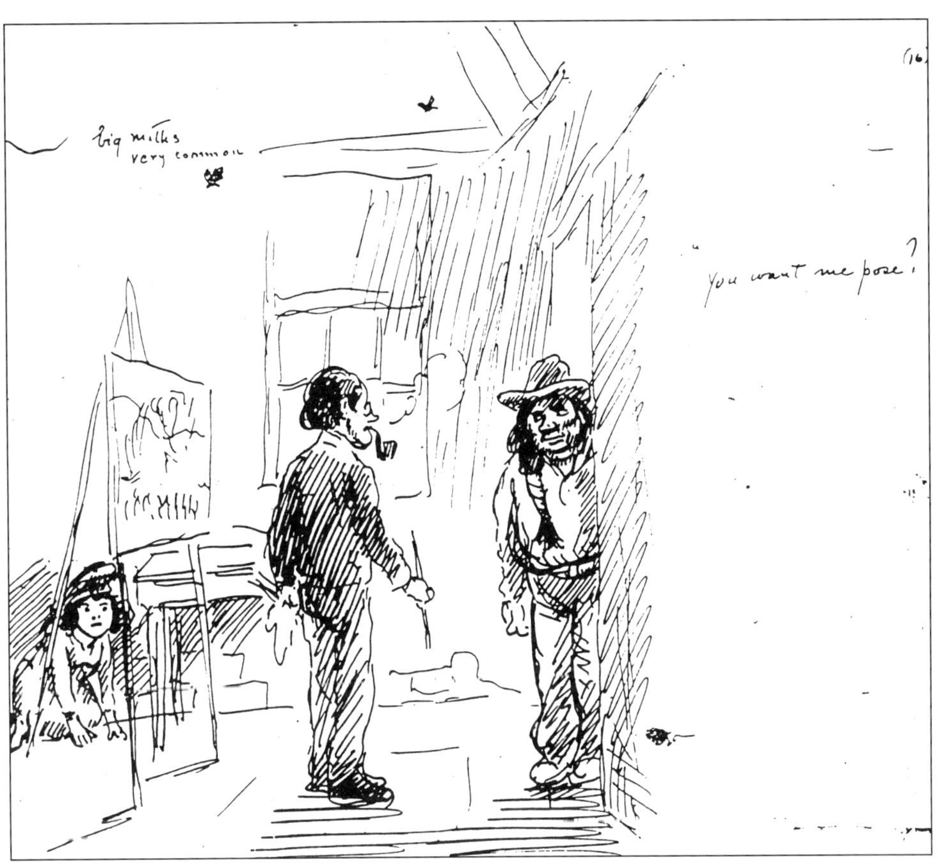

Dear Pach:

Well! here we are again in the old town—it looks just the same we feel the altitude more this year than last I suppose because we climbed more slowly by automobile last year We took three days to get here and were delayed 5 miles out of Lamy for 3 hours very provoking, for we would have arrived on the dot of schedule time if a freight wreck in Apache canyon had not occurred ahead of us.

Dr. Hewett[1] I have seen just once for a few minutes he seemed glad to welcome me back We walked out to the "Casa de Davey"[2] last Sunday—He is going to have a beautiful place when his alterations are completed they're well under way. He has three horses one apiece for self wife & boy a place near him $900 is the price but I guess I wont indulge myself in real estate purchases.

I have started painting nearly a week went by before I felt ready—a Corpus Christi procession[3] through the roads and over the bridge Sunday—gave me a theme.

By the way I got in to the Metropolitan Anniversary Ex before I left N.Y. and thank you for reminding me of its importance I enjoyed the special additions very much Suppose you read Coomaraswamy's[4] article in The Dial "Art & Craftsmanship." I thought it very concise and true didnt you?

I hope that Raymond is quite well by now remember us both to Mrs Pach and if you have some time to kill drop us a line—we feel far away out here Regards to "Bayley"[5] if you see him Good luck and good health to you

Yours sincerely, John Sloan

1. Dr. Edgar L. Hewett, director of the Museum of New Mexico in Santa Fe.

2. Home of Randall Davey; he had studied at the Henri School of Art in New York and later took up residence in Santa Fe.

3. *Corpus Christi Procession, Santa Fe*, completed that month.

4. Dr. Ananda Coomaraswamy, a Hindu artist and writer, was Curator of Hindu Art at the Boston Museum. His article appeared on pages 744–746 in the June 1920 issue.

5. A. S. Baylinson (1882–1950), a New York artist and officer of The Society of Independent Artists along with Sloan and Pach.

---

c/o Morgan & Co.
14 place Vendôme
Paris, Feb. 22, 1931

Dear Sloan,

I got a letter from Bayli to tell me about the fire, but I am glad I wrote the one I sent through you before I got his. It is a really big loss that his things were destroyed. I did not want to think it, before the news came. I am full of confidence though that he will go on to even better things. But just the same, it must give you a pleasure, regretful if it is, that you got that fine canvas of his. We have one painting and four drawings.

The special reason for this letter is that I want to transmit a proposal from a friend of mine, the director of the Chalco-graphie of the Louvre. That collection, begun under Louis XIV, contains some 6 or 7000 engraved plates from which prints are made and sold to the public. There is a constant exhibition of selections from the collection in the galleries of the museum and there are rooms where the public can see prints of all the plates. Also there is a good catalogue.

M. Angoulvent, the director and a fine fellow, has asked me to suggest American etchers, particularly such as are not over here and from whom he might get a plate. The Louvre can not pay for them but they give 10% of the money from sales of prints to the artists and continue the payment to the artists' heirs for fifty years after their decease. (I give full particulars, as furnished to me). The proposition does not amount to much, financially, but it *is* an honor, and can be of value to one as propaganda, especially if the work is kept before the great number of visitors to the museum. Also, the plate can be one from which the artist has pulled all the prints he can ever sell himself—with his own signature as printer—which the Louvre prints do not have. They have capable printers.

I suggested your name, and M. Angoulvent said he would be delighted to have a plate from you. They usually have a sort of jury, to keep from getting over-slight works, but he waived that formality in this case, saying that anything of yours that I recommended (which I transmit as—anything you cared to present) would be accepted. Don't think I am asking you to do it at all; if you *care* to send me a plate, I'll be glad to pass it on. . . . All goes well with us, and I hope it does with you and Dolly.

Always cordially yours—Walter Pach

[Cable]

Members and Students Protest Committee
of the Art Students League

PARIS, APRIL 16, 1932

JOHN SLOAN REPRESENTS LONG STRUGGLE AGAINST MEDIOCRITY CONSTANTLY THREATENING AMERICAN ART. IF HIS SELF-SACRIFICE IN ACTING AS PRESIDENT IS UNAPPRECIATED, IF POLITICAL SENTIMENT DOMINATES LEAGUE, I SHALL DECLINE INVITATION TO TEACH.

WALTER PACH[1]

1. This communication in support of Sloan was read aloud at a mass meeting held at the League on April 19, prior to a meeting the following day at which Henry Schnakenberg defeated Sloan in a vote for League president. John Sloan had resigned that post the previous month when his suggestion that George Grosz, the satiric German graphic artist, be invited to teach at the League in the fall was initially approved, then rejected.

53 Washington Square,
New York, April 30, 1932

Dear Pach:

I have felt that a letter *to you* was due for some time—and now that the explosion of the League is over (as far as Im concerned) I can pay my debt and write you. You perhaps know that at the earnest request of a large body of students I ran for election to the presidency which I had resigned and was defeated (very fortunately I think) by Schnackenberg who has stipulated that he is to be an *inactive president* which I suppose I was not. I probably agree with you as to Geo. Grosz but the board turned him down 10 to I vote and it seemed the last straw and I resigned. He has and shows (too plainly perhaps) a European academic background which I thought would be a good element in the league teaching staff. But the incident is closed and I feel I am well out of it. The strong tendency toward *inbreeding* in the League cant be killed (by *me* at any rate). Students—then Board members then a year or so in Paris then return and made teachers—The retention of DuMond[1] on the staff when the board is ashamed of his work and the sentimental refusal to fire him—a reserve fund they are afraid to use in these bad times—(times when they should put the best foot forward even if they lose money)—My own suspicion of the Institution on account of its being 1/3 owner of the valuable site on 57th Street[2]—all these factors play their part in my sense of escape

I dont know how they feel about your letter in which you so bravely came to my support—Jonas Lie[3] had said at a meeting of the board that he would resign if you lectured in the League! But he was voted down A large number of the Student body are demanding his resignation now. Incidently, I have signed up with Archipenko's[4] Ecole d'Art for next Winter—he sought me after the fight was over, and I agreed to join him teaching on a percentage basis. Times are so bad that I must go back to the teaching—but I think that I really rather like it.

Since I am out by the way—the row in the Student body is going on and the Board, I am told, has made Grosz an offer! They know more about him now I guess So what they really wanted was an *in*bred and inactive president. Just my good luck at work for me, as I believe it *always has*!

It is good to hear that you have been at work painting and I look forward to seeing your results next fall I suppose that *we must* afford to go to Santa Fe as usual though I *cant say* that we *can* afford to do so—But Dolly[5] has had a good salary all winter working on the management of the Exhibition of Indian Tribal Arts which is now on tour booked for a year ahead[6]—Miss A. Elizabeth White[7] who puts up most of the financial backing for the Ex. is going to make a trip to the west coast from Portland I think to

San Diego in July and Dolly is to go along—booking the ex. for that section for 1933.

Good old Baylinson though a teacher in the League came out for me in the fight—just as you did—he has now put the Sixteenth Annual Independent to bed for another year.[8] We had a showdown with Walthausen at last, called his bluff, and found that we can store the screens in the G.C. Palace[9] and save cartage and $50.00 a year on rental! Hows that?!

The show looked splendid, more space, 450 exhibitors a drop to 6300 or so in attendance and a deficit perhaps $1700.00 or more (Mrs. J.D.R. Jr.[10] has promised a maximum of $2000.00 this year—$500.00 for next we will have to dig up a couple more $500.00 guarantors for 1933) Auditors Report is not yet ready—

I have just heard that the Board has cabled you as to whether you care to give your lectures with the new President—please do just as you think best I certainly think they would be of real usefulness to the students of the League—(Of course you will have decided this before you get the letter)

The Catalogue of your Ex in Paris[11] came as I am closing this letter today (May 1st Sunday) and I am glad to see the extensive list of titles—and enjoyed in a vague way your preface (my small ability to read French accounts for the vagueness)

Well there is just room to wish you and Magda & Raymond a happy Summer—We go to Santa Fe about June 1st unless unforseen calamity should prevent

Best regards from Dolly
and yours Sincerely, John Sloan

1. Frank Vincent DuMond (1865–1951), who had been teaching at the League for forty years.

2. The American Fine Arts Society Building, home of the League.

3. Jonas Lie (1880–1940) had criticized Sloan's frequent "misuse" of presidential authority, and subsequently resigned from the League.

4. Alexander Archipenko (1887–1964), a Russian-born modernist sculptor who came to the United States in 1923.

5. Anna M. "Dolly" Wall Sloan (1877–1943), John's first wife.

6. Sloan was president of the Exhibition of Indian Tribal Arts, planned by him and others as the first major show of its kind in the United States.

7. Amelia Elizabeth White was one of John Sloan's major patrons.

8. Held from April 1 to 24, 1932.

9. The Grand Central Palace, at 46th Street and Lexington Avenue.

10. Mrs. John D. (Abby Aldrich) Rockefeller Jr.

11. Held at the Galerie Dru from March 12 to 26, 1932, it consisted of seventeen oils and thirty-one watercolors.

Paris, July 12, 1932

Dear Sloan,

I was very glad to get your letter, about two months ago. It showed that your feeling about the League affair was what I might have hoped: that it was better for you to be out of the place. And yet, having worked so for it—or, more exactly—for the better art-conditions in America that should result from proper training, I know that the failure of people to appreciate what you have done and the ideal you have represented must have caused you a certain disappointment, at the least. Had I not known you personally, I should have felt the same indignation that was aroused in my mind when I got the cable of the Protest Committee and then, afterward, when I learned the result of the election. . . .

. . . I think you're absolutely right to look on your being out as fortunate. You are too much in earnest about your work to be satisfied in a position where you feel some responsibility for things you cannot approve—and as president of the League, that was the case. When you were simply a teacher there, the bad work in other men's classes was not your affair—any more than the bad work at the Independents is our affair.

. . . I am hoping for good long talks with you when we are back.

Magda and Raymond join me in sending the best of good wishes to you and to Dolly.

As always

Cordially yours, Walter Pach

---

148 West 72nd Street
New York, Oct. 20, 1939

Dear John,

I have wanted to read the book[1] before writing you about it, and I do not easily find time to read. But each time I have picked this book up, I have found myself running along with it for more time that I meant to spend in reading at the moment. Probably the division into short, pithy sections accounts for that. At all events I have found it a rich source of entertainment—outside all question of the solid value of its ideas.

Those last will make the book live. I certainly think artists ought to be given a faculty for looking down to earth a hundred years or so after they take their departure. I'm very sure if I get such a viewing of the world, a century hence, I shall see a lot of people reading *Gist of Art*. . . .

I see two essential things in this book: the analyses of methods and motives, which you meant to give and which offer a better compendium of knowledge of the arts than

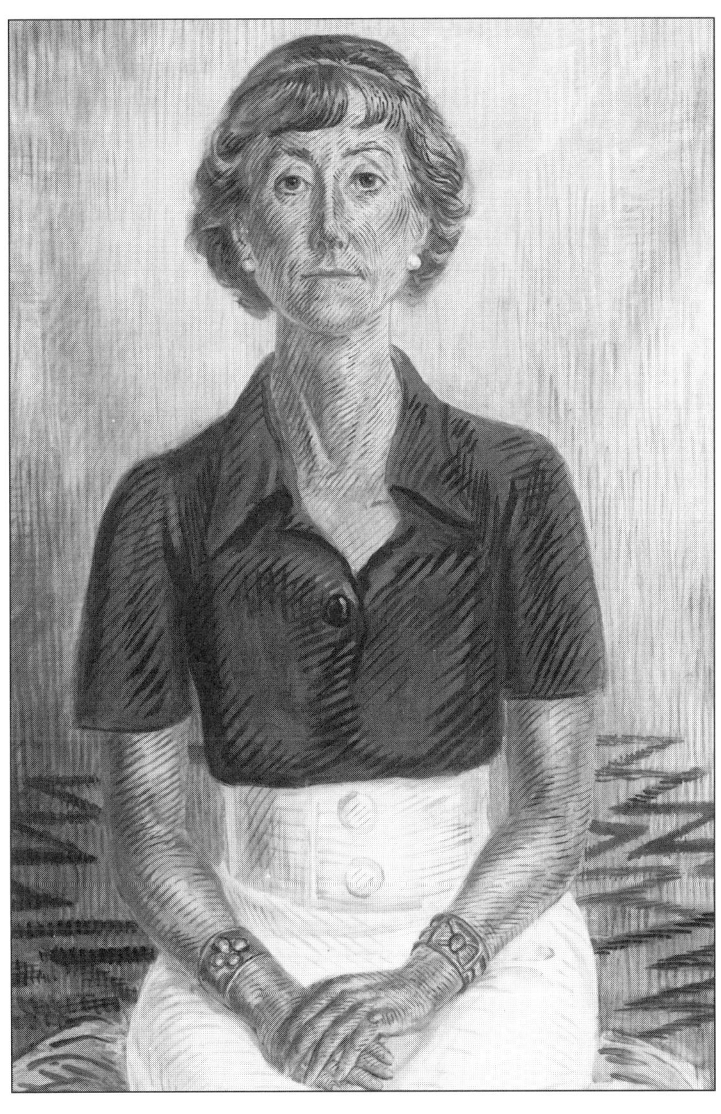

John Sloan, *Portrait* (Amelia Elizabeth White), 1934. Tempera and oil on wood, 36 x 24 in. Whitney Museum of American Art, New York, Gift of Miss Amelia Elizabeth White. 52.13.

I, for one, have met in any other book, and then—point number two—what you didn't try to give: an image of the character and understanding of art at this early time in the history of America. Again and again I was astonished (after all the years we have been talking together) at the insight into the masters who are to be seen at full length in Europe alone. What that proves is that with a few originals and then reproductions, a discerning mind can penetrate to that gist of things which you so properly use in the title of the book. I ought to say a word for the way Helen Farr[2] has done her part of the work. Whatever editing you did, she has an immense share of credit for the benefit that will come to all the readers of your pages.

It's not depriving you of your new-found literary laurels to say that the pages which still impressed me most were those of the illustrations. I have said on other occasions how important I thought the work you have done—and, above all, what you are doing, but there is a cumulative value to this series of plates that I never got before, beside which there were for me new acquaintances there, the absolutely corking portrait of Miss White,[3] for example. I think it will hold up in very strong company. I am not done with the book and shan't be for a very long time.

Yours cordially, Walter Pach

1. Sloan's *Gist of Art: Principles and Practise Expounded in the Classroom and Studio, Recorded with the Assistance of Helen Farr* (New York: American Artists Group, Inc., 1939).

2. Helen Farr, who had been studying with Sloan since 1927, contributed and organized many of his classroom comments and suggestions for the book. In 1944, a year after the death of Sloan's first wife, Dolly, he married Helen.

3. *Portrait of Amelia Elizabeth White*, 1934. The sitter was one of Sloan's major patrons.

Av. Michoacan 81,
Mexico City, Aug. 10, 1942

Dear Sloan,

I don't know if news of us and our blessed event has reached you, so I write it to you now . . . one of my old colleagues at the University of Mexico, now an important man in the Mexican government, was in New York, and asked me to come down here and give some lectures as I did just twenty years ago. Of course I accepted with enthusiasm, as the powerful impressions of 1922 have never weakened. . . .

The last two years—since the World's Fair job—have been a time of almost absolute financial drought for me. We have been living almost wholly on past earnings, and the prospects for the coming season looked worse than ever. The jobs I tried for were refused me; no sale of pictures; few lectures; and every attempt to earn by writing

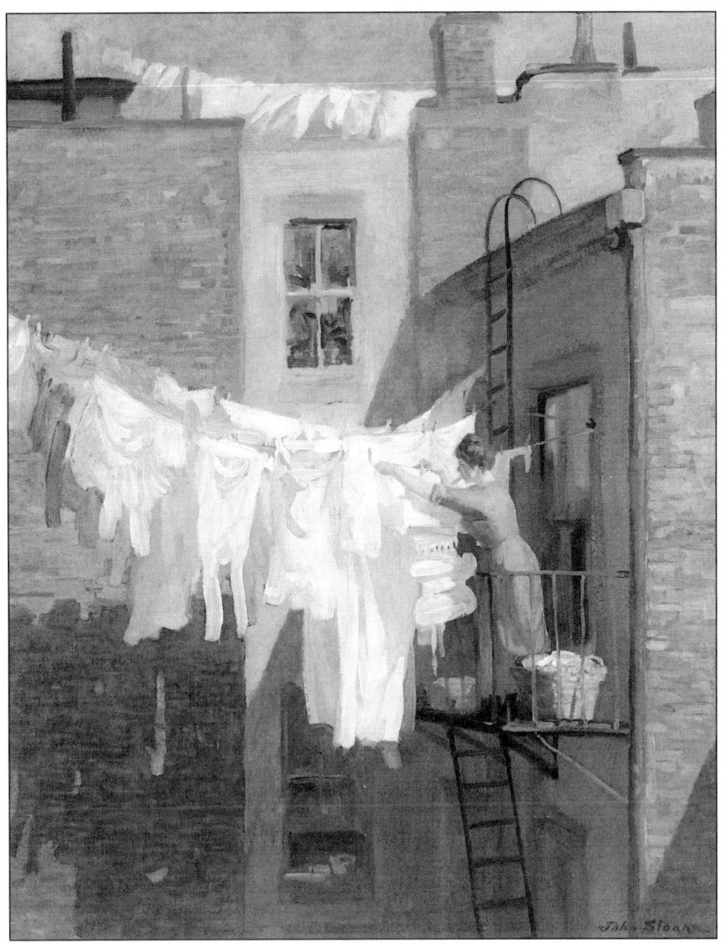

John Sloan, *A Woman's Work*, 1912. Oil on canvas, 31 5/8 x 25 3/4 in. © The Cleveland Museum of Art, Gift of Miss Amelia Elizabeth White, 1964.160.

knocked on the head. So, as expenses here are from a fourth to a third of what they were in New York . . . I am happy over our outlook. I believe I'm going to have a steady spell of work—and in a place that just *means* painting. . . .

Diego Rivera has been doing some fine easel painting, and is now at work on a fresco again. I was glad to see him and Frida, and they were most cordial in their welcome to us. José Clemente Orozco has also made progress. . . .

Magda joins me in warmest regards to you

Most cordially, Walter Pach

Mexico City, Oct. 7, 1942

Dear Sloan,

It was certainly a pleasure to get your letter of a month ago, and to hear that the summer had been a good one . . .

It was nice that you sold the two pictures.[1] If the right people had the money, you would be cleaned out on your whole stack. Diego Rivera dropped in on me today and, running through some photos I have for a thing to show him, I came on one of yours, a seated nude—with cross-hatching—that I liked especially when you did it, a few years ago. He spoke particularly of a canvas of girls under the Elevated, which he said had more of New York in it than anything else he knew. His own recent work is simply ripping, the best he has done. . . .

All warmest good wishes to Dolly and you.

As always, cordially yours, Walter Pach

1. *A Woman's Work*, 1912 and *Nude, Terra Cotta*, 1930, 1933, had been included in a one-man show at the Martha White Memorial Gallery in Santa Fe from August 15–29, 1942.

P.O. Box 1067
Santa Fe, Dec. 30, 1943

Dear Walter & Magda:

. . . I enjoyed your article on the "Eight"[1] I would have liked to see the Brooklyn showing and Id like to have done what I could to stop this talk of the group as an "organization" *which it never was*. The *name* "Eight" was tacked on to us by *Fred'k James Gregg*—writer of the "Eve. Sun" staff who of course along with Fitzgerald[2] were of great assistance in raising the rumpus over our little exhibition. The "chosen" of Robert Henri, we were not at all a mutual admiration group as I recall the time.

After the rumpus had started which I think surprised us as much as it did others, there was of course some talk of organizing and repeating the group show but we never did it. Rather as you say, we "*opened up*" for the so-called Independent Show on 36th St [*sic*] 1910[3] We thereby showed I think our unselfishness and interest in the best of American Art.

Well good friends I'll cut off here—theres nothing much in the way of painting coming out of me these days Ive made a few little nudes from etchings and N.Y. sketch books and it is good fun.

The Best of New Year Wishes for you

Your Sincerely, John Sloan

1. See footnote on page 179.

2. Charles FitzGerald, art critic for the *New York Evening Sun.*

3. Since the exhibition of The Eight in 1908, Henri, Sloan, and Davies had been seeking a larger facility in which to showcase the works of unaffiliated artists. This was accomplished when they, together with Walt Kuhn, organized the 1910 Independent Show, held from April 1 to 27 in a pair of rented buildings at 29–31 West Thirty-fifth Street. One hundred and three artists paid an entry fee to exhibit 631 of their drawings, paintings, and sculptures.

Source of Letters: Helen Farr Sloan Library, Delaware Art Museum, which contains additional Sloan/Pach correspondence.

MICHAEL STEIN
(1865–1938)

An early collector of avant-garde French art and brother of Gertrude and Leo. Michael Stein was born in Pittsburgh, the eldest of the Stein collecting trio. He studied at Johns Hopkins University in Baltimore and then went to San Francisco to aid his father in managing that city's cable car railways. Initially interested in music and the theatre, he focused on art by the turn of the twentieth century.

In 1903 Michael, his wife Sarah, and their young son Allan moved to Paris, where they were soon surrounded by Renoirs, Cézannes, and Picassos in their apartment at 58 Rue Madame, not far from the living quarters of Gertrude and Leo at 27 Rue de Fleurus. Like his sister and brother, Michael instituted a weekly open house, and it was in this way that Walter Pach came to meet Michael and Sarah Stein, and view their growing collection.

The Michael Steins' Saturday salons involved serious philosophical discussions, and Matisse reportedly attended in order to meet with a variety of aestheticians and scholars. Among the Americans were the Cone sisters from Baltimore—Dr. Claribel Cone had attended Hopkins Medical School with Gertrude Stein—and, on a rare occasion, Dr. Albert Barnes of Pennsylvania. (Both Barnes and the Cones purchased works from the Michael Steins.)

Among their numerous holdings, hung three and four high in their apartment, were *The Reader* by Renoir, Matisse's *Portrait of Madame Matisse*, and Picasso's *Portrait of Allan Stein*.

83 Bd. Montparnass
Paris, Dec. 6, 1912

Dear Mr. Stein,

Thanks very much for your letters and the option on the Picassos in London,[1] (I will insure them for 2000 francs each immediately). I have written Mr. Dell. Our exhibition opens Feb. 1st[2] unless—unexpectedly—we should be forced to wait till the 15th and I am afraid to take the risk of waiting; so I've asked him to let us have them at the earlier date. I'll be dropping in for a while tomorrow evening.

Till then, thanks again.

Yours very cordially, Walter Pach

1. The Picassos were being exhibited in London at the Grafton Gallery's "Second Post-Impressionist Exhibition"; it was organized by Roger Fry, a former Curator of Painting at the Metropolitan Museum of Art.

2. The exhibit referred to here is the "International Exhibition of Modern Art" which was held in New York's 69th Regiment Armory; it thus became known as the Armory Show. The show was indeed postponed, with a press preview held on Sunday evening, February 16th, and the public opening the following day. Of the eight works by Picasso shown in the armory—five oils, a gouache, a charcoal drawing, and a bronze sculpture—two were loaned by Leo Stein. His brother Michael loaned a pair of Matisse oils.

Hotel Blackstone
Chicago, March 30, 1913

Dear Mr. Stein,

Your letter of the 11th reached me here, where I arrived nine days ago. I had a twist of conscience when I read that you had not heard from me yet, but you must have gotten my letter immediately afterward; you did, didn't you? I have written New York to send you catalogues etc. Each time I spoke of it they said "Wait till you get your whole list ready for Europe" and I weakly let it go at that. The list is still far from finished but I'm sure yours will go on ahead, I made it good and plain how I felt about it. . . . I hope that will be somewhat of a commentary on the way I have been kept on the jump. I never saw the like of it. Of course it's because only a couple of us are working Davies, Kuhn, Gregg,[1] Mac Rae and me to be more exact and the proposition, with its thousand ramifications, Chicago, Boston etc. etc. etc. is gigantic. But we are going to put a mark on American thought that will be simply indelible. We have done it already. Total attendance in N.Y. about 100,000—most all paid. Yesterday and today in Chi[cago] about 20,000 people! each (they are free-days at the [Art]

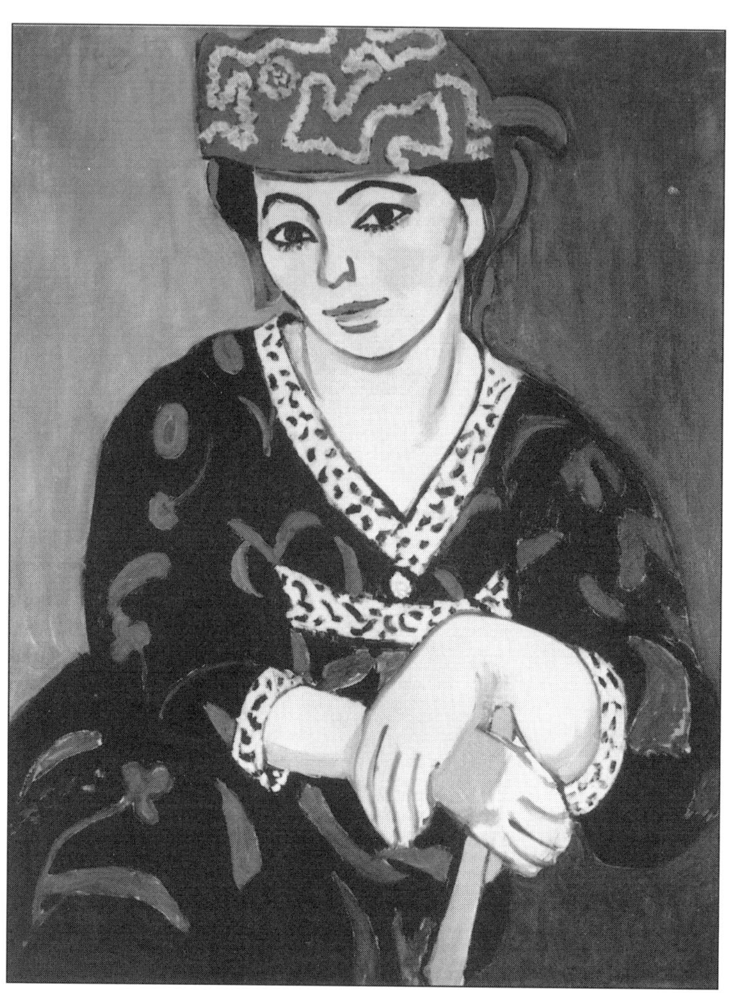

Henri Matisse, *The Red Madras Headdress (Mme. Matisse: Madras rouge)*, 1907. Oil on canvas, 39 1/8 x 31 in. © 1995 The Barnes Foundation, BF #448.

Institute but the pay-days have been big too)—and the show is not yet open a week here. Total number of sales in N.Y.—237 (this includes about 50 lithographs Cézanne, Renoir, Denis, Gauguin, Vuillard, Bonnard). Our *great* sale was a glorious Cézanne landscape to the Metropolitan Museum. That just about made me wild with joy. I will send you a catalogue with all sales marked later. Among the important sellers were Redon, Derain, Duchamp-Villon and his brothers, [Pierre] Girieud, Signac

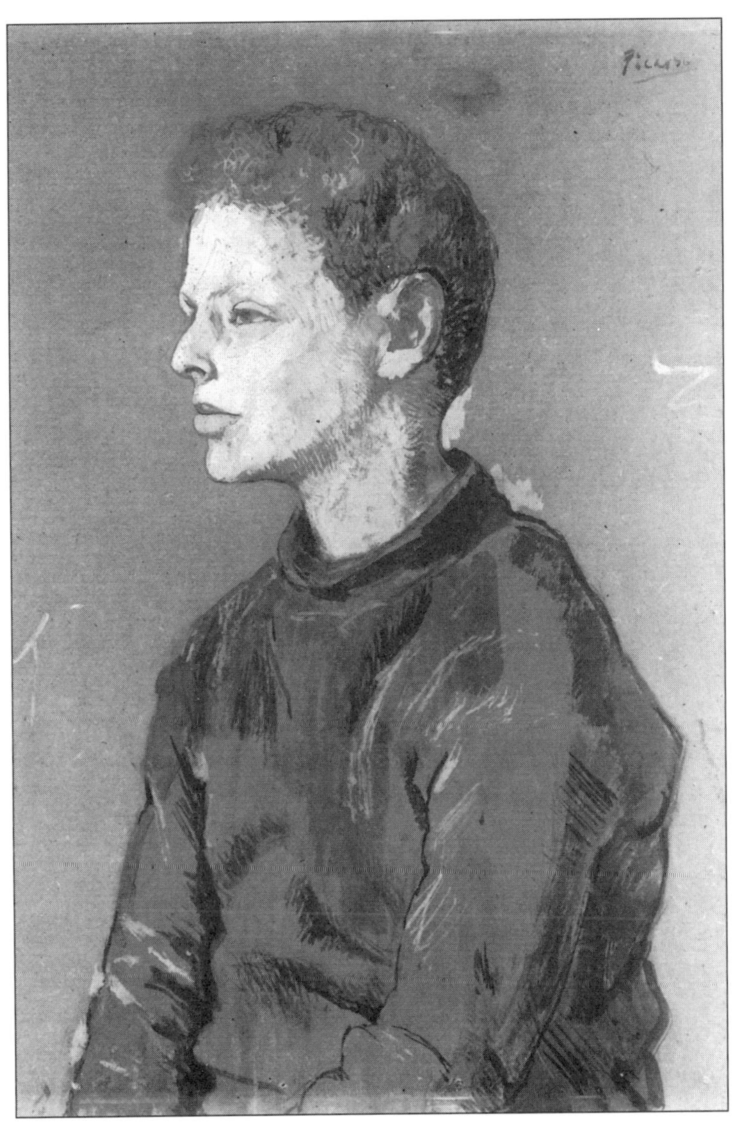

Pablo Picasso, *Allan Stein*, 1906. Gouache on cardboard, 29 1/8 x 23 1/2 in. The Baltimore Museum of Art: The Cone Collection, formed by Dr. Claribel Cone and Miss Etta Cone of Baltimore, Maryland. BMA 1950.275.

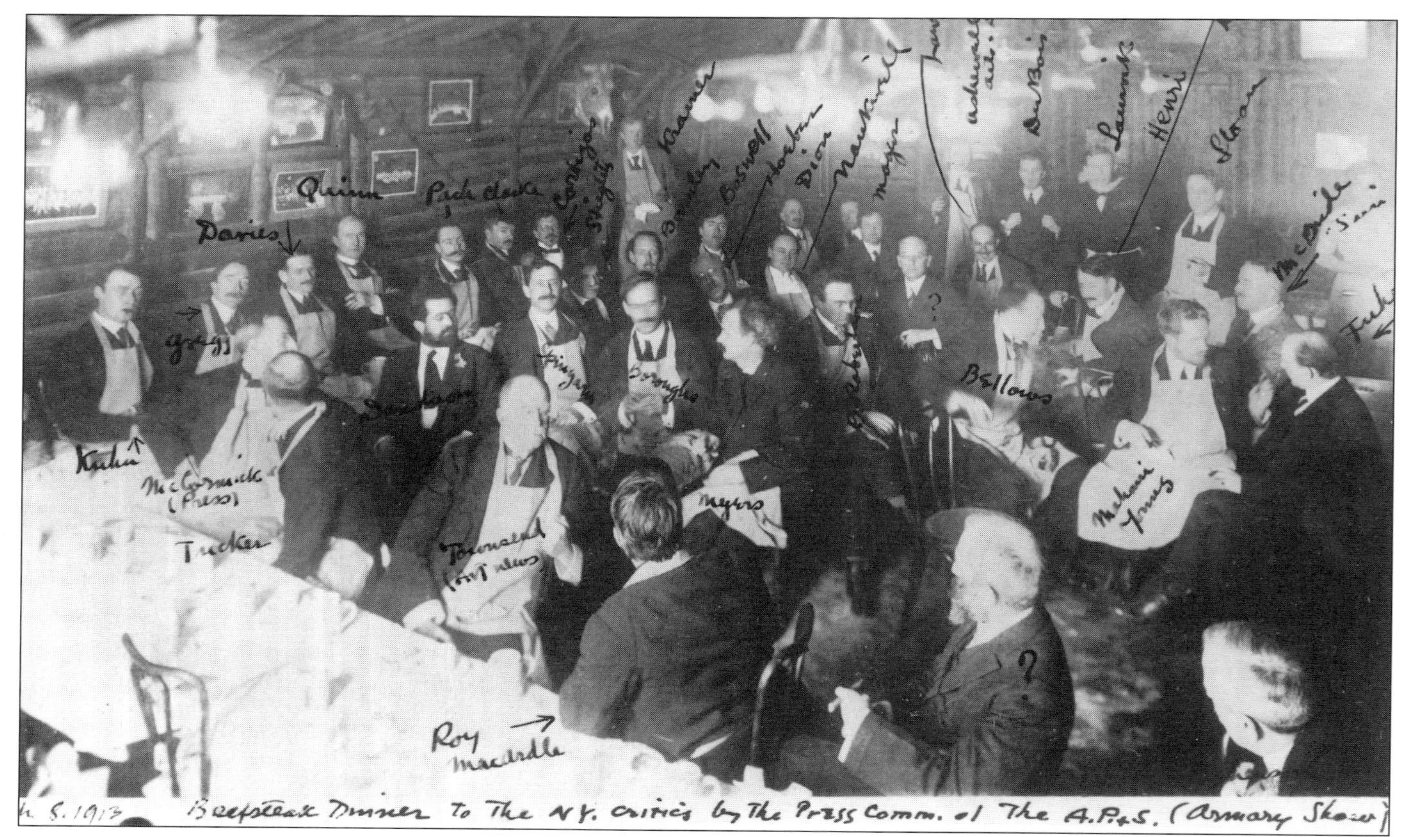

Photographer unknown, *Beefsteak Dinner to the N.Y. critics by the Press Comm. of the A.P.+S.* [Association of American Painters and Sculptors] *Armory Show*, March 8, 1913. Archives of the American Art, Smithsonian Institution, Walt Kuhn – Armory Show Papers. Walter Pach, back row, fifth from the left.

water colors and [Amadeo de] Sousa-Cardozo;—I give the ones of whom we sold the largest proportion of things but there were others of interest with one thing sold or two. No Matisse painting yet (confound it) nor Picasso. Matisse, I really believe, awakens more interest than any one else in the show and I do not have to work hard to keep up my hopes of a sale or two from the splendid long wall he has to himself here, the first thing you see as you enter. Davies made the plans for the hanging here, and designed it that Matisse should first meet the eye and set a pace,—enunciate the character of the exhibition—I send you a day's clippings from the Chicago press. The New York critics were sometimes a little better informed, spoke less of the cubists, but in the end were nearly as idiotic. Not one article showing real critical insight of importance has appeared. But no matter—we have two enormous scrapbooks more than filled with press notices that sent the public in by the thousands—and they are talking of it everywhere and all the time. You would be *astounded* at the amount of intelligence I find in my rounds of the galleries (I am chief salesman you know),—even as a small fraction of the comment, it more than makes up for the idiots. Oh how the old academic rotters feel that they are hit! John Quinn in a public speech quoted Admiral Philip at Santiago about them "Don't cheer, boys, the poor devils are dying."[2] We certainly have hot times,—but oh, *won't* I be glad when I see Paris again. My best to Mrs. Stein and yourself

Pach

1. Frederick James Gregg, art critic for the *Evening Sun*, who served as Chairman of the Armory Show's Press Committee. He and Pach were the only two individuals paid for their services, each receiving twelve hundred dollars.

2. John Phillip, who captained the battleship *Texas* in the Spanish-American War battle in which every Spanish ship was either beached or sunk.

Agay, Oct. 19, 1914

My dear Pach,

Certainly nothing could have surprised me more than the receipt of your letter from Paris, nor do I gather from same what you are there for. What kind of an exhibition are you gathering stuff for?[1] You do not mention that. I last heard from Matisse from Colloure about three weeks ago. He had heard nothing from his brother, who lives near St. Quentin. He wrote me that the House in Issy-les Moulineaux was occupied by French officers. Should you get into communication with him, dont fail to impress on him that he must now look to America for a market for his art for sometime to come and he might as well send all the things that are at Issy, especially the older and smaller things, black & whites etc. etc. and not to put the prices too high, as now is the time to have the Americans begin to own Matisse. They have read about him, discussed him, seen him in exhibitions at infinitum. It is about time he were ranked among the accepted classics & bought freely. We are staying on here, as it is quiet and there was nothing calling us to Paris for the time being. Let me hear fully from you, as to your plans and take kindest greetings from me as well a[s] from Mrs. Stein and Allan.[2]

Yours sincerely, M. D. Stein

P.S. Some one just sent us an October Century . . .[3]

1. Pach journeyed to France in the fall of 1914, just at the outset of World War I, as a representative of the Montross Gallery in New York. As a result, the first fully representative one-man show by Matisse was held there from January 20 to February 27, 1915, resulting in the sale of fourteen paintings, nearly fifty prints and drawings, and eleven sculptures.

2. Allan Stein was the son of Michael and Sarah Stein.

3. That issue of *Century Magazine* contained an article by Pach on pages 851 to 869 entitled "The Point of View of the 'Moderns.'"

Source of Letters: Yale Collection of American Literature, Beinecke Rare Book and Manuscript Library, Yale University.

ALFRED STIEGLITZ (1864–1946)

A pioneer photographer, gallery owner, and early champion of both photography and modern art as acceptable art forms. Born in Hoboken, New Jersey, he studied at the City College of New York and the University of Berlin. In 1896 he helped found the Camera Club of New York and became editor of its magazine, *Camera Notes*, which efforts helped dispel the notion that "snap-shooting" was merely an avocational pastime meant for Sunday outings.

In 1905 Stieglitz opened the Little Galleries of the Photo-Secession at 291 Fifth Avenue; after an initial season of exhibiting only photographs, he introduced paintings, drawings, and prints. Not only did Alfred Steiglitz show such avant-garde French art as watercolors by Cézanne and Picasso, and sculpture by Matisse, but he exhibited works by the American Moderns: Marin, Maurer, Hartley, Weber, and Arthur Dove. His 291 Gallery was followed by the Intimate Gallery (1917–1929) and An American Place (1929–1946).

Alfred Stieglitz and Walter Pach were kindred spirits in seeking recognition for European and American modernism; Stieglitz, for his part, considered Pach one of the best-informed Americans on the subject.

c/o Mountain House
Valhalla, N.Y., Sept. 16, 1917

My dear Mr. Stieglitz,

Some little time ago I had a letter from Severini,[1] and it has occurred to me that I might do well to tell you of it as the mails are not as certain now as in normal times and it is possible that you have not heard from him.

He says—"J'ai reçu une lettre très aimable de M. Stieglitz m'annonçant le succés matériel de mon exposition, dont vous êtes sans doute informé. Inutile de vous dire qu'il dépasse mon espoir et que je suis très *content*."[2] He goes on to thank me again very warmly,—as he has assuredly done with you.

I am still very strongly of the opinion that the exhibition[3] was the right thing from the art-standpoint and I am glad that it was at 291.[4] From the personal standpoint, that of Severini himself in the difficult period he has been through, the exhibition and the results you obtained were simply a godsend.[5] I take this opportunity to express my own appreciation again of your doing the thing in the way you did.

With good wishes for the coming season

Yours very sincerely, Walter Pach

1. Gino Severini (1883–1966), the Italian Futurist painter who was living in Paris.

2. "I have received a very nice letter from Mr. Stieglitz informing me of the success of my exhibit, of which you are probably aware. Needless to say it goes beyond my expectation and that I am very *pleased*."

3. "25 paintings, drawings, pastels by Gino Severini," held March 6–17, 1917, represented the artist's American debut.

4. Stieglitz's gallery at 291 Fifth Avenue.

5. Sales were strong, including several to collector John Quinn.

---

13 East 14th St.,
New York, May 9, 1921

Dear Mr. Stieglitz,

I have just had a 'phone from the Freeman asking me to come and correct the proofs of my article on the Philadelphia show,[1] so I imagine that it will appear in the number of this week. I think the work of your committee was splendidly done and that the show looks almost the best it could.

When Nevinson[2] was over here he asked me for your address as Severini[3] had requested him to speak to you about the paintings that are still in America. I do not think he wanted them returned but would probably be glad of a line from you to say the

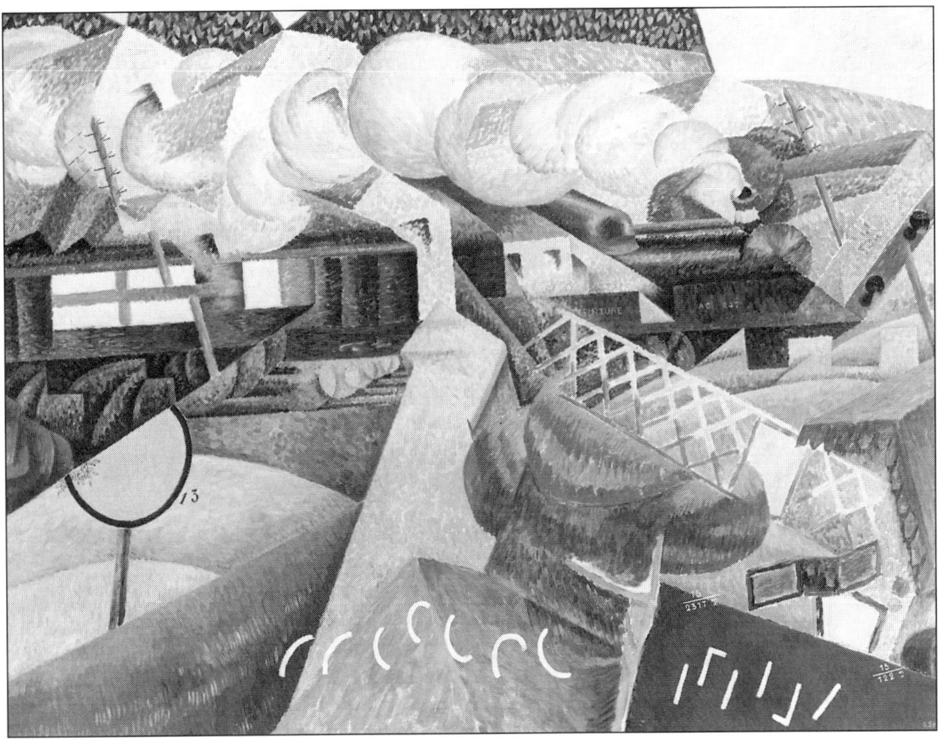

Gino Severini, *Red Cross Train Passing a Village*, 1915. Oil on canvas, 35 x 45 3/4 in. Solomon R. Guggenheim Museum, New York. 44-944. Photograph by David Heald © The Solomon R. Guggenheim Foundation, New York.

pictures were safe. I did not have your address at the time but made a note of the matter (which I have just come on). I told Nevinson to get your address from de Zayas[4] but never heard whether he communicated with you. Severini's address, as I remember it, is 6 rue Sophie-Germain, Paris,—in case you need to write.

Yours very sincerely, Walter Pach

1. "Art. At the Pennsylvania Academy," *The Freeman* 3 (May 18, 1921), 232–233.

2. Christopher Nevinson (1889–1946), an English artist credited with painting the first British Futurist composition in 1913, a year after he had met Severini in London. He came to the United States following the end of World War I.

3. Gino Severini (1883–1966), a member of the Italian Futurists who signed that art movement's manifesto when it was drawn up in 1910. Stieglitz gave him his American debut in March, 1917 at the 291 Gallery.

4. Marius De Zayas (1880–1961), a gallery director, artist, and exhibitor at the 291 Gallery.

Lake George, July 21, 1923

Dear Pach:

O'Keeffe[1] & I have been reading your translation of Faure.[2] And I want you to know how much pleasure both have gotten out of it & that we are looking to the future volumes. —I know the original volumes. —O'Keeffe doesn't read French. —I hope the books are going well. They deserve to. It's a great way to teach real history.*

Sincerely, Stieglitz

*And Americans certainly need teaching properly very badly. —More than ever.

1. Georgia O'Keeffe (1887–1986) and Alfred Stieglitz spent their summers at the Stieglitz family home on Lake George, New York; the couple was married in 1924.

2. By 1923 Pach had translated four Elie Faure volumes: *History of Art, Ancient Art* (1921), *History of Art* (1922), *Art of Cineplastics* (1923), and *History of Art, Renaissance Art* (1923), two of which were already in circulation.

---

c/o Mrs. A. Drares
Westport, Conn., July 27, 1923

Dear Stieglitz,

Thank you very much for your letter about the Faure books. I may have said, the time you were down at my place, that I worked for seven years—off and on—from the first weeks I was back in America, when I ran up to Scribner's from the great old Armory,[1]—trying to get the work published here: my idea being just the one you express—that there is a capacity for educating in those books that exactly fills the need of the country. Last season, while out West on a lecture tour, I had a chance to see that the thing was working right: they had the book everywhere,—in libraries, clubs and private houses—they were reading it and it was thawing away at the frozen mass, . . . But it is a slow business, and you have seen enough of its discouragements—with an occasional reward in some communicating of the better intelligence of things. . . .

So, I repeat, it is a great satisfaction to hear that you and Miss O'Keeffe are enjoying it,—and thank you for writing.

I come back to New York in October, and hope I may see you soon after my return.

Yours very sincerely, Walter Pach

1. An allusion to the 1913 Armory Show.

Source of Letters: Yale Collection of American Literature, Beinecke Rare Book and Manuscript Library, Yale University.

J. ALDEN WEIR (1852–1919)

An artist and one of the chief exponents of the Impressionist technique in America. Born in West Point, New York, where his father was a drawing instructor at the U.S. Military Academy, at the age of seventeen he occupied a studio/shed in the winter, and began painting outdoors in the summertime.

After two years at the National Academy of Design, he sailed for Europe, was admitted to the École des Beaux-Arts, and painted during the summer in Pont-Aven, a haven for many American art students who sought to flee the heat of Paris.

Weir's conversion to the Impressionist technique was due, in part, to his friendship with Theodore Robinson who, during several years in the late 1880s and early 1890s, spent time with Claude Monet in Giverny, and with John Twachtman, who developed his own Impressionist style. By 1897 he was receptive to Childe Hassam's plan to organize The Ten, so Weir, together with Hassam and Twachtman, became the organization's catalysts.

Unlike Hassam, who was not represented in the Armory Show, J. Alden Weir exhibited seven oils, five watercolors, and an unknown number of etchings.

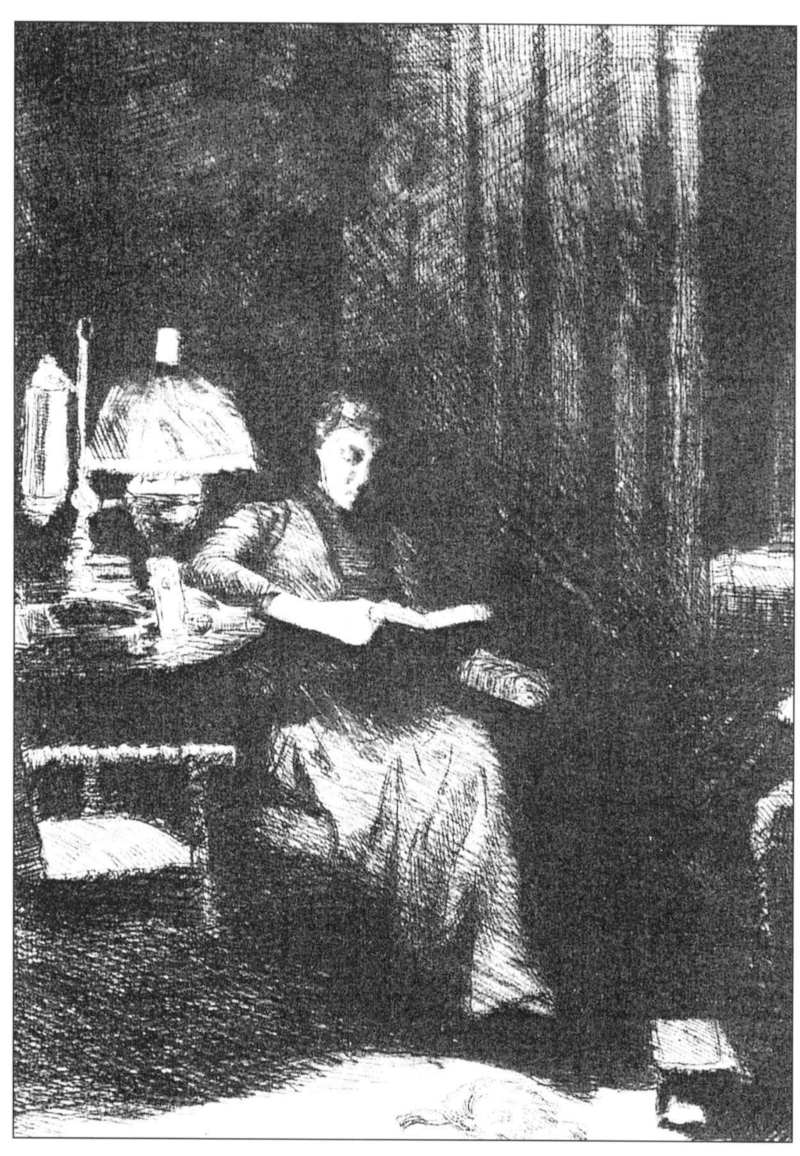

J. Alden Weir, *The Evening Lamp*, ca. 1888. Drypoint and etching, 6 1/4 x 4 5/8 in. Brigham Young University Museum of Art, Mahonri M. Young Collection.

CENTURY CLUB
7 WEST FORTY-THIRD STREET
NEW YORK, NOV. 25, 1910

My dear Mr Pach

on seeing the heading of your note 3 bis Rue des Beaux arts is where I lived for three years in the large studio once used by the great & immortal Ingres. & you can imagine how strange & interesting it was to see the heading of your note. I have always declined to interpret myself & my work & do not know how to go about it. I etched & drew on copper for the sole reason that it had the mystery of a new path. The only engraving I ever made was "Arcturus" having had an order for a drawing for a magazine. Scribner's I chose this because I knew it would make me more careful & this plate I spent a month on from the model & a delightful month it was for a period of about eight years I was deeply interested in etching & especially dry point as it was so easy to carry about in ones pocket a half a dozen plates, which would fill up odd moments. —I gradually got so interested in a certain charm that etching only possesses, had my own press & would often pull prints to the early hours of the morning a number of my best plates were ruined by the dropping of a shelf which contained some twenty odd pounds of copper plates, breaking a large bottle of nitric acid. Dutch mordant which my foolish man had stood under this shelf My ardor was somewhat cooled only later to go on again. "The lamp" an etching & dry point of a figure reading by night injured my eyes at that time I worked at night as painting took a new interest & I gradually dropped etching, hoping & desiring ever since to take it up again. I never etched for any other reason than the interest & charm that I saw in it Did a number of portraits & landscapes some of the latter I think are among my best work. I think this little plate will have to suffice but had I known that a larger plate would have been acceptable I should have much preferred it Maybe later I will have a new interest & do some good things as I feel as if I must accomplish some good things yet. 1885 to '93 was the period that I did this work. Thanking you for your interest believe me

Very cordially yours, J. Alden Weir

Source of Letter: Archives of American Art, Smithsonian Institution, Julian Alden Weir Papers, reel 125.

BIBLIOGRAPHY

Books, General

The Britannica Encyclopedia of American Art. Milton Rugoff, editor. Chicago: Encylopedia Britannica Educational Corporation, 1973.

Brown, Milton W. *The Story of the Armory Show*. New York: Abbeville, 1988.

Dictionary of American Biography. John A. Garraty, editor. New York: Charles Scribner's Sons, 1981.

The Dictionary of Art. Jane Turner, Editor. New York: Grove's Dictionaries, 1996.

The Educator's Quotebook. Compiled by Edgar Dale. Bloomington, Ind.: Phi Delta Kappa, 1884.

The New York Times Obituary Index 1858–1968. New York: New York Times, 1970.

Twentieth Century Authors: A Biographical Dictionary of Literature. Stanley J. Kunity and Howard Haycraft, editors. New York: H. W. Wilson, 1966.

Union List of Newspapers 1821–1936. Compiled by Karl Brown and Daniel C. Haskell. New York: H. W. Wilson, 1937.

Who's Who in America. Chicago: A. N. Marquis, 1997.

Who's Who 1893–1894: An Annual Biographical Dictionary. New York: St. Martin's, 1983.

Who Was Who in America 1887–1992, vol. 1. Chicago: A. N. Marquis, 1950.

Who Was Who in American Art. Peter Hastings Falk, editor. Madison, Conn.: Sound View, 1985.

Publications by Subject

BOOKS BY WALTER PACH

Catalogue of European and American Paintings 1500–1900. Introduction and descriptions by Walter Pach. Masterpieces of Art, New York World's Fair, 1940.

Ingres. New York: Hacker Art Books, 1973.

The Masters of Modern Art. New York: B. W. Huebsch, 1924.

Modern Art in America. New York: C. W. Kraushaar Art Galleries, 1928.

The One Hour Series: An Hour of Art. Philadelphia: J. B. Lippincott, 1930.

Queer Thing, Painting: Forty Years in the World of Art. New York: Harper and Brothers, 1938.

ABOUT WALTER PACH

Malloy, Nancy, and Catherine Stover. A *Finding Aid to the Walter Pach Papers.* Washington, D.C.: Archives of American Art, Smithsonian Institution, 1997.

McCarthy, Laurette Eileen. *Walter Pach: Artist, Critic, Historian, and Agent of Modernism* [1883–1920 only]. Ann Arbor: UMI Dissertation Services, 1997.

Perlman, Bennard B. "Walter Pach (1883–1958) and Magda Pach (1884–1950)." In *Exhibition of the Art of Walter and Magda Pach.* Youngstown, Ohio: Butler Institute of American Art, 1988.

ARTICLES BY WALTER PACH (ARRANGED IN CHRONOLOGICAL ORDER)

"The 'Memoria' of Velasquez," *Scribner's Magazine* 42 (July 1907), 38–52.

"At the Studio of Claude Monet," *Scribner's Magazine* 43 (June 1908), 765–767.

"Cézanne—An Introduction," *Scribner's Magazine* 44 (December 1908), 765–768.

"Manet and Modern American Art," *The Craftsman* 17 (February 1910), 483–492.

"New York as an Art Centre," *Harper's Weekly* 54 (February 26, 1910), 12.

"On Albert P. Ryder," *Scribner's Magazine* 49 (January 1911), 126–127.

"Pierre Auguste Renoir," *Scribner's Magazine* 51 (May 1912), 606–612.

"The Point of View of the 'Moderns,'" *The Century Magazine* 87 (April 1914), 851, 852, 861–864.

"Why Matisse?" *The Century Magazine* 89 (February 1915), 633–636.

"Modern Art Today," *Harper's Weekly* 62 (April 19, 1916), 470, 471.

"Some Reflections on Modern Art Suggested by the Career of Arthur Burdett Frost, Jr.," *Scribner's Magazine* 63 (1918), 637–639.

"Connoisseurship or Criticism," *The Dial* 65 (November 12, 1918), 365, 366.

"The Significance of Redon," *The Dial* 66 (February 22, 1919), 191–193.

"The Independents," *The Dial* 66 (March 22, 1919), 307, 308.

"The Schamberg Exhibition," *The Dial* 66 (May 17, 1919), 505, 506.

"Painting. A Modern Art Exhibition," *The Freeman* 1 (June 23, 1920), 354, 355.

"Art. A Half-Century Celebration," *The Freeman* 1 (August 25, 1920), 568, 569.

"Art in America. I," *The Freeman* 2 (November 10, 1920), 206, 207.

"Art in America. II," *The Freeman* 2 (November 17, 1920), 232, 233.

"Art. A Modern Artist" [Vincent van Gogh], *The Freeman* 2 (December 8, 1920), 302, 303.

"Methods of Criticism," *The Freeman* 2 (January 19, 1921), 450, 451.

"Art. Paris in New York," *The Freeman* 2 (February 2, 1921), 492–494.

"Art. At an Exhibition of Photography" [Alfred Stieglitz], *The Freeman* 2 (February 23, 1921), 565, 566.

"Art.The Independents," *The Freeman* 2 (March 9, 1921), 616, 617.

"Elie Faure," *The Freeman* 3 (March 30, 1921), 58–60.

"Art. At the Pennsylvania Academy," *The Freeman* 3 (May 18, 1921), 232, 233.

"Art.The Contemporary Classics," *The Freeman* 3 (July 13, 1921), 423–425.

"Anatomizing the Muses," *The Freeman* 3 (September 7, 1921), 619.

"Ex Libris," *The Freeman* 7 (April 4, 1923), 95.

"A Grand Provincial" [Thomas Eakins], *The Freeman* 7 (April 11, 1923), 112–114.

"Art.The Independents," *The Freeman* 7 (April 18, 1923), 135–137.

"Picasso's Achievement," *The Forum* 23 (June 1925), 769–775.

"What Passes for Art," *Harper's Magazine* 155 (June 1927), 89–97.

"The Evolution of Diego Rivera," *Creative Art* 4 (January 1929), 31–39.

"Europe and American Art," *American Magazine of Art* 25 (October 1932), 203–206.

"American Art in the Louvre," *Fine Arts* 20 (May 1933), 18–20, 48, 50.

"On Owning Pictures," *The Fine Arts* 20 (August 1933), 27–29, 46, 47.

"Rockefeller, Rivera, and Art," *Harper's Magazine* 167 (September 1933), 476–483.

"New-Found Values in Ancient America," *Parnassus* 7 (December 1935), 7–10.

"The Outlook for Modern Art," *Parnassus* 8 (April 1936), 5–8, 43.

"Gericault," *Parnassus* 8 (November 1936), 12–15.

"Delacroix Speaks for Himself," *Artnews* 43 (November 1–14, 1944), 8–11.

"The Role of Modern Art," *Virginia Quarterly Review* 21 (Summer 1945), 399–412.

"The [Alexander] Shilling Fund," *The New Republic* 114 (February 4, 1946), 159.

"La Barricade [by Delacroix] in America," *Artnews* 45 (July 1946), 42, 43, 46.

"Thus Is Cubism Cultivated," *Artnews* 48 (May 1949), 23 25, 52, 53.

"Art Must Be Modern," *The Atlantic Monthly* 185 (May 1950), 44–48.

"John Sloan," *The Atlantic Monthly* 194 (August 1954), 68–72.

"Submerged Artists" [Ryder, Eakins, Prendergast, etc.], *The Atlantic Monthly* 199 (January 1957), 68–72.

"Renoir, Rubens, and the Thurneyssen Family," *Art Quarterly* 21 (Autumn 1958), 279–282.

ABOUT THE ARMORY SHOW

Brown, Milton W. *The Story of the Armory Show*. New York: Abbeville Press, 1988.

Kuhn, Walt. *The Story of the Armory Show*. New York: privately printed, 1938.

ABOUT WALTER ARENSBERG

Kimball, Fiske. "Cubism and the Arensbergs," *Art News Annual* 53 (November 1954), 117–122, 174–178.

Naumann, Francis M. *New York Dada 1915–23*. New York: Harry N. Abrams, 1994.

Stewart, Patrick L. "The European Art Invasion: American Art and the Arensberg Circle, 1914–1918," *Arts* 51 (May 1977), 108–112.

ABOUT BERNARD BERENSON

Calo, Mary Ann. *Bernard Berenson and the Twentieth Century*. Philadelphia: Temple University Press, 1994.

Secrest, Meryle. *Bernard Berenson: A Biography*. New York: Holt, Rinehart and Winston, 1979.

Springge, Sylvia. *Berenson: A Biography*. Boston: Houghton Mifflin, 1960.

ABOUT VAN WYCK BROOKS

Nelson, Raymond. *Van Wyck Brooks: A Writer's Life*. New York: E. P. Dutton, 1981.

Spiller, Robert E., editor. *The Van Wyck Brooks—Lewis Mumford Letters: The Record of a Literary Friendship, 1921–1963*. New York: E. P. Dutton, 1970.

ABOUT BRYSON BURROUGHS

Bryson Burroughs: Catalogue of a Memorial Exhibition of His Works. New York: Metropolitan Museum of Art, 1935.

ABOUT ARTHUR B. DAVIES

Cortissoz, Royal. *Arthur B. Davies*. New York: Whitney Museum of American Art, 1931.

Perlman, Bennard B. *The Lives, Loves, and Art of Arthur B. Davies*. Albany: State University of New York Press, 1998.

Wright, Brooks. *The Artist and the Unicorn*. New City, N.Y.: The Historical Society of Rockland County, 1978.

ABOUT KATHERINE DREIER

Bohan, Ruth L. *The Société Anonyme's Brooklyn Exhibition: Katherine Dreier and Modernism in America*. Ann Arbor: UMI Research Press, 1982.

De Angelus, Michele. "Katherine S. Dreier (1877–1952)." In *Avant-Garde Painting and Sculpture in America 1910–25*. Exhibition catalogue. Wilmington: Delaware Art Museum, 1975.

Dreier, Katherine S. *Western Art and the New Era*. New York: Brentano's, 1923.

ABOUT MARCEL DUCHAMP

Gough-Cooper, Jennifer, Jacques Caumont, and Marcel Caumont. *Marcel Duchamp.* Cambridge: MIT Press, 1993.

Mink, Janis. *Marcel Duchamp 1887–1968: Art as Anti-Art.* Köln: Benedikt Taschen, 1995.

Naumann, Francis M., with Beth Vann. *Making Mischief: Dada Invades New York.* Exhibition catalogue. New York: Whitney Museum of American Art, 1996.

Rubin, William S. *Dada, Surrealism, and Their Heritage.* Exhibition catalogue. New York: Museum of Modern Art, 1968.

ABOUT SUSAN (MRS. THOMAS) EAKINS

Hendricks, Gordon. *The Life and Work of Thomas Eakins.* New York: Grossman, 1974.

Pach, Walter. "American Art in the Louvre," *Fine Arts* 20 (May 1933), 18–20, 48, 50.

Rubinstein, Charlotte Streifer. *American Women Artists: From Early Indian Times to the Present.* New York: Avon, 1982.

Wilmerding, John, general editor. *Thomas Eakins (1844–1916) and the Heart of American Life.* Exhibition catalogue. London: National Portrait Gallery, 1993.

ABOUT ARTHUR BURDETT FROST JR.

Davidson, Abraham A. *Early American Modernist Painting 1910–1935.* New York: Harper and Row, 1981.

Lader, Melvin P. "Arthur Burdett Frost, Jr. (1887–1917)." In *Avant-Garde Painting and Sculpture in America 1910–25.* Exhibition catalogue. Wilmington: Delaware Art Museum, 1975.

Levin, Gail. "Patrick Henry Bruce and Arthur Burdett Frost, Jr.: From the Henri Class to the Avant-Garde," *Arts Magazine* 53 (April 1979), 102–106.

Pach, Walter. "Some Reflections on Modern Art Suggested by the Career of Arthur Burdett Frost, Jr.," *Scribner's Magazine* 63 (1918), 637–639.

Reed, Henry M. *The A.B. Frost Book.* Rutland, Vt.: C. E. Tuttle, 1967.

ABOUT CHILDE HASSAM

Adams, Adeline. *Childe Hassam.* New York: American Academy of Arts and Letters, 1938.

Adelson, Warren, Jay E. Cantor, and William H. Gerdts. *Childe Hassam: Impressionist.* New York: Abbeville, 1999.

Hiesinger, Ulrich W. *Childe Hassam: American Impressionist.* New York: Pestel Verlag, 1999.

Hoopes, Donelson F. *Childe Hassam.* New York: Watson-Guptill, 1979.

ABOUT ROBERT HENRI

Homer, William Innes. *Robert Henri and His Circle*. Ithaca: Cornell University Press, 1969.

Perlman, Bennard B. *Robert Henri, His Life and Art*. New York: Dover, 1991.

———. *Robert Henri: Painter*. Exhibition catalogue. Wilmington: Delaware Art Museum, 1984.

———, editor. *Revolutionaries of Realism: The Letters of John Sloan and Robert Henri*. Princeton: Princeton University Press, 1997.

ABOUT FISKE KIMBALL

"The New Director [Fiske Kimball]," *The Pennsylvania Museum Bulletin* 21 (October 1925), 2–3.

Roberts, George and Mary. *Triumph on Fairmount: Fiske Kimball and The Philadelphia Museum of Art*. Philadelphia: J. B. Lippincott, 1959.

ABOUT ALICE KLAUBER

"Alice Ellen Klauber: San Diego's First Lady of the Arts," by Martin E. Petersen. Unpublished biography. San Diego Museum of Art Archives.

ABOUT LEWIS MUMFORD

Spiller, Robert E., editor. *The Van Wyck Brooks—Lewis Mumford Letters: The Record of a Literary Friendship, 1921–1963*. New York: E.P. Dutton, 1970.

ABOUT DUNCAN PHILLIPS

Green, Eleanor. *Master Paintings from The Phillips Collection*. Exhibition catalogue. Fort Lee, N.J.: Penshurst Books, 1981.

Passantino, Erika D., editor. *The Eye of Duncan Phillips: A Collection in the Making*. New Haven: Yale University Press, 1999.

Phillips, Marjorie. *Duncan Phillips and His Collection*. New York: W. W. Norton, 1982.

ABOUT MAURICE PRENDERGAST

Green, Eleanor, and Jeffrey R. Hayes. *Maurice Prendergast: Art of Impulse and Color*. Exhibition catalogue. College Park: University of Maryland, 1976.

Mathews, Nancy Mowll. *Maurice Prendergast*. Exhibition catalogue. Munich: Prestel Verlag, 1990.

Wattenmaker, Richard J. *Maurice Prendergast*. New York: Harry N. Abrams, 1994.

ABOUT JOHN QUINN

Reid, B. L. *The Man from New York: John Quinn and His Friends*. New York: Oxford University Press, 1968.

Zilczer, Judith. *"The Noble Buyer": John Quinn, Patron of the Avant-Garde*. Washington, D.C.: Smithsonian Institution Press, 1978.

ABOUT ABBY ALDRICH ROCKEFELLER

Bloch, Lucienne. "The Making of Rivera's Rockefeller Center Mural: A Memoir," *Art in America* 74 (February 1986), 103–123.

Chase, Mary Ellen. *Abby Aldrich Rockefeller*. New York: Macmillan, 1950.

Kert, Bernice. *Abby Aldrich Rockefeller: The Woman in the Family*. New York: Random House, 1993.

ABOUT ALBERT PINKHAM RYDER

Broun, Elizabeth. *Albert Pinkham Ryder*. Exhibition catalogue. Washington, D.C.: Smithsonian Institution Press, 1990.

Homer, William Innes, and Lloyd Goodrich. *Albert Pinkham Ryder: Painter of Dreams*. New York: Harry N. Abrams, 1989.

Pach, Walter. "On Albert P. Ryder," *Scribner's Magazine* 49 (January 1911), 126–127.

ABOUT PAUL J. SACHS

Vincent, Steven. "The Crimson High Tide," *Art and Auction* 18 (January 1996), 80–81, 112–113.

ABOUT MORTON L. SCHAMBERG

MacAgy, Douglas. "5 Rediscovered from the Lost Generation," *Art News* 59 (Summer 1960), 38–41.

Scott, Wilford. "Morton L. Schamberg (1881–1918)." In *Avant-Garde Painting and Sculpture in America 1910–25*. Exhibition catalogue. Wilmington: Delaware Art Museum, 1975.

Wolf, Ben. *Morton Livingston Schamberg*. Philadelphia: University of Pennsylvania Press, 1963.

ABOUT CHARLES SHEELER

Brown, Milton W. *The Modern Spirit: American Painting 1908–1935*. Exhibition catalogue. London: Arts Council of Great Britain, 1977.

Stebbins Jr., Theodore E., and Norman Keys Jr. *Charles Sheeler: The Photographs*. Exhibition catalogue. Boston: Museum of Fine Arts, 1987.

Troyen, Carol, and Erica E. Hirshler. *Charles Sheeler: Paintings and Drawings*. Exhibition catalogue. Boston: Museum of Fine Arts, 1987.

ABOUT JOHN SLOAN

Brooks, Van Wyck. *John Sloan: A Painter's Life*. New York: E. P. Dutton, 1955.

Perlman, Bennard B., editor. *Revolutionaries of Realism: The Letters of John Sloan and Robert Henri*. Princeton: Princeton University Press, 1997.

Scott, David. *John Sloan: Paintings, Prints, Drawings*. New York: Watson-Guptill Publications, 1975.

St. John, Bruce, editor. *John Sloan's New York Scene from the Diaries, Notes, and Correspondence 1906–1913*. New York: Harper and Row, 1965.

ABOUT MICHAEL STEIN

Cone, Rose Belle. *Stein, Bergman, and Cone Families*. Baltimore: Ida Charles Wilkins Foundation, 1954.

Four Americans in Paris: The Collections of Gertrude Stein and Her Family. Exhibition catalogue. New York: Museum of Modern Art, 1970.

ABOUT ALFRED STIEGLITZ

Greenough, Sarah, and Juan Hamilton. *Alfred Stieglitz: Photographs and Writings*. Exhibition catalogue. Washington, D.C.: National Gallery of Art, 1983.

Homer, William Innes. *Alfred Stieglitz and the American Avant-Garde*. Boston: New York Graphic Society, 1977.

Lowe, Sue Davidson. *Stieglitz: A Memoir/Biography*. London: Quartet Books, 1983.

ABOUT J. ALDEN WEIR

Burke, Doreen Bolger. *J. Alden Weir: An American Impressionist*. Newark: University of Delaware Press, 1983.

Gerts, William H. *American Impressionism*. New York: Abbeville, 1984.

Phillips, Duncan. "Julian Alden Weir." In *Julian Alden Weir: An Appreciation of His Life and Works*. New York: The Century Club, 1921, 3–47.

Young, Dorothy Weir. *The Life and Letters of J. Alden Weir*. New Haven: Yale University Press, 1960.

INDEX